Arenas of Language Use

Arenas of Language Use

Herbert H. Clark

The University of Chicago Press

&

Center for the Study of Language
and Information

The University of Chicago Press, Chicago 60637
The University of Chicago Press, Ltd., London
Center for the Study of Language and Information

© 1992 by the Center for the Study of Language and Information
Leland Stanford Junior University
All rights reserved. Published 1992
Printed in the United States of America
01 00 99 98 97 96 95 94 93 92   1 2 3 4 5 6

CIP data, acknowledgments, and other information
appear at the end of the book

Acknowledgments

Doing science is like playing in a string quartet. It depends on the talent, training, integrity, and dedication of all of the participants. It also depends on their ability to work in ensemble. No one in the quartet sounds any better than the other players allow them to sound. That is as true for the mighty first violin as for the lowly viola. And when everything works just right, the music is exhilarating and a delight to hear.

For me, doing science has been a pleasure precisely because of the ensembles I have fallen in with. I have been privileged to work with superb violinists, hard working violists, and cheerful cellists. Even when our recitals haven't gone as well as they should have, even when we have received only polite applause, we have enjoyed the music anyway, and we have learned from it. Our next recitals were always better.

My collaborators on the chapters in this collection were Sam Buttrick, Thomas Carlson, Richard Gerrig, Catherine Marshall, Edward Schaefer, Michael Schober, Robert Schreuder, and Deanna Wilkes-Gibbs. To them I owe inexpressible gratitude. But many of the ideas represented here developed out of other collaborations with Susan Brennan, Ellen Francik, Susan Haviland, Ellen Isaacs, Barbara Malt, Daniel Morrow, Gregory Murphy, Karen Ravn, Gisela Redeker, Dale Schunk, and Heather Stark. To them I owe the same gratitude. Many others have read, commented on, or offered advice on one or another of these chapters, and they include Kent Bach, Philip Barnard, Lawrence Barsalou, Irving Biederman, Alexandra Belyaeva, Keith Brown, Helen Clark, Florence Edwards, David Evans, Anne Fernald, Charles Fillmore, James Fox, Simon Garrod, Gerald Gazdar, Raymond Gibbs, Jerry Hobbs, Mark Jackson, Philip Johnson-Laird, Paul Kay, George Lakoff, Mark Lepper, Willem Levelt, Susan Lyte, A. P. Martinich, Jerry Morgan, Geoffrey Nunberg, Lawrence Paul, Mary Louise Pratt,

Christine Riley, Ivan Sag, Edward Smith, Neil Smith, Robert Stalnaker, and Keith Stenning. My collaborators and I thank them all for holding us to higher standards. Throughout this work there has been one player especially committed to the quality of our work, and that is Eve V. Clark. She has been a collaborator, a reader, a critic, a promoter, and more. She has played second violin to no one.

For financial support, I am indebted to the Center for Advanced Study in the Behavioral Sciences, the Center for the Study of Language and Information, the Max Planck Institute for Psycholinguistics, the National Institute of Mental Health, the National Science Foundation, the Nederlandse Organisatie voor Wetenschapelijk Onderzoek, and Stanford University. However I am to address you, thank you.

Contents

Arenas of Language Use

Introduction

When we think of language use, we think of activities in which language plays a necessary role. We think of face-to-face conversations; telephone conversations; reading and writing letters, novels, and newspapers; putting on and watching plays, movies, and television shows; taking part in court trials, formal meetings, and religious ceremonies; and even talking to oneself. These are all arenas of language use. They are all theaters of action in which people do things with language. But what actions do people take in these arenas, and how do they do them? That is the focus of this collection.

We can view language use in many ways. One way is to treat it as a class of human actions. Then we might ask: What do people do with language? What are their goals, their intentions? By what processes do they achieve these goals? Another, more common view is to treat language use as a product, or expression, of people's competence in a language. So we might ask instead: How do people produce and understand the sentences of their language? What is the link between language use and the grammar of the language? Throughout this collection, I have taken the first view and treated language use primarily as human activity. Let me briefly explain why.

Two Traditions

For a long time, students of language didn't really separate the study of language use from the study of language structure. Both were part of a broader study of language. In about 1960, that began to change. With the introduction of generative linguistics by Noam Chomsky, the two began to be considered distinct, though connected, fields of study. For Chomsky, it was essential to distinguish people's linguistic competence, their capacity to produce and recognize the sentences of their language, from their linguistic performance, how they actually produce and understand uses of these sentences on particular occasions. In his view, competence is people's tacit knowledge of their language, and this is represented by the grammar—the rules of phonology, morphology, syntax, and semantics. Performance is a reflection of this competence, but it is subject to additional principles.

In this tradition—let me call it the *product tradition*—it was largely up to experimental psycholinguistics to discover the principles of linguistic performance. Many of these investigations were attempts to confirm the "psychological reality of linguistic structures." One classic series of experiments, for example, compared the difficulty of understanding passive sentences, like *John was kissed by Mary*, with their active counterparts, like *Mary kissed John*. The idea was that since passive sentences take more steps in their derivation in the grammar than active sentences, they ought also to take longer to understand. The experiments were an initial success, although their conclusions were later reinterpreted as both linguistic and processing theories changed.

During the same period, but largely outside linguistics and psycholinguistics, there developed quite a different approach to language use. I will call it the *action tradition*. At the beginning it was most closely associated with the Oxford philosophers John Austin, Paul Grice, and John Searle. According to Austin, when people use language they are doing things with words. At one level, they are making sounds. At another level, they are expressing words and sentences. At another level, they are issuing utterances. At another level, they are making assertions, requests, apologies. At still another level, they are trying to get others to believe things, divulge information, become frightened. In addition, according to Grice, people ordinarily mean things by what they utter. They intend their addressees to recognize certain of their intentions, and that requires their close cooperation. Although the work in this tradition started in philosophy, it soon spread to linguistics, psychology, and artificial intelligence.[1]

Gradually the action tradition began to include linguistic actions that fell outside Austin, Grice, and Searle's original framework. There was William Labov's sociolinguistic work on narratives and on language in its social context. There were Harvey Sacks', Emanuel Schegloff's, and Gail Jefferson's analyses of conversational interaction. There were Erving Goffman's sociological studies of language in interactional settings. The work that followed most directly from the Oxford philoso-

---

[1] Austin gave his William James Lectures "How to do things with words" in 1955 and Grice published "Meaning" in 1957. These are the same two years that Chomsky finished his dissertation and published his first influential monograph *Syntactic Structures*.

phers came to be called pragmatics—in parallel with phonology, morphology, syntax, and semantics—but the tradition as it evolved was much broader than that. It included not only analysis but also observation and experiment.

The product and action traditions, then, are built on very different foundations. The product tradition starts with language structure and investigates how it is manifest in speaking and listening. The action tradition starts directly with what people do with language and investigates how that works. As an experimental psychologist, I began in the product tradition. But the more phenomena I worked on, the more I turned to the action tradition for explanations.

Three Tenets of Language Use

Let me illustrate several differences between the product and action traditions by describing three tenets I have come to hold for the study of language use.

TENET: In language use, utterances are more basic than sentences.

Sentences are a fundamental category of language structure. They are one of the basic units that the grammar of a language is assumed to generate. They have a well defined structure. So in the product tradition, it is only natural to ask what role that structure plays in the processes of speaking and understanding. The grammar predicts, for example, that the sentence *The game warden watched the poacher with binoculars* is structurally ambiguous. One question to investigate, then, is how listeners process that ambiguity. For most investigators in the product view, utterances are simply tokens of sentences. That makes utterances of secondary interest.

In the action tradition, it is utterances that are more basic. Take *I'm hot*. As a sentence, it is a unit that has been abstracted away from all speakers, times, places, and circumstances in which it might be uttered. It can mean "The person uttering this sentence is, at the time of utterance, lucky," although it can also mean other things. In contrast, an utterance of *I'm hot* necessarily involves a speaker, time, place, and set of circumstances. When I uttered it to my son during a game of poker, I meant I was lucky, so he had better bet cautiously.

Why are utterances more basic in language use? First, it is utterances and not sentences that we actually produce, hear, or read. We never hear a piece of language that isn't produced by a particular speaker for a particular audience on a particular occasion. Strictly speaking, it is a category mistake to speak of sentence comprehension or sentence production, as many investigators do. Also, many utterances are not tokens of sentences at all. They are phrases (e.g., *A cup of coffee?*), words (*Sorry*), or atomic units that cannot be parts of sentences (*Ah!, Hello*). And, as Grice noted, they are often not linguistic at all, but gestures or other actions. In addition, most utterances contain elements that grammars have no account for, such as the boldface elements in this actual utterance:

> but you see it is sui generis **so it'll** so . anybody who is looking for **uhm** . **a a niche to fit it** a ready-made niche . in English grammar to fit it . into . is sort of begging for the moon - - **you see**

Spontaneous speech is littered with interjections and self-repairs like these. There is no a priori reason to rule these out of the study of language use just because they aren't generated by the grammar, nor is there any reason to rule out utterances that are not sentences. Both are part of the authentic, spontaneous life of everyday language. Excluding them could only distort our theories of language use.[2]

The assumption that sentences are basic has a more insidious influence. It tempts us into studying linguistic expressions without thinking about the speaker, time, place, and circumstances of their utterance. But it is precisely the speaker, time, place, and circumstances of an utterance that distinguish the study of language use from the study of language structure. Let me return to the ambiguous sentence *The game warden watched the poacher with binoculars.* I would utter this sentence on some occasion only if, for example, I had a particular poacher in mind and believed that my addressee could identify him from our shared background (see Chapters 1, 2, and 3). I would have to believe he was uniquely identifiable as "the poacher with binoculars." The utterance is only ambiguous when it is stripped of its speaker, addressee, time, and circumstances. "Yes, of course," you reply, "so what is the problem?" The problem is that, in most psychological experiments, utterances like these are stripped bare, or nearly bare, before they are presented to subjects. The subjects are treated as if they had just begun overhearing a conversation between two strangers. Now there is nothing wrong with studying overhearing. But that must not be confused with studying understanding by addressees. Theories of understanding will not be the same for addressees and for overhearers (see Chapters 6, 7, 8, and 9).

The product tradition makes a strong assumption about language use: To produce or understand an utterance, a person has to formulate

---

[2]This is certainly not to deny the existence of sentences and their structure. They are just not as basic to language use as utterances.

or analyze the sentence uttered—the utterance stripped of speaker, addressee, and circumstances. This is a strong assumption and clearly not true in general (see Chapters 10 and 11). If it were, everyone would have rejected as nonsense a sign that stood on the wall of a London hospital for a number of years: "No head injury is too trivial to ignore."

TENET: In language use, speaker's meaning is primary, and word or sentence meaning are derivative.

Word and sentence meaning have always come first in theories of language structure. These theories assume that the meaning of a sentence like *The game warden watched the poacher with binoculars* is a composition of the meanings of its parts. Just as the words *game warden, watch, with*, and the rest get combined into larger and larger syntactic constructions, so their meanings get combined in larger and larger semantic representations. The result is the meaning of the sentence. In the product tradition, just as the sentence is basic, so is it natural to take word and sentence meaning as primary.

For many investigators in the action tradition, in contrast, it is the speaker's meaning, what the speaker means with an utterance, that is primary. Speaker's meaning is very different from word and sentence meaning. As Grice argued, it is a type of intention that speakers have toward addressees. When I say "Sit down" I intend you to recognize that I want you to sit down, and I expect you to see that in part by recognizing that very intention. Word and sentence meaning, on the other hand, are statements about conventions that hold within communities of people that enable the words and sentences to be used as a way of meaning things. *Hot* can mean "lucky," so when I say, "I'm hot" I can mean that I am lucky. In Grice's argument, words and sentences have meaning only in so far as a speaker can mean something by using them. That makes speaker's meaning primary.

Does it matter which type of meaning we take to be primary—word and sentence meaning, or speaker's meaning? Yes, it does, again because of the way it encourages us to think. In the product tradition, there is no need to look further than word or sentence meaning. Once investigators have discovered how people understand the meaning of the sentence *The game warden watched the poacher with binoculars*, they have said all they need to say. Speaker's meaning, they assume, follows directly from word and sentence meaning once they add certain information from context.

But we cannot take this model of understanding for granted. When I utter "I'm hot," what I mean isn't exhausted by what the sentence *I'm hot* means, even once *I* is tied to me, the tense of *am* to the moment I produced it, and *hot* to the meaning "lucky." Depending on the circumstance, I could also mean "This is why I have so many poker chips" or "I don't want to go home just yet" or many other things (see Chapters 7, 8, and 9). What is more, people often utter sentences, like *Our electric typewriter got married*, that are ungrammatical or semantically anomalous by grammatical criteria, but perfectly ordinary and acceptable in the circumstances (Chapters 10 and 11). In these and many other cases, we simply cannot derive what speakers mean from the meanings of the words and sentences they use. In language use, there is a great deal more to account for than sentence meaning.

TENET: Speaking and listening aren't autonomous activities, but parts of collective activities.

In the product tradition, speaking and listening are generally treated as autonomous processes like shaking a stick, playing a piano solo, or paddling a one-person kayak. They are processes that investigators can study by looking at individuals in isolation. The idea is this. Sentences are basic, so it is important to study how they are produced and understood. The most reliable way to investigate their production is to shut individuals up in a telephone booth away from all distractions and measure their actions as they utter sentences. And the most reliable way to study understanding is to shut individuals up in the same telephone booth, serve them utterances of sentences through earphones or on a video screen, and measure their reactions. That is roughly how most experiments in psycholinguistics proceed.

In the action tradition, however, a growing view is that speaking and listening are parts of collective, or joint, activities (see Chapters 4, 5, and 6). When two people use language, it is like shaking hands, playing a piano duet, or paddling a two-person canoe: It takes coordination, even collaboration, to achieve. Speaking and listening are two parts of a collective activity just as surely as playing the two parts of the piano duet are two parts of a collective activity. Playing the primo part in a duet demands much more of a pianist than playing the same primo part alone. Any musician will tell you that. So although we may be able to study some aspects of duet playing by looking at the two pianists in isolation, we must ultimately study them as they perform the duet. Likewise, many essential aspects of speaking and listening will emerge only when we study two people talking to each other.

Arenas of Language Use

These three tenets help explain why I speak of arenas of language use. Language use is more than people's production and understanding of a set of sentences with particular meanings. It is a class of collective activities in which speaker's meaning plays a necessary role. In these activities, speakers take actions by which they mean things, and their partners coordinate with them in trying to understand what they mean. The two of them try to reach certain goals, some joint and others not. Language use therefore takes place not in a vacuum, but in highly structured arenas of actions. Here are three properties of these arenas:

Participants. There are always two or more people involved in an arena of language use (Chapter 7 and 8). The participants are the people who take direct part in the current speaker's actions—the speaker, the addressees, and certain so-called side participants. Any other people around are considered bystanders or eavesdroppers precisely because they do not take direct part in these actions. In most arenas, the participants have additional roles that help define what they say and mean. They may be clerk and customer, interviewer and interviewee, boss and employee, or teacher and student.

Social processes. The participants' primary business in any arena of language use isn't talk per se. It is to accomplish some social process—to gossip, complete a business transaction, entertain each other, solve a problem together, instruct and learn, or even pass the time. How language is used in each arena depends on what the social process is.

Collective actions. The participants in an arena of language use engage in collective as well as autonomous actions. They have to if they are to accomplish the social processes they have set out to accomplish. They speak and listen in coordination, in collaboration, just as two pianists play a duet together, a couple waltzes together, or two gymnasts perform tricks together. Take away one of the two participants and you lose the phenomenon of interest.

Four Issues of Language Use

In this collection I take up four issues that emerge from viewing language use as a collective activity:

1. **Common ground.** All language use rests on a foundation of information that is shared by the participants—what is technically called their common ground. For language use to be a collective activity, it couldn't be otherwise. But just what is this common ground, and how is it necessary for language use?

2. **Collaborative processes.** What does it mean for language use to be a collective activity? At one level, it means that the partic-

ipants have to coordinate with each other—perhaps to cooperate in the way Grice proposed. But in conversation—the cradle of language use—it means something more. The participants also have to collaborate with each other. How does this collaboration work, and what are the consequences?

3. Audience design. Speakers don't just talk to the air. In arenas of language use, they design their utterances for their particular audiences as a way of accomplishing their goals. In fact, it isn't easy to engineer utterances for more than one hearer at a time or to deal with overhearers. Just what is audience design, and how is it engineered?

4. Coordination of meaning. The usual assumption is that, when speakers use a word, they are simply exploiting one of the word's fixed dictionary meanings. All we need to do is list these meanings and see how speakers select among them. But this assumption won't do. Speakers use words only in coordination with the other participants in an arena of action. What they mean by a word often goes far beyond what could ever be found in the word's dictionary entry. But how? In what ways do the traditional models of word use and understanding fall short?

These are hardly the only issues that distinguish the product and action traditions, but they are important ones. What the contributions to this book demonstrate, I hope, is that the collective nature of language goes far deeper than many have supposed. But we can only see this if we view language within natural arenas of use.

Part I

Common Ground and Language Use

Introduction to Part I

Common ground is a type of shared information. The common ground between Ann and Bob, for example, is the sum of their mutual knowledge, mutual beliefs, and mutual suppositions. The term was introduced in this technical sense, as far as I know, by Karttunen and Peters (1975) and Stalnaker (1978). Karttunen and Peters characterized it as the set of propositions that

any rational participant [in an exchange of talk] is rationally justified in taking for granted, for example, by virtue of what has been said in the conversation up to that point, what all the participants are in a position to perceive as true, whatever else they mutually know, assume, etc.

Stalnaker used it for describing a speaker's presuppositions:

Roughly speaking, the presuppositions of a speaker are the propositions whose truth he takes for granted as part of the background of the conversation ... Presuppositions are what is taken by the speaker to be the *common ground* of the participants in the conversation, what is treated as their *common knowledge* or *mutual knowledge* [Stalnaker's emphases].

The idea behind the three contributions in this first part of the book is that Ann and Bob cannot talk to each other successfully without appealing to their common ground.

My interest in common ground grew out of work I did with Susan Haviland in the early 1970s on *given* and *new information* in English utterances. In a paper in 1967, Michael Halliday had noted that speakers segment what they say into information units, usually clauses or sentences, which they divide into two parts. One part refers to information they assume their addressees take as "given," and a second part introduces information they assume their addressees will take as "new." They signal which part is which by placing focal stress on the constituent that expresses the new information. So with "What John did was *hit* Bill" the speaker takes it as given that John did something to Bill, and as new that that something was to hit him. Halliday's distinction was similar to Akmajian's, Chomsky's, and Jackendoff's distinction between "presupposition" and "focus" and Chafe's and Kuno's contrast between "old" and "new" information.[1]

Speakers and listeners, Haviland and I argued, ought therefore to adhere to an implicit "given-new contract" about the cooperative use of given and new information. Speakers should try to convey information they think the listener already has or can infer (that John did something to Bill) as given information, and information they think the listener doesn't yet know and cannot infer (that that something was hitting) as new information. Listeners should count on speakers doing this. They should seek a unique referent for the given information in memory (an event in which John did something to Bill) and add the new information to it. If there is no such referent represented in memory, they should draw a *bridging inference* to something that is and add that too.[2] Take the sequence:

Bill has a black eye. What John did was hit him.

To make sense of the second utterance when all you know is the first, you must draw the bridging inference "Bill had a black eye because John did something to him." That, then, allows you to add the new information (that that something was hitting) to memory. In a series of papers between 1973 and 1978, Haviland and I offered experimental and observational evidence for that model.

We were rather vague, however, about the content of the listener's memory. In our 1977 paper we said it was "information [the speaker] thinks the listener already knows" (p. 4). It included "not only those propositions underlying the sentences of a conversation—and perhaps not even all of these—but also propositions inferred from these sentences and from the extralinguistic context of the conversation" (p. 5). But this characterization doesn't say what information the listener can and can't access in a search for the referent of the given information. What we lacked was a precise notion of shared information.

Still, the model we proposed had three properties that have become part of most models of discourse:[3]

(1) The participants in a conversation work together against a background of shared information (later called common ground).

---

[1]For a comparison of Chafe's, Kuno's, and my conceptions of given and new information, see Prince 1981.

[2]David Lewis (1979) later called the same process *accommodation*.

[3]Among the earliest of these were Gazdar 1979, Lewis 1979, and Stalnaker 1978.

(2) As the discourse proceeds, the participants accumulate shared information by adding to it with each utterance.

(3) Speakers design their utterances so that their addressees can readily identify what is to be added to that common ground.

These three properties will return in different guises in this collection. For me, they got their start in this work.

What, then, was the information that speakers thought the listener already knew? I had read Grice's account of speaker's meaning and Strawson's and Searle's counterexamples to certain ways of characterizing the speaker's intentions. While I was on sabbatical leave at University College London, I talked to Ruth Kempson and Deirdre Wilson about some of these issues, and one of them suggested I read Stephen Schiffer's 1972 book *Meaning*. It is an indigestible book even by philosophical standards, but it introduced me to the technical notion of mutual knowledge and beliefs and showed me how essential this was to Grice's notion of meaning. That sent me back to David Lewis's characterization of mutual knowledge (he called it common knowledge) in his 1969 book *Convention*. Lewis, in turn, sent me back to Thomas Schelling's characterization of coordination in his 1960 book *The Strategy of Conflict*. These three books together show how essential common ground is in accounting for coordinated actions.

But for me, these three books raised a more psychological issue: How do people establish and represent mutual beliefs in a human-sized memory? One way of representing mutual beliefs implies that they are impossible to represent, and another doesn't. After I returned from my sabbatical in 1976, Catherine Marshall and I tried several approaches to the issue and carried out several preliminary experiments to test them. Our efforts bore no fruit until we hit on what we came to call the "copresence heuristics." From then on we never looked back. We presented a brief version of our work as "Reference diaries" at the 1978 conference, Theoretical Issues in Natural Language Processing-2 (known as TINLAP 2), and a more complete version as "Definite reference and mutual knowledge" at the 1978 Sloan Workshop on Computational Aspects of Linguistic Structure and Discourse Setting at the University of Pennsylvania. It is that paper, published in 1981, that appears as Chapter 1.

In the years since the publication of that paper, I have been surprised at how often Marshall and I have been misread. Here are two common examples.

1. We conclude that people's mental representations of mutual knowledge or mutual beliefs are *simple* in form. They are simple in-

ferences based on certain evidence and assumptions. They are *not*, I repeat *not*, an infinitely long list of statements, or even a truncated list. Some investigators have rejected mutual knowledge and mutual beliefs out of hand because they assume—incorrectly—that we imply that people's mental representations would have to be infinitely large. But that is standing our argument on its head. We argue, first, that it is absurd to think that people's mental representations could be infinite in size. We then go on to show how people can represent mutual knowledge or mutual beliefs fully and accurately in an elementary form. It seems difficult to say this more plainly.

2. We also conclude that people hold mutual beliefs with greater or lesser conviction. How strongly they hold a mutual belief depends on the evidence and assumptions it is based on. I may be confident you and I mutually believe the world is round, but less confident that you and I mutually believe Columbus wasn't the first European in America. Some investigators have rejected our arguments because they assume—incorrectly—that we require all "mutual knowledge" to be held with certainty. They appear to be misled by our cover term "mutual knowledge" even though we say in footnote 1: "Which propositional attitude is appropriate—knowledge, belief, assumption, supposition, or even some other term—depends on the evidence [the agent] possesses and other factors. For simplicity we will use *know* as the general term, but we could replace it with *believe* or certain other terms without affecting our argument." We chose the term *mutual knowledge* to match Lewis's and Schiffer's uses. It is because of this confusion that I turned to the term *common ground*. It explicitly covers mutual knowledge, mutual beliefs, mutual assumptions, and other mutual attitudes.

In the study of language use, investigators appeal time and again to "context" to explain this or that phenomenon. The problem is that they almost never say what they mean by "context" even when it is essential to their explanations. The notion of context, however, needn't be vague, Thomas Carlson and I argued. In language use the relevant context is simply the common ground of the participants. Our paper, "Context for comprehension," was presented at the 1980 Attention and Performance conference held in Jesus College, Cambridge. It appears as Chapter 2. To my surprise, a reviewer of the 1981 proceedings argued that the term *context* is useful to psychologists precisely because it is vague. That may be. But it also allows psychologists to hoodwink themselves as well as others into thinking they have explanations for context effects when they don't. I prefer to eschew the term *context* for something less dangerous.

David Lewis, in his book *Convention*, argued that conventions are solutions to recurrent problems people have in coordinating, and that a language like English is simply a conventional signalling system. In that argument, he appealed to Schelling's analysis of coordination problems. Robert Schreuder, who was on sabbatical leave at Stanford in 1980–1981, and I started to look closely at Schelling's analysis and realized that it offered an account for the pervasive nonconventional aspects of language use too. As I recall, we first applied our ideas to the understanding of word meaning, but were unable to devise experimental tests to show what we needed to show. So, in work with Sam Buttrick, we applied them instead to the understanding of demonstrative reference. The result was "Common ground and the understanding of demonstrative reference," which appeared in the *Journal of Verbal Learning and Verbal Behavior* in 1983. It appears as Chapter 3. Some of the same themes turn up again in Chapters 10, 11, and 12.

1

Definite Reference and Mutual Knowledge

WITH CATHERINE R. MARSHALL

> Jack thinks
> > he does not know
> > what he thinks
> > > Jill thinks
> > > he does not know
> But Jill thinks Jack does know it.
> So Jill does not know
> > she does not know
> > that Jack does not know
> > that Jill thinks
> > that Jack does know
> and Jack does not know he does not know
> > that Jill does not know she does not know
> > that Jack does not know
> > > that Jill thinks Jack knows
> what Jack thinks he does not know
> Jack doesn't know he knows
> and he doesn't know
> > Jill does not know.
> Jill doesn't know she doesn't know,
> > and doesn't know
> > > that Jack doesn't know Jill does not know.
> They have no problems.
>
> *Knots*, by R. D. Laing

In speaking and listening, people make essential use of a great deal of world knowledge that they "share" with each other. The question is, what kind of "shared" knowledge do they use, and how? Recently, in looking at how people plan definite reference, we came on one answer to this question that made us distinctly uneasy. It seemed to suggest that expressions like *the cold asparagus*, *the mess I made*, and *that animal* require speakers to check a list of facts or beliefs that is infinitely long. Under the most plausible assumptions about how they would actually check that list, they should take an infinitely long time to decide on each noun phrase. However, if there was anything we were certain about, it was that noun phrases like these are ordinarily selected in a *finite* amount of time—in a few seconds or less. We were at an impasse. The argument for an infinite amount of processing time seemed impeccable, but so did the evidence against it. What we had was a processing paradox, which for reasons that will become clear later we called the *Mutual Knowledge Paradox*.

Like all paradoxes, of course, this one rests on several critical assumptions, and when these assumptions are weakened in one way or another, the paradox can be resolved in several ways. These different resolutions, however, each have their own consequences, and depending on which one we accept, we are led to rather different models for the production and understanding of speech. It is important to decide, then, which way the Mutual Knowledge Paradox is most plausibly resolved.

But we are interested in this paradox only as a way of getting at the two central questions of this chapter: (a) What type of shared knowledge is needed for language use? and (b) how is that shared knowledge in practice assessed and secured? The area of language in which we will take up these questions is definite reference, but even our interest in definite reference is secondary to our concern with the two questions of mutual knowledge. The way we will proceed, then, is to set out the Mutual Knowledge Paradox, describe two ways of resolving it, and argue that one of them is the more usual resolution. We will then suggest that the answers to these two questions bear directly on current theories of language structure and language use, in particular on the characterization and processing of definite reference.

1 The Mutual Knowledge Paradox

Imagine that there is a Marx brothers film festival on at the Roxy, with one film showing each night for a week. Against this background consider the following scenario.

VERSION 1: On Wednesday morning Ann reads the early edition of the newspaper which says that *Monkey Business* is playing that night. Later she sees Bob and asks, *Have you ever seen the movie showing at the Roxy tonight?*

Our interest is in Ann's use of the definite referring expression *the movie showing at the Roxy tonight*, term *t*, by which Ann intends to refer to *Monkey Business*, referent *R*. What does Ann have to assure herself of in order to make this reference felicitously? That is, under what conditions does Ann have good reason to believe that Bob won't get the wrong referent or have to ask for clarification, as with *Which movie do you mean?* The answer we will develop is that she must be certain that once she has made her reference he and she can establish certain shared knowledge about the identity of that referent. Although not all aspects of this scenario are applicable to all other instances of definite reference, we will take up the more general case later.

An obvious first condition is that Ann herself know that the expression *the movie showing at the Roxy tonight* uniquely describes the movie *Monkey Business*—for example, there aren't two movies showing tonight instead. We will describe this knowledge as "*t* is *R*," that is, *the movie at the Roxy tonight is Monkey Business*. So, Ann must be certain that after her reference the following condition will be true:[1]

(1)   Ann knows that *t* is *R*.

But is this enough? Obviously not, for what is missing is even the simplest notion of shared knowledge. Specifically, (1) gives no assurance that on the basis of her reference Bob himself will realize that *the movie at the Roxy tonight* uniquely describes *Monkey Business*, a realization that is surely a sine qua non of a felicitous reference. The way Ann's reference may fail can be illustrated by a variation on our original scenario:

VERSION 2: On Wednesday morning Ann and Bob read the early edition of the newspaper and discuss the fact that it says that *A Day at the Races* is showing that night at the Roxy. Later, after Bob has left, Ann gets the late edition, which prints a correction, which is that it is *Monkey Business* that is actually showing that night. Later, Ann sees Bob and asks, *Have you ever seen the movie showing at the Roxy tonight?*

---

[1]One important caveat here. Often all Ann will be able to check is her belief or assumption or supposition instead of her *knowledge* that *t* is *R*. Which propositional attitude is appropriate—knowledge, belief, assumption, supposition, or even some other term—depends on the evidence Ann possesses and other factors. For simplicity we will use *know* as the general term, but we could replace it with *believe* or certain other terms without affecting our argument.

Although this version satisfies condition (1), Ann has clearly made her definite reference without the proper assurances. She has no reason to think that Bob will realize that the film she is referring to is *Monkey Business*. He is most likely to think it is *A Day at the Races*. The reason why her reference isn't felicitous is clear. She has not assured herself that after she had made her reference Bob will know that the *movie showing at the Roxy tonight* uniquely describes *Monkey Business*. So Ann must satisfy this condition:

(2)   Ann knows that Bob knows that t is R.

At first, conditions (1) and (2) may appear to be enough, but it is easy to show that they aren't. Consider this variation:

VERSION 3: On Wednesday morning Ann and Bob read the early edition of the newspaper, and they discuss the fact that it says that *A Day at the Races* is showing that night at the Roxy. When the late edition arrives, Bob reads the movie section, notes that the film has been corrected to *Monkey Business*, and circles it with his red pen. Later, Ann picks up the late edition, notes the correction and recognizes Bob's circle around it. She also realizes that Bob has no way of knowing that she has seen the late edition. Later that day Ann sees Bob and asks, *Have you ever seen the movie showing at the Roxy tonight?*

The scenario satisfies conditions (1) and (2). Ann knows that the movie is *Monkey Business* and that Bob knows that it is, too. But she believes that he believes that she still thinks it is *A Day at the Races*. He is very likely to take her reference as one to *A Day at the Races* instead of *Monkey Business*. Her reference is infelicitous because she hasn't satisfied this condition:

(3)   Ann knows that Bob knows that Ann knows that t is R.

The third condition, however, is still not enough, as we can illustrate with yet another version of the original scenario:

VERSION 4: On Wednesday morning Ann and Bob read the early edition of the newspaper and discuss the fact that it says that *A Day at the Races* is playing that night at the Roxy. Later, Ann sees the late edition, notes that the movie has been corrected to *Monkey Business*, and marks it with her blue pencil. Still later, as Ann watches without Bob knowing it, he picks up the late edition and sees Ann's pencil mark. That afternoon, Ann sees Bob and asks, *Have you ever seen the movie showing at the Roxy tonight?*

This version satisfies conditions (1), (2), and (3). Ann knows that the movie is *Monkey Business*; she knows that Bob knows it, too—she saw him look at the late edition; and she knows that he knows that she knows it, too—she saw him notice her pencil mark on the correct movie in the late edition. Yet Ann is still not completely justified in thinking Bob will know she is referring to *Monkey Business*. If she looks at the world from his point of view, she should reason like this: *She knows that the movie is* Monkey Business. *But she thinks that I, Bob, think it is A Day at the Races, and so by her reference, she must think I will pick out* A Day at the Races. But if her reference may get Bob to pick out *A Day at the Races*, it is infelicitous. So we must add another condition for Ann to be sure of:

(4)   Ann knows that Bob knows that Ann knows that Bob knows that *t* is *R*.

Can we now stop with the confidence that condition (4) is enough? Not if we can dream up a scenario that satisfies (1) through (4) but still doesn't justify a felicitous reference. With a little difficulty, we can:

VERSION 5: On Wednesday morning Ann and Bob read the early edition of the newspaper and discuss the fact that it says that *A Day at the Races* is playing that night at the Roxy. Later, Bob sees the late edition, notices the correction of the movie to *Monkey Business*, and circles it with his red pen. Later, Ann picks up the newspaper, sees the correction, and recognizes Bob's red pen mark. Bob happens to see her notice the correction and his red pen mark. In the mirror Ann sees Bob watch all this, but realizes that Bob hasn't seen that she has noticed him. Later that day, Ann sees Bob and asks, *Have you ever seen the movie showing at the Roxy tonight?*

Complicated as this scenario is, it is possible to see that Ann should not in good conscience have made this definite reference. Putting herself in Bob's shoes again, she should reason like this: *Ann knows that the movie is* Monkey Business, *and she knows that I know that, too. Yet she believes that I think she thinks the movie is* A Day at the Races, *and so by her reference, she should think I will decide she is referring to* A Day at the Races. But if her reference gets Bob to pick out *A Day at the Races*, it is infelicitous. So we must add condition (5):

(5)   Ann knows that Bob knows that Ann knows that Bob knows that Ann knows that *t* is *R*.

Can we be confident that condition (5) is enough? Indeed, we can be sure that it isn't, no matter how fast we seem to be narrowing in on what Ann must be sure of. What these versions show is that there is a way *in principle* of demonstrating that the last piece of embedded knowledge is insufficient. The method is this: Corresponding to Ann's condition (1) is an analogous condition that Bob must assure himself of if he is to be certain she is referring to *Monkey Business*. The condition is this:

(1′)   Bob knows that t is R.

For Ann to be sure that her reference succeeds in bringing about this knowledge, she must put herself in Bob's shoes, reason as he would, and make sure she could identify the intended referent uniquely. What we did in constructing Version 2 was to create a scenario in which (1) held after Ann's definite reference, but Ann couldn't know whether (1′) held or not. This led us to add condition (2), *Ann knows that Bob knows that t is R*, the equivalent of *Ann knows that (1′)*. But just as Ann needs to make sure her reference will bring about (2), Bob has to come to know (2′):

(2′)   Bob knows that Ann knows that t is R.

But then (2′) is something else Ann must make sure her reference will bring about, as we showed in creating Version 3, and this led to condition (3). Corresponding to (3), however, is Bob's (3′), which we used in creating Version 4. In principle, we could use this procedure to construct countermanding versions ad infinitum.

The Paradox

This view of what Ann has to be sure will result from her use of *the movie showing at the Roxy tonight* suggests a processing paradox. On the one hand, Ann has an infinity of conditions, like (1) through (5), to assure herself of, and that should take her an infinite amount of time. On the other hand, she is surely able to use *the movie showing a the Roxy tonight* as a definite reference, when the circumstances are right, in a finite amount of time. Hence the paradox.

You might rightly complain, however, that the paradox contains a number of hidden assumptions, one or more of which are probably suspect. We see the underlying assumptions to be roughly the following:

ASSUMPTION I: Ann ordinarily tries to make definite references that are felicitous—ones for which Bob won't get the wrong referent or have to ask *Which one?*

ASSUMPTION II: To make such a felicitous definite reference Ann must assure herself of each of the infinity of conditions (1), (2), (3), (4), and so on.

ASSUMPTION III:Each of the conditions (1), (2), (3), (4), and so on, takes a finite (though small) amount of time or capacity to check.

ASSUMPTION IV: Ann ordinarily makes each definite reference in a finite amount of time, on the order of a few seconds.

Assumption I is simply that Ann always tries to make herself understood. She doesn't just blurt out a definite reference and hope against hope that it will work. She chooses her references deliberately and with care. Assumption II merely restates what we have just argued in Ann's reference to *Monkey Business*—that it appears to require her to check an infinity of conditions. Assumption III states a processing assumption that is common to almost every psychological model for such a process—that an infinite number of mental operations cannot be carried out in a finite amount of time (Sternberg 1966; Townsend 1972). And Assumption IV states the obvious empirical observation that when people refer to things, they don't take much time in doing it.

The Mutual Knowledge Paradox can be resolved, therefore, by throwing out one or another of these assumptions. Assumptions III and IV seem impossible to get rid of. At least, doing so would take a great deal of argument. The burden of the paradox, then, falls on Assumptions I and II. Which one, if not both, should we drop? We will return to this question once we have looked more closely at the Frankenstein monster we have created for "shared" knowledge.

2   "Shared" Knowledge

In common parlance, "shared" knowledge has several definitions. Ask your aunt what it means for the two of you to share knowledge that the mayor is an embezzler, and she would probably say, *It means that you know he is an embezzler, and so do I.* If p is the proposition that the mayor is an embezzler, then the first definition of shared knowledge comes out like this:

A and B share$_1$ knowledge that p =$_{\text{def}}$

(1) A knows that p.

(1′) B knows that p.

Or your aunt might give a more complicated answer: *It seems that both of us know that he is an embezzler, and furthermore, I know that you know he is, and you know that I know he is.* This leads to a second definition of shared knowledge:

> A and B share$_2$ knowledge that $p =_{\text{def}}$
>
> (1) A knows that p.
> (1$'$) B knows that p.
> (2) A knows that B knows that p.
> (2$'$) B knows that A knows that p.

We can define a series of types of "shared" knowledge merely by extending the list of statements. These can be denoted by the appropriate subscript on *share*. Shared$_4$ knowledge contains statements down to (4) and (4$'$), shared$_n$ knowledge, statements down to (n) and (n$'$). None of these finite definitions, of course, describes the "shared" knowledge required of Ann and Bob after her reference to *Monkey Business*. For that we need something more.

Mutual Knowledge

What is required, apparently, is the technical notion of *mutual knowledge*. It has been defined and exploited by Lewis (1969) and Schiffer (1972) for dealing with close cousins of the problem we have raised here. Mutual knowledge is Schiffer's term, whereas Lewis' term for the same thing is common knowledge. We have chosen Schiffer's term, which seems more transparent and less open to misinterpretation. Schiffer defines mutual knowledge as follows:

> A and B mutually know that $p =_{\text{def}}$
>
> (1) A knows that p.
> (1$'$) B knows that p.
> (2) A knows that B knows that p.
> (2$'$) B knows that A knows that p.
> (3) A knows that B knows that A knows that p.
> (3$'$) B knows that A knows that B knows that p.
> etc., ad infinitum.

Mutual knowledge is the same as shared$_\infty$ knowledge. With the appropriate changes in the definitions, we can also talk about mutual beliefs, mutual expectations, and other mutually held propositional attitudes.

Harman (1977) notes that the infinity of statements in this definition of mutual knowledge can be represented more succinctly in a single self-referential statement of the following kind:[2]

---

[2]Another way to represent this is as two interreferring statements of this kind:

A and B mutually know that $p =_{\text{def}}$

    (q) A and B know that p and that q.

Cohen (1978) uses a similar representation. In some ways, this definition captures our intuitions about mutual knowledge even better than Schiffer's definition. A visual metaphor will help. Imagine that the proposition p is that the mayor is an embezzler, which Ann and Bob come to know by viewing a picture of the mayor altering the books in the city treasurer's office—he was caught red-handed by a local newspaper photographer. Now by Harman's definition, it is as if Ann and Bob are viewing not only the picture of the mayor's embezzlement, but also a picture of them looking at this picture. That second picture, of course, shows them looking at both pictures, the second of which shows them looking at both pictures, and so on ad infinitum. This definition seems to capture the kind of omniscience Ann and Bob possess about their knowledge of the mayor's embezzlement.

Yet this definition per se doesn't change what Ann and Bob have to assess. Ann must check whether for the Marx brothers example she and Bob know that is *Monkey Business*. But she must also check to see whether she and Bob know that q, and q is that she and Bob know that t is *Monkey Business* and know that q'. That is, she must check to see whether she and Bob know that she and Bob know that t is *Monkey Business*, and, for q', whether she and Bob know that she and Bob know that she and Bob know that t is *Monkey Business* and that q'', and so on. So just the fact that mutual knowledge can be captured in a single statement doesn't absolve Ann and Bob from checking each of an infinity of statements. Although the representation *looks* simpler, its assessment isn't necessarily simpler.

The form in which mutual knowledge will be most useful, however, is slightly different from either of these two definitions. Note that both definitions represent mutual knowledge as an omniscient observer would see it, an observer who can say both what A knows and what B knows. But in our Marx brothers examples, Ann was not omniscient. She needed only half the conditions in Schiffer's definition—those numbered *without* primes. It is easy to see that what she needed is equivalent to this:

A and B mutually know that $p =_{\text{def}}$

    (r) A knows that p and that r'.

    (r') B knows that p and that r.

In some ways this representation is preferable, for unlike the single self-referential statement, it does not assume that if A knows that A knows that p, then A knows that p. Although this assumption may be justifiable for the verb *know*, it is not so obviously justifiable with *believe* or *assume* or *suppose* in place of *know*.

A knows that A and B mutually know that p.

The effect of this single recursion is to erase all the primes in Schiffer's definition. This assertion says, for example, that A knows that $(1')$. With $(1')$ spelled out, it says that A knows that B knows that p. But this is equivalent to (2). All the other primes get obliterated in the same way. So from Ann's vantage point, she must determine that she knows that she and Bob mutually know that p, and from his vantage point, he must determine that *he* knows that he and she mutually know that p.[3] Most of the time, however, we will speak informally of A determining merely that A and B mutually know that p, and of B determining merely that A and B mutually know that p. These might be called *one-sided definitions of mutual knowledge*.

Uses of Mutual Knowledge

The notion of mutual knowledge was originally devised by Lewis to handle some ordinary problems of coordination raised by Schelling in his book *The Strategy of Conflict* (1960). Take the grandfather of all coordination problems:

> You are to meet somebody in New York City. You have not been instructed where to meet; you have no prior understanding with the person on where to meet; and you cannot communicate with each other. You are simply told that you will have to guess where to meet and that he is being told the same thing and that you will just have to try to make your guesses coincide. (Schelling 1960, 56)

According to Lewis, you will want to go where the other person will go, namely, where you expect him to go. But you expect him to go where he will expect you to go. Where is that? Where he will expect you to expect him to go, of course, And so on. In short, the two of you will go where you mutually expect the other to go. Whether your mutual expectations are accurate or not is another matter.

If you repeatedly meet your friend at the same place, Lewis argues, you will eventually firm up your expectations and set up a regularity that can be called a convention. It may become a convention, for example, that the two of you meet, whenever you are supposed to meet in New York City, at the lost-and-found booth of Grand Central Station. But to do so, the two of you must mutually know, among other things, that both of you will go to that booth and that both

---

[3]This one-sided mutual knowledge can be represented in a self-referential definition (see footnote 2) as follows:

A knows that A and B mutually know that $p =_{\text{def}}$

$\quad (r)$ A knows that p and that: B knows that p and that r.

of you expect each other to go to that booth. In Lewis' formulation, mutual knowledge is indispensable to the definition of convention. It is also, therefore, indispensable to the definition of language because, as Lewis shows, a language like English is in part a system of such conventions.

An application of mutual knowledge closer to our own examples is found in Schiffer's reformulation of Grice's definition of speaker meaning in natural language. Very briefly, his application goes like this. As Grice (1957, 385) defined this meaning, " 'S [the speaker] meant something by x' is (roughly) equivalent to 'S intended the utterance of x to produce some effect in an audience by means of the recognition of his intention.' " But this definition will not work, Schiffer shows, unless the speaker and audience mutually know, among other things, the effects particular utterances are intended to produce. Schiffer was forced to this conclusion by a series of counterexamples to Grice's definition devised by Strawson (1964), by Searle (1965), and by Schiffer himself. Strawson's and Searle's counterexamples had led to minor repairs in Grice's definition, but Schiffer's, like ours, showed that it was always possible in principle to devise problematic scenarios for "shared" knowledge with fewer than an infinite number of steps. Schiffer's solution was to incorporate the notion of mutual knowledge directly into the definition of speaker meaning, just as Lewis had incorporated it directly into the definition of convention.

Mutual knowledge, then, is ubiquitous. It is an essential ingredient in convention, in meaning, and in language in general. It isn't surprising that it should be an essential ingredient in definite reference, too.

Uses of "Shared" Knowledge

How have other investigators defined "shared" knowledge? Most haven't. The great majority have avoided the problem by not mentioning any interaction between the speaker and listener (for example, J. Anderson (1976; 1977; 1978), R. Anderson et al. (1976), Ortony and Anderson (1977), Schank and Abelson (1977)). Others have avoided the problem by limiting the universe of discourse to precisely what the speaker and listener both know. In Winograd's (1972) understanding program, for instance, the commander of the computer "robot" knows what the robot knows and cannot entertain the possibility that there are things the robot knows that he doesn't know. This has been characteristic of most models within psychology and artificial intelligence.

Within linguistics and philosophy only a handful of investigators have addressed the problem of "shared" knowledge. Several have discussed shared knowledge in a general way, but without saying which kind of shared knowledge they mean. Karttunen (1977, 155), for example, talked about a "conversational context," the set of propositions the speaker and addressee can take for granted at that point in the discourse. Later, Karttunen and Peters introduced the notion of "common ground" or the "common set of presumptions". This consists of the set of propositions "any rational participant [in an exchange of talk] is rationally justified in taking for granted, for example, by virtue of what has been said in the conversation up to that point, what all the participants are in a position to perceive as true, whatever else they mutually know, assume, etc." (286). Karttunen and Peters did not say whether they meant "mutually know, assume, etc." in the technical sense or not. (See also Hawkins 1978, and McCawley 1979.)

On several occasions, investigators have committed themselves to specific kinds of shared knowledge. Clark and Haviland (1977), for example, discussed a processing strategy, the given–new strategy, that appeared to require nothing more than shared$_2$ knowledge. Prince (1978) proposed the notion of tacit assumptions, took up examples that required various amounts of shared knowledge, but didn't bring in anything more than shared$_3$ knowledge. Kempson (1975) explicitly committed herself to shared$_4$ knowledge in discussing the set of propositions that constitute the speaker and hearer's "shared knowledge— knowledge they believe they share" (167). She specifically listed knowledge statements (1), (2), (3), and (4), and no others. In an early paper, Stalnaker (1977) characterized pragmatic presupposition as equivalent to shared$_4$ knowledge: "A proposition P is a pragmatic presupposition of a speaker in a given context just in case the speaker assumes or believes that P, assumes or believes that his addressee believes that P, and assumes or believes that his addressee recognizes that he is making these assumptions, or has these beliefs" (137).

Finally, a few investigators have been explicit in their use of mutual knowledge. In a later paper, Stalnaker (1978) replaced his earlier shared$_4$ knowledge with the notion of "common ground": "presuppositions are what is taken by the speaker to be the *common ground* of the participants in the conversation, what is treated as their *common knowledge* or *mutual knowledge* [Stalnaker's emphasis]" (321). Similarly, Nunberg (1977), in accounting for definite reference and other pragmatic problems, introduced the notion of "normal beliefs," which are based on mutual knowledge. And Cohen (1978), in his computational model of speech acts and reference, made essential use of mutual beliefs, too.

As this brief survey shows, at least some investigators have felt the need for a notion of shared knowledge. When they have been specific, they have used notions ranging from shared to mutual knowledge. There have been almost as many names for shared knowledge as investigators: conversational context, common ground, common set of presumptions, shared sets, contextual domain, tacit assumptions, pragmatic presuppositions, normal beliefs, and mutual beliefs. Yet these investigators have not taken up the question that would resolve the Mutual Knowledge Paradox: How is shared knowledge assessed in the process of speaking or understanding? Before turning to this question, however, we must take up definite reference itself.

3 Definite Reference

Although definite reference has begotten a vast literature in linguistics, philosophy, artificial intelligence, and psychology, there is still little consensus about its essentials. In this brief section, we cannot hope to do justice to that literature or provide that consensus. Yet to be able to examine the role mutual knowledge plays in definite reference, we need a model for definite reference, no matter how tentative. For this purpose, we will adopt Hawkins' (1978) model of definite reference and modify it a bit to handle some observations of Nunberg (1977), and to make it more closely resemble a related model of Clark and Clark (1979). The only claim we make for this model is that it is a reasonable first approximation—good enough at least to allow us to examine the role of mutual knowledge.

The Location Theory of the Definite Article

In Chapter 3 of his book *Definiteness and Indefiniteness* Hawkins reviews the major nongeneric uses of the definite article *the* and then proposes what he calls the location theory of the definite article. He takes up only some uses of the demonstratives *this* and *that*; he doesn't discuss pronouns or proper names. Although his theory is more restrictive than we desire, it is a place to start.

According to the location theory, the speaker performs three acts in using the definite article:

a. He introduces a referent (or referents) to the hearer.
b. He instructs the hearer to locate the referent in some shared set of objects.
c. He refers to the totality of the objects or mass within this set that satisfy the referring expression.

To take an example, imagine that Ann told Bob *Bring me the apples*. By this she introduces to him some referents, namely apples. She instructs him to locate apples in some set of objects that she and he share knowledge about. She then refers to the totality of apples in that set—namely, all of the apples. If Ann had said *Bring me the apple*, the shared set of objects would contain exactly one apple, and by referring to the totality of objects within this set, she would have referred to that apple uniquely.

As (b) makes clear, the referent is to be located in a shared set of objects. Where do these shared sets come from? Hawkins argues that they are based on shared knowledge—he doesn't specify which kind—and are inferred "either from previous discourse or from the situation of utterance" (1978, 168). As evidence, Hawkins discusses the eight major uses of the definite article put forth by Christopherson (1939) and Jespersen (1949):

1. **The Anaphoric Use.** In *I bought a lathe, but the machine didn't work right*, the utterance of *a lathe* sets up a "shared previous discourse set," which can subsequently be identified as the referent of *the machine*.

2. **The Visible Situation Use.** In a situation where a bucket is visible to both the speaker and listener, the speaker can say *Pass me the bucket*. The visible bucket constitutes a shared set of objects, which can then be identified as the referent of *the bucket*.[4]

3. **The Immediate Situation Use.** A speaker can use *Do not feed the pony* even though the pony is not visible, so long as its existence can be inferred from the situation. Then it is the inferred pony that constitutes the shared set of objects to which *the pony* refers.

4. **The Larger Situation Use Based on Specific Knowledge.** Bob may know the particular store Ann shops at every day, and so it is a shared set of objects. Ann can then refer to it without further explanation, as in *I'm going to the store*.

5. **The Larger Situation Use Based on General Knowledge.** Ann and Bob know as a general fact that American towns of a certain size each have one city hall. The city hall of Spearfish, the town they happen to be going through at the time, therefore constitutes a shared set of objects that Ann can refer to, an in *I wonder where the city hall is*.

6. **The Associative Anaphoric Use.** In *A car just went by and the exhaust fumes made me sick*, the car is a "trigger" to the "as-

---

[4] "Visibility" is obviously too restricted a term here and should be replaced by "perceptibility" to encompass taste, smell, and hearing, as in *Where is the awful smell/taste/noise coming from?* This is part of our reason for later using the term "physical" as opposed to "visual" for such cases.

sociate" exhaust fumes, and so with the mention of a car, people have a set of associates, which constitutes a shared set of objects. According to Hawkins, "speaker and listener share knowledge of the generic relationship between trigger and associate" (1978, 125).

7. **The Unavailable Use.** Take *Bill is amazed by the fact that there is so much life on earth*, in which *the fact that there is so much life on earth* introduces new information unknown to the listener. To account for this apparent counterexample to (b), Hawkins takes a transformational approach, arguing that the sentence is derived from *That there is so much life on earth is a fact which Bill is amazed by*. In this source, *a fact* is now indefinite, and so the location theory can be preserved. The unknown information introduced in *The woman whom Max went out with last night was nasty to him*, which contains a "referent–establishing relative clause," is handled in a similar way, and so is the unknown information in *I don't like the color red*, which contains a nominal modifier.

8. **The Unexplanatory Modifier Use.** In *The first person to sail to America was an Icelander*, the definite noun phrase picks out a unique person, whoever he may be, from the set of people who have sailed to America. This is what Donnellan (1966) has called an *attributive* rather than a *referential* use of the definite noun phrase. It picks out "whatever or whoever has that description," whereas a referential use is "merely one tool for calling attention to a person or thing," and "any other device for doing the same job, another description or name, would do as well" (285). Attributive uses are not intended to secure the mutual knowledge of the identity of the thing being picked out (although they may), and so they should not be assimilated, as they appear to be by Hawkins, with the referential uses, which *are* intended to secure mutual knowledge of the identity of the referent. Our concern is with referential uses, and so we will not consider the unexplanatory modifier use or any other attributive uses any further.

Modifications of the Location Theory

Like all other current theories of definite reference, the location theory has its problems. At least two of these problems are critical to our enterprise.

The first problem has to do with a condition Hawkins places on the composition of the shared set of objects is (b): "The hearer must either know or be able to infer that the intended object has the property that is used to refer to it in the descriptive predicate" (1978, 168). This condition says that for *the ham sandwich*, the hearer must know or be able to infer that the referent is a ham sandwich. This, however, cannot be correct—at least not without qualification.[5]

Nunberg (1977) has pointed out systematic examples in which the referent does not have to have the property of the descriptive predicate. Imagine a waiter in a restaurant pointing to a ham sandwich and saying to another waiter *The ham sandwich is sitting at table six*. In this utterance, *the ham sandwich* is used to refer to the customer who ordered the sandwich, and that customer is obviously not a ham sandwich. Or imagine Ann pointing at her watch and saying *This watch now costs a hundred dollars*, by which she means "an instance of the type of watch this watch is would now cost a hundred dollars" (her own battered watch no longer having much value). Indeed, as Nunberg shows, deferred reference like this is common. To handle such cases, Nunberg introduces the notion of reference function. This is a function the hearer computes on each occasion to get him from the "designatum," (the ham sandwich or watch) to the intended referent (the customer or kind of watch).

The way we will handle this is to distinguish direct from indirect reference precisely on the analogy of direct and indirect illocutionary force. To begin with illocutionary force, *Do you know the time?* can be said to have a *direct* illocutionary force, *Do you have the knowledge of the time?*, by virtue of which a speaker can convey a second *indirect* illocutionary force, *Please tell me the time* (Searle 1975). In his utterance, the speaker intends to convey both illocutionary forces, although the direct meaning may not be intended to be taken seriously (Clark 1979), and it may convey the indirect meaning by one or another conventional means (Morgan 1978). Analogously, *the ham sandwich* can be said to have a *direct* referent, the ham sandwich on the plate in front of the waiter, by virtue of which the waiter can indicate a second *indirect* referent, the man who ordered the sandwich. In uttering *The ham sandwich is sitting at table six*, the waiter intends to refer to both objects—the sandwich and the person—although the thing that he is saying is sitting at table six is always the indirect referent. The relation

---

[5]It cannot be correct for other reasons either. In Donnellan's (1966) example *Who is the man drinking a martini?* the definite reference *the man drinking a martini* refers to a particular man even if the speaker is mistaken and the man happens to be drinking water. Moreover, such a reference will generally succeed (see also Donnellan 1968). The complications of this sort of misdescription and its relation to mutual belief are thoroughly discussed by Perrault and Cohen (Joshi, Webber, and Sag 1981). There is a related problem in deception (see Bruce and Newman 1978).

between the direct and indirect referents is determined by Nunberg's reference function.

The condition Hawkins places on the composition of the shared set of objects, then, doesn't need to be changed, as long as we say he is dealing with *direct* definite reference. That is what we will do. We assume that theories of indirect definite reference will proceed along the lines set out by Nunberg as to what constitutes the intended reference function on any particular occasion. As he demonstrates, discovering those functions will not be an easy matter.

The second problem lies in the chronological order of (a) the time of acquisition by the speaker and listener of their shared knowledge of the required set of objects and (b) the moment of the reference act itself— the moment when the speaker utters the referring expression. Call these two moments $Moment_{SK}$ and $Moment_{RA}$, respectively (SK for shared knowledge and RA for reference act). Although Hawkins doesn't say so explicitly, he seems to assume that $Moment_{SK}$ must precede $Moment_{RA}$. That is, the speaker can only refer to sets of objects he and his listener *already* share knowledge about. This assumption pervades Hawkins' discussion of the first six uses of the definite article, and it seems to motivate his transformational treatment of the seventh.

Is this assumption correct? Clearly not. It appears possible to find counterexamples to the assumption for all eight uses of the definite article. Take the anaphoric use. Contrary to the assumption, it is easy to get an anaphor before its "antecedent," as in *Before he could steal anything, a burglar who had broken into our house was frightened away*. Or take the visible situation use. Contrary to the assumption, Ann can felicitously ask Bob *Please pass the salt* without his realizing there is any salt around. Indeed, it is her reference that induces him to assume there must be salt in view and to look for it. Or take the larger situation use based on general knowledge. Also contrary to the assumption, Ann can felicitously tell Bob *The fourth root of 81 is the number of sisters I have* without assuming that Bob *already* knows what the fourth root of 81 is. She need only assume that he can readily figure it out. In each of these examples, $Moment_{SK}$ comes *after* $Moment_{RA}$, and the shared knowledge is brought about in part by the reference act itself.

But if $Moment_{RA}$ can precede $Moment_{SK}$, there is less reason to posit transformational sources for the seventh use of the definite article. For an alternative analysis, consider Ann's assertion to Bob *The woman Max went out with last night was nasty to him*, where Ann is introducing the woman referred to for the first time. Referent–establishing relative clauses like this, as Hawkins notes, must be anchored to object sets that are already shared, in this instance Max. Ann could not have said, for example, *The woman some man went out with last night was nasty to him*, because *some man* doesn't provide such an anchor. If this is so, Bob can form an object set for this utterance by very much the same procedure as he would for *I wonder where the city hall is*, the fifth use of the definite article. For Ann and Bob it is general knowledge that men like Max often go out with women, ordinarily one woman on any one night, and so Bob can form the set of objects Ann is referring to, namely, the woman Max went out with last night. The requirement, then, seems to be not that Bob already have a shared set of objects, but that he be able to form one based on general or particular mutual knowledge and on the fact that the reference act occurred.

With these two modifications, we can reformulate the location theory in slightly different terms. Tentatively, we suggest the following convention:

The Direct Definite Reference Convention. In making a direct definite reference with term *t* sincerely, the speaker intends to refer to

1. the totality of objects or mass within a set of objects in one possible world, which set of objects is such that
2. the speaker has good reason to believe
3. that on this occasion the listener can readily infer
4. uniquely
5. mutual knowledge of the identity of that set
6. such that the intended objects or mass in the set fit the descriptive predicates in *t*, or, if *t* is a rigid designator, are designated by *t*.

We will not try to justify this formulation in detail, but a few observations are in order. The main point of the convention is this: For a speaker to refer to a thing, he must be confident that because of his speech act the identity of that thing will become mutually known to him and his listener. It doesn't have to be mutually known beforehand, but, of course, if it were, the listener's inferences would be all that much easier. Ordinarily, to *become* mutually known, the referent must at least be anchored to something that is already mutually known via an anchor cable that is already mutually known. To understand Ann's *I wonder where the city hall is*, Bob doesn't need to believe that the city hall of that town is mutually known, but merely that he and she mutually know about that town (the anchor) and that they mutually know that towns of that size ordinarily have a single city hall (the anchor cable). In condition (6), we have added the notion of a rigid designator, as defined by Kripke (1972, 1977), to take care of proper nouns. In Kripke's theory, *George Washington*, say, is a rigid designator, because it designates the same thing in all possible worlds. In our convention, to use *George Washington* Ann must have good reason to believe that Bob can figure out who it is that the term rigidly designates.

4 Heuristics for Assessing Mutual Knowledge

For felicitous reference, the speaker and listener must establish certain kinds of mutual knowledge. Simpler notions of "shared" knowledge will not do—as witness Ann's reference to *Monkey Business*. In the light of Lewis' and Schiffer's arguments, this conclusion isn't terribly surprising. Definite reference is an example par excellence of something speakers and listeners achieve through coordination, and coordination is ordinarily achieved on the basis of mutual expectations. Moreover, definite reference is governed by conventions, and mutual knowledge is an indispensable part of conventions.

But what about the Mutual Knowledge Paradox? It is unthinkable that speakers and listeners assess mutual knowledge by working serially, statement by statement, through an infinity of statements. As we noted earlier, this paradox rests on two debatable assumptions:

ASSUMPTION I: Ann ordinarily tries to make definite references that are felicitous.

ASSUMPTION II: To make a felicitous definite reference, Ann must assure herself of each of the infinity of statements (1), (2), (3), (4), and so on.

The inevitable conclusion is that one or both of these assumptions must be weakened and the infinite process replaced by finite heuristics.

The obvious thing to weaken first is Assumption I. In ordinary speech Ann may sometimes guess at what Bob knows—perhaps guessing wildly—and turn out expressions of definite reference that are far from felicitous. Much of the time this may not matter because her references may be close enough to succeed anyway. And when they don't go through, Bob will look puzzled, ask for clarification, or show other evidence of misunderstanding, and Ann can reassess what she thinks Bob knows and repair her reference. Indeed, repairs of this kind appear to occur often in spontaneous speech, suggesting that speakers don't always satisfy Assumption I with the precision that our Marx brothers examples might have suggested. Perhaps, then, the felicitous reference is an ideal that in practice is rarely reached.

Yet surely it is an ideal people strive for because they will want to avoid misunderstanding whenever possible. What heuristics will enable these to approach this ideal if not reach it? We will suggest two families of heuristics. The first, which we will call truncation heuristics, results in a permanent weakening of Assumption I. The second family, which we will call copresence heuristics, retains the possibility of felicitous definite reference, as in Assumption I, but solves the problems posed by Assumption II.

Truncation Heuristics

The stickler in assessing mutual knowledge statement by statement is that there is an infinity of such statements, and that is too many to check. What if people checked only a few of them—like the first four? The task could then be carried out in a finite, even short, period of time, and that would resolve the Mutual Knowledge Paradox. But if they did this, they could not be guaranteed a felicitous definite reference on each occasion, and Assumption I would no longer hold. Heuristics of this kind will be called *truncation heuristics*.

What makes these heuristics plausible is that they ought ordinarily to lead to few references that are infelicitous. Imagine that Ann always verifies the statement *Ann knows that Bob knows that Ann knows that Bob knows that t is R*, which is condition (4) for mutual knowledge. On actuarial grounds, if condition (4) holds, it should be highly likely that conditions (5) through infinity hold, too. So, although errors can occur, they should occur rarely and only in complicated situations.

What makes this a *family* of heuristics is that there are several checking procedures a speaker might use. First, imagine that Ann, in referring to *Monkey Business* with the noun phrase *the movie showing at the Roxy tonight*, checks conditions (1) through (4). This might be called the *progressive checking strategy* because Ann starts at the beginning of the list and works so far down. Where she stops depends on her desire for precision. The more precise she wants to be, the further down the list she will want to check. Second, imagine that Ann checks condition (4) and no others. This might be called *the selective checking procedure*. Once again, the condition Ann picks out to check depends on her precision. The more precise she wants to be, the further down the list she will want to enter.[6]

---

[6]There may seem to be no real differnce between the selective and the progressive checking strategies because for shared knowledge the truth of condition (4), for example, entails the truth of conditions (1), (2), and (3). For shared beliefs or suppositions or other propositional attitudes, however, this entailment no longer holds. If Ann believes that Bob believes that the movie showing at the Roxy tonight is *A Day at the Races*, that doesn't imply that *she* believes it is *A Day at the Races*. In the more general case, these two strategies are distinct.

Neither of these procedures guarantees a felicitous definite reference because both lead to something less than full mutual knowledge of the referent. Yet in special circumstances there are heuristics that *can* lead to a felicitous reference—so long as the listener draws the right inferences. These heuristics will be called the *augmented truncation heuristics*.

Consider this variation on Version 4:

VERSION 4a: On Wednesday morning Ann and Bob read the early edition of the newspaper and discuss the fact that it says that there is a double feature playing tonight at the Roxy—*Monkey Business* followed by *A Day at the Races*. Later, Ann sees the late edition, notes that *A Day at the Races* has been canceled, and marks the notice with her red pencil. Still later, as Ann watches without Bob's awareness, Bob picks up the late edition and sees Ann's pencil mark. That afternoon, Ann sees Bob and asks, *Have you ever seen the movie showing at the Roxy tonight?*

Like Version 4, this scenario satisfies conditions (1), (2), and (3), but it also satisfies (4*):

(4*)   There is no R^* such that Ann believes that Bob believes that Ann believes that Bob believes that t is R^*.

Here R^* is a unique referent that fits the description *the movie showing at the Roxy tonight*. Because the reference is singular and there are actually two movies for which condition (4) holds, there is no R^* than fits this description.

These conditions can be enough for a felicitous reference if Ann can count on Bob drawing the right inferences. She could reason this way: *Bob knows that I know that the movie tonight is* Monkey Business. *But because we discussed the early edition, he believes that I believe he thinks there are two movies showing. I can disabuse him of this belief by using a* singular *definite reference. Because he knows I know than* Monkey Business *is the only movie playing, he will infer that I know that he knows that, too—even though he doesn't know I know that. He should be able to infer:*

(3')   Bob knows that Ann knows that Bob knows that t is R.

But because this is my, Ann's, conclusion, I know or believe the equivalent of (4):

(4)   Ann knows that Bob knows that Ann knows that Bob knows that t is R.

Reasoning further, I know that this is something Bob could infer, which gives way to (4'), *hence my* (5), *and his* (5'), *hence my* (6), *and so on* *ad infinitum. Voila! He and I mutually know that t is R.* In Version 4, it should be noted, Ann could not have reasoned this way precisely because that version doesn't fulfill condition (4*).

When will augmented truncation strategies work? That depends on the precision Ann wants. Imagine a Version 2a (analogous to Version 4a), in which Ann had seen the late edition of the newspaper canceling *A Day at the Races*, but had no idea whether Bob had seen that notice. So she would fulfill:

(1)   Ann knows that *t* is *R*.

(2)   There is no *R** such that Ann knows that Bob knows that
       t is *R**.

In this version, although she might be sure that Bob realized she was referring to a single movie—he *could* have thought she made a speech error and intended to say *movies*—she has no reason to think he would be able to figure out which one. In an analogous Version 3a, in which she saw Bob look at the late edition but realized he didn't know she had seen it, she could have some confidence he would figure out which. But what Bob really needs to know is that she knows the movie is *Monkey Business*, as in Version 4a. Higher-order versions should make her even more confident he will draw the right inferences.

What we have described, then, is a constellation of conditions that Ann, with certain auxiliary assumptions, can take as good evidence Bob will pick out the right referent. There are probably other such constellations, but all of those we have considered require at least three or four conditions for a reference to be felicitous.

Difficulties with Truncation Heuristics

In principle, truncation heuristics seem capable of doing the job. They may even allow for felicitous definite reference. We suspect that they may be used on at least some occasions. Version 4a is not such an implausible scenario for people to handle roughly as we suggested. In fact, for scenarios like Version 4a, we have asked subjects to tell us what is being referred to by expressions analogous to *the movie showing at the Roxy tonight*. These subjects appeared to use procedures very much like the truncation heuristics, especially the augmented truncation heuristics. As the scenarios became more complex, they tended to have more difficulty as this analysis would predict. So these heuristics are possible.

But are they plausible as the way people *normally* assess mutual knowledge in making definite reference? We believe not. Our doubts lie in two areas. First, it isn't easy to deal with reciprocal statements as complicated as condition (4). It is implausible that people ordinarily check these conditions per se. Second, the evidence people need in order to verify these conditions anyway suggests a radically different family of heuristics, namely, the copresence heuristics.

Reciprocal knowledge statements, like condition (4), seem unlikely mental objects for people to assess. Recall that in Version 4 of our Marx brothers scenario, we created a situation in which Ann didn't believe that Bob knew that she knew that he knew that the movie that night was *Monkey Business*, a violation of condition (4). The scenario wasn't easy to understand. The main sticking point was in grasping condition (4) and deciding that it wasn't true. Why is condition (4) so difficult to grasp, and to disconfirm?

There probably two main reasons. One is that recursive statements about propositional attitudes are themselves difficult to grasp. For example, *John Dean knew that Nixon knew that Haldeman knew that Magruder knew that McCord had burgled O'Brien's office in the Watergate Apartments* describes a pipeline of gossip that is difficult to keep straight. When these statements are also reciprocal, with the pipeline turning back on itself, the difficulty seems to increase with the square of the number of recursions. Parallel to the last example is the following *reciprocal* statement: *John Dean knew that Nixon knew that John Dean knew that Nixon knew McCord burgled O'Brien's office in the Watergate Apartments.* It isn't just that *utterances* of these sentences are difficult to grasp. Rather, their content appears to be inherently hard to keep track of. Any statement more complex than condition (4) can be obliterated by one glass of decent sherry.

Studies of children suggest that the ability to deal explicitly with reciprocal knowledge develops quite late in childhood. In one study (Miller et al. 1970), children were asked to describe cartoons of people thinking of people thinking of people. These children found reciprocal relations much more difficult to describe than nonreciprocal ones. In addition, no more than half the twelve-year-olds were able to deal with reciprocal relations like condition (2), and fewer than a third were able to deal with reciprocal relations like condition (3). In another study (Barenboim 1978), it was found that children spontaneously talk very little about other people's thoughts (like condition 2) until age twelve, or about other people's thoughts about other people's thoughts (like condition 3) until age sixteen (see also Flavell et al. 1968). All these studies required rather a lot from children—explicit talk about recursiveness and reciprocity—yet they suggest that recursive reasoning even two levels deep is not easy for children under age twelve. The trouble is that children much younger—six to eight years of age (Maratsos 1976; Warden 1976)—appear to use definite reference felicitously, at least much of the time. And even younger children sometimes spontaneously repair definite references to take account of what their listeners know (E. Clark and Andersen 1979). So, although studies of children give us anything but a knockdown argument, they do suggest that the truncation heuristics are not very plausible.

The more basic argument against the truncation heuristics is to be found in what counts as evidence for the truth of conditions (1), (2), (3), and so on. Take condition (3), *Ann knows that Bob knows that Ann knows that t is R*. Obviously, Ann won't have this statement represented per se in memory for any arbitrary t and R. Ann doesn't go through life creating such statements for every object she or anyone else might potentially refer to. Rather, what she needs is a piece of information from which she can deductively or inductively *infer* condition (3). Imagine, for example, a version of our original scenario in which Ann and Bob look at the late edition's correction to *Monkey Business* together. It would be hard to think of better evidence Ann could appeal to for the truth of condition (3).

Ann's knowledge that she and Bob looked at the correction together, however, is infinitely more useful than that. It is also about the best evidence Ann could appeal to for the truth of all the rest of the infinity of conditions. That is, with this evidence, Ann can jump immediately to full mutual knowledge. If that is so, why would she ever check conditions one by one—even a truncated list of them? She would be better off making sure of the back-up evidence itself. This is precisely the principle that underlies the next family of heuristics, the copresence heuristics.

Copresence Heuristics

What kind of evidence can Ann appeal to in order to simultaneously verify the infinity of conditions? If Ann knew, she could in principle satisfy Assumption I and make definite references that were felicitous. She would resolve the Mutual Knowledge Paradox instead by circumventing Assumption II, which otherwise forces her to verify as infinity of conditions one by one. We will argue that what she generally needs is evidence of triple copresence of certain events in which Ann, Bob, and the target object are copresence, as when Ann, Bob, and the notice about *Monkey Business* were openly present together Wednesday morning. The trick is to say what counts as triple copresence—as being "openly present together"—and to say how this can lead to inferences of mutual knowledge.

When Lewis and Schiffer hit on the notion of mutual knowledge, they each recognized the need for a finite means of handling the infinity of conditions. Their solutions were essentially the same. If A and B make certain assumptions about each other's rationality, they can use certain states of affairs as a basis for *inferring* the infinity of conditions all at once. This solution is elegant, for it satisfies everyone. It fits people's intuitions that they mutually know certain facts, and that they yet arrive at this knowledge simply and easily, as if in one short step.

This solution is best illustrated with an example adapted from Schiffer: Ann and Bob are sitting across a table from each other, and there is a single candle between them. Both are looking at the candle, and both see the other looking at it, too. The proposition p is that there is a candle on the table. Consider the scene from Ann's point of view. Clearly, she has direct evidence for the truth of (1):

(1)   Ann knows that p.

But she knows other pertinent information, too. First, she has evidence that she and Bob are looking at each other and the candle simultaneously. We will call this the *simultaneity assumption*. Second, she assumes that he is not only looking at her and the candle, but also *attending* to them. We will call this the *attention assumption*. Finally, Ann assumes that Bob is normal and if he were in her shoes he would be drawing the same conclusions she is. We will call this the *rationality assumption*.

Now if Bob is attending to the candle and is rational, he has evidence for (1'):

(1')   Bob knows that p.

This, however, is Ann's conclusion, and so she has evidence for (2):

(2)   Ann knows that Bob knows that p.

But, if Bob is rational, he will be drawing the inference that corresponds to hers—his equivalent of (2)—namely (2'):

(2')   Bob knows that Ann knows that p.

Once again, this is Ann's conclusion, and so she has evidence for (3):

(3)   Ann knows that Bob knows that Ann knows that p.

In like fashion, Ann would be justified in iterating this process through the remaining knowledge statements (4) through infinity, and Bob would be justified is doing the same for his.

This method for inferring mutual knowledge can be formalized as follows (adapted from Lewis):

Mutual Knowledge Induction Schema. A and B mutually know that p if and only if some state of affairs G holds such that:

1. A and B have reason to believe that G holds.
2. G indicates to A and B that each has reason to believe that G holds.
3. G indicates to A and B that p.

G is called the *basis* for the mutual knowledge that p. In the candle example, G (for "grounds") is Ann and Bob's evidence of triple copresence and their auxiliary assumptions. Ann and Bob each have reason to believe that G holds. These grounds G indicate to each of them that the other has reason to believe that they hold. And the grounds G indicate to both of them that there is a candle on the table. By the induction schema, Ann and Bob mutually know that there is a candle on the table.

The point of this schema is that Ann and Bob don't have to confirm any of the infinity of conditions in mutual knowledge at all. They need only be confident that they have a proper basis G, grounds that satisfy all three requirements of the induction schema. With these grounds Ann and Bob tacitly realize, so to speak, that they could confirm the infinity of conditions as far down the list as they wanted to go. Because they could do so in principle, they need not do so in fact. This is what gives the copresence heuristics their power. Once one has found proper grounds for mutual knowledge, that is enough.

Mutual knowledge can then be treated as a single mental entity instead of an infinitely long list of even more complex mental entities. That is, what Ann would represent to herself is not (1), (2), (3), and so on ad infinitum, but merely this: *Ann and Bob mutually know that p.* This obviously leads to an important savings in memory. Just as it is implausible that Ann ordinarily checks a large number of conditions like (1), (2), and (3), so is it implausible that she ordinarily stores these conditions separately is memory. Whenever she needs one of these conditions, she can generate it by a rule such as this (an adaptation of Harman's definition of mutual knowledge): If A and B mutually know that p, then q, where q is that A and B know that p and that q. On demand Ann can deduce, for example, that if she and Bob mutually know there is a candle on the table, then she knows that Bob knows that she knows there is a candle on the table. So with the mutual knowledge induction schema there is simplification in memory, too, and the simpler memory structure makes good intuitive sense.[7]

---

[7]When mutual knowledge is treated as a primitive, it follows that most cases of non-mutual knowledge will require a more complex memory representation than mutual knowledge. As a consequence, they ought to be more difficult to understand. Our Marx brothers scenarios bear out this prediction. Versions 2, 3, 4, and 5

What do the grounds G for the mutual induction schema look like? In the candle example, Ann's grounds consisted of two parts. The first was her direct visual evidence of triple copresence—that there was a candle on the table and that Ann and Bob were simultaneously looking at each other and at the candle. As an event she experienced, this information is relatively fleeting. The second part was her assumptions about the situation—that Bob was consciously attending, that he was doing so simultaneously with her, and that he was rational. These assumptions are more lasting. Ann can assume that Bob is chronically rational, and that if he appears to be looking alertly at a scene, he is attending to it at that moment. These are assumptions she would make for any event of this kind.

There are other grounds, too. Some of them are like the candle example but consist of weaker evidence of triple copresence and stronger auxiliary assumptions. For there is a trade-off between the evidence and assumptions loosely as follows:

Evidence + Assumptions + Induction Schema = Mutual Knowledge

Because the induction schema is fixed, the weaker the evidence Ann has at her disposal, the stronger the assumptions she must make in order to satisfy the induction schema and infer mutual knowledge. Still other grounds don't use triple copresence at all. It is instructive to classify the grounds that are most commonly used.

5 Varieties of Mutual Knowledge

Mutual knowledge can be classified in various ways. For our purposes it ought to be classified to show its grounds—its sources in a person's experience—because we are interested in how it is secured in the making of definite reference. One main division is between lasting and temporary kinds of mutual knowledge, and another is between several kinds of temporary mutual knowledge. A third division is between *generic* and *particular* knowledge.

Generic knowledge is knowledge about *kinds* of things (about kinds of objects, states, events, and processes), whereas particular knowledge is knowledge about *individual* or *particular* things (about particular objects, states, events, and processes). What we know about dogs is

---

were successively more difficult to understand. The knowledge we had to keep in mind required more and more conditions, and these conditions themselves became more and more complex. The version for mutual knowledge where Ann and Bob openly discussed the showing of *Monkey Business* at the Roxy, was the easiest to understand. Apparently, the mutual knowledge we had to represent for it was simple.

general (that they are animals, that they are domesticated, that they come in many species, and so on) is generic knowledge. What we know about Rin Tin Tin (that he once lived in Hollywood, that he was in several movies, that he was fed caviar, and so on) is particular knowledge. These two types of knowledge are ordinarily expressed in two different ways. Generic knowledge comes is generic sentences like: *Lions roar*; *A canary is a bird*; *Rooms each have a floor, a ceiling, at least three walls, at least one door, and they may have windows, carpets, lights, and so on.* Particular knowledge normally comes in nongeneric sentences that refer to particular things, like: *The lion roared just now*; *Our canary is yellow*; and *The room I am in now has a floor, a ceiling, four walls, two doors, a skylight, a desk, a bookshelf, and so on.* With definite reference, speakers refer to individuals—things in particular knowledge. Yet in doing so, they often need to draw on generic knowledge, too.

Community Membership

Even when Ann is not acquainted with Bob, she can assume there are generic and particular things the two of them mutually know. The basic idea is that there are things *everyone* in a community knows and assumes that everyone else in that community knows, too.[8] In the broad community of educated Americans, for example, people assume that everyone knows such *generic* things as these: Cars drive on the right; senators have terms of six years and representatives terms of two years; and steak costs more than hamburger. They also assume everyone knows such *particular* things as these: George Washington was the first president of the United States; Colorado is west of Pennsylvania; there was a great depression between World Wars I and II. Once two people establish that they belong to the community of educated Americans, they can assume that they mutually know all of these things. We will call this mutual knowledge based on community membership.

But Ann belongs simultaneously to many communities and subcommunities, each of which has its own distinct areas of knowledge. At one and the same time Ann could be a high school graduate, a nineteenth-century-history buff, a San Francisco Forty-Niner football

---

[8]Of course, we must qualify the notion that *everybody* in a community needs to know a thing before it is taken to be mutual knowledge within that community. We can do that informally by replacing *everybody* with *almost everybody*, and *universal* by *almost universal*, or we can do it more formally by introducing parameters that specify the probabilities (see Lewis 1969, 76–80). This qualification is needed if we want to account for why certain references that are otherwise justifiable on the basis of community membership and community knowledge occasionally fail.

fan, a psychiatrist, a Palo Alto home owner, an American, a Californian, a skier, a speaker of Spanish, and a person of Scottish extraction. For each of these communities, she will have acquired facts she assumes are nearly universal within that community, and she must keep straight which facts are universal for which communities. She would not want to meet another person of Scottish ancestry and assume mutual knowledge of Freud's theory of neurosis or the Spanish word for beautiful.

The trick is to judge community membership, and there are many ways to do that. Ann may judge Bob to be as American by his accent, a Palo Alto home owner by his attendance at a meeting of such home owners, a nineteenth-century-history buff by his description of the German revolution of 1848, a psychiatrist by his announcement of that fact, and a person of Scottish ancestry by his surname Macpherson. Not only will Ann use these signs in her judgments, but Bob will provide them, intending her to use them for that purpose. In ordinary conversation people go to some trouble to establish the communities of which they are members just so that their definite references will succeed. An illustration of this point can be found in Schegloff's (1972) account of how people formulate references to places, as when giving directions.

Before Ann and Bob can assume mutual knowledge of what is universally known within a community, they must mutually know that they both belong to that community. Ann might know, for example, that Bob and she belong to the Stanford University community. But unless he comes to know that, to know that she knows that, to know that she knows that he knows that, and so on, he can misinterpret such references as *the church*, *the library*, and *the president*. It is easy to imagine a series of Marx-brothers-like examples that demonstrate this. Ann could establish mutual knowledge of their Stanford community membership by her reference itself, as in *Memorial Church*, *Meyer Library*, and *Stanford president*, but this won't always be possible. Requiring mutual knowledge of community membership introduces a new problem: How do Ann and Bob initially come to mutually know they belong to the same particular community? We suggest that they use one of the copresence heuristics discussed in the next section.

Mutual knowledge of community membership makes an excellent basis G for the mutual knowledge induction schema. Let us suppose that G is *Ann and Bob mutually know that they are both educated Americans*. The induction schema requires three things. By requirement (1), Ann and Bob must have good reason to believe G. Indeed, they do. They mutually know they are both educated Americans, which entails that they mutually know G itself. By requirement (2), G must indicate to Ann and Bob that each has reasons to believe that G holds. This requirement is fulfilled in the same way. And by requirement (3), G must indicate to Ann and Bob that, for example, American independence was declared on July 4, 1776. This holds because they assume that every educated American knows the date of American independence. By the induction schema it follows that they *mutually* know that American independence was declared on July 4, 1776.

It is instructive to spell out the two main assumptions required here for mutual knowledge of proposition p. First, Ann must believe that she and Bob mutually know they belong to a particular community. Let us call this assumption *community comembership*. And second, Ann must believe that everyone in that community knows that particular proposition p. Let us call this assumption *universality of knowledge*. Mutual knowledge of this type, then, has a basis G with two assumptions:

1. Community membership: community membership, universality of knowledge.

Right away we should note two obvious problems. First, communities are not well defined. At what point should a person be considered an educated American, or a member of the Stanford University community, or a nineteenth-century-history buff? Deciding community membership is not a simple task. And second, the two assumptions may vary in strength of certainty. Ann may be certain Bob is an educated American, but less certain that he is a psychiatrist. This is akin to the first point. And she may be more certain an educated American will know that George Washington was the first president of the United States than that Colorado is southwest of South Dakota. The strength of these two assumptions, of course, will affect how certain Ann is that the definite references she is making are felicitous.

Mutual knowledge based on community membership is generally preserved over long periods of time. Once Ann and Bob mutually know they are educated Americans, they are likely to retain that knowledge for use in reference to all sorts of things. And with a constant source of fresh evidence, that mutual knowledge is continually being renewed. Mutual knowledge of the next three types, in contrast, is ordinarily relevant only for short periods of time. It may be used only once and then dropped. Its most distinguishing characteristic is that it is based on evidence that is, in a sense, more direct.

Physical Copresence

The strongest evidence for mutual knowledge that people are generally prepared to accept is what we will call *physical copresence*. An example par excellence is the scene with Ann, Bob, and the candle.

Not only are the three of them physically and openly present together, but Ann, say, can readily assume that Bob is attending to this fact, is doing so at the same time she is, and is rational. The physical, or perceptual, evidence Ann possesses is so strong that her three auxiliary assumptions can be relatively trivial. It is rare that she would have reason to think, contrary to the attention assumption, that Bob was catatonic, hypnotized the right way, or very nearsighted, or, contrary to the rationality assumption, that he was too brain-damaged or too young to possess the mutual knowledge induction schema. So with this evidence, once Ann has assured herself of these minimal assumptions, it is trivial for her to refer to *this candle*. Mutual knowledge of the candle has already been secured, and all she has left to do is make sure its identification is unique.

When the time period of physical copresence is placed with respect to the moment of the reference act itself, we can distinguish three varieties of physical copresence. Imagine that Bob isn't paying attention to the target candle, but it is easily within view. Ann can then say *this candle*, which gets Bob to look at it and complete the physical copresence of him, her, and the candle. This could be called *potential physical copresence*. When Ann and Bob are actually focusing on the candle as she says *this candle*, we have a case of *immediate physical copresence*. And when Ann and Bob have looked together at the candle but have stopped before she says *that candle*, we have an instance of *prior physical copresence*.

On the face of it, these three types of physical copresence differ in how strong they are as evidence. The immediate type is the strongest. The potential type is sightly weaker, for Ann must assume that Bob can discover the target candle and bring it into view simultaneously with her. Let us call this the *locatability assumption*. The prior case is also weaker, for Ann must assume Bob can recall the earlier copresence of him, her, and the candle. Let us call this the *recallibility assumption*. If Ann is to use evidence of physical copresence to secure the mutual knowledge necessary for her definite reference, she will need the following auxiliary assumptions:

2. Physical copresence
    a. Immediate: simultaneity, attention, rationality
    b. Potential: simultaneity, attention, rationality, locatability
    c. Prior: simultaneity, attention, rationality, recallability

(Simultaneity, attention, and rationality refer to the assumptions we described earlier.) So far so good. The stronger the evidence, the fewer auxiliary assumptions are needed here.

Linguistic Copresence

Many things that are referred to have only been mentioned in conversation. Imagine Ann saying to Bob *I bought a candle yesterday.* By uttering *a candle*, she posits for Bob the existence of a particular candle. If Bob hears and understands her correctly, he will come to know about the candle's existence at the same time as she posits it. It is as if Ann places the candle on the stage in front of the two of them so that it is physically copresent. The two of them can be said to be is the *linguistic copresence* of the candle. Ann can then make a definite reference to the candle, as in *The candle cost me plenty.*[9]

The world in which a thing is claimed to exist can be real or imaginary, past, present, or future. *A deer and a unicorn were grazing beside a stream when the unicorn complimented the deer on his beautiful extra horn.* These two beasts live in as imaginary world, on an imaginary stage, which is quite enough for their linguistic copresence with the speaker and listener. (The question of worlds is too complicated to consider further here, but see McCawley 1979, and Prince 1978.)

Unlike physical copresence, linguistic copresence can never be "immediate," that is, simultaneous with the definite reference for which it is used. *A candle* cannot be spoken at the same time as *the candle.* It must come either before, as in *I bought a candle, but the candle was broken*, or afterward if *the candle* is pronominalized, as in *Because it was broken, I returned a candle I had just bought to the store.* In parallel with physical copresence, these two cases can be called prior and potential linguistic copresence, respectively.

To refer to an object that is linguistically copresent, Ann need not use the same term as was used with the potential or prior mention of it. Because a lathe is a machine, and also an inanimate thing, she could say *I bought a lathe, but the machine/it didn't work right.* Note that because not all machines are lathes, it would ordinarily be odd to say, with the same intended interpretation, *I bought a machine, but the lathe didn't work right.*

What auxiliary assumptions are needed for linguistic copresence?

---

[9]Written language, as in books and on signs, we assume, is derivative from spoken language and requires an extended notion of copresence. In *Pride and Prejudice*, for example, Jane Austen assumed her readers would be rational, comprehending people who would take in her words serially, as if spoken, etc., etc. She could pretend, in other words, that she was speaking her novel to each reader and that linguistic copresence would be established that way. Signs often rely on an extended notion of physical copresence as well. For example, *Break this glass to sound alarm* makes sense on a fire alarm, but not pinned to the back of a professor's coat. Nevertheless, we are mindful of the differences between written and spoken language and expect them to complicate the copresence heurisitcs in various ways.

To begin with, there are the assumptions of simultaneity, attention, and rationality. Ann and Bob must be attending to Ann's utterance of *a candle* simultaneously, and both must be rational. There is also a complex assumption we will call *understandability*. Ann must assume that Bob will penetrate her indefinite reference, *a candle*, and understand that she is sincerely positing the candle's existence in some world. And as before, prior linguistic copresence requires the assumption of recallability, and potential linguistic copresence the assumption of locatability. Recalling and locating linguistic objects, however, may not be the same as recalling and locating physical objects; so these two assumptions may be either stronger or weaker than those for physical copresence. putting them all together, we have:

3. Linguistic copresence
   a. Potential: simultaneity, attention, rationality, locatability, understandability
   b. Prior: simultaneity, attention, rationality, recallability, understandability

Fairly clearly, linguistic copresence is ordinarily weaker evidence for mutual knowledge than physical copresence. Whereas seeing is believing, hearing about something requires more—the extra understandability assumption. Both types of copresence are difficult to compare with mutual knowledge based on community membership, whose auxiliary assumptions are so different.

Mixtures

Very often mutual knowledge is established by a combination of physical or linguistic copresence and mutual knowledge based on community membership. Imagine Ann saying to Bob *I bought a candle yesterday, but the wick had broken off.* In uttering *a candle*, Ann establishes the linguistic copresence of him, her, and the candle, but not of him, her, and the wick. To refer to the wick she has to assume that when Bob accepts the existence of the candle, he also accepts the existence of the wick. He and she mutually know that they belong to the community of educated people for whom it is universally known that candles have wicks. By referring to *the wick* she can therefore secure mutual knowledge of the identity of the wick that belongs to this particular candle. Ann's use of *a candle*, then, establishes what we will call the *indirect linguistic copresence* of her, Bob, and the wick.

Indirect copresence of this kind may be based on a less certain association than that between candles and wicks (see H. Clark 1977, 1978; Clark and Haviland 1977; Haviland and Clark 1974; and others). For

TABLE 1
Types of Mutual Knowledge and the Assumptions

Basis for Mutual Knowledge	Auxiliary Assumptions
Community membership:	Community comembership, universality of knowledge
Physical copresence:	
a. Immediate	Simultaneity, attention, rationality
b. Potential	Simultaneity, attention, rationality, locatability
c. Prior	Simultaneity, attention, rationality, recallability
Linguistic copresence:	
a. Potential	Simultaneity, attention, rationality, locatability, understandability
b. Prior	Simultaneity, attention, rationality, recallability, understandability
Indirect copresence:	
a. Physical	Simultaneity, attention, rationality, (locatability or recallability), associativity
b. Linguistic	Simultaneity, attention, rationality, (locatability or recallability), understandability, associativity

example, a candle has only a *likelihood* of having a wrapper associated with it and only a *low possibility* of being made of bayberries. Yet that is enough to allow Ann to establish their mutual knowledge with her references in *I bought a candle yesterday, but the wrapper was torn* and in *I bought a candle yesterday, and the bayberry smelled great*. Indirect copresence can be very indirect indeed.

There can also be indirect *physical* copresence. A physically present candle, for example, may have a price, which is then indirectly present, too. When Ann and Bob are looking at a candle, Ann says *The price was three dollars*, referring to the candle's price that is indirectly copresent and thereby establishing mutual knowledge of its identity.

Both types of indirect copresence require mutual knowledge based on community membership. That knowledge may be generic, as with candles having wicks, wrappers, bayberries, and prices, but it may also be particular. Imagine that Ann and Bob belong to a small community in which it is universally known that Charlie has a broken left leg. That broken leg is then indirectly copresent with the mention of Charlie. Ann could say to Bob *I saw Charlie yesterday, and the leg is getting better*.

What assumptions are required for inducing mutual knowledge from indirect copresence? If we think of the copresence of the wick as parasitic on the copresence of the candle, then there are first the assumptions of physical or linguistic copresence, whichever is the parasite's host. There is next an assumption we will call *associativity*. It must be mutually known in the community that the parasite is certainly, probably, or possibly a particular part of, or in a particular role with, the host. The two major types of indirect copresence, then, require these assumptions (where parentheses enclose assumptions that are optionally needed depending on the subtype of the host):

4. Indirect copresence
   a. Physical: simultaneity, attention, rationality, (locatability or recallability), associativity
   b. Linguistic; simultaneity, attention, rationality (locatability or recallability), understandability, associativity.

As this listing shows, indirect copresence is always weaker than direct copresence with the parasite's host. The four major types of mutual knowledge are summarized in Table 1.

6 Types of Reference

Traditional linguistic theories tell us that definite reference comes in different kinds. But if definite reference secures mutual knowledge of the identity of R, and if this mutual knowledge is ordinarily inferred from states of affairs G, then definite reference should be classifiable by these grounds G. We will argue that the traditional classifications are indeed based on these grounds G. This argument is important for two reasons. It is indirect evidence that copresence heuristics are used is making definite reference. And it suggests that definite reference cannot be fully explained without bringing them in.

Deixis, Anaphora, and Proper Names

The three basic types of definite reference are deixis, anaphora, and proper names (Lyons 1977). *Deictic* expressions are used to point to things in the nonlinguistic situation. In Ann's *I want that*, *I* refers to the speaker Ann, and *that* refers to the object she is pointing at. Anaphoric expressions are used to refer to things introduced into the conversation itself. In Ann's *I bought a candle, but the thing was broken*, *the thing* refers to the candle introduced by Ann's utterance of *a candle*. Deixis is often construed to cover anaphora, too, but we will stick with its narrower sense. Contrasting with both deixis and anaphora are proper nouns, as in *George Washington had a knotty mouth*. In Kripke's (1972, 1977) proposal, each proper noun rigidly designates the same individual regardless of context.

With this classification, the fit between definite reference and mutual knowledge seems clear. Deixis corresponds to physical copresence; anaphora corresponds to linguistic copresence; and proper names correspond to community membership. The fit could hardly be more obvious. Yet deixis, anaphora, and proper names are categories that are primarily based on functional characteristics. It is worthwhile to look more closely at a few of their structural properties.

The prototypical deictic expressions are demonstratives, as when the speaker gestures at something and says *that*, or *that woman*. These gestures are used to establish immediate physical copresence. They make certain that the speaker and listener come to look at the same object simultaneously. As Hawkins (1978, 111) points out, *that* can replace a "visible situation use" of the definite article, as in *Look out for the table*, where the table is visible, but not an "immediate situation use," as in *Beware of the dog*, where the dog is somewhere around but not visible. This contrast coincides with our distinction between direct and indirect physical copresence. When there is a candle between Ann and Bob, the candle is physically present, but its price is only indirectly present (unless there is a price tag). Ann can say *That candle is beautiful*, but not *That price is high*. The choice of *that* is governed in part by whether the basis for mutual knowledge is direct or indirect physical copresence.

In anaphora, the prototypical expressions are definite pronouns and definite descriptions, although demonstratives can be used, too. In *I met a woman yesterday; the woman/she was a doctor*, the noun phrases *the woman* and *she* are used to refer to a woman already established by linguistic copresence. The type of linguistic copresence is critical. When it has been established in a previous sentence, the speaker can choose either definite descriptions or pronouns, depending on other factors. When it is established in the same sentence as the definite reference, the choice is highly constrained, as summarized, for example, by Lasnik (1976). In *The woman decided she would operate*, the second reference to the woman must be the pronoun *she*. When there is potential linguistic copresence, it must "command" the definite reference in a technical sense of command. In *She decided that the woman would operate*, it is impossible for *she* to refer to the same person as *the woman*.

Indeed, there appear to be stringent requirements on the basis for mutual knowledge that will allow pronouns. Chafe (1974) has argued that the referents of pronouns must be in the listener's consciousness, "on stage," at that point is the conversation. If so, the conditions of pronouns tie in directly with the assumptions of recallability and locatability. When the referents are recallable, or locatable, within immediate, as opposed to long-term, memory, the speaker can use a pronoun; otherwise, he can not.

Demonstratives can be used for anaphora only under special conditions. In *I met a woman yesterday: That woman was a doctor*, *that* attracts contrastive stress and implies there is a contrasting set of women. It is not used for simple cases of linguistic copresence. And in discourse *this* and *that* are distinguished precisely by the kind of linguistic copresence they require. To refer to something established by prior copresence, one can use either *this* or *that*, but to refer to something yet to be established—potential linguistic copresence—one must use *this*.

Anaphora can be summarized this way. It is prototypically expressed with pronouns or definite descriptions. The expression that is appropriate depends on the type of linguistic copresence: whether it is potential or prior, whether it "commands" the definite reference or not, and whether it is available in immediate or long-term memory, among other things. Anaphora can also be expressed with demonstratives, yet the demonstrative that is appropriate again depends on whether the linguistic copresence is potential or prior. The choice of definite reference, then, is heavily determined by the basis for the mutual knowledge it establishes.

Proper names are the prototypical way of referring to things that are mutually known by community membership. When a particular is widely known in a community, it tends to get a proper same—a rigid designator that doesn't change from one conversation to the next. That is, it is the universally known things within a community that get so named. Note what get proper names: people (*George Washington*), places (*Valley Forge*), and prominent events (*the Revolutionary War*). The few trees, rocks, or animals that get proper names have to be prominent, like *The Great Redwood*, *Standing Rock*, and *Rin Tin Tin*. There is probably no grain of sand, glass of water, or ream of typing paper that has ever received a proper name.

Many universally known particulars, however, are referred to with definite descriptions instead of proper names; for example, *the sun*, *the moon*, and *the last winter*. Historically, many of these have come to be treated as proper names, as is the change from *the great swamp* to *the Great Swamp*, from *the civil war* to *the Civil War*, and from *the supreme court* to *the Supreme Court*. Sometimes the definite descriptions even become proper nouns, as is *the earth* to *Earth* and *the first world war* to *World War I*. Pronouns and demonstratives apparently cannot be used for reference to things that are mutually known on the basis of community membership, except in rare cases. They require a direct basis for mutual knowledge.[10].

Eight Uses of the Definite Article

Another classification of definite reference already noted is Christopherson's, Jespersen's, and Hawkins' eight uses for the definite article. Two of these uses are obvious cases of deixis and anaphora. The rest reflect mixtures and fall under our heading of indirect copresence.

The Visible Situation Use, as in *Pass me the bucket* for a visible bucket, is a clear example of physical copresence, but there are three other uses that are indirect physical copresence. The Immediate Situation Use, as in *Do not feed the pony* for a nonvisible pony, relies on the physical copresence of a fenced-in yard, supplemented by generic knowledge that such a yard could contain a pony. The Larger Situation Use Based on Specific Knowledge relies on the physical copresence of, say, Ann and Bob in a particular situation, with mutual knowledge based on community membership completing the identification of the referent. Ann and Bob mutually know, for example, which store Ann ordinarily goes to in a community; so as long as she and Bob are physically copresent in the neighborhood, she can refer to that store as *I'm going to the store*. The Larger Situation Use Based on General Knowledge, as in *I wonder where the city hall is* for a new town, has a similar basis.

The Anaphoric Use is a plain example of linguistic copresence, and the Associative Anaphoric Use, as in *A car just went by and the exhaust fumes made me sick*, a case of indirect linguistic copresence. Within a community, cars are known to produce exhaust fumes, knowledge that along with the linguistic copresence of the car is enough to secure mutual knowledge of the fumes being referred to.

There are several subtypes of Unavailable Use of the definite article. The first is the Referent Establishing Relative Clauses, as in *The woman Max went out with last night was nasty to him*. These always "relate the new, unknown object [here, the woman] either to other objects in the previous discourse set, or to participants in the speech act, or else they identify entities in the immediate situation of the utterance" (Hawkins 1978, 137). So they are cases of indirect linguistic or physical copresence via mutual knowledge based on community membership. A second subtype is the Associative Use, as in *the beginning*

---

[10]One exception, pointed out to us by a native, is the Highland Scottish use of *himself* as a proper name for the local laird or head of a clan, as in *Himself was angry with Ian today*. Its highly marked form helps to make its proper-name status clear

of World War II, another case of indirect copresence because it is mutually known among educated people that wars have beginnings, and so one can indirectly identify the beginning of a mutually known war. A third subtype is the Noun Complement, as in *the idea that he is in Caracas*, and *the fact that the world is round*. One way to view these is to say there is a set of possible ideas, and a set of possible facts, and these sets are mutually known based on membership in the community of thinking, perceiving humans. Any individual fact or idea can then be identified merely by being specified. The fourth type, Nominal Modifiers, as in *the color red*, would work the same way.

Deixis as Fundamental

According to many linguists (for example, Lyons (1975)), deixis is the source for all definite reference. In Indo-European languages, the pronouns (like English *he*, *she*, *it*, and *they*) and the definite articles (like English *the*) are historically derived from demonstratives (like English *this* and *that*). Thorne (1972, 1974) has argued that the definite article is fundamentally locative—that is, deictic. *The woman* designates not merely a particular woman, but a particular woman in a particular place. All the world's languages appear to have demonstratives and personal pronouns, but many do not have definite articles. In these languages, when a definite reference has to be made absolutely clear, a demonstrative is used, as in *that woman* (Moravcsik 1969). That is, demonstratives are stretched to cover other nondeictic kinds of definite reference. And in language acquisition, E. Clark (1978; Clark and Sengul 1978) has argued that deixis is also fundamental. Children refer to things by pointing long before they begin to speak, and their first referring expressions, usually *that*, *there*, or *look* in English, are almost invariably accompanied by pointing. The weaker forms of definite reference—the pronouns and definite article—are acquired only later. Proper nouns, our incommensurate case, however, come in very early (E. Clark 1973).

If, as we have argued, physical copresence is the fundamental type of copresence, then it follows that deixis should have primacy in definite reference. The idea is this: physical copresence is the prototype of what it means for a thing to be mutually known. It is such good evidence that it needs only weak auxiliary assumptions to serve as a basis G in the mutual knowledge induction schema. The other types of copresence each require stronger assumptions, as if they were defective types of copresence in which one or another of the essential conditions of physical copresence hadn't been fulfilled. If physical copresence is primary, then deixis, too, should be primary. It is significant that there is such a convergence of evidence from historical linguistics, language universals, and language acquisition.

To summarize, when definite reference is divided into types, these correspond to different bases G by which mutual knowledge of the identity of the referent is established. And among these types, deixis appears to be primary. All this evidence is in line with the copresence heuristics—in particular with the use of physical, linguistic, and indirect copresence, and of community membership.

7   Reference Repairs

In conversations people often say one thing, repair what they have just said, and then go on (see Clark and Clark 1977, 260–71). Ann might say *I ran into Ralph—you know, the guy who works in our clinic—the other night at the symphony*. Or she might say *I ran into Ralph the other night at the symphony*, to which Bob would ask, *Who is Ralph*, to which Ann would reply, *You know, the guy who works in our clinic*. Both types of repairs—self-repairs and other repairs—are common is everyday speech, although self-repairs predominate (Schegloff et al. 1977).

Repairs of definite reference, what DuBois (1975) has called *reference editing*, give further evidence for the copresence heuristics. The argument is this. One reason speakers repair definite references is to make them more likely to succeed. In our examples, Ann wants to make it more likely Bob will identify the person she was referring to. In making these repairs speakers have two broad options. They can provide more information in the reference itself. This way the basis G on which they and their listeners come to mutually know the identity of the referent will become clearer. This might be called a *horizontal repair*. Or they can strengthen the type of copresence on which their reference is based. This might be called a *vertical repair*. Of these repairs, some should increase the success of a reference, and others should not. If our proposal is correct, those that increase success ought to be just those that provide stronger types of copresence—direct instead of indirect, physical instead of linguistic, immediate instead of potential. The evidence is that they are.

Horizontal Repairs

Most reference repairs are horizontal. They ensure greater success by providing more precise information about the referent without changing the type of basis G on which its identity becomes mutually known. Consider these four cases.

1. **Physical Copresence.** Imagine telling a librarian with a gesture, *I want that.* He prompts, *Which one?* You reply, *The book right there on the second shelf.* He prompts again, *I still don't see which one.* You reply, *The green book on the second shelf from the bottom of that bookcase.* These references all rely on potential physical copresence. What changes with each repair is the precision with which the referent is specified. This you accomplish by adding descriptors that refer to other potential physically copresent items—*right there, the second shelf, the bottom, that bookcase.* Each addition, you believe, makes it more likely that the right book will be identified uniquely. Each new piece of information strengthens the basis *G* on which the identity of the referent can be mutually known. Horizontal repairs of *prior* physical copresence work the same way.

2. **Linguistic Copresence.** Imagine this interchange. Ann: *A doctor I met last night introduced me to a lawyer, and she gave me some advice.* Bob: *Who did?* Ann? *The lawyer.* In this repair Ann has disambiguated her reference by providing one more descriptor—that the referent is a lawyer. This descriptor, like the reference itself, is based on prior linguistic copresence. She could not have added: *the woman in black*, or *the person near the piano*, or *the rich one*, which do not make contact with information Ann has provided linguistically, but she could have said: *the person the doctor introduced me to*, or *not the doctor*, or *the one I talked to second.* To be effective, horizontal repairs must add or alter descriptors, not delete them. It wouldn't make sense for Ann to say: *A woman I met last night introduced me to her daughter, and the older one, I mean she, gave me good advice.* Cooperative repairs— and that is what we are talking about—must lead to a more precise identification of the referent.

3. **Indirect Copresence.** Imagine Ann's report: *I tried to get downtown yesterday but the bus—the one I was riding in—broke down.* The bus is identifiable only on the basis of indirect copresence, and the repair adds other evidence of indirect copresence, namely that Ann *rode* on the bus. Like the previous two types of repairs, the more information the listener is provided with, the more successful the reference is judged to be.

4. **Community Membership.** When references rely on community membership, there are several ways of making horizontal repairs. One is to add information, as in *I met Nina—Nina Baker*, or as in *I hated the war—the Vietnam War.* Another is to change the community basis for the reference, as in *I like my new colleague—you know,*

Elizabeth Adams. Here both the original reference and the repair rely on community membership. What the repair does is change the community from one in which it is universally known who the speaker's colleague is to one in which it is universally known who Elizabeth Adams is. This change in community must strengthen either the certainty it is mutually known that the speaker and listener belong to that community or the certainty that the referent is universally known in that community.

Vertical Repairs

The principle of repairs is that they *strengthen* the basis G on which mutual knowledge of the identity of the referent can be inferred. With this principle we can examine vertical repairs, ones that replace one kind of copresence by another, to see if we can order the types of copresence for their strength. If our proposal is correct, the types of copresence should order themselves from strongest to weakest according to the number and kind of auxiliary assumptions they require. Indeed, that is what we will demonstrate.

1. **Physical Copresence.** Among types of physical copresence, immediate physical copresence should be the strongest because it requires the fewest auxiliary assumptions—and it is. Ann: *The book over there is mine.* Bob: *Which one?* Ann, picking up a book and showing it to Bob: *This one.* In her repair Ann has moved from potential to immediate physical copresence. If she had moved in the reverse direction, from immediate to potential physical copresence, her repair would have been nonsense. Or imagine Ann: *The book I just showed you is mine.* Bob: *Which book was that?* Ann, picking up a book and showing it to Bob: *This one.* Ann's repair here goes from prior to immediate physical copresence, and it too would be nonsensical in the reverse direction. Recall that the basis G for potential and prior physical copresence requires the auxiliary assumptions of locatability and recallability, respectively. What these and similar repairs show is that some such assumptions are necessary and that G can be strengthened by turning to direct evidence that doesn't need them—namely, immediate physical copresence. As Searle (1969, 88) has argued, the limiting case of referring to something is physically showing it (along with a suitable expression).

Physical copresence is stronger when it is direct than when it is indirect. Ann, still staring at Bob and the candle: *The price was too high.* Bob: *What price?* Ann: *The price of this candle.* And physical copresence is stronger, all other things being equal, than linguistic copresence. Ann: *I was just reading a book on your bookshelf, and it was terrific.* Bob: *What book?* Ann, picking out a book and showing it to Bob: *This one.* Repairs like these, then, are evidence for the auxiliary assumptions of associativity and understandability that we said were required for indirect physical copresence and for linguistic copresence.

2. **Linguistic Copresence.** When things are not physically showable, repairs have to be made that move up to the strongest kind of linguistic copresence. Ann: *I bought a candle today; the seal was broken,* Bob: *What seal?* Ann: *The seal on the wrapper around the candle.* This repair moves the evidence up from indirect to direct linguistic copresence. It suggests that the assumption of associativity is not a trivial one. And within linguistic copresence, a repair can be made that strengthens the recallability or locatability of the linguistic copresence. Ann: *I think your idea is excellent.* Bob: *What idea?* Ann: *A moment ago you mentioned going to a movie tonight.* This repair brings back into linguistic copresence an idea Bob had failed to recall.

3. **Community Membership.** Community membership cannot be ordered for strength in relation to physical, linguistic, or indirect copresence because its auxiliary assumptions are not comparable with those of the other three types. It can apparently be either stronger or weaker than physical or linguistic copresence, depending on the purpose for the repair. Take this exchange: Ann: *I was just talking to the woman standing right over there* (pointing). Bob: *Who is she?* Ann: *Nina Baker, the artist.* Contrast it with this interchange: Ann: *I was just talking to Nina Baker, the artist,* Bob: *Who is she?* Ann: *The woman standing right over there* (pointing). In the first exchange, the woman's physical appearance was not as significant an identification for Bob as her role in Ann and Bob's community. In the second, it is the other way around, as if Bob knows little about Nina Baker in the community and now at least can identify her physically. These repairs bear out the claim that the community membership has auxiliary assumptions that are not comparable with the others.[11]

---

[11] What an adequate answer to a *who*-question consists of has been taken up by Boer and Lycan (1975) in their paper on "knowing who." They argue that the answer to *Who is X?* is always relative to some purpose and that its ultimate answer is always an attributive use of the definite description. So the *ultimate* answers—and the ultimate repairs—go beyond our chapter, which is about referential uses.

The several bases G we proposed earlier—physical, linguistic, and indirect copresence and community membership—are only one way of cutting up the territory. They provide a tidy geography in which each basis has associated with it a few assumptions, such as simultaneity, recallability, understandability, and community comembership. A more thorough survey of repairs might suggest a different geography with slightly different auxiliary assumptions. Still, such a survey would rely on the logic we have just been using. Every repair that is judged to strengthen a reference should be associated with the elimination or simplification of one or more auxiliary assumptions. Such a survey should lead to a more complete map of the copresence heuristics themselves.

To summarize, repairs of definite reference bear witness to people's use of copresence heuristics. When a speaker makes such a repair, he tacitly reassesses his evidence for mutual knowledge of the identity of the referent, and his repair is as attempt to strengthen that evidence. The way he strengthens it is to try to find fresh evidence that needs weaker or fewer auxiliary assumptions.

8 Organization of Memory

The copresence heuristics, with their voracious appetite, can be satiated only by the right kinds and amount of factual fodder. How is this fodder organized? What does the storehouse of data the heuristics feed on look like? The arguments we have offered so far suggest a rather different view of memory from those of most current models of understanding and production.

One traditional view of definite reference is that its primary function is to pick out particular individuals—individual objects, states, events, or processes (see Strawson 1974). What this view has suggested to most investigators in that is processing definite reference people search memory for the particulars actually referred to. They can't, of course, find the particulars themselves, but they can find *referential indices* corresponding to them. Each index is a stand-in, so to speak, for the referent itself. Imagine that Bob's memory contains a set of referential indices for entities represented as $E_1, E_2, E_3, \ldots, E_n$ and that E_3 is the referential index for *Monkey Business*. When Ann uses the definite description *the movie showing a the Roxy tonight*, he is supposed to search this list and settle on the intended referent E_3. Although current models of comprehension differ is their specifics, virtually all of them assume this kind of search for the intended referent, including those of Anderson (1976), Clark and Haviland (1977), Kintsch (1974), Kintsch and van Dijk (1978), Rumelhart et al. (1972), Schank and Abelson (1977), and Winograd (1972), to name just a few.

All of these models, however, are incomplete. Bob cannot search memory for E_3 alone, for that would hardly guarantee that E_3 was mutually known to him and Ann. In most cases, he must search for an *event* that involves not only E_3 but also E_1, Ann, and E_2, him. This event, call it E_4, has to be evidence of their physical, linguistic, or indirect copresence. Or when community membership is concerned, he must search for an individual E_3 that everyone in a community he (E_1) and Ann (E_2) both belong to knows. In none of the models just mentioned does the listener search for such an event or for such a community-wide individual.

Components of Memory

Our point can be made with a metaphorical view of memory as a personal archive, or library, in which there are several different kinds of reference books. Most theories of understanding require memory to contain a grammar of English and a dictionary. With these two books, the listener can parse sentences and figure out what they mean. But to handle definite reference, the listener needs more.

What most current models of comprehension add is an elaborate kind of telephone book. In a definite reference like *the man in the red shirt*, Bob is told the name and address of the individual whose referential index he is seeking. All he needs to do is search the telephone book for this same and address, and the book will tell him the right referential index—the telephone number that connects his name and address (the reference) with his physical person (the referent). The telephone book must be a sophisticated one, like the Yellow Pages, in which the names and addresses are organized and cross-classified according to some scheme. But in effect it is a mere listing of descriptions of individuals paired with their referential indices.

Such a telephone book won't do, however, because it doesn't contain the right kind of information. Take Ann's telephone book. For her to be able to make a successful definite reference, the book would have to distinguish those names and addresses she knew Bob knew from the rest, and it would have to make the same distinction for everyone else she might potentially talk to. Although that satisfies condition (2) for mutual knowledge, it doesn't do anything more. Her book would also have to distinguish those names and addresses she knew Bob knew she knew from the rest, satisfying condition (3), and those she knew Bob knew she knew Bob knew from the rest, satisfying condition (4), and so on. Very quickly, her book would grow unmanageably large. The telephone book, in effect, is an embodiment of Assumption II, which is just the assumption we want to circumvent in order to avoid the Mutual Knowledge Paradox.

What the copresence heuristics require instead is a pair of books, a diary and an encyclopedia. Bob's diary is a personal log that keeps an account of everything significant Bob does and experiences. When Ann uses the reference *the man in the red shirt*, Bob must find in memory an individual who fits that description—a man in a red shirt. But he knows that he must search his diary for an entry that gives evidence of the physical, linguistic, or indirect copresence of him, Ann, and that man. That is, he must seek out an *event* that he can use along with certain auxiliary assumptions as the basis G for inductively inferring mutual knowledge of the identity of that man. This is far more complicated than searching a telephone book for a number. Every event he searches for involves the referent plus two other individuals, and that takes more specifications than the referent alone.

Not all parts of the diary will be equally accessible. The more recent events ought to be more accessible, and there is evidence to suggest that they are. In several studies, people were found to take less time to understand definite references that relied on linguistic copresence the more recently the antecedent event occurred (Carpenter and Just 1977; Clark and Sengul 1979; Lesgold et al. 1979). And events that are more significant ought to be more accessible, too. However, too little is known to be able to say much more about the organization of the diary. Our point is that such a diary is needed to account for genuine cases of felicitous definite reference.

Bob's second book is an encyclopedia, which he needs for mutual knowledge based on community membership. It will have recorded in it all the generic and particular knowledge Bob believes is universal to each community he belongs to. Instead of being organized is the conventional way—alphabetical by subject matter—it might take this form: Chapter 1 would contain the knowledge every human being is assumed to know, Chapter 2 the additional knowledge every American is assumed to know, Chapter 3 the additional information (over Chapters 1 and 2) that every Californian is assumed to know, and so on. Within each chapter there would be sections on biographical, geographical, historical, and other types of information. And there would be special chapters for the additional specialized knowledge possessed by psychiatrists, by Palo Alto homeowners, and by whatever other communities and subcommunities Bob may happen to belong to. Happily, subject matter and communities tend to go hand is hand—psychiatry is known by psychiatrists, and the rules and regulations for owning homes in Palo

Alto by Palo Alto homeowners—and so the encyclopedia doesn't have as complicated an organization as it might first appear.

It is the encyclopedia that Bob consults for references that require mutual knowledge based on community membership. Imagine that Bob and Ann mutually establish through months of companionship that they both belong to certain communities—those corresponding say, to Chapters 1 through 8, 11, 15, and 33 in Bob's encyclopedia. When Ann uses the reference *George Washington*, Bob must search just those chapters for an individual with that name. He must also consult those chapters for her references that rely on indirect copresence. When she says *I went to buy a candle but the price was too high*, he will find what is knows about candles, determine that each has a price, use this information to create as individual (or rather, its referential index) that corresponds to the price of the candle she mentioned, and identify it as the referent of *the price*. Creating such referential indices via indirect copresence is known to take people longer than merely identifying referential indices that are already present. People understand *The beer was warm* more quickly after *Mary got some beer out of the car*, where the beer is directly copresent, than after *Mary got some picnic supplies out of the car*, where the beer is only indirectly copresent (Haviland and Clark 1974).

A great deal has been said about the organization of such an encyclopedia. Minsky (1975) has proposed that people have "frames" for what such things as rooms consist of in general and what specific rooms consist of. Schank and Abelson (1977) have made a similar proposal for "scripts" of what people should and actually do do in such activities as going to a restaurant. Rumelhart and Ortony (1977) have proposed "schemata." Yet in none of these proposals is there any consideration for how this knowledge might be compartmentalized according to what information is mutually known by a community or by two individuals, as required for definite reference.

The diary and encyclopedia are not independent of each other. They must be cross-indexed by the individuals they contain—as when someone speaks of George Washington, the Revolutionary War, and 1776 and then refers to them all in *He led the army then*. And certain diary entries will be duplicated in the encyclopedia, as when Bob sees a news item on CBS television and supposes that it is universally known by the community of people who habitually watch CBS television.

Speaker Models and Listener Models

The memory described so far seems entirely too large and unwieldy for everyday use. It seems to go against people's intuition that talk is easy, that getting the right information at the right time is effortless and straightforward. Their intuition is based, we suggest, on the fact that the diary and the encyclopedia are compartmentalized into useful units. In conversation the units that are pertinent at any time can be prepared for selective access.

Imagine, at a party, turning from talk with an English speaker to talk with a French one. You are likely to feel you are changing gears— as if you are putting away your English dictionary and grammar and pulling out your French ones. Our suggestion is that you make similar shifts whenever you change interlocutors. You prepare yourself selectively to talk to, or listen to, that particular person or group of people. You do this by selecting pertinent parts of the diary and encyclopedia for ready access.

The way a speaker prepares is by accessing his model of the listener, and the listener accesses his model of the speaker. When Ann talks to Bob, she creates in memory a model of what is in Bob's mind—his knowledge, his perceptions, his current thoughts—and she constantly updates it. Bob carries along a similar model of what is in Ann's mind. These models must include the right diary entries and encyclopedia chapters. Ann's model of Bob would contain all those chapters of her encyclopedia that correspond to communities she knows he belongs to. However, she knows she can refer only to individuals in those communities she knows they mutually know they *both* belong to. She may know Bob is a chess addict, but realize he doesn't know she knows. So her model may include Chapters 1 through 11, 16 through 24, 38, and 55, but of those only Chapters 1 through 8, 16 through 18, and 55 are mutually known. Her model of him also contains all those diary entries that involve Bob in some way. It is these she consults when deciding whether she can establish mutual knowledge of the identity of most individuals she wants to refer to. Ann's model of Bob, in short, contains just those parts of her diary and encyclopedia that will be useful for getting him to understand her, whatever she may want to talk about. It will also contain just those parts that will allow her to understand him and all his actions.

The suggestion is that we carry around rather detailed models of people we know, especially of people we know well. If Bob is a close friend of Ann, she may even have a special chapter in her encyclopedia for him as if he and she form a community of two people. It is hard to estimate the importance of these models. At a cocktail party, as Ann turns from Bob, her close friend, to Charles, her cousin from out of town, her model of the listener will change radically, and so will the way she refers. Diary entries are particularly important here. If she has just told Bob about her theory of the Marx brothers' success in Hollywood, she cannot immediately expect Charles, who has not heard what she told Bob, to understand references to things she told Bob. She must keep track—careful track—of what she told each of them. Though her Marx-brothers theory may be uppermost in her mind as she turns to Charles, she has to explain it over again to him if he is to understand her. People who tell someone the same gossip, or joke, or piece of news twice without realizing it are considered impolite or absentminded. They have failed in the social imperative of keeping their models of each particular listener straight.

How do we build these models in the first place? In certain circumstances we can watch our model of a person being erected block by block. One of these is in formal introductions, which are designed to lay the foundations of our model of the other person in the first few seconds and to add onto it prefabricated sections quickly and easily.

Imagine Ann at a party of academics bumping into Ed. *Isn't the weather just great!* she tells Ed. The weather one can always refer to, because it is mutually identifiable by people in the same locale. The convention of always talking about the weather at the beginnings of conversations and in new conversations has an obvious basis is mutual knowledge.

Yes, it is, replies Ed. *My name is Ed Taylor. I'm a psychiatrist working here at the Palo Alto VA hospital.* With this, Ann can add to her model of Ed not only, say, encyclopedia Chapters 1 and 2—for being human and being American, which she could gather from his reply alone—but also Chapters 3 through 11, 15 and 25, for being a Californian, a Palo Altoan, a psychiatrist, and so on. This is typical of third-party- and self-introductions. They allow one to build up great chunks of the model of the other person. They are intended to accomplish just that so that the two now have something to talk about, things they can felicitously refer to.

How do you do. And I'm Ann Horton, and I work in the psychiatry department at Stanford. With this, Ann has established mutual knowledge of the universal information in these chapters. She was able to refer to Stanford University and its psychiatry department just because she knew Ed was a member of the Palo Alto community and the community of psychiatrists, and so her reference would secure mutual knowledge of the identity of these two places. *What kind of psychiatry do you specialize in?* she might go on, continuing to establish mutual knowledge of larger and larger spheres of experience.

In summary, people's memory must be organized to enable them to get access to evidence they will need to make felicitous references.

What that implies is that their memory must contain a diary of significant personal experiences cross-indexed with an encyclopedia organized both by subject matter and by the communities who possess the knowledge. It also suggests that people have selective access to information that is pertinent to each person they talk to. They have a model of what is in the other person's mind, a model they have built up from previous contact and which they continue to update as they go on talking. It is that model that enables people to make and understand references so quickly and accurately.

9   Conclusions

Definite reference is one of those phenomena in language that seem so obvious that it is hard to see what there is to explain. We have tried to shatter this illusion by posing the Mutual Knowledge Paradox, which is this: To make or interpret definite references people have to assess certain "shared" knowledge. This knowledge, it turns out, is defined by an infinite number of conditions. How then can people assess this knowledge in a finite amount of time? From the beginning, we knew the paradox was illusory—one or more of its assumptions had to be incorrect. Yet we found it a useful magnifying glass for looking into the processes by which people use and understand definite reference.

The resolution of the paradox we favor for most circumstances is that people assess mutual knowledge by use of the copresence heuristics. They search memory for evidence that they, their listeners, and the object they are referring to have been "openly present together" physically, linguistically, or indirectly. Or they search memory for evidence that the object is universally known within a community they and their listeners mutually know they belong to. With such evidence they can infer mutual knowledge directly by means of an induction schema. There is no need to assess an infinite number of conditions, and the paradox collapses.

The copresence heuristics have important consequences for definite reference. They help determine people's choice of noun phrase for each definite reference. For physical copresence, as in deixis, people prototypically use demonstratives. For linguistic copresence, as in anaphora, they prototypically use pronouns or definite descriptions. And for community membership, they prototypically use proper names, especially proper nouns. The heuristics also determine in part how people repair inadequate or unsuccessful definite references. The idea is that each repair should strengthen the basis on which mutual knowledge of the referent is established. The copresence heuristics, by spelling out the trade-off between direct evidence and certain auxiliary assumptions, tell how that basis can be strengthened.

And these heuristics require a memory that is organized around diary entries and around communities in which knowledge is universally shared. Currently, the memory assumed in most models of comprehension and production is not organized this way,

What all this suggests is that our views of comprehension and production are in need of reform. We have tried to shatter the illusion that definite reference is simple and self-evident by demonstrating how it requires mutual knowledge, which complicates matters enormously. But virtually every other aspect of meaning and reference also requires mutual knowledge, which also is at the very heart of the notion of linguistic convention and speaker meaning. Mutual knowledge is an issue we cannot avoid. It is likely to complicate matters for some time to come.

2

Context for Comprehension

WITH THOMAS B. CARLSON

Although the notion of context plays a central role in most current explanations of language understanding, what can count as context is generally left undefined. If it includes any information a listener can make available to himself, then it loses much of its power to explain. After reviewing experimental attempts to elucidate context, we take up a more analytic approach. We first define the *intrinsic context* as that information available to a process that is potentially necessary for it to succeed. Our proposal is that the intrinsic context for understanding what a speaker means on some occasion is the common ground that the listener believes holds at that moment between the speaker and the listeners he or she is speaking to. By common ground, we mean the knowledge, beliefs, and suppositions that the two people share in a technical way. Finally, we review some of the evidence for this proposal.

1 Introduction

In the past twenty years, the word *context* has become a favorite in the vocabulary of cognitive psychologists. It has appeared in the titles of an astonishing number of articles. It has been used to describe phenomena under labels ranging from "environmental" and "pharmacological context" to "thematic" and "knowledge context." "Context effects" are everywhere. "Contextualism" has been coined as the name of a theory of memory (Jenkins 1974).

What then *is* context? According to the dictionary, it is the "parts of a discourse that surround a word of passage and can throw light upon its meaning." We call this the *standard definition*. In psychology, its use has been extended far beyond the standard definition. And the further its uses have been extended, the murkier its denotation has become. Smith, Glenberg, and Bjork (1978) have complained that context has become "a kind of conceptual garbage can."

For most purposes in psychology, this may not matter. Context, one could argue, is a term that is useful precisely because it is vague and general and can accommodate many different ideas. In some areas, however, context has been used not merely to *describe* phenomena, where vagueness and generality could be virtues, but to *explain* them, where vagueness and generality are vices. One of these areas is language comprehension, in which the theories appeal directly to context to explain how people decide what a speaker means. Theories of how people decide between two meanings of a word like *bank*, for example, appeal to people's knowledge of the "context," which includes not only the "parts of the discourse that surround" the word but also a good deal more. In theories like these, the characterization of context must be precise before their predictions can be precise.

Our goal is to outline a theory of the context that is intrinsic to language comprehension. First, we review some of the uses of the term "context" in the experimental literature, concentrating on the literature in language comprehension, and draw out their essential features; that is, we try to summarize the *experimental approach* to the role of context in psychological processes. Second, we make our own proposal, which is based largely on an *analytic approach* to context. What we argue, briefly, is that for a listener to understand a speaker's meaning, he can confine himself to a certain limited domain of information, namely, the speaker's and his listener's common ground, that part of the speaker's and his listener's knowledge, beliefs, and assumptions that are shared. We then review some of the evidence for this proposal.

2   Varieties of Context

Context has long been used in psychology to describe certain parts of the experimental subject's surroundings. In visual perception, it has been used for the content of the visual stimuli surrounding or preceding the object to be perceived or identified (Brigell, Uhlarik, and Goldhorn 1977) and for the "contextual relations" among objects depicted in a scene (Biederman 1972; Palmer 1975). In learning and retention, it has been used in a broad sense both for "stimulation from the external environment, such as the furniture in the room, the experimenter, and the apparatus" (McGeoch 1939, 347) and for the "inner states of the experiencing person which affect the way he views or remembers the same stimulus material" (Reiff and Scheerer 1959, 19). The inner states have been given such names as "pharmacological context" (Eich 1980) and "mood contexts" (Bower, Monteiro, and Gilligan 1978). Context has also been used in a narrower sense for the items presented along with the target item on each study trial in learning (Tulving and Thomson 1973), as well as for larger units of organization, under such names as "list context" (Anderson and Bower 1974).

In word perception, most uses of context have been close to the standard definition. It has appeared in such notions as "context-conditioned" acoustic cues (Liberman, Cooper, Shankweiler, and Studdert-Kennedy 1967), "syllable contexts" (Dorman 1974), and "acoustic contexts" (Warren and Obusek 1971). In the identification of words in printed texts, context has also been used in a sense close to the standard definition (Tulving and Gold 1963). In other studies, the notion has been drastically extended under such labels as "sentence context," "word association context," "category contexts" (the name of a semantic category), and "letter contexts" (the first few letters of the word being identified) (Rubenstein and Pollack 1963), and "semantic context" (associated words or incomplete sentences) (Meyer, Schvaneveldt, and Ruddy 1975; Schuberth and Eimas 1977). These uses refer, as Miller, Heise, and Lichten (1951) put it, to the subject's "knowledge of the conditions of stimulation." This tradition has been continued in Morton's (1964, 1969) "logogen model," in which there are word unit detectors, or "logogens," that are sensitive to information provided by the unspecified workings of a "context system" ("cognitive system" in later formulations). In this model, all information is treated equally, with no restriction on what is to count as context (Morton 1970).

Contexts for Language Use

In studies of language use, context could have been limited to the standard definition, but even here it has been extended from the very beginning. In 1951, in his classic text *Language and Communication*, Miller said, "The verbal context of any particular verbal unit is made up of the communicative acts that surround it." But then he added, "What a man says cannot be predicted entirely from the verbal context ... A discussion of the complete context of a communicative act must include the talker's needs, perceptions, audience, and cultural background (81–82)."

In studies of the ongoing processing of sentences, most uses of context refer to selective parts of the context as specified in the standard definition, as in "semantic and syntactic context" (Marslen-Wilson and Welsh 1978) and "prior semantic context" (Foss and Jenkins 1973;

Swinney and Hakes 1976). What "syntactic and semantic context" refer to here are the constraints placed on a word by the syntax and meaning of the sentence up to that point. Similarly, Carroll, Tanenhaus, and Bever (1978) have spoken of the "discourse context" provided by a preceding sentence. On the other hand, what Dooling (1972) meant by "context" was not just syntactic and semantic constraints but some sort of mental representation of the *content* of the previous discourse.

Two related uses of context can be found in the study of memory for utterances. In Brewer and Harris's (1974) study, they spoke of "deictic context"—the relation of an utterance to "the particular time, place, person, or discourse context." And in a study by Keenan, MacWhinney, and Mayhew (1977), memory for utterances was examined in "the context of natural, purposeful communication" or "interactional context," which includes "degree of previous involvement with the speaker, the formal identity of speech acts represented by particular statements, the organizational structure of the interaction ..., and the amount of active participation on the part of the listener (559)." For these to be considered part of the standard definition, discourse must be taken as including a good deal more than just the linguistic expressions that have gone before.

Context has also been used to refer to things that are clearly non-linguistic. In studies of the verification of sentences against pictures, the pictures have sometimes been called the "context" (Tanenhaus, Carroll, and Bever 1976). And in work by Huttenlocher and Weiner (1971), the physical situation in which children were to carry out instructions was called the "extralinguistic context" of the instructions. The idea of calling these "context" may be traced to Wason's (1965) classic study of the "contexts of plausible denial," in which he referred to the pictures that his assertions and denials were meant to describe as the "objective context." This he contrasted with the "subjective context," the speaker's beliefs about the listener's beliefs about a situation.

It is Bransford and his colleagues (Bransford and Johnson 1972, 1973; Bransford and McCarrell 1974) who have been most closely associated with the study of context in comprehension; yet they have been even less clear about what they meant by it. Bransford and Johnson (1972), for example, speak of the "context picture," "appropriate semantic structures," "appropriate context" as "part of the pre-experimental knowledge," and "the context underlying a stimulus," all in relation to their general claim that "relevant contextual knowledge is a prerequisite for comprehending prose passages." Doll and

Lapinski (1974) attribute to Bransford and Johnson two additional terms, "thematic context" and "referential context." Later, Bransford and Johnson (1973) speak of "activated semantic context" or "activated knowledge structures," arguing that in general "the ability to understand linguistic symbols is based not only on the comprehender's knowledge of his language, but also on his general knowledge of the world (383)." Still later, Bransford (1979) equates "context" with "appropriately activated knowledge." What knowledge is "relevant" or "appropriately activated" Bransford never says.

3 Essentials of Context

There are six features of context that appear to be common to most of the uses we have reviewed.

1. Information. Context is information in the sense used in "information-processing" psychology. It is information about objects, events, states, or processes. It may be generic, characterizing what, for example, trees are like in general, or it may be particular, characterizing what a particular tree—say, the tree after which Palo Alto was named—is like. It may come from direct experience, from being told, or from inferences based on these sources. It may include, but is not limited to, a person's knowledge, beliefs, or suppositions.

2. Person Relativity. If context is information, it must be in someone's possession. In most of the uses we have reviewed, the context is usually relativized, not to people in general but to each particular person.

3. Process Relativity. Not all information a person possesses is considered to be context. Investigators always speak of the context of something—of a word, of a list, or of the subject in an experiment. What they mean, we suggest, is that context is relative to *a process* a person is carrying out. In a sentence, the context of a word is really information a person has relative to his interpretation of that word.

4. Occasion Relativity. For most investigators, context is information a person possesses in the carrying out of a particular process *on a particular occasion*. To be able to speak of the context changing from one pass through a list to the next or from one hearing of a sentence to the next, we must treat context as occasion relative.

With features 2–4, context can be thought of as a function with three arguments—the agent A, the process p, and the occasion or time t.

Context is *context*(*A, p, t*), not just *context*(*A, p*), *context*(*p, t*), or *context*(*A, t*). This is another way of saying that when investigators talk about context, they talk about the context for a particular person doing a particular task at a particular time (see Bower 1972).

5. **Availability.** In most usages, context is only that information that is *available* to the person carrying out the particular process on that particular occasion. When Joe Bonnano was reading the word *today* in his newspaper at 9:13 A.M. on July 4, 1980, his memory was full of all sorts of information. He knew the map of Eastern Europe, knew how to change tires, knew the Catholic catechism, believed that at age thirteen one day he saw a flying saucer, and so on. But only the part of this information that was available to Joe for the task at hand would be considered part of the context.

6. **Interactibility.** For information to be called "context" in most usages, it must also be able to interact with the process at hand. Even if the catechism were available to Joe Bonnano as he was reading *today* in the newspaper, it wouldn't be considered part of the context unless it could somehow interact with the reading and understanding of that word.

To sum up, context is information that is available to a particular person for interaction with a particular process on a particular occasion. From now on, we take this to be *the* definition of context.

Intrinsic and Incidental Context

Psychologists study context—in our now technical sense—because of its role in the processes they are interested in. Their accounts of those processes would not be complete without describing its role. Take the psychologists who study how people identify objects in visual scenes. The surroundings of an object in a scene are often crucial to people's identification of that object. One and the same visual configuration—say, a blacked-in circle—will be identified in one surrounding as a ball, in another as a tire, and in a third as a hole in a door. Most visual configurations are ambiguous in this way—look at Magritte. Psychologists recognize, therefore, that their theories of object identification must specify the role that the surroundings play.

Yet most psychologists try to distinguish between two parts of the context (still in our technical sense). For example, take Margaret in an experimental room viewing a slide and trying to identify an object in the middle of it. The process she goes through, and hence her identification, errors, and reaction time, can be influenced by many things. One category includes her identification of the surroundings of the object, her knowledge of the plausibility of the object in those surroundings, and her knowledge of the categories of objects the experimenter said she would be identifying. Another category includes her thoughts about the exam she has been studying for, her irritation with the experimenter, her perseveration on the mistake she made on the last slide, her awareness of her sore throat, her hunger, and her discomfort in the chair. Technically, both categories are part of Margaret's context in identifying the object. Both have been studied, and both continue to be worth studying.

These two categories, however, bear different relations to the task Margaret is carrying out. The things in the first category would generally be considered parts of the context that are *intrinsic* to the process of object identification. They belong to the process and, most psychologists would feel, need to be accounted for in any adequate theory of the process. The things in the second category would generally be considered *incidental* to the process as carried out on that occasion. They affect the process only indirectly, by limiting Margaret's attention to the task, interrupting the process, or making her less efficient. They do not belong to the process of object identification per se and do not need to be accounted for directly in a theory of that process. Let us call these two parts of the context the *intrinsic context* and the *incidental context*.

The intrinsic context, we stipulate, is that part of the context that, a priori, has the potential of being necessary on some occasion for carrying out the process in question. Although Margaret may sometimes be able to identify the typewriter in the middle of the slide without checking its visual surroundings, in general she could not. For the process of object identification to succeed *in general*, it must make use of the visual surroundings. The incidental context is what remains, the parts of the context that never need to be consulted.

An adequate theory for any psychological process must make reference to the intrinsic context, without which the process won't generally succeed. An important goal in studying such a process, then, is to distinguish the intrinsic from the incidental context. Indeed, in the study of comprehension, psychologists have tried to identify those parts of the discourse, broadly conceived, that a listener appears to have to consult in order to succeed in understanding what the speaker meant. Most of this effort has been experimental. Psychologists have tried out this and that part of the context to see which parts are potentially needed in comprehension. We now turn to a more analytic approach to intrinsic context. We argue that there are certain a priori grounds for characterizing the intrinsic context for comprehension in one particular way.

4 Intrinsic Context in Comprehension

Most of the characterizations of context we have reviewed allow almost anything a person knows to belong to the context in comprehension. This is implied by such terms as "interactional context," "appropriate semantic context," "relevant contextual knowledge," "thematic context," "referential context," "activated knowledge structures," "appropriate knowledge structures," and "cognitive system." The modifiers that might limit this range—"relevant," "activated," "appropriate"— have been left undefined. As characterizations of intrinsic and incidental context together, these descriptions may be accurate, but they aren't very helpful as characterizations of intrinsic context alone, which is what we are seeking. The problem is a practical one. When a listener tries to understand what a speaker means on some occasion, it would be advantageous if the process he uses could limit what it retrieves from memory to some portion of the total information that could be made available. In particular, it should limit itself to the intrinsic context, that portion of the information that may be needed for the process to succeed.

Our proposal is straightforward: *The intrinsic context for a listener trying to understand what a speaker means on a particular occasion is the common ground that the listener believes holds at that moment between the speaker and the listeners he or she is speaking to.* There are two technical notions here that need explaining. The first is *what the speaker meant*, or *speaker's meaning* (Grice 1957, 1968; Schiffer 1972). Our proposal is about how a listener tries to determine what the speaker intended him to determine, in part by means of his recognition of the speaker's intentions. Our proposal is *not* about the further inferences that a listener carries out on the basis of what the speaker meant; that is, it is about the "authorized" and not the "unauthorized" inferences made by the listener, two sorts of inferences that listeners ordinarily keep quite distinct (Clark 1977).[1] The second technical notion is common ground.

---

[1] So in the understanding of what the speaker meant, one could also define two further notions of context. One is the *intended context*, the information that the speaker intended the listener to consult in understanding his utterance on a particular occasion. The second is the *actual context*, the information that the listener actually did consult. Ideally, the actual context should be identical to the intended context, and both should be part of the intrinsic context. In everyday performance, these relations doubtless fall short of the ideal.

Common Ground

As a first approximation, the common ground between two people can be thought of as the information the two of them share. When Ann and Bob, for example, are standing together in a gallery looking at a Picasso painting, they share a good deal of information—about the objects depicted in the painting, about its colors, about its position on the wall, about Picasso, about modern painting, about each other, and so on. When Ann and Bob are later discussing their opinions of the painting with each other, they also share information about what each other has just said, meant, and implied. The common ground between them consists, roughly, of the knowledge, beliefs, and even suppositions shared in this way.

The obvious first problem is that what Ann takes to be the common ground between them won't exactly match what Bob takes to be the common ground between them. Discrepancies of this sort are a major source of misunderstanding between people. Furthermore, we can speak of a third party's beliefs in the common ground between Ann and Bob—say, the beliefs of Connie. In general, Connie's beliefs about Ann's and Bob's common ground will be less veridical and less complete—often very much so—than will either Ann's or Bob's. Non-veridicality and incompleteness are two major sources of misunderstandings by third persons.

As we will see, however, this first approximation to common ground will not do. It isn't enough for both Ann and Bob to know or believe certain things. They must each know or believe that they both know or believe these things—and they must know or believe that the other knows or believes that they both know or believe these things, and so on. What is required is the technical notion of "common" or "mutual" knowledge, beliefs, and suppositions (Lewis 1969; Schiffer 1972). Mutual knowledge of a proposition p is defined by Schiffer as follows:

A and B mutually know that $p =_{\text{def}}$

1. A knows that p.
1'. B knows that p.
2. A knows that B knows that p.
2'. B knows that A knows that p.
3. A knows that B knows that A knows that p.
3'. B knows that A knows that B knows that p.
    etc., ad infinitum.

Mutual beliefs and mutual suppositions are like mutual knowledge but with the verb *know* replaced everywhere by the verb *believe* or the verb *suppose.* In short, the common ground between two people consists of their mutual knowledge, mutual beliefs, and mutual suppositions.[2]

Sources of Common Ground

An immediate problem with the definition of common ground is that it is infinite in length. For A and B to mutually know something, it appears that they must represent in memory an infinite number of knowledge statements—namely, 1, 1', 2, 2', etc., ad infinitum. This is clearly impossible. Clark and Marshall (this volume), however, have argued that the problem is only apparent.

The central idea is that mutual knowledge is an elementary mental representation that is inductively inferred from certain special kinds of evidence. Imagine that Ann and Bob are standing together looking at the Picasso painting and that each is aware of the other doing this; that is, Ann sees Bob looking at the painting, and she sees him noticing her doing this at roughly the same time. If she assumes that Bob is rational and that he is attending to both her and the painting, it is easy to show that she can immediately jump to the conclusion that they mutually know about the painting. The evidence Ann requires is an event in which she, Bob, and the painting are "co-present," that is, openly present together in a certain way. She can jump to this conclusion by using this evidence along with certain auxiliary assumptions in a "mutual knowledge induction schema." She can then add to her beliefs about the common ground between her and Bob certain beliefs about the Picasso painting. For the induction schema to apply, the evidence has to be of just the right kind. Clark and Marshall identified three major types of evidence: physical co-presence, linguistic co-presence, and community membership.

Among the strongest evidence that something is common ground is *physical co-presence.* An example of this is Ann and Bob viewing the Picasso painting at the art gallery. The two of them are experiencing it together, simultaneously, in the near-certain awareness that the other is experiencing it, too. What better evidence could Ann want that she knew about the painting, knew that he knew about the painting, knew that he knew that she knew about the painting, and so on? The auxiliary assumptions she needs are minimal—mainly that Bob is rational and is paying attention, just as she is. This experience

---

[2] As Gerald Gazdar has pointed out to us, this definition is probably insufficient, because there are almost certainly mixtures of knowledge, belief, and suppositions in which 3, for example, might read *A supposes that B believes that A supposes that p,* or *A knows that B knows that A believes that p,* etc. This is not the place to take up these complications.

constitutes an event of physical co-presence, and it is that event, along with the assumptions, that allows her to infer mutual knowledge of the picture. The experience, of course, can be visual, auditory, tactile, and so on, or any combination of the senses.

In contrast with physical co-presence is linguistic co-presence. Imagine that Ann had seen the painting and Bob hadn't, and Ann says to Bob *I saw an extraordinary painting by Picasso today.* In mentioning the painting in this way, she is bringing it into linguistic co-presence with Bob; that is, whereas in physical co-presence Ann, Bob, and the picture are openly present together in a single event, in linguistic co-presence Ann, Bob, and Ann's *mention* of the picture are what are openly present together. If Ann assumes that Bob understands her correctly and is otherwise rational and paying attention, she can infer that they now mutually suppose the existence of the Picasso painting. Whereas physical co-presence relies on "natural" evidence of the joint presence of Ann, Bob, and the painting, linguistic co-presence relies on "symbolic" evidence of their joint presence. In this way, the two types of evidence are distinct.

The last major type of evidence for common ground is *community membership*. Once Ann and Bob mutually establish that they both belong to a particular community, they can infer that what is universally known within that community is mutually known to the two of them. Imagine, for example, that Ann and Bob mutually discover that they are both on the Stanford University faculty. Ann can then infer that they mutually know where the Stanford Post Office is, who the president of the university is, and so on. Ann and Bob, of course, each belong to many communities and subcommunities, some in common and others distinct. To assume mutual knowledge for anything known by some community, they must first establish that they mutually know that they are both members of that community. If Ann knew that Bob was on the Stanford University faculty but knew that he didn't know that she was, she couldn't assume mutual knowledge of the post office, the president, and so on.

As evidence for common ground, physical and linguistic co-presence constitute single time-bounded events, whereas community membership constitutes an enduring state of affairs. Once Ann and Bob have mutually established that they are both members of some community, they can return again and again to that membership as a basis for inferring what is in their common ground. With physical and linguistic co-presence, in contrast, the single events are generally of limited use. Ann can later refer to the painting she and Bob had just seen or talked about, but only so long as the events are still fresh in memory. Evidence of physical and linguistic co-presence is generally pretty transitory.

Most inferences of common ground are based on a combination of these three types of evidence. After Ann tells Bob *I saw an extraordinary painting by Picasso today*, she can infer that they mutually believe not only that she saw the painting but also that it was modern. She can draw the second inference because they both belong to the community of educated people who almost universally know that Picasso was a modern painter. Similarly, after Ann and Bob view the painting together, she can infer mutual knowledge not only of its existence but also of the manner in which it was probably created—from oils applied to canvas with a brush. This inference is also justified and drawn quite naturally on the basis of their joint membership in the community of educated people. If Bob had been a child or a stone-age food gatherer, Ann would not have been willing to draw this inference.

A Classification of Contexts

If the intrinsic context for comprehension is the speaker's and addressee's common ground, then the contexts mentioned in the literature as relevant to comprehension should be classifiable into one or more of the three main sources of common ground. And they are.

A major source for common ground in comprehension is, naturally enough, linguistic co-presence. The listener takes as common ground between him and the speaker all of their conversation up to and including the utterance currently being interpreted. Likewise, the reader takes as common ground between him and the narrator of the written discourse all the text up to and including the utterance he is currently considering. So linguistic co-presence quite naturally subsumes such types of context as "prior linguistic context," "semantic context," "discourse context," "syntactic context," and even "interactional context."

A second source for common ground is physical co-presence. The listener takes as common ground what he and the speaker are currently experiencing and have already experienced. This subsumes such notions as "extralinguistic context," "perceptual context," and Wason's "objective context." As they stand, these earlier notions are untenably broad, because they include perceptual information that is available to the listener but is known, believed, or supposed by the listener not to be part of his and the speaker's common ground. By reference to common ground, we can cut these gargantuan contexts down to size.

The least understood source of evidence is community membership. If something is universally known in a community, then two people in that community can assume that they mutually know it. This will cover, while narrowing down, a good deal of Bransford's allusions to "pre-experimental knowledge," "appropriate knowledge framework," and "relevant contextual knowledge." It will also subsume other notions often included under the rubric of context, such as frames (Minsky 1975), scripts (Schank and Abelson 1977), schemata (Rumelhart and Ortony 1977), and story grammars (Mandler and Johnson 1977). These notions are each too inclusive as they now stand. An American wouldn't assume that an Egyptian has the script for what happens in American fast-food restaurants. The mutuality of such knowledge is essential for understanding the speaker's intent.

5   Why Common Ground?

What evidence is there that common ground is the right notion of intrinsic context? Most of it is formal. There are, for example, formal demonstrations that common ground is the necessary ingredient in conventions (Lewis 1969), in speech acts (Schiffer 1972), and in definite reference (Chapter 1, this volume). Other investigators have appealed to these demonstrations in their own arguments in favor of common ground. Yet most of the argument depends on a common sense analysis of language use. In our review, we try to convey as much of this common sense analysis as we can.

Conventions

The first formulation of mutual knowledge was proposed by Lewis (1969) to account for conventions. Consider the convention of using *chien* to denote dogs. For Ann to use *chien* with Bob to denote dogs, she must know that he knows it means "dog." But what if he knows it means "dog," but believes *she* thinks it means "cat"? Then Ann must suppose that he knows that *she* knows it means "dog." But what if he knows that she knows that it means "dog" but believes that *he* thinks it means "cat"? Ann must therefore suppose that he knows that she knows that he knows it means "dog." And so on, as Lewis demonstrated, ad infinitum. More generally, Lewis showed that for any convention to be usable by two people, it has to be mutually known (in the technical sense) by those two people.

If mutual knowledge—one aspect of common ground—is an essential part of conventions, then it must also be an essential part of language use because so much of language is conventional. The relations between most words and their meanings are conventional and so are phonological, morphological, and syntactic rules, the rules of semantic composition, and even, some would argue, much of pragmatics. What is represented in a person's mental lexicon and mental grammar are conventions that are common ground for that person and any other person who speaks the same language or dialect.

The source of common ground for conventions, then, is community membership. Trivially, to use English phonology, syntax, and semantics, the speaker must establish that he and his listener mutually know that they are both members of the community of English speakers. For many aspects of language, even the subcommunities to which the speaker and listener belong are critical. Words like *Jacobian*, *Bessel function*, and *quark*, for example, have conventional meanings only for the subcommunity of physicists, and ordinary words like *bug*, *tea*, and *attention* have additional conventional meanings in the subcommunities of computer workers, drug users, and psychologists. Whenever a speaker from one of these subcommunities talks to someone outside it, he can take as common ground only the vocabulary of the larger communities to which they both belong (Nunberg 1978).

Speech Acts

In uttering sentences like *It's raining out* and *Who is coming tonight?*, a speaker is performing certain speech acts. He has certain attitudes he wants to express for certain listeners—for example, his belief that it is raining out or his desire to know from his addressees who is coming that night—and in uttering these sentences he intends those listeners to recognize these attitudes by means of their recognition of his intentions (Grice 1957, 1968; Searle 1969; Bach and Harnish 1979). Our working assumption is that understanding what the speaker meant consists largely in trying to recognize the attitudes the speaker intended his listeners to recognize—the speech acts he performed.

How do listeners recognize the attitudes the speaker is expressing? According to a formal demonstration by Schiffer (1972), they do so by means of certain evidence—the words the speaker used and certain other "contextual" information. The critical point in Schiffer's demonstration is that this evidence has to be mutually known or believed by the speaker and his addressees. If it isn't, the speech act can fail, and it will be only accidental if the listeners manage to recognize the speaker's attitudes. What Schiffer's demonstration shows, then, is that the intrinsic context for understanding speech acts is mutual knowledge or beliefs—that is, common ground.

One source of evidence listeners use here is community membership, which leads them to the conventions governing the phonology, syntax, and semantics of the sentence uttered. The interrogative mood of *Who is coming tonight?*, for instance, can conventionally be used for asking questions (although it can also be used for other speech acts). The two other main sources of evidence for common ground—physical and linguistic co-presence—are also important. With *Who is coming tonight?*, they are needed for identifying when "tonight" is and where the people are "coming" to. Identifying the speech act being performed generally requires some combination of the three main sources of evidence for common ground.

Every conversation can be viewed as a series of speech acts that each increment the common ground of the parties in the conversation (Gazdar 1979; Stalnaker 1978). The idea, roughly, is this: Before Joe says in the middle of a conversation *Bill left for New York yesterday*, he will have assessed the common ground of his conversational partners and found it to be common ground who Bill is but not that he left for New York yesterday. Joe, of course, believes that Bill left for New York the day before (if he is being sincere) and perhaps that a few others might believe it but that not all the parties believe that all the parties believe it. Joe makes his assertion, therefore, in an attempt to increment the common ground among the parties—otherwise, there would be no point to it. They now all believe—indeed, mutually believe—that he believes that Bill left for New York yesterday. Once this is common ground, the next speaker, Sally, can say, for example, *Did he go by plane?*, in which she presupposes that it is common ground that Bill left for New York the day before.

Common ground is essential to speech acts that are indirect, too. Imagine that Joe says to Sally *Do you know what time it is?* In the right situation, he could mean, literally, that she is to say whether or not she knows what time it is. He could also mean, indirectly, that she is to go to an appointment she has forgotten. What is the intrinsic context for Sally's recognition of this reminder? All the evidence suggests (Clark 1979; Cohen and Perrault 1979) that it is once again common ground. To be able to make this reminder, Joe must know about the appointment, know that she knows about it, know that she knows that he knows about it, and so on. Joe cannot expect her to refer to information that is not part of their common ground.

Definite Reference

Imagine Judy saying to David at a party *The woman in the blue dress is the mayor of San Francisco*. In uttering *the woman in the blue dress*, Judy is making a definite reference. She is trying to enable David to identify the person to whom she is referring—a particular woman—and with the rest of her utterance she is asserting something about that woman.

What information is necessary for David's identification of that woman? According to a formal demonstration by Clark and Marshall (this volume), it is once again mutual knowledge or beliefs. If Judy's definite reference is sincere, she has good reason to believe that on this occasion David can readily and uniquely infer mutual knowledge of the identity of her referent. Most often, that means that the referent itself is *already* mutually known, and it is a matter of picking out the right referent from a mutually known array of possible referents. Describing the referent as the woman in a blue suit will do the trick. On other occasions, the referent *isn't* yet mutually known, but its identity can be inferred on the basis of mutual knowledge, beliefs, or suppositions. In short, the part of the context that David is intended to use as intrinsic to understanding Judy's reference is his and her common ground.

The three traditional types of definite reference—deixis, anaphora, and proper names—generally reflect the three main sources of mutual knowledge by which they are interpreted (Chapter 1, this volume). With deixis, as in *this woman, that box over there*, or *you*, the speaker prototypically depends in part on the physical co-presence of the speaker, addressee, and referent, which he often secures by gestures and eye contact. With anaphora, as in *the woman, the box I just mentioned*, and *itself*, the speaker depends primarily on the *linguistic* co-presence of the speaker, addressee, and referent. And for proper names, as with *George Washington, Napoleon*, and *World War II*, the speaker relies mainly on community membership—that he and his addressee belong to a community in which it is universally known who George Washington and Napoleon were, and what World War II was. What listeners take as intrinsic context for interpreting definite reference is just the evidence that allows them to infer common ground.

6   Contextual Expressions

Contextual expressions are constructions whose senses vary indefinitely depending on the occasion on which they are used (Clark and Clark 1979). Imagine that Ed and Joe have a mutual friend named Max, who has the odd habit of carrying a teapot and occasionally sneaking up and rubbing the back of people's legs with it. One day Ed says to Joe, *Well, Max did it this time. He tried to teapot a policeman.* On this occasion, the verb *teapot*, based on the noun *teapot*, has the meaning "rub the back of the leg of with a teapot." However, with a change in the story about Max, it could have meant something else entirely. Because there are indefinitely many distinct stories one could tell about Max and teapots, there are indefinitely many distinct senses one could ascribe to the constructed verb *teapot*.

The main defining feature of contextual expressions is that, like the verb *teapot*, they have indefinitely many potential senses. They are different from ordinary ambiguous constructions like *virtualness*, which have a small finite number of distinct senses that either are conventional and are listed separately in the mental lexicon or are identifiable from conventional rules of composition applied to the conventional meanings of their parts (here, *virtual* and *-ness*). It is only in context that listeners can create the intended senses of expressions like *teapot*, hence the name *contextual expression*. Contextual expressions are not on the periphery of language, linguistic oddities to account for in a special way. They are ubiquitous and are thought to be a natural part of language (Clark 1981).

The point is that for contextual expressions the intrinsic context is the speaker's and the target audience's common ground. Ed could not have said *Max tried to teapot a policeman* to just anyone and expected him to recognize the meaning "rub the back of the leg of with a teapot." Ed had to be sure that his addressee knew about Max's odd habits, knew that Ed knew about them, knew that Ed knew that he knew about them, and so on. It is easy to demonstrate that, like definite reference, contextual expressions have interpretations that require, in general, reference to the speaker's and audience's mutual knowledge, beliefs, and suppositions. The intrinsic context is their common ground.

7   Conclusions

What we have proposed is that when a listener tries to understand what a speaker means, the process he goes through can limit memory access to information that is common ground between the speaker and his addressees. At the very least, it must distinguish between information that is and is not part of the common ground, because otherwise in certain situations it will systematically misinterpret conventions, direct and indirect speech acts, definite reference, and contextual expressions. So the comprehension process must keep track of common ground, and its performance will be optimal if it limits its access to that common ground. Whether its design is actually optimal in this respect is a question that can only be answered empirically.

The intrinsic context for comprehension is different in one fundamental way from most other notions of intrinsic context. In areas like visual perception, the notion of common ground isn't even definable, because there are generally no agents involved other than the perceiver himself. Defining the intrinsic context in terms of common ground appears to be limited to certain processes of communication. Context, therefore, cannot be given a uniform treatment across all psychological domains. In language comprehension, indeed, the intrinsic context is something very special.

3

Common Ground and the Understanding of Demonstrative Reference

WITH ROBERT SCHREUDER AND SAMUEL BUTTRICK

Suppose a speaker gestures toward four flowers and asks a listener, *How would you describe the color of this flower?* How does the listener infer which of the four flowers is being referred to? It is proposed that he selects the one he judges to be most salient with respect to the speaker's and his common ground—their mutual knowledge, beliefs, and suppositions. In a field experiment, it was found that listeners would accept demonstrative references (like *this flower*) with more than one potential referent. Three further experiments showed that listeners select referents based on estimates of their mutual beliefs about perceptual salience, the speaker's goals, and the speaker's presuppositions and assertions. Common ground, it is argued, is necessary in general for understanding demonstrative reference.

A demonstrative reference is a reference that requires an accompanying gesture for its complete interpretation. Suppose Margaret points at a copy of the *New York Times* that Duncan is holding and asks Duncan,

(1)   Could I look at that newspaper?

To understand what she is referring to, Duncan must not only grasp the words *that newspaper*, but also register what Margaret is indicating by her gesture, or *demonstration*, which could have been a nod, a gaze, a presentation, or some other gesture.

Demonstrative references at first seem trivial to understand. In

(1), let us call *newspaper*, the descriptive part of the noun phrase, the *descriptor*, and the newspaper Margaret is pointing at the *demonstratum*. Standard theories of demonstrative reference (e.g., Bennett 1978; Fillmore 1982; Lakoff 1974; Lyons 1975, 1977; Maclaran 1980) make two tacit assumptions about such a reference.

ASSUMPTION I: The referent is identical to the demonstratum. If Margaret is referring to a newspaper, she must be pointing at that newspaper.

ASSUMPTION II: The referent is uniquely determined by the demonstratum together with the descriptor. With her gesture, Margaret specifies a set of potential referents—the newspaper itself, the newsprint, a headline, and many other possibilities—and with the descriptor *newspaper*, she uniquely specifies which element in that set, the newspaper itself, is the intended referent.

With Assumptions I and II, it seems obvious how people understand demonstrative references.

The problem is that both assumptions are incorrect. Suppose Margaret points at the same newspaper and asserts

(2)   I used to work for those people.

Although she is demonstrating a newspaper, she is referring to its publishers, the New York Times Company. This utterance is perfectly acceptable, and in the right circumstances, Duncan will readily understand it. Contrary to Assumption I, the referent need not be identical to the demonstratum (Nunberg 1979). Next, suppose Margaret, gesturing in the direction of two newspapers Duncan is holding, asks Duncan,

(3)   Could I look at that newspaper?

By Assumption II, this reference should be unacceptable since there are two newspapers. But if one has a screamer, say, "War Over," and the other has ordinary headlines, this utterance is also perfectly acceptable, and Duncan will understand her as referring to the first newspaper. The point is that understanding demonstrative references often requires complicated inferences. In (2), Duncan had to infer the connection between the newspaper being demonstrated and the people being referred to. In (3), he had to infer which of the two newspapers was the referent. Both examples raise the same issue: how do listeners infer the mapping from the demonstratum to the referent?

Our goal is to characterize how people understand demonstrative reference in general. In this chapter, however, we will investigate only cases that violate Assumption II, as in example (3). There Margaret's reference can be said to be "underdetermined," since her demonstration and the descriptor *newspaper*, by themselves, do not allow Duncan to pick out the intended referent. How, then, does he do it? We will describe a partial model of demonstrative reference draw out its consequences for underdetermined reference, and report four experiments illustrating these consequences.

1 Demonstrative Reference

In our proposal, a demonstrative reference has three parts: a demonstratum d, a demonstrative relation F, and a referent r. In example (2), d is the newspaper Margaret is pointing at; r is the people who publish it; and F is the relation of being the people who publish, which we will write people-who-publish. The relation F maps the demonstratum d into the referent r (see Nunberg 1979). In example (3), similarly, d is the set of two newspapers Margaret is pointing at; r is the one with the screamer; and F is the relation having-a-screamer-in. Example (1) is simply the degenerate case in which the demonstratum d, the newspaper, coincides with the referent r, and so F is the identity relation. In general, F can be any relation the speaker can get the addressees to infer quickly and uniquely.

Our proposal is that the speaker provides the addressees with enough information about d, F, and r as a triad that they can infer d, F, and r uniquely. In (2), Margaret's descriptor *people* narrows r to people; her demonstration indicates that those people bear some relation to the newspaper; so F takes the form people-somehow-connected-with. Duncan is intended to infer the specific d, F, and r as the combination, or package, that makes the best sense under these constraints. For that, he must use other information and infer F to be people-who-publish and not, say, people-who-print, people-who-distribute, or people-mentioned-in-the-headlined-story-in, which could indeed be the intended F in other situations.

The method listeners use in packaging d, F, and r, according to our proposal, changes with the information provided. With a precise demonstration and a vague descriptor, they should choose one method; with a vague demonstration and a precise descriptor, they should use another (see Pechmann and Deutsch 1982). Ultimately, they should appeal to a general principle they believe to be part of the speaker's and addressees' common ground:

Principle of Optimal Design. The speaker designs his utterance in such a way that he has good reason to believe that the addressees can readily and uniquely compute what he meant on the basis of the utterance along with the rest of their common ground.

Working backwards, the addressee can assume he has been given enough information and can thereby reason through to the speaker's meaning.

The Principle of Optimal Design relies crucially on the notion of *common ground*, technically the mutual knowledge, beliefs, and assumptions shared by the speaker and addressees (see Chapters 1 and 2, this volume). In our proposal, the speaker intends each addressee to base his inferences not on just *any* knowledge or beliefs he may have, but only on their *mutual* knowledge or beliefs—their common ground. One goal of our research is to explore the role common ground plays in demonstrative reference.

Underdetermined Demonstrative Reference

Let us turn now to underdetermined demonstrative reference. Suppose Julia nods at a cluster of men jogging along a road and tells Ken

(4)   That man is my neighbor.

If Ken takes d to be the set of ten men, and r to be one of them, what F should he infer? If one jogger was naked, he might infer F to be naked-man-in. If exactly one jogger was especially tall, a midget, or in a gorilla suit, or if one had just fallen, won the race, or slugged a bystander, he would infer a different F and r. In each case, he would choose F to make r the most distinctive man in the cluster. The F would have the general form most-salient-part-of.

This characterization, however, cannot be complete. Each jogger is the most salient by some criterion—by being the only one with red hair, in second place, or wearing blue socks. In what respect is the *intended* referent most salient? Suppose Julia had just told Ken that her neighbor was completely bald, and suppose all the joggers except one were hirsute. In saying (4), Julia would expect Ken to see that this prior information, part of their common ground, was relevant. He was to pick the jogger most salient not on *general* grounds, but against their *particular* common ground. He was to select the bald man even if the tallest man, the midget, or the winner would be most salient on general grounds. As the Principle of Optimal Design dictates, the only information he should consult is their common ground. So the general form of F should be most-salient-part-of-with-respect-to-common-ground.

The common ground between two people is based on roughly three sources of information (see Chapter 1). The first is *perceptual evidence,* what the two have jointly experienced or are jointly experiencing at the moment. The second is *linguistic evidence*, what the two have jointly heard said or are now jointly hearing as participants in the same conversation. The third is *community membership*. They take as common ground everything they believe is universally, or almost universally, known, believed, or supposed in the many communities and subcommunities to which they mutually believe they both belong. Most parts of common ground are based on a combination of these sources.

Two people's common ground may be a tiny plot or a large acreage. If Julia and Ken are strangers, their common ground comes entirely from their joint membership in the community of, say, adult Americans (mutually recognized from their American accents) and from the scene they are witnessing. If Julia assumed nakedness would be the most salient attribute in the scene for most Americans, she would expect Ken to understand her in (4) as referring to the naked jogger. But if Julia and Ken are intimates, their common ground will be extensive and include their discussion of her bald neighbor, and Ken should understand her as referring to the jogger who is bald. For the same demonstratum and descriptor, the relation F, and hence the referent r, should change with common ground.

At first, one might view the underdetermined demonstrative references in (2) through (4) simply as defective, as no different from the equivalent underdetermined definite descriptions. If they were, they should be replaceable by underdetermined definite descriptions with no change in understandability. They are not. Suppose Margaret uttered (1′) through (4′) in the same contexts as (1) through (4), but without the accompanying gestures.

(1′)   Could I see the newspaper in your hand?

(2′)   *I used to work for the people in your hand.

(3′)   *Could I see the newspaper in your hand?

(4′)   *The man in the group in front of us is my neighbor.

While most people we have asked find (1′) acceptable, they find (2′) through (4′) unpalatable. They feel as if they are left with the questions *What people?*, *Which newspaper?*, and *Which man?* whereas they accept (2) through (4) without such questions. When a reference is accompanied by a demonstration, listeners seem to feel they are to understand it partly by examining the demonstratum more closely. Demonstrative references are simply different from other definite descriptions (Hawkins 1978).

Before examining this *common ground model* further, we need to demonstrate that Assumption II is false—that people *will* accept demonstrative references with more than one potential referent. That was the aim of Experiment 1.

2 Experiment 1

We stopped students on the Stanford University campus, showed them a photograph with four types of flowers in it, and asked, gesturing to the photograph as a whole, "How would you describe the color of this flower?" We expected them to respond in one of three main ways:

(a) Implicit acknowledgment of understanding, *It's yellow.*

(b) Request for confirmation, *Do you mean this flower* [pointing at one of the flowers]?

(c) Request for clarification, *Which flower do you mean?*

Response (a) indicates the student thought they understood the reference; (b) indicates less certainty; (c) indicates the least certainty, since the students do not even offer the conjecture they do in (b). Put negatively, (b) indicates they thought the reference was partly defective, and (c), rather more defective. With (a), (b), and (c), we have a natural scale of understandability.

Method

The color photograph we used, from the *Sunset New Western Garden Book* (1979, 128), depicted four varieties of flowers beside a wooden fence: a cluster of yellow daffodils in the front center; white daisies dispersed throughout the background; a number of orange California poppies at the right; and a cluster of blue irises on the far left. We compared two versions of the photograph. Picture 1 was a color Xerox copy of that photograph, measuring eighteen by twenty-four centimeters, in which the daffodils were only slightly more prominent than the other three flowers. Picture 2 was a second color Xerox copy, cropped to eleven by fifteen centimeters, in which the daffodils were clearly more salient than the others. The two pictures each showed all four types of flowers but differed in the prominence of the daffodils.

One of us, Buttrick, approached forty students at various places on the Stanford University campus. With a clipboard in hand, he introduced himself to each student, handed the student one of the two pictures, and, nodding at the picture while preparing to write down the answer, asked, "How would you describe the color of this flower?" He wrote down everything the student said, including all requests for confirmation or clarification. The flower chosen was always clear from the color named or flower pointed at. Each picture was described by twenty students.

TABLE 1
Responses to the Question
How would you describe the color of this flower?
(Experiment 1)

RESPONSE	PICTURE 1 (LOW SALIENCE)	PICTURE 2 (HIGH SALIENCE)
a. Immediate choice	3	11
b. "This one?"	3	3
c. "Which one?"	12	5
Other	2	1
Totals	20	20

NOTE: Two students offered a color for Picture 1 and then questioned their choice; one student narrowed the four referents down to two possibilities.

Results and Discussion

Suppose that listeners look where the speaker is pointing, note the set of potential referents there (the referent array), and select the object uniquely specified by the descriptor. This model, which is much like Olson's (1970) model of definite reference, is based on Assumptions I and II. We will call it the *classical* model. According to that model, if the referent array contains four flowers, listeners should accept a descriptor like *daffodil*, which picks out a unique flower, but they should not accept *flower*, which does not. Yet as shown in Table 1, many students in Experiment 1 accepted *flower* without hesitation. For Picture 2, eleven of twenty students immediately described the color of the daffodils. For the two pictures together, fourteen of forty students did so. To anticipate a finding in Experiment 4, twelve of fifteen students gave response (a) for a similar picture. These responses constitute evidence against the classical model and Assumption II.

By the classical model, *this flower* should be no more acceptable a reference for Picture 2 than Picture 1, since *flower* picks out a unique flower no more for one than for the other. Yet it was. More students chose the daffodils immediately (response (a)) on Picture 2 than Picture 1, 55 to 15%, $\chi^2(1) = 7.03$, $p < .01$. More students offered at least some hypothesis (response (a), (b), or a mixed response) for Picture 2 than Picture 1, 75 to 40%, $\chi^2(1) = 5.01$ $p < .05$. And if responses (a), (b), and (c) are assigned confidence values 3, 2, and 1, respectively, students were more confident for Picture 2 than Picture 1 by 2.15 to 1.55, $t(38) = 2.92$, $p < .01$. All this evidence also counts against the classical model.

By the common ground model, the more salient the most salient flower is, the more confidently it should be picked as the referent (and the less likely the reference should be deemed defective). On intuitive grounds, the daffodils were more salient and should have been chosen more confidently in Picture 2 than Picture 1, and they were. We will consider perceptual salience of this sort more closely in Experiment 2.

It is surprising how widely the students ranged in their acceptance of the demonstrative references. On each of the two pictures, some students immediately committed themselves to the daffodils (response (a)), yet others wouldn't even offer a conjecture (response (c)). What made the confident students so confident and the uncertain students so uncertain? If we could answer this, we would be a long way toward the main issue of interest: how do people infer the intended referent when it is underdetermined by the demonstration and descriptor?

personality type [handwritten margin note]

3 Salience and Common Ground

According to the common ground model, the students in Experiment 1 responded (a), (b), or (c) based on their judgment of how salient the most salient flower was. They judged salience, in turn, against their estimate of their common ground with the questioner. Unfortunately, there are currently no theories about how people judge salience against common ground, nor will we propose one here. Instead we propose an empirical measure derived from the *Schelling task*, which we have named after one of the first to use the task, Thomas C. Schelling (1960).

Suppose a student named Mary is shown a picture of three balls—a basketball, a golf ball, and a squash ball—and is told, "Select one of these three balls. I am giving the same picture and instructions to another student in the next room, a person you don't know. You will both get a prize if the two of you select the same ball, but nothing if you don't." As Schelling pointed out (54):

What is necessary is to coordinate predictions, to read the same message in the common situation, to identify the one course of action that their expectations of each other can converge on. They must "mutually recognize" some unique signal that coordinates their expectations of each other.

For this problem, Mary might assume large size to be the most distinctive attribute in her common ground with the anonymous student. If she takes this as a "unique signal" for coordinating their expectations, she will pick the basketball. Let us call such a choice on a Schelling task a *Schelling choice*.

But suppose Mary is told her partner is Peter, with whom she regularly plays squash. Because she could assume the squash ball was particularly salient in their common ground, she could select it, believing Peter, too, would see it as a "unique symbol" for coordinating expectations. No matter how avid a squash player she was, she could not make the same assumption when her partner was just "another student." It matters to Mary who her partner is because it matters what is in their common ground.

Schelling choices, therefore, should reflect what the two partners take to be salient with respect to their common ground. In the common ground model, listeners choose referents by the same criterion—salience with respect to common ground—and so the distribution of Schelling choices should predict their choices of referents. It should also predict their confidence. In a Schelling task, if object A is selected more often than object B, then in the corresponding reference task those listeners who happen to select A should be more confident than those who happen to select B. Experiments 2 and 3 were designed to test these predictions.

4 Experiment 2

Students were asked to interpret demonstrative references from a speaker they did not know. In assessing common ground, therefore, they could make only the most general assumptions about the display and how it would be viewed by most people. In fact, people generally have a pretty good idea of what others will attend to in such a display, especially what they will see as salient, distinctive, or out of place. These estimates should be the same ones they use in making Schelling choices and, more simply, in choosing the most salient object.

Method

We constructed twenty-seven displays of common objects by cutting pictures out of merchandise catalogs from such department stores as Sears, J. C. Penney, and Best Products. Each display depicted two to seven objects of the same type, like four watches, six lamps, or three tents, each with a number or letter next to it for identification. The displays was designed so that one object in each display seemed more prominent than the rest—larger, more distinctive in shape, more foregrounded—and so that the prominence of the most prominent object varied from display to display. The twenty-seven displays were placed in one order and photocopied to make three booklets that differed only in the sentence typed at the bottom of each page: "What do you think of this X" for a reference task, "You are both to choose the same X" for a Schelling task, and "You are to choose the most prominent or salient X" for a salience task. For X we substituted a one- or two-word description of the objects in the picture—for example, *watch*, *lamp*, or *tent*.

Reference task. Ten students were instructed, "Imagine that you and another person are looking through this catalog. He shows you this page and asks you the question printed at the bottom (for example, 'What do you think of this alarm clock?'). You are to indicate for each display which object you think he is referring to. After you have made your choice, please indicate how confident you are that you have chosen the correct referent." They rated their confidence on a seven-point scale, with 1 meaning "no confidence" and 7 "very confident."

After the students had finished, they were asked to go through the displays again and rank the remaining objects for how likely each one was to be the intended referent. They were then asked to describe for each display the criteria on which they had based their initial choices. Since the reference choices and confidence ratings were collected first, they could not be influenced by the later judgments.

Schelling task. Ten other students were instructed, "Imagine that you and another person whom you do not know are looking at these displays. If you can both independently select the same object, you will win a prize. If you fail to choose the same object then you lose." Otherwise, they followed the same procedure as in the reference task. They went through the twenty-seven displays one time making choices and confidence ratings, a second time ranking the remaining objects, and a third time describing the criteria for their choices.

Salience task. Ten more students were asked to choose for each display "the most prominent or salient X." They, too, went through the displays three times, once making choices and salience ratings, a second time giving ranks, and a third time describing their criteria.

The thirty students were Stanford University undergraduates participating either as a course requirement or for pay. They worked in groups of two to four in sessions lasting about forty-five minutes. The first three displays were considered practice and later discarded.

Results

The choices in the reference task generally coincided with those in the Schelling and salience tasks. In each display for each task, one object tended to be chosen more than any other. Let us call this the major choice. In the reference task, the percentage of students

TABLE 2

Means, Medians, and Ranges of Twenty-four Correlations
Computed on Mean Ranks of Students' Choices Between
the Reference, Schelling, and Salience Tasks
(Experiment 2)

PAIRS OF TASKS	MEAN	MEDIAN	RANGE
Reference and Schelling tasks	.80	.89	0.33–1.00
Reference and salience tasks	.80	.83	0.27–1.00
Schelling and salience tasks	.84	.89	0.21–1.00

making the major choice averaged 70% (ranging from 40 to 100%). The percentages in the Schelling and salience tasks averaged 81 and 89%, respectively. So within tasks, the students showed considerable agreement. The major choices also tended to coincide across tasks. For eighteen of the twenty-four displays, they were identical for the three tasks; for all twenty-four displays, they were identical for at least two of the three tasks. For each display we can identify the one object on which the largest number of students agreed across all three tasks. The percentage of students making that choice averaged 67%, which is near the maximum possible of 70%, the average percentage of students making the major choice on the reference task. So the major choices in the three tasks are in good agreement.

A second way to show agreement across the three tasks is to compare the rankings of the objects in each display. For each task, we computed the mean ranks for the two to seven objects in each display; we then correlated the mean ranks for each display separately, between the reference and Schelling tasks, between the reference and salience tasks, and between the Schelling and salience tasks. These seventy-two correlations (three comparisons for twenty-four displays) had a mean of .81 and a median of .85. Table 2 shows the means, medians, and ranges of these correlations for the three comparisons separately. The mean correlations for the three comparisons were very similar, ranging from .80 to .84, as were the medians, which ranged from .83 to .89. So this measure, too, is in line with the common ground model: the choices in the reference, Schelling, and salience tasks were very similar.

The students in Experiment 2, as in Experiment 1, ranged widely on most displays in how confident they were in their initial choices, from 1 ("no confidence") to 7 ("very confident"). These ratings yielded a surprising finding: the more popular a given choice turned out to be—without anyone knowing this, of course—the more confident were the people who had made it.

There are several ways of demonstrating this. Consider the reference task. For each display, we can compare the mean confidence on the major choice with the mean confidence on the other choices. For the seventeen displays where we could compute both means, the majority choice averaged 4.6 (on the seven-point scale) and the other choices averaged only 3.6, min $F'(1,19) = 5.19$, $p < .05$ (see Clark 1973). The corresponding two means for the Schelling task were 5.0 and 3.9, min $F'(1,23) = 15.20$, $p < .01$, and for the salience task, 6.1 and 5.2, min $F'(1,15) = 7.37$, $p < .025$.

The same point can be illustrated in another way. For each task, we classified each student's choice on each array by how many of the ten students concurred on that choice, and then computed the mean confidence rating of each of these ten categories (one to ten students concurring on the choice). In the reference task, for example, there were four separate displays in which eight students agreed on a single object within the display. These thirty-two confidence ratings averaged 5.2. The ten mean ratings computed this way for each task are plotted in Figure 1.

In all three tasks, the more students who concurred on a choice, the more confident were the students who made that choice. In the reference, Schelling, and salience tasks, the mean correlations were .79, .91, and .92, respectively. These three coefficients are each significantly greater than zero, $F(1,9) > 14.94$, $p < .01$, and they are not significantly different from one another. Figure 1 also shows, for the major Schelling choices only, the mean confidence ratings from the reference task as predicted from the number of students concurring on their Schelling choices. The correlation here, despite a restricted range, was .75.

Although the three tasks should be very similar to each other, the salience task should stand out in one respect. In the reference and Schelling tasks, the students rated their confidence in whether their choice would be the same as the choice of *another* person, someone they did not know. But in the salience task, they rated the salience as they alone judged it, without any implied comparison with another person's judgments. So the students in the reference and Schelling tasks should be less confident that they knew what other people would do than the students in the salience task should be in what themselves thought. Indeed, for the reference and Schelling tasks, the mean confidence ratings were 4.4 and 4.8, but for the salience task it was 5.8, which is significantly larger than the other two, $F(1,27) > 5.76$, $p < .05$.

The criteria the students gave for their choices were virtually identical across the three tasks. As representative of all three, here is a

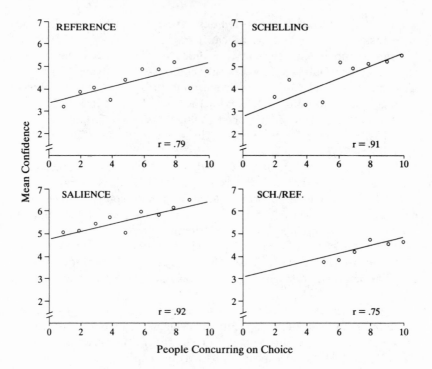

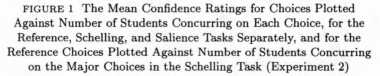

FIGURE 1 The Mean Confidence Ratings for Choices Plotted
Against Number of Students Concurring on Each Choice, for the
Reference, Schelling, and Salience Tasks Separately, and for the
Reference Choices Plotted Against Number of Students Concurring
on the Major Choices in the Schelling Task (Experiment 2)

breakdown of the two hundred and forty reasons for the reference task:
52% mentioned visual features such as size, shape, color, or special
markings; 17% mentioned functional properties such as having a carrying case or being simplest to operate, 12% mentioned position in
the display, such as being in front; 12% were vague, as in "most unusual," "unique," "different from others," or the like; 4% expressed
personal preferences such as "the one I'd be most likely to buy"; and
4% were claims of "don't know" or "no special reason." So about
80% of the reasons mentioned perceptually salient features explicitly;
many of the rest could be claims about salience in common ground
with people in general. Only one, "My roommate has that kind of
basketball" was impossible as a statement about common ground with
the speaker.

Discussion

Although the classical model does not say anything about the relations among reference, Schelling, and salience choices, the common ground model does. Students in the reference task should select in each display that object they think is most salient in their common ground with the speaker. So they should reason in the critical respects just as they would in making a Schelling choice, and they did. The reference choices were well accounted for by the Schelling choices. But the only common ground the students could appeal to in either task was their estimate of how people in general would see the displays—what they would judge to be perceptually salient or prominent. So the reference and Schelling choices should also agree with the salience choices, and they did.

People's confidence in their choice of referents ranged widely on the very same display. What is remarkable is how accurate they were in estimating their confidence. When John and Mary—pseudonyms for two students—were faced with three clocks in Display 9, John chose Clock A with a confidence of 6, and Mary chose Clock B with a confidence of 3. They presumably made the best choices they could, but just came to different conclusions. Still, each one judged the validity of his or her own choice accurately. John's confidence in Clock A was justified, since 80% of the students concurred on this choice. Mary's lack of confidence in Clock B was also justified, since no other person agreed with her. So people are quite deft in estimating not merely which object is most likely the intended referent, but also *how* likely it is to be the intended referent. They need both estimates if they are to know when they should ask for confirmation or clarification.

All the findings so far could be accounted for by a *perceptual model* in which the addressee would compare the perceptual salience of all objects in a display and then choose the most salient one. He would not consider the speaker's point of view at all, let alone the common ground they shared. Experiment 3 was designed to test this model.

5 Experiment 3

For most demonstrative references, the common ground contains more than the scene pointed at and assumptions about how it is generally viewed. It also contains what has just been discussed and implied in conversation and, among acquaintances, other information, too. In the perceptual model, addressees should ignore all other information and select the perceptually most salient object regardless. In the common ground model, they should select the object most salient against *all* the information in common ground.

In Experiment 3, it was made common ground that the speaker was buying a present either for his old conservative Uncle George or for his young modern Cousin Amanda. In the common ground model, that should make a difference. To a question like "What do you think of this watch?" addressees should select one watch with Uncle George in mind and perhaps quite a different watch for Cousin Amanda. Perceptual salience should be relevant, but only as weighed against the rest of common ground. By contrast, in the perceptual model the speaker's purpose should make no difference. Addressees should select the same watch regardless of who the speaker was shopping for.

Method

We constructed twenty-one displays like those in Experiment 2, but each with four objects. Each display was designed so that two objects (say, watches) seemed more appropriate for Cousin Amanda and the other two more appropriate for Uncle George. Again the first three displays were considered practice.

Reference task. We prepared several booklets by photocopying the 21 displays with "What do you think of this X?" at the bottom of each display, where X was the appropriate one- or two-word description. Ten students were instructed, "Imagine that your neighbor is looking for a present for his Uncle George. He shows you this catalog and asks 'What do you think of this X?' You are to indicate for each display what object you think your neighbor is referring to." There were ten other students for Cousin Amanda. Uncle George was described as a middle-aged, conservative, thrifty bachelor and Cousin Amanda as a rich, young, modern jet-setter.

As in Experiment 2, the students went through the booklets three times, once making reference choices and confidence ratings, a second time ordering the other objects in each display, and a third time describing criteria for their choices.

Schelling task. In this set of booklets, the sentence read "You are both to choose the same X." Ten students were instructed, "Imagine that your Uncle George has looked through this catalog and has chosen one object from each display. Your task is to pick the same object as your Uncle George. If and only if you have both chosen the same object will you win a prize. If you fail to agree in your choice, then you lose." There were ten other students for

TABLE 3

Means of Eighteen Correlations Computed on Mean
Ranks of Students' Choices Between the Reference
and Schelling Tasks with Uncle George and
Cousin Amanda as Recipients of Gifts

(Experiment 3)

TASK	2	3	4
1. Reference task for Amanda	+.72	−.35	−.25
2. Schelling task for Amanda		−.44	−.37
3. Reference task for George			+.75
4. Schelling task for George			—

Cousin Amanda. Uncle George and Cousin Amanda were described
as in the reference task. All twenty students followed the same
procedure as in Experiment 2, giving choices, confidence ratings,
rank orders, and rating criteria.

The forty students, from the same source as in Experiment 2 worked
in groups of two to four in sessions lasting about forth-five minutes.

Results and Discussion

The reference and Schelling choices for Uncle George were like each
other, but unlike those for Cousin Amanda. To show this, we computed
the mean ranks of the four objects in each display in each task, and
then correlated for each display separately the mean ranks from the
four tasks. The means of these correlations are listed in Table 3 If the
students made the same choices in the reference and Schelling tasks
for the same person, the correlations between these two tasks should
be highly positive, and indeed they were. These eighteen correlations
averaged .75 for Uncle George, and .72 for Cousin Amanda, $F(1,17)$
= 87 and 53, respectively, $p < .001$. If the students made roughly
complementary choices for Uncle George and Cousin Amanda, the four
cross-correlations among the Uncle George and Cousin Amanda tasks
should be negative, and they were. The means ranged from −.25 to
−.44, all $F(1,17) > 5.17$ $p < .05$, except for −.25, $F(1,17) = 2.45$.

If the perceptual model, were correct, the students should have selected the same perceptually salient object from each display regardless
of who the present was for, but they did not. By the common ground
model, they should have considered the common ground information
about who the present was for, and they did. Their choices in the reference task were predicted by the Schelling choices, but only when the
recipient of the gift was the same in the two tasks. So for both choices,

the students considered perceptual salience only part of the pertinent information in common ground.

The reasons students gave for their choices were nearly identical for the reference and Schelling tasks, but differed markedly between Uncle George and Cousin Amanda. In the reference task, about 75% of the 360 reasons mentioned visual or functional features, as in Experiment 2. But unlike the previous experiment, most of these features fit the stereotype for Uncle George or Cousin Amanda, as with "modern design" and "it looks sleek" for Cousin Amanda, and "simplest to use" or "reliable" for Uncle George. Indeed, it is difficult to distinguish these reasons from another 19% that simply identified one object as tailored to one of the two stereotypes, as with "conservative," "plainest," or "fashionable." Another 2% mentioned personal preference, and 4% were vague or "don't know." Only one reason could possibly be typed as egocentric—"It's the only kind I've ever seen." So over 90% of the reasons mentioned features presumed to be in common ground, and most were tailored to the stereotype of whom the gift was for.

6 Assertions and Presuppositions

One of the surest ways to introduce information into common ground is to mention it in conversation. In Experiment 3, the speaker's goal could have been mentioned in a prior utterance, as in "I am looking for a present for Uncle George—What do you think of this stopwatch?" or in the question itself, as in "What do you think of this stopwatch as a present for Uncle George?" and it probably would have made little difference. But there are many ways of mentioning a piece of information—by asserting or presupposing it, in a prior utterance, the same utterance, or a future utterance, and explicitly or by implication.

A listener must often take account of what is being asserted about the referent. Suppose two men are walking down the street, one very fat and the other very thin, and you say (5), (6), or (7) to a companion as you nod in their direction.

(5)   That man weighs too much for his own good.

(6)   That man weighs too little for his own good.

(7)   That man is my neighbor.

In (5) and (6), the only way your companion can find a demonstrative relation F is by using what you are asserting about the referent; you would assert (5) of the fat man and (6) of the thin man, but not vice versa (unless you were being ironic). In (7), where he can find no reasonable relation, he is uncertain.

The interpretation of the assertion must itself be common ground. Suppose you point at the same two men but say instead

(8)   That is what George will look like very soon.

If you had been talking about George gaining weight, your companion would take you as referring to the fat man as in (5). If you had been talking about George losing weight, he would select the thin man as in (6). Without such information, he would be uncertain. In (8), then, your companion appeals to the common ground specifically established between him and you. An overhearer not privy to your earlier conversation would be uncertain regardless of what your companion thought (see Chapter 7, this volume).

The common ground needed may include quite specialized information as well. Suppose for the same two men you utter (9), (10), or (11).

(9)   That man is a real Falstaff.

(10)   That man is a real Don Quixote.

(11)   That man is a real George Smith.

Your companion must appeal to the knowledge he assumes the two of you share, as educated adults, of Falstaff and Don Quixote for (9) and (10), and as friends of thin George Smith for (11). An educated but unacquainted overhearer might guess (9) and (10), but could not interpret (11).

These arguments have been based on intuitions about demonstrative references in context. Experiment 4 was a field experiment designed to substantiate even subtler intuitions about the use of presuppositions.

7   Experiment 4

Method

For this experiment, we used a picture from *Newsweek Magazine* of President Ronald Reagan sitting with David Stockman, then the director of the Office of Management and Budget. We supposed that virtually everyone at that time would assume Reagan was very familiar to most people and Stockman less familiar. As interviewer, Buttrick approached thirty students one at a time on the Stanford University campus, showed them the picture, and, while recording their responses on a clipboard, asked half of them Question 1 and the other half Question 2.

Question 1. You know who this man is, don't you?
Question 2. Do you have any idea at all who this man is?

TABLE 4
Responses to Question 1 (*You know who this man is, don't you?*)
and Question 2 (*Do you have any idea at all who this man is?*)
(Experiment 4)

RESPONSE	QUESTION 1	QUESTION 2
1. Selects Reagan	12	0
2. Points at Reagan, "This one?"	2	2
3. Selects Stockman	0	3
4. Points at Stockman, "This one?"	0	4
5. "Which one?"	1	5
6. Identifies Reagan and Stockman	0	1
Totals	15	15

With Question 1, Buttrick appeared to presuppose the student would surely know who "this man" is. With Question 2, he appeared to presuppose the opposite. If people rely on such presuppositions, the students should tend to select Reagan for Question 1 and Stockman for Question 2. To check our assumptions about Reagan's and Stockman's familiarity, Buttrick then asked each student to rate how recognizable Reagan and Stockman would each be to the general public on a 1 to 7 scale with 1 being "very low" and 7 being "very high." He also asked them to identify either man they had not yet named.

Results and Discussion

Questions 1 and 2 led to different choices of referents. The 30 responses are summarized in Table 4. For Question 1, 14 of 15 students chose Reagan, 12 outright and 2 tentatively; none chose Stockman. For Question 2, 7 of 15 students chose Stockman, 3 outright and 4 tentatively; only 2 chose Reagan and they did so tentatively. This difference is highly significant, $\chi^2(1) = 15.65$, p < .001. As expected, Reagan was judged more recognizable than Stockman, 6.2 to 2.3, $t(29) = 30$, $p < .01$. All 30 students identified both Reagan and Stockman correctly.

The perceptual model cannot account for these findings. If it were correct, there should be no difference between Questions 1 and 2, since the referent should be chosen entirely on the basis of perceptual salience. But there *was* a difference. By the common ground model, the students should use Buttrick's apparent presuppositions in their rationales for selecting Reagan versus Stockman. When he appeared to presuppose they knew the referent, they should select Reagan, reasoning that Reagan is better known than Stockman; when he appeared to presuppose the opposite, they should select Stockman. And that is what occurred.

no, because the asking g QI eliminates that choice

revise in order some

The students were more certain in answering Question 1 than Question 2. Let us call a response uncertain if it was a request for confirmation or clarification. Only three of fifteen students were uncertain for Question 1, as compared with eleven of fourteen students for Question 2, $\chi^2(1) = 7.74$, $p < .01$. There are several possible reasons why. The students might have been more certain of their answer to Question 1 than to Question 2. Or they might have been more ready to assume Buttrick was referring to the more recognizable man, namely Reagan. Or Reagan might have been slightly more prominent perceptually. Whatever the reason, it does not affect the conclusion that the students relied heavily on the speaker's apparent presuppositions.

8 General Discussion

Demonstrative references are not simple. To understand the reference in *How would you describe the color of this flower?*, the students in Experiment 1 had to appeal to the "relevant context" and draw certain inferences. The "relevant context," we have argued, consists of the common ground between the speaker and addressees, and the inferences needed are based on the Principle of Optimal Design, which governs language use in general (see Clark 1983). The students had to find a demonstrative relation F to get them from the demonstratum d (the picture of four flowers) to the referent r (one of the four flowers). The F could not be just any relation. It had to be the one they believed they were intended to infer on the basis of common ground.

To infer F for underdetermined demonstrations, we have argued, people try to select the object that both fits the descriptor and is the most salient against common ground. They do this in much the same way they find the best solution in a Schelling task. They assume the speaker and addressees "must 'mutually recognize' some unique signal that coordinates their expectations of each other" (as Schelling put it), and they take that signal to be the most salient object in their common ground. In Experiments 2 and 3, choices in the reference task were well accounted for by the corresponding Schelling choices. People must weigh every part of common ground that might be pertinent. We have demonstrated the influence of four such parts:

1. **Perceptual salience.** Each demonstratum in our experiments consisted of an arrangement of objects, and students could estimate how people in general would view these arrangements. When there was no other pertinent information in common ground, they would simply select from the display the perceptually most salient object, which is the only object they could be expected to pick out

uniquely. In Experiment 2, as predicted, the reference choices were well accounted for by the salience judgments.

2. **Speaker's goals.** When the speaker's goals are part of common ground, they are often crucial to the interpretation of an utterance (see Clark 1978, 1979; Cohen and Perrault 1979; Gibbs 1981). The utterance *City Hall, please* would be interpreted one way by a taxi driver, but another way by a telephone operator because of what they presume to be common ground about the speaker's goals. The speaker's presumed goals are just as important for demonstrative reference. In Experiment 3, when it was common ground that the speaker was looking for a present for Uncle George, the listener's choice of referent was based on this goal in combination with perceptual salience.

3. **Speaker's assertions.** What the speaker asserts also becomes part of common ground, and it, too, can influence the listener's choice of referent. To interpret *That man weighs too much for his own good*, the addressee had to use what was asserted about the referent. An overhearer unable to understand the assertion, as in *That is what George will look like soon*, might be unable to pick out the right referent.

4. **Speaker's presuppositions.** What the speaker presupposes in his utterance is also part of common ground and potentially relevant. This was demonstrated in Experiment 4 for two kinds of presuppositions. When Buttrick said *You know who this man is, don't you?* he appeared to presuppose explicitly that *this man* was a man the student would surely know. He also appeared to presuppose, implicitly, that it was common ground that Reagan was better known than Stockman. So for this question, the students readily chose Reagan, but for *Do you have any idea at all who this man is?* they tended to choose Stockman instead.

When people are addressed by someone, they ordinarily assume the speaker has done his best to enable them to understand him. It is on this assumption, the Principle of Optimal Design, that they can reason through to the referent. Yet people also recognize that the speaker can make misjudgments—especially about common ground. When they detect misjudgments, they have several options. They can guess, with the possibility of revising their guess later; they can guess but ask for confirmation; or they can directly ask for clarification. In Experiments 1 and 4, students were indeed more likely to ask for confirmation or clarification the less well designed the reference was.

Demonstrative reference is perhaps the prototype of expressions that cannot be understood without appeal to context. But what context? If our proposal is correct, all the information the listener should ever appeal to is the speaker's and addressees' common ground. Similar claims have been made for the use and understanding of conventional and novel words, assertions, presuppositions, direct and indirect speech acts, and definite reference (see Chapters 10, 2, and 1, this volume, for reviews). If these claims are correct, it will be crucial to study how people create, represent, and access common ground.

Part II

Discourse as a
Collaborative Process

Introduction to Part II

People have to coordinate with each other when they talk. That was clear from Grice's 1975 essay on the cooperative principle (which I had read in a faint underground version in 1971). It was also clear from my own work on given and new information, definite reference (Chapter 1), demonstrative reference (Chapter 3), indirect speech acts, and novel word uses (Chapters 10, 11, and 12). But there are many questions about precisely *how* people coordinate.

One problem is that the formulation and interpretation of utterances is dynamic. As noted earlier, the participants in a discourse accumulate common ground as they talk. They also design each utterance to be understood against their current common ground. So if you want to tell a friend something, you have to design your utterance against the common ground you assume you and your friend have right now—not one utterance ago or even one second ago. And what is in your common ground changes from moment to moment. Many models of language use are unable to cope with these changes.

That was especially true for models of definite reference around 1980. Within psychology, the best known model was David Olson's, published in 1970, which went like this. Speakers assume that the thing they wish to refer to (say, a tall blue block) is a member of a *comparison set* (say, tall and short, red and blue blocks). Their goal, Olson argued, is to design a definite reference ("the tall blue one") so that its descriptive terms ("tall" and "blue") select the intended referent uniquely out of the full comparison set. So the model only works if there is a well defined comparison set for each reference. For isolated examples, the comparison set may be clear, but in a fast moving discourse, it is anything but clear. Olson's model was of little help in spontaneous dynamic language use.

How to study reference with accumulating common ground? I already knew about the pioneering work by Robert Krauss and Sidney Weinheimer in the mid 60s on the so-called referential communication task. I had watched their project germinate and flower at the Bell Telephone Laboratories, Murray Hill, New Jersey, where I had spent the summers of 1963, 1964, and 1965 working on quite a different project; one of those summers Weinheimer and I had been roommates. In their task, two people were given identical sets of, say, ten hard-to-describe figures. One person was to get the other to arrange the figures in the same order as the first had them. The two people could talk to each other but not see each other. What Krauss and Weinheimer found was that people's reference phrases shortened as they referred repeatedly to these figures. Their first reference to a figure might be "the upside down martini glass on a wire stand" but after repeated references it was simply "the martini." This shortening posed a problem for Olson's model. The comparison sets remained the same throughout the referential communication task, yet the reference phrases the participants used shortened radically as they proceeded.

In 1981 Deanna Wilkes-Gibbs and I decided to study how reference changed with the accumulating common ground of the participants. We set up our own version of the referential communication task and, at a suggestion of Alexandra Belyaeva's in Moscow in 1979, replaced Krauss and Weinheimer's figures with Tangram figures. Our plan was to track the references of one person, say Ann, as she arranged 12 Tangram figures a number of times first with one partner, Ben, and then with another, Charles. Her reference phrases should shorten while talking to Ben, but they should immediately lengthen again when she started talking to Charles. Just how much she changed should depend on her common ground with Charles. If Charles hadn't been privy to her conversation with Ben, she and Charles could assume no special common ground for these figures. But if Charles had overheard their conversation, or had participated in it even as a silent partner, she could assume some or a great deal of common ground about the figures.

Wilkes-Gibbs and I should have been prepared for what we found, but we weren't. Yes, Ann's reference phrases shortened the more she talked to Ben and lengthened again when she talked to an ignorant Charles. But by far the most striking feature of their conversations was how closely the two partners collaborated with each other. They carried on an intricate back and forth interchange on each and every reference. We had known Schegloff, Jefferson, and Sacks' work on interactive features of conversation, but we hadn't realized how essential these were to the making of definite references. So Wilkes-Gibbs and I temporarily dropped our original goals and concentrated on the collaborative nature of reference, in Ann's first conversation with Ben. The result was Chapter 4, "Referring as a collaborative process," which was published in *Cognition* in 1986. It was only much later that we reported the experiments we originally set out to do in "Coordinating beliefs in conversation," published in the *Journal of Memory and Language* in 1992.

One problem with the collaborative model of reference was that it was restricted to reference. What about other actions speakers take—including what they do with utterances as wholes? Edward Schaefer and I began to address this problem in 1984. In one of our first projects, we analyzed a large corpus of telephone calls to directory enquiries in Cambridge, England, from customers asking for telephone numbers and other information. That led us to develop a theory of contributing to discourse. We presented that model in a paper called "Collaborating on contributions to conversation," which appeared in *Language and Cognitive Processes* in 1987. But that model was open to the criticism that it only applied when the participants in the conversation had to be especially accurate, as in the referential communication task or in the calls to directory enquiries. So Schaefer and I set out to show how it also accounted for ordinary conversation. The result was "Contributing to discourse," which we presented at a Sloan Workshop on Sentence Processing at Stanford University in 1986 and published in *Cognitive Science* in 1989. It appears here as Chapter 5. Since then, alas, Schaefer has become a mathematician and ascended into higher spheres.

In the models proposed there is collaboration between speakers and addressees—the participants in a conversation—but not between speakers and overhearers. Speakers are under no obligation to make sure overhearers understand what they mean. They don't look for evidence of understanding from overhearers, and overhearers don't offer any evidence either—it would be rude and meddlesome if they did. So an important prediction of both the collaborative model of reference, and the theory of contributions, is that addressees should come to understand almost everything speakers tell them, but overhearers should not. Michael Schober and I tested this prediction with the referential communication task and reported our findings in "Understanding by addressees and overhearers," published in *Cognitive Psychology*, 1989. It appears as Chapter 6.

Schober's and my findings bring out several points that we think too few students of language fully appreciate. The first is that talk is an *opportunistic* process. Speakers work with their addressees until the addressees have understood them well enough for current purposes—

and no further. The two of them don't put in any more total effort than they have to. Hence a second point: Addressees and overhearers are forced to adhere to very different criteria for understanding. Addressees can always understand as well as they *need* to. Overhearers can only ever understand as well as they are *able* to—and that may not be very well at all. The reason is that addressees are intended to *recognize* the speaker's intentions. Overhearers can only *conjecture* about them (see also Chapters 7, 8, and 9). Understanding by addressees and overhearers isn't the same at all. Hence a third point: In most studies in psycholinguistics, subjects are treated not as addressees but as overhearers. There is no guarantee that these findings hold for addressees too. Many theories of language processing may turn out to be only theories about overhearing.

4

Referring as a Collaborative Process

WITH DEANNA WILKES-GIBBS

In conversation, speakers and addressees work together in the making of a definite reference. In the model we propose, the speaker initiates the process by presenting or inviting a noun phrase. Before going on to the next contribution, the participants, if necessary, repair, expand on, or replace the noun phrase in an iterative process until they reach a version they mutually accept. In doing so they try to minimize their joint effort. The preferred procedure is for the speaker to present a simple noun phrase and for the addressee to accept it by allowing the next contribution to begin. We describe a communication task in which pairs of people conversed about arranging complex figures and show how the proposed model accounts for many features of the references they produced. The model follows, we suggest, from the mutual responsibility that participants in conversation bear toward the understanding of each utterance.

Conversation is the fundamental site of language use. For many people, even for whole societies, it is the only site, and it is the primary one for children acquiring language. From this perspective other arenas of language use—novels, newspapers, lectures, street signs, rituals—are derivative or secondary. How, then, do speaking and understanding work in conversation? For psychologists this ought to be a central question, but surprisingly, it has not been. The main attempts to answer it have come instead from philosophy and sociology.

Among philosophers the study of conversation grew out of an analysis of what speakers mean and what listeners understand them to mean. The idea was that, when speakers utter sentences, they do so with certain intentions toward their addressees. They assert, request, promise, and perform other illocutionary acts, and their interlocutors are expected to recognize these intentions (Austin 1962; Grice 1957, 1968; Schiffer 1972; Searle 1969). In 1967 Grice argued that, for this scheme to work, people in conversation must be cooperative. Speakers must try to "make their contribution such as is required, at the stage at which it occurs, by the accepted purpose or direction of the talk exchange in which (they) are engaged" (Grice 1975, 45). Only then can their partners go beyond what is "said" to infer what is conversationally "implicated" (Grice 1975, 1978).

Among sociologists the issue has been how people direct the course of conversation and repair its inherent troubles. As this work has shown, people in conversation manage who is to talk at which times through an intricate system of turn taking (Sacks, Schegloff, and Jefferson 1974). Further, when one person speaks, the others not only listen but let the speaker know they are understanding—with head nods, yes's, uh huh's, and other so-called back channel responses (Duncan 1973; Goodwin 1981; Schegloff 1981; Yngve 1970). When listeners don't understand, or when other troubles arise, they can interrupt for correction or clarification (Schegloff, Jefferson, and Sacks 1977). The participants also have techniques for initiating, guiding, and terminating conversations and the topics within them (Schegloff 1968; Schegloff and Sacks 1973).

In both traditions a central issue is coordination: How do the participants in a conversation coordinate on the content and timing of what is meant and understood? The issue, however, cannot be resolved within either tradition alone. In the first tradition conversation is idealized as a succession of illocutionary acts—assertions, questions, promises—each uttered and understood clearly and completely (Gazdar 1979; Kamp 1981; Stalnaker 1978). Yet from the second tradition we know that many utterances remain incomplete and only partly understood until corrected or amplified in further exchanges. How are these two views to be reconciled?

In this chapter we propose a resolution for an essential use of language: how people in conversation coordinate in the making of a definite reference. Our concern is not with semantic reference, but with speaker's reference—not, for example, with what the phrase *the clown with the red nose* means, but with what the speaker does in referring, say, to a clown as part of an assertion that the clown is funny (Donnellan 1978; Kripke 1977; Searle 1969). Our premise is that making such a reference is a collaborative process requiring actions by both speakers and interlocutors. To some it may appear self-evident that the process is collaborative, but it is one thing to assume it is and quite another to understand why it is and how it works. The goal here is important, since, if conversation is fundamental, its processes are likely to underlie or shape processes in other uses of language as well.

In the first section of this chapter, then, we offer evidence for the premise itself and outline what we will call a collaborative model for the process of reference. In the second and third sections we describe an experiment on referring and use it to corroborate and fill in details of the model. In the final section we return to the general issue of coordination and note problems still to be resolved.

1 Referring in Conversation

Traditionally, philosophers, linguists, and psychologists have presupposed what might be called a *literary model* of definite reference. Speakers refer as if they were writing to distant readers. When Elizabeth selects the noun phrase *the clown with a red nose* in talking to Sam, the assumption is that she intends it to enable him to identify the clown uniquely. She satisfies her intentions by issuing the noun phrase. Her act of referring is cotemporal with that noun phrase, beginning with *the* and ending with *nose*. Further, she retains complete responsibility and control over the course of this process. Sam hears the definite description as if he were reading it and, if successful, infers the identity of the referent. But his actions have no bearing on hers in this reference.

The literary model makes these tacit idealizations. (1) The reference is expressed linguistically with one of three standard types of noun phrase—a proper noun (e.g., *Napoleon, King George*), a definite description (*this year, the man with the moustache*), or a pronoun (*he, this, they*). (2) The speaker uses the noun phrase intending the addressee to be able to identify the referent uniquely against their common ground. (3) The speaker satisfies her intention simply by the issuing of that noun phrase. And (4) the course of the process is controlled by the speaker alone.

A conversational model of the process, however, ought to look quite different for three reasons. First, in conversation unlike writing, speakers have limited time for planning and revision. They need to overcome this limitation, and in doing so they may exploit techniques possible only in conversational settings. Second, speech is evanescent. The listener has to attend to, hear, and try to understand an utterance at virtually the same time it is being issued. That requires a type of process synchronization not found in reading. And third, listeners in conversations aren't mute or invisible during an utterance. Speakers may alter what they say midcourse based on what addressees say and do.

Indeed, once we look at actual conversations, we find that the four idealizations of the literary model are very wide of the mark. To see this, let us turn to eight types of examples that fail on one or more of these assumptions.

Eight Problems

1. Self-corrected noun phrases. Consider this attested utterance: *She was giving me all the people that were gone this year I mean this quarter y'know* (from Schegloff et al. 1977, 364, in simplified notation). The speaker began the referential process by uttering *all the people that were gone this year*, but corrected the last two words to *this quarter* in what Schegloff et al. (1977) called a self-initiated repair. The referential process, clearly, isn't cotemporal with one particular noun phrase, since two noun phrases were uttered in succession. It is more naturally described as a process in which the speaker decided midcourse to repair the initial noun phrase, indicated her change with *I mean*, and then uttered *this quarter* (see Levelt 1983). The process began with *all the people* and was completed with *y'know*.

2. Expanded noun phrases. Although the first noun phrase a speaker utters may be technically correct, he or she may still judge it insufficient and change course, as here (from Cohen 1985):

S. Take the spout—the little one that looks like the end of an oil can—

J. Okay.

S. —and put that on the opening in the other large tube. With the round top.

S began with *the spout*. But when he saw that it was insufficient for J to pick out the referent, he expanded on it with the parenthetical noun phrase. Ordinarily, parenthetical phrases are nonrestrictive—not needed for identifying the referent. Here, the parenthetical phrase *was* deemed necessary, and S changed course midutterance to add it.

3. Episodic noun phrases. For similar reasons, once S completed *the other large tube*, he judged that to be insufficient as well and added the restrictive phrase *with the round top* under a separate intonation contour, as part of a new tone group. He produced a single noun phrase, but intonationally, he divided it into two information units. We will call this an episodic noun phrase, and it is another nonstandard type.

4. **Other-corrected noun phrases.** The process becomes more complicated when the addressee makes the repair, as with A's reference to Monday in this example (from Schegloff et al. 1977, 369):

> B. How long y'gonna be here?
> A. Uh- not too long. Uh just til uh Monday.
> B. Til- oh yih mean like a week f'm tomorrow.
> A. Yah.
> B. [Continues]

A initiated the referential process by uttering *Monday*. Uncertain of the intended referent, B offered a correction, which A accepted, all before B proceeded. The process took place over several turns and was participated in by both A and B.

In the four cases so far, then, the speakers changed the course of their reference after uttering an initial noun phrase. They did so in reaction to both their own and their addressee's judgments of inadequacy or error. But speakers are not merely reactive. At other times they bring addressees into the referential process by the very design of their utterance. Consider the next four classes of examples.

5. **Trial noun phrases.** Some noun phrases are uttered with a rising intonation, or *try marker* (Sacks and Schegloff 1979), imposed on them, as in this example (from Cohen 1985):

> S. Okay now, the small blue cap we talked about before?
> J. Yeah.
> S. Put that over the hole on the side of that tube—
> J. Yeah.
> S. —that is nearest to the top, or nearest to the red handle.

With *the small blue cap we talked about before?* S asks J to say whether or not he has understood S's reference. The process begins when S utters this phrase and ends only with J's *yeah*. If J hadn't understood, the process would have continued as here (from Sacks and Schegloff 1979):

> A. ... well I was the only one other than than the uhm tch *Fords?*, uh Mrs. Holmes Ford? You know uh=
> ⎡ =the the cellist?
> B. ⎣ Oh yes. She's she's the cellist.
> A. Yes. Well she and her husband were there.

When A received no reply to *Fords?* she offered the expanded noun phrase *Mrs. Holmes Ford?* and then went to *the cellist?* before B implicated that she had identified the referent. The referential process was continued until A said *yes* confirming that B's display of understanding was correct.

6. **Installment noun phrases.** Speakers can also utter noun phrases in *installments*, as we will call them, and invite addressees to affirm their understanding of each installment. In the earlier example, S began *the hole on the·side of that tube*, paused for confirmation from J, and then completed the noun phrase with *that is nearest to the top, or nearest to the red handle.* As with his trial noun phrase, S made the course of his reference contingent on the addressee's midcourse response.

7. **Dummy noun phrases.** Speakers sometimes initiate the referential process with terms like *what's-his-name*, *whatchamacallit*, *whatzit*, or *thingamabob*, which we will call dummy nouns or noun phrases. Consider: *If he puts it into the diplomatic bag, as um— what's-his-name, Micky Cohn, did, then it's not so bad* (from Svartvik and Quirk 1980, 35). The speaker recognized from the start that *what's-his-name* was inadequate as a definite description. Yet, pressed for time, he used it to initiate the referential process until he could replace it with an adequate noun phrase, *Micky Cohn.* Dummy noun phrases are *not* standard, and when speakers use them, they do *not* intend them to enable their addressees to identify the referent uniquely. Dummy noun phrases are uttered only as part of a more extended process.

8. **Proxy noun phrases.** In some circumstances, the speaker makes it clear that a noun phrase is to come next, but the addressee actually utters it. Here is one of many spontaneous examples recorded by Wilkes-Gibbs (unpublished):

A. That tree has, uh, uh ...
B. tentworms.
A. Yeah.
B. Yeah.

A initiated the referential process by halting at a place where he needed a noun phrase and uttering two *uhs*. B helped out by offering a proxy, or stand-in, noun phrase she thought appropriate. A confirmed the proxy with *yeah*, and then B responded to A's full assertion. B took part in the process from the very beginning.

As all eight examples make plain, a conversational model of the referential process must be quite different from the literary model. First, many noun phrases are distinctly nonliterary in form or nonstandard in intonation. These include trial, episodic, installment, dummy, and proxy noun phrases. Second, the process takes a very different course in conversation than in literature. In all eight examples, speakers went beyond the issuing of standard noun phrases; in three examples they deliberately drew the addressees into the process; and in three they began by knowingly issuing a questionable or inadequate noun phrase. What characterizes these examples is that the speaker and addressee put in extra effort, generally together, to make sure the reference has been understood. To understand the process of referring, we need to know how this works.

Establishing Understanding

Suppose A, a man, is speaking to B, a woman, and refers to a dog. In making the reference, according to most theories, A intends the identity of the dog to become part of A's and B's mutual knowledge or beliefs (see Chapter 1, this volume). Establishing such mutual knowledge or belief is a stringent requirement. To meet it, A must convince himself that the identity of the dog is truly going to become part of their common ground. If at any moment in making the reference he thinks it won't, he should change or expand on what he has done so far. The same requirement applies to B, since she is trying to understand A's reference. To meet it, she should find ways of letting A know, as she listens, whether or not she is understanding him. Indeed, A should suppose that she is cooperating in precisely this way.

For each reference, then, A and B should have procedures for establishing the mutual belief, at some level of confidence, that B has identified A's reference. We have already seen evidence in our examples that they do. These procedures, we will argue, are inherently collaborative.

The evidence is clearest when B believes she may *not* have identified A's referent and attempts to repair the problem, as in our earlier example:

B. Til- oh yih mean like a week f'm to*mor*row.
A. Yah.

These turns constitute a *side sequence*, a block of exchanges embedded within or between anticipated contributions to the conversation (Jefferson 1972; Schegloff 1972). So although the side sequence was initiated by B, it was completed by A before the conversation was allowed to proceed. That was needed for them to *mutually* believe that B had now understood A's reference correctly.

More often, A and B have to establish that B *has* understood the reference, and for this, B can use a simple expedient: allowing the next contribution to continue. Suppose the conversation had continued this way:

B. How long y'gonna be here?
A. Uh- not too long. Uh just til uh Monday.
B. Oh that's too bad.

By asserting *Oh that's too bad*, B would be passing up the opportunity to correct a possible misunderstanding and would thereby be implicating that she understood A's reference. "Regularly, then," as Sacks et al. (1974, 728) put it, "a turn's talk will display its speaker's understanding of a prior turn's talk, and whatever other talk it marks itself as directed to" (see also Goffman 1976). Note that going on wouldn't necessarily mean B had truly understood. She might not recognize her misunderstanding, or she might want to claim she had understood when she hadn't. But in either case, going on is a signal that B believes she has understood. In the first case she is making a mistake; in the second she is using the signal to deceive.

The same mutual belief can be established more directly by what Schegloff (1981) has called *continuers*, as in his example from a radio call-in show (80):

A. Now, I wanna ask you something, I wrote a letter. (pause)
B. Mh hm,
A. T'the governor
B. Mh hm::,
A. -telling'im what I thought about i(hh)m!
B. (Sh:::!)
A. Will I get an answer d'you think,
B. Yes.

By inserting the continuers *mh hm* and *sh:::* while A's turn was still underway, according to Schegloff, B was showing, first, that she was paying attention and realized that A was in the middle of an extended unit of talk. At the same time, she was explicitly signaling that she was passing up the opportunity to initiate a repair on the turn so far and, by implication, that she understood the turn so far. With the second *Mh hm::,* for example, she was claiming to understand the phrase *t'the governor* and, therefore, the definite reference it contained. The same holds for the other definite references.

B may even be intended to interrupt A as soon as she believes she has identified the referent, as in this example (from Sacks, quoted by Jefferson (1973, 59)):

A. I heard you were at the beach yesterday. What's her name, oh you know, the tall redhead that lives across the street from Larry? The one who drove him to work the day his car// was-
B. Oh *Gina*!
A. Yeah Gina. She said she saw you at the beach yesterday.

A indicated he would go on until B identified the referent. Indeed, he stopped at B's interruption and completed the process by confirming B's identification with *Yeah Gina*.

Taken together, this evidence suggests that A and B accept mutual responsibility for each definite reference. Roughly speaking, they try to establish the mutual belief that B has understood A's reference before they go on. So far we have only informal examples of how they do this. The challenge is to characterize the system and the logic behind it.

Mutual Acceptance

The idea behind the view of reference we are taking is this: A and B must *mutually accept* that B has understood A's references before they let the conversation go on. Conversations proceed in an orderly way only if the common ground of the participants accumulates in an orderly way (see Clark 1985; Chapter 2, this volume; Gazdar 1979; Stalnaker 1978). A and B must therefore establish the mutual belief that B has understood, or appears to have understood, A's current utterance before they go on to the next contribution to the conversation. They establish that belief, we argue, through an acceptance process.

The two basic elements in this process are (a) a presentation and (b) an acceptance. Suppose A wants to refer to a mutually identifiable dog. To do so, he *presents*, as we will put it, the standard noun phrase *the dog that just barked*. With this presentation A presupposes a number of things. First, he believes B is now paying attention, is able to hear and identify the words, and understands English. Second, he believes B can view the referent as fitting the description *dog that just barked*. That is, he believes that referent r can be viewed under description d. And third, he believes B will be able to pick out r uniquely with this description d along with the rest of their common ground.

Once A has made this presentation, B must accept it, and A and B must mutually recognize that acceptance. We propose that B has two main methods of accepting it. First, she can *presuppose acceptance*, as illustrated earlier, by continuing on to the next contribution or by allowing A to continue. Letting the next contribution begin is mutually recognized as an acceptance of the last presentation. Second, she can *assert acceptance*, as with continuers, *yes*, *right*, *I see*, and head nods. These, too, are mutually recognized as acceptances of the last contribution.

But B may have reasons for *not* accepting A's presentation. She may not have heard it fully; if so, she might respond *What?* or *The dog that just what?* She may not accept *d* as a description of *r*; then she might respond, *That's a toy not a dog.* Or she may not accept that *d* is sufficient with their common ground to pick out *r* uniquely; then she might respond *Which one?* When B doesn't accept the presentation, A must deal with B's implicit or explicit questions until B does accept it. That may take several exchanges.

As our examples show, however, A's presentation can take more complicated forms. It can be a trial or installment noun phrase, which B can accept only by assertion. It can be a dummy noun phrase, which B isn't intended to accept until amended. It can be a self-corrected or expanded noun phrase, which B is to accept only as amended. It can even be a proxy noun phrase made by B, which A is then intended to accept.

These informal examples, though suggestive, still do not specify precisely how the acceptance process works. For that we need more systematic evidence.

2   References in an Experimental Task

In search of such evidence we turned to a communication task originally devised by Krauss and Glucksberg (Krauss and Weinheimer 1964, 1966, 1967; Krauss and Glucksberg 1969, 1977; Glucksberg, Krauss, and Higgins 1975; see also Asher 1979). In our version two students were seated at tables separated by an opaque screen. In front of each student were twelve cards, each showing one of the so called Tangram figures in Figure 1. For the person we will call the *director*, the cards were already arranged in a target sequence of two rows of six, and for the person we will call the *matcher*, the same figures lay in an identical matrix but in a random sequence. (For ease of exposition, we will talk as if the director were male and the matcher female, even though both sexes took both roles in our task.) The director's job was to get the matcher quickly and accurately to rearrange her figures to match the target ordering. They could talk back and forth as much as they needed, but the director was to go through the positions in the array sequentially (numbered one to six on the top row, and seven to twelve on the bottom). After they had matched their arrangements, the director's and matcher's figures were

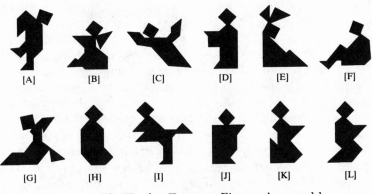

FIGURE 1 The Twelve Tangram Figures Arranged by
Directors and Matchers

placed in two new random orders, the director's new sequence became
the new target, and the procedure was repeated. They carried out the
task six times, for six trials.

The collaborative view of reference makes several global predictions
about this task. First, it should take the two partners many words to
reach acceptance the first time they encounter a figure since they will
often need nonstandard techniques such as episodic, installment, or expanded noun phrases. Later references to the same figure should be
shorter since they can appeal to prior acceptance of a related description and succeed more often with standard noun phrases, which are
typically shorter. This reasoning would account in part for Krauss and
Weinheimer's (1964) original finding that, as people referred repeatedly to the same figure, they tended to shorten their noun phrases,
although only if their listeners could speak in return. The collaborative view also predicts that, since the later references are more likely
to be standard noun phrases, they should require fewer turns. For this
prediction there is no evidence. We will defer more detailed predictions
about the acceptance process itself.

3 Method

Eight pairs of partners each arranged twelve figures on each of six trials. The twelve figures, each formed from different arrangements of
seven elementary shapes, were selected from a book with four thou-
sand such figures collected by Elffers (1976) from the ancient Chinese
game of Tangram. These twelve were chosen because their varying ab-

straction and similarity seemed to provide a good range of difficulty. Two copies of each figure were cut out of black construction paper and pasted individually on white 15 centimeter by 20 centimeter cards. The identifying letters in Figure 1 did not appear on the stimuli.

The two students in each session drew lots for director and matcher roles. They were told they had identical figures and would play the game six times while timed and tape-recorded. A timer was started on each trial when both students were ready, and stopped when they were satisfied they had finished. After each trial the two orderings were checked and the students were told of the positions of any mismatches. The error rate was only 2%. The six trials took about twenty-five minutes. The students, seven men and nine women, were Stanford University undergraduates fulfilling a course requirement.

One of us transcribed the conversations, including changes of speaker, back-channel responses, parenthetical remarks, interruptions, hesitations, false starts, and basic intonational features; the other checked the transcripts, especially for intonation. The transcripts contained 9792 words, reflecting the positioning of 576 figures (twelve figures on six trials by eight pairs of students).

General Patterns

For a broad picture of what occurred, consider this very simple series of utterances by one director for figure I on Trials 1 through 6:

(1) All right, the next one looks like a person who's ice skating, except they're sticking two arms out in front.
(2) Um, the next one's the person ice skating that has two arms?
(3) The fourth one is the person ice skating, with two arms.
(4) The next one's the ice skater.
(5) The fourth one's the ice skater.
(6) The ice skater.

As this series illustrates, directors generally referred to the location (e.g., *the fourth one*) and then asserted something about the Tangram figure to be placed in that location. On Trial 1 directors always *described* the figure, generally with an indefinite reference (e.g., *a person who's* ...). On Trials 2 through 6, in contrast, they *referred* to the figure with a definite description (e.g., *the ice skater*). Directors tended to use nonstandard noun phrases in the early trials (e.g., this director's trial and episodic noun phrases in Trials 2 and 3) and standard noun phrases later (e.g., *the ice skater*).

Partly because of these features, this director took many more words to secure acceptance of his presentation on Trial 1 than on Trial

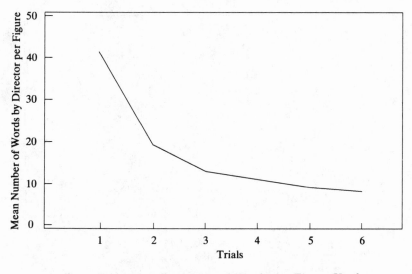

FIGURE 2 Average Number of Words per Figure Used
by Directors on Each Trial

6. As predicted, this pattern held in general. Figure 2 shows that directors used an average of forty-one words per figure in Trial 1 but only eight words per figure in Trial 6. This decline is highly significant, $F(1,35) = 44.31$, $p < .001$. The decline was steepest from Trial 1 to Trial 2 and had almost disappeared by Trial 6.

The example we have cited, however, is atypical in that the director took only one turn on each trial for this figure; it is also incomplete in that we have omitted the matcher's single turns. More often, the two partners took many turns for a single placement, and as predicted, the number of turns they needed declined from Trial 1 to 6. Figure 3 shows that the director averaged 3.7 turns per figure on Trial 1 but only about one per figure by Trial 6. This trend was also highly significant, $F(1,35) = 79.59$, $p < .001$. So Figure 2 includes the director's words not just from his first turn on each figure but from *all* of his turns on that figure.

The director and matcher became more efficient not only from one trial to the next, but also from the beginning to the end of each trial. Figure 4 plots the number of words per figure over the twelve spatial positions in the arrangements for Trials 1, 2, and 6. Since the figures were randomly assigned to the positions on each trial, there is some confounding of figures with positions, but the pattern is still clear. On Trial 1, there was a steep decline in word count (4.6 words per position)

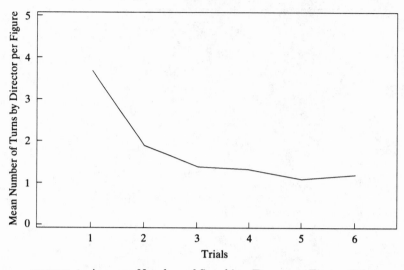

FIGURE 3 Average Number of Speaking Turns per Figure Taken
by Directors on Each Trial

as the two partners worked from position 1 to position 12 ($F(1,77) =$ 40.01, $p < .001$). On Trials 2 and 6 there were successively smaller declines (1.0 and .4 words per position) both also significant ($F(1,77) = 5.83, 7.16, p < .05$). Number of turns per figure shows a similar pattern.

The general decline in number of words used from position 1 to position 12 is predicted by the collaborative view but also by others. By any reasonable theory of information or reference (e.g., Olson 1970), the fewer figures there are in the array, the less information it should take to distinguish the target from the remainder. In the limit, the figure in position 12 needs only a minimal description since it is the only one left—for example, *Number 12 is the last one.* Indeed, sometimes it wasn't even mentioned. The number of turns should decrease by the same reasoning, as it did.

The decline from position 1 to 12, however, got smaller from Trial 1 to Trial 6, and that is predicted by the collaborative view but not by general theories of information. By the collaborative view, as we will justify later, the two partners come to rely on descriptions mutually accepted on previous trials, forming shorter noun phrases accepted in fewer turns until they arrive at optimal descriptions. This is nicely illustrated in the example cited. But as the descriptions become optimal, they should be less influenced by the physical context. The

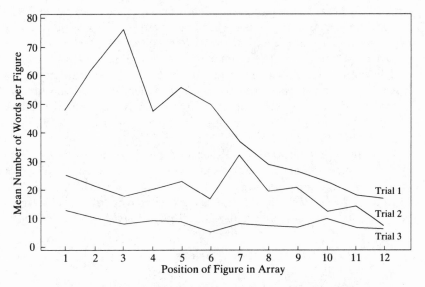

FIGURE 4 Average Number of Words per Figure Used by Directors on
Trials 1, 2, and 6, Plotted by Position of the Figure in the Array

decline from position 1 to 12 should be largest on Trial 1, when reaching acceptance takes many words, and smallest on Trial 6, by which time the two partners have preferred descriptions. This is precisely what occurred. The difference in slopes between Trials 1, 2, and 6 was significant ($F(2,284) = 15.49$, $p < .001$). By information theory, in contrast, going from one position to the next should reduce the array size as much on Trial 6 as on Trial 1, hence the slopes should remain the same. This prediction is disconfirmed.

Finally, the twelve figures also varied in difficulty, $F(11,77) = 5.94$, $p < .001$. The most difficult one, figure B, averaged 26.5 words per trial, eliciting 39.6 words on Trial 1. The easiest, figure C, averaged only 9.7 words per trial, with 24 words on Trial 1.

Having sketched the global performance in this task, we now turn to details of the referential process itself.

4   Collaborating on References

Our primary goal here is a process model of how speakers and addressees collaborate in the making of a definite reference. The collaborative model, as we will call it, must do more than list the devices used—trial noun phrases, interruptions, continuers, and the like. It must spell out how the process of mutual acceptance gets initiated, carried through, and completed. The process usually begins with the speaker issuing a noun phrase. But these noun phrases come in many types, as already noted, and do no more than initiate the process. The model must show how these noun phrases are organized as a system and how they enter in a uniform way into the referential process as a whole. We must resist the temptation, engendered by the literary model of reference, to treat standard noun phrases as genuine and all others as aberrations, for that doesn't explain the role of any of the noun phrases in the process.

Definite references to the Tangram figures, as noted earlier, occurred only on Trials 2 through 6. In the simplest pattern, the director would refer to a position (e.g., *Number 4*) and assert which figure appeared there (*is the guy leaning against the tree*), and the matcher would signal she had placed it with *okay, all right, got it*, or *right*, as in:

A. Number 4's the guy leaning against the tree.
B. Okay.

Sometimes the matcher responded with two moves, as in *Okay, I've got it*, or with a brief confirmation of the description plus an okay, as in *Dancer, okay*. The director would then go to the next position. These all constitute what we will call the *basic exchange*.

Our main interest is in the director's use of the noun phrase for the figure as a whole, here *the guy leaning against the tree*. By the collaborative view, he presents it as a means for the matcher to identify the intended figure, and she is expected to accept it. In the basic exchange, indeed, the matcher uses her *okay* to assert (a) that she believes she has identified the figure correctly, and (b) that she has placed the figure in the right location. In doing so, she presupposes (c) that she accepts the director's presentation, including his perspective on the referent. Sometimes the matcher handled these components separately. One matcher signaled her identification *a* and acceptance *c*, but signaled trouble with *b*, finding and placing the figure: *Okay, um. Wait, just a sec, just a sec. I can't find it again. God ... Okay, okay.* So in the basic exchange, the acceptance process is canonical: the director presents a noun phrase, and the matcher presupposes her acceptance.

The basic exchange should only be possible when the matcher can accept the director's initial presentation without refashioning it. If so, basic exchanges should have occurred seldom on early trials, but often on later trials, where they could be based on prior mutually accepted descriptions. The percentages of basic exchanges on Trials 1 through

6 were 18, 55, 75, 80, 88, and 84. This trend is highly significant, $F(1,55) = 84.19$, $p < .001$. Since the basic exchange requires fewer words and turns than most other exchanges, this accounts for much of the decrease in word count and turns in Figures 2 and 3.

Within the structure of the basic exchange, we can now examine the three processes by which the two partners reached mutual acceptance of each reference—initiating, refashioning, and evaluating presentations.

Initiating a Reference

Suppose the director has just uttered *Number 4 is* ..., intending the next noun phrase to pick out a particular figure. It is at this moment that the referential process gets initiated. We will call the first full noun phrase uttered at that point the *initial* presentation. These noun phrases fall into at least six distinct types.

1. **Elementary Noun Phrase.** The director utters this type of noun phrase in a single tone group, such as *the guy leaning against the tree*. Presumably, he believes the matcher can accept it canonically. This is the type of noun phrase that usually occurred in basic exchanges.

2. **Episodic Noun Phrase.** The director utters this type of noun phrase in two or more easily distinguished episodes or tone groups, as in *Number 7's the goofy guy that's falling over, with his leg kicked up*. The first episode ends with *over* and is immediately followed with more of the same noun phrase in a second episode.

3. **Installment Noun Phrase.** The director utters this type of noun phrase in episodes, too, but gets explicit acceptance of each installment before going on, as in:

   A. And the next one is the one with the triangle to the right ...
   B. Okay.
   A. With the square connected to it.

   The director doesn't end the first installment with a try marker, but does indicate by his intonation that he intends to go on. His pause is effective in getting the matcher to respond.

4. **Provisional Noun Phrase.** Often, the director presents a noun phrase which he comes to realize is inadequate—a provisional noun phrase—and immediately expands on it without prompting, as in: *And the next one is also the one that doesn't look like anything. It's kind of like the tree?* Note that the expansion is *not* part of the initial noun phrase, but comes in a new clause.

5. Dummy Noun Phrase. A speaker usually utters this type of noun phrase, such as *the whatchamacallit*, as a stand-in until he or his partner can produce a more complete noun phrase. We found no dummy noun phrases in our transcripts, though, as we noted, they are found elsewhere.

6. Proxy Noun Phrase. If the director pauses long enough, and if the matcher has some confidence she knows what he is about to say, she can present all or the final part of a noun phrase by proxy, as here:

A. And number 12 is, uh, . . .
B. Chair.
A. With the chair, right.
B. Got it.

In some cases, the speaker actively solicits proxy noun phrases with *what's the word?* or *you know*, or by the way he or she pauses or gestures. We found only five clear initial proxy noun phrases in our transcripts, although elsewhere we have documented their existence in great detail (Wilkes-Gibbs, unpublished).

Any of these six types of noun phrases can end with a try marker, as in *Um, the next one's the person ice skating that has two arms?* With it, one partner asks the other for an explicit verdict on the noun phrase, or installment, before they go on. Note that try markers don't turn assertions into questions; this utterance doesn't mean *Is the next one the person ice skating that has two arms?* The noun phrase is the only element within the scope of the try marker. With it the speaker queries whether the noun phrase is acceptable as it stands.

Try markers should be used for noun phrases the director is less certain will be accepted. In our task, as it happened, it was impossible to distinguish try markers on initial noun phrases, which almost always came at the ends of utterances, from rising intonation for the utterances as wholes. Our directors often used rising intonation to mark utterances as members of a list, with the final member getting a falling intonation. Indeed, as the directors went from Trial 2 through Trial 6, they used the list intonation to end steadily more of the utterances containing their initial noun phrases, from 41% through 78%.

Each type of noun phrase is generally marked by the speaker for its *status*, which reflects the speaker's confidence in the noun phrase being produced. Episodic, installment, and provisional noun phrases almost always had distinctive intonation patterns in our data; dummy noun phrases have distinctive lexical content, as with *what's-her-name*; and proxy noun phrases are identifiable by the change in speakers and often

TABLE 1
Rules of Projection for Next Move

	PROJECTED NEXT MOVE	
TYPE OF NOUN PHRASE	UNMARKED	WITH TRY MARKERS
Elementary	Implicated acceptance	Explicit verdict
Episodic	Implicated acceptance	Explicit verdict
Installment	Explicit acceptance	Explicit verdict
Provisional	Self-expansion	Self-expansion
Dummy	Self-expansion	Proxy
Proxy	Explicit acceptance	Explicit verdict

by the first speaker's hesitation as well. Each of these noun phrases can be modified by a try marker, by which the speaker implies there is some possibility of a negative verdict. Truly elementary noun phrases are identifiable by their lack of special features.

These status markings, we propose, are used by speakers to project the next move in the acceptance process. For an analogy, consider questions and answers as a type of adjacency pair (Schegloff and Sacks 1973). When A asks B a question, it is "expectable" that B answer it in the next utterance. B's next utterance, of course, need not be an answer, but it is interpreted by its relation to what is expected. The answer is the preferred response. Likewise, an installment of a noun phrase by A projects an explicit acceptance by B; with an added try marker, it projects an explicit verdict: accept or not accept. These projections, however, are unlike true adjacency pairs, in which the first and second parts are always produced by different speakers. A provisional noun phrase by A projects an expansion by A and *not* by B. The moves that we propose are projected by each noun phrase are shown in Table 1. They are consistent with our data, though need more support. If confirmed in further work, they become excellent evidence that the two partners tacitly recognize they are engaged in an acceptance process.

In selecting a noun phrase, the director presumably aims at several ideals. He prefers uttering the initial noun phrase himself. He prefers it to be elementary—not an episodic or installment noun phrase; to be adequate, free of errors, and uttered fluently—not in need of refashioning; and to be no more prolix than necessary (Grice 1975). Elementary noun phrases should therefore be the most preferred, and proxy noun phrases the least. Our data are consistent with this ordering though hardly definitive. Table 2 lists the percentages of initial references on Trials 2 through 6 that belonged to each category; the descriptions listed are those utterances in which a figure was described rather than

TABLE 2
Percentages of Six Types of Initial Noun Phrases
for Trials 2 through 6

	TRIAL				
TYPE OF NOUN PHRASE	2	3	4	5	6
Elementary	52	68	69	80	72
Episodic	11	10	8	6	5
Installment	0	0	0	0	1
Provisional	17	14	8	2	6
Dummy	0	0	0	0	0
Proxy	0	1	2	1	1
Description	17	7	12	9	14
Unclassified	3	0	1	2	1

identified, e.g., *Okay, number 7 is like, she's dancing. The head is tilted.* As the table shows, there were too few installment, dummy, and proxy noun phrases to test. But, as predicted, episodic and provisional noun phrases, which were used only when necessary, declined and by Trial 6 had mostly disappeared (linear trend, $F(1,28) = 9.02$, $p < .01$). What remained were the preferred elementary noun phrases, which increased significantly over trials, $F(1,28) = 17.02$, $p < .01$.

Refashioning a Noun Phrase

An initial noun phrase that isn't acceptable must be refashioned. This is accomplished in three main ways.

a. Repair. In planning and uttering each noun phrase, speakers monitor what they are doing and, on detecting a problem, set about repairing it (Laver 1973; Levelt 1983; Schegloff et al. 1977). These self-repairs were legion in our transcripts, as in: *Um, next one is the guy, the person with his head to the right but his legs are, his one leg is kicked up to the left.* There were also many of what Levelt (1983) has called *covert* repairs, as in: *Okay, number, uh, 4 is the, is the kind of fat one with the legs to the left—er, I mean, to the right.* In repeating *is the*, the director might well have been repairing something he was about to say even if we have no way of determining what. The numbers of self-repairs on Trials 1 through 6 were 85, 30, 20, 8, 7, and 6; the instances of repeated words were 47, 14, 10, 4, 7, and 1. These declines contribute to the decrease in word count in Figure 2.

Repairs could also be initiated by the addressee, but all of these in our data could be classified in one of the next two categories.

b. Expansion. Once the director has completed a noun phrase, he or the matcher may judge it to be inadequate for the purposes at hand and in need of a phrase, clause, or sentence of expansion. If the initial noun phrase is provisional, the director will expand on it without prompting, as in these two examples:

> Okay, number 1 is the just kind of block-like figure with the jagged right-hand side. *The left side looks like a square.*

and:

> Okay, number 6 is the guy, uh, sitting down with his legs to the left, *and he's kind of leaning his head over.*

Note that the clauses in italics are *not* part of the initial noun phrases, but expansions added to improve on them. If we call the description in the initial noun phrase x and that in its expansion y, then what the director and matcher end up mutually accepting is the compound description $x + y$.

Self-expansions like these should be needed less often the more clearly the director can formulate his initial noun phrases, and they were. The percentages of figure placements with self-expansions, under a strict criterion, were 25, 17, 11, 6, and 10 on Trials 2 through 6. This decline also helps account for the decrease in word count in Figure 2.

When the matcher didn't find the director's initial noun phrase x clear enough, she could signal the need for an expansion y, as in this example:

A. Okay, the next one is the rabbit.
B. Uh–
A. That's asleep, you know, it looks like it's got ears and a head pointing down?
B. Okay.

In the side sequence here, the matcher used *Uh–* with an extended, level intonation to signal that she needed more description, and the director complied. Requests for expansion like this took many forms, often occurring more than once on a single figure. Many times the matcher signaled uncertainty with a tentatively voiced *um, uh huh,* or *yes?,* as if saying, "I'm still uncertain, so please expand on your noun phrase." Other times she displayed silence where a reply could have been expected—such as at a pause after a completed utterance. Still other times she repeated the main part of the director's description with a rising intonation, as in:

A. Uh, person putting a shoe on.
B. Putting a shoe on?

A. Uh huh. Facing left. Looks like he's sitting down.
B. Okay.

Prompts of this latter type occurred on 15, 3, 3, 2, 1, and 1% of the figure placements on Trials 1 to 6.

Overall, matchers should have had less need to request expansions if they had previously found a mutually acceptable description for a figure. On Trial 1, 36% of the figure placements included at least one request for expansion (counting prompts as a subtype); on Trials 2 through 6, the percentages decreased to 12, 8, 3, 1, and 3. So requests for expansion also contribute to the decrease in word count and turns in Figures 2 and 3.

The matcher herself often expanded on the director's noun phrase, almost always in the form of a request for confirmation, as in this example:

A. Um, third one is the guy reading with, holding his book to the left.
B. Okay, kind of standing up?
A. Yeah.
B. Okay.

The matcher initiated a side sequence by accepting what the director had said so far (x) with *Okay*—a postponement, as we will call it—but by asking him to confirm her expansion y. Once he accepted it, the side sequence was complete, and with her next *Okay*, the matcher presupposed acceptance of the amended noun phrase $x + y$. Requests for confirmation, like the other forms of expansion, also declined over trials, occurring in 37, 12, 8, 6, 1, and 2% of the figure placements on Trials 1 to 6.

Logically, at least some episodic noun phrases might be considered initiating noun phrases plus self-expansions. In this view the director presents an elementary noun phrase *the goofy guy that's falling over*, immediately judges it inadequate, and then adds the restrictive phrase *with his leg kicked up* in a new tone group, all before allowing the matcher to respond. So he adds an expansion just as he does to a provisional noun phrase, but here the expansion is still part of the initial noun phrase and not a new clause. Consistent with this view, the number of episodic noun phrases declined over trials—11, 10, 8, 6, and 5 in Trials 2 through 6 (Table 2)—just as other forms of expansion did.

c. Replacement. Once the director had finished his noun phrase, the matcher could reject it and present a noun phrase of her own, which we will call a *replacement*. The following is one example:

A. Okay, and the next one is the person that looks like they're carrying something and it's sticking out to the left. It looks like a hat that's upside down.

B. The guy that's pointing to the left again?

A. Yeah, pointing to the left, that's it! (laughs)

B. Okay.

Since the director's noun phrase x was still unacceptable, the matcher presented a description z from an alternative perspective, which the director then accepted. Indeed, the director took up her replacement on the next trial when he said, *And the next one's the guy pointing to the left.* Replacements are different from expansions. In presenting z, the matcher was rejecting x and replacing it with z, expressing a different description and not merely an additional one. What the two of them accepted in the end wasn't $x + z$, but simply z.

Most replacements in our transcripts included try markers, as in this example. With the demands of the task, it was rare for a matcher to have a strong enough hypothesis to make a replacement. Also, then, replacements by the matcher shouldn't be that prevalent. They occurred on only 10, 5, 0, 2, 2, and 0% of the figure placements in Trials 1 through 6.

Passing Judgment on Presentations

A presentation, expansion, or replacement that is put forward needs to be judged acceptable or unacceptable. That can be accomplished by three methods.

a. **Acceptance.** . Once one person has presented a noun phrase, his or her partner can *presuppose acceptance* by continuing on to the next contribution, as when the matcher completes the basic exchange with *Okay.* Or the partner can *assert acceptance*, as in the last example, when the director replied *Yeah* to the matcher's trial replacement. Both types occurred in our transcripts.

b. **Rejection.** A partner can reject a noun phrase either directly or by implication. The clearest rejections are asserted, as in *Oh, the ice skater?* followed by *Y-er, no.* Implicated rejections can also be clear, as when the matcher made the replacement *The guy that's pointing to the left again?* Face to face, a partner can offer other signals, like quizzical looks, which should also be effective.

c. **Postponement.** The partner can also signal that she accepts the presentation so far but is postponing final judgment until it is expanded, as with a tentatively voiced *Okay.*

The matcher can also render verdicts by interrupting the director, but then she is generally signaling more than mere acceptance or rejection. Here is one example:

A. Okay, our kneeling person with the hook on the—
B. [Okay.
A. [—left side

Although the matcher may simply have suffered from mistiming, she was more likely signaling that she didn't need such an extensive description or any further qualifications (see Jefferson 1973, 59).

The Acceptance Process

As these results demonstrate, the acceptance process is played out in conversation, as in other human affairs, as a series of steps. It takes at least two such steps—a presentation and its acceptance—but it may take more. With the devices summarized in Table 3, the possibilities are, indeed, unlimited.

The basic process, which might be called the *acceptance cycle*, consists of a presentation plus its verdict. Let x, y, and z stand for noun phrases or their emendations. A presents x and then B evaluates it. If the verdict is not positive, then A or B must refashion that presentation. That person can offer: a repair x', an expansion y, or a replacement z. The refashioned presentation, whether x', $x + y$, or z, is evaluated, and so on. Acceptance cycles apply iteratively, with one repair, expansion, or replacement after another, until a noun phrase is mutually accepted. With that, A and B take the process to be complete.

A positive verdict from B alone, however, may not bring the process immediately to completion, since A may not be satisfied that B has understood A's reference. This leads to what we will call *follow-ups*, turns initiated immediately after one partner has accepted the noun phrase, as here:

A. The first one's the one I said looked like a rabbit last time.
B. Okay.
A. You've got that one, right?
B. Yeah.

Sometimes follow-ups seemed to have been initiated because the director couldn't tell whether the matcher's *okay* meant *I understand you so far* or *I have identified the figure and have placed it in my array*. Other times they came on the heels of an error or confusion in the previous trial; the director had good reason for seeking reassurance. Still other times they were initiated because the director didn't seem

TABLE 3
Mutual Acceptance as a Recursive Process

INITIATING A REFERENCE	
To initiate a reference,	present x_1, or invite x_1.
If an x_1 is invited,	present x_1.
REFASHIONING A NOUN PHRASE	
If x_i is inadequate,	present revision x'_i, or expansion y_i, or replacement z_i; or request x'_i, y_i, or z_i.
If an x'_i, y_i, or z_i is requested,	present x'_i, y_i, or z_i.
If x'_i, y_i, or z_i is presented,	let $x_{i+1} = x'_i$, $x_i + y_i$, or z_i.
CONCLUDING A REFERENCE	
If x_i is adequate,	accept x_i.
If x_i is adequate and accepted,	conclude mutual acceptance.

satisfied with his description, even though the matcher had accepted it, as in:

A. Okay, the next one looks, is the one with the person standing on one leg with the tail.
B. Okay.
A. Looks like an ice skater.
B. Yeah, okay.

On all later trials, this director referred to the figure as an ice skater.

Follow-up sequences may be a good indicator of the director's confidence in the accuracy of their mutual beliefs about the referent. As this would suggest, the number of follow-ups decreased with successive acceptances for each figure. The percentages of figure placements with follow-ups on Trials 1 through 6 were 35, 12, 6, 6, 1, and 5.

A mutual acceptance, once reached, can also later be reconsidered. Recall that the goal of the acceptance process is to establish the mutual belief that the listener has understood what the speaker meant. Once a mutual acceptance has been arrived at, many things can shake those beliefs. The mutual acceptance might have been premature or mistaken, and all it takes to revoke it is some reason for thinking it was in error. Mutual acceptances were reconsidered in several cases in our task.

Minimizing Collaborative Effort

In classical theories of least effort (e.g., Brown 1958; Brown and Lenneberg 1954; Krauss and Glucksberg 1977; Olson 1970; Zipf 1935), speakers try to utter the shortest noun phrases that will enable their addressees to pick out the referent in context. These theories tacitly assume that speakers work alone, again a literary model of reference with all its problems for conversation. Still there seems to be minimization of effort in conversation. Our proposal is that speakers and addressees try to minimize *collaborative effort*, the work both speakers and addressees do from the initiation of the referential process to its completion. The principle of least collaborative effort, as we shall call it, is needed to account for many features of the acceptance process.

In the collaborative model there is a trade-off in effort between initiating the noun phrase and refashioning it. The more effort a speaker puts into the initial noun phrase, in general, the less refashioning it is likely to need. Why don't speakers always put in enough effort to avoid refashioning? There are three main reasons.

1. **Time pressure.** Speakers may realize they cannot design the ideal noun phrase in the time allowed. So (a) they may be forced to invite or accept a proxy noun phrase rather than have addressees wait for them to plan their own. Or (b) they may have to use a dummy or provisional noun phrase to give themselves time to plan a better description, which they offer in an immediate expansion. Or (c) they may utter a noun phrase and, finding it inadequate so far, amend it in a second episode.

2. **Complexity.** Speakers may realize that the noun phrase they are designing is too complex to be easily understood, so they present it in installments.

3. **Ignorance.** Speakers may realize that they don't know enough to decide what addressees would accept anyway, so they are forced into trial and error. They try out a description and leave it to the addressees to refashion if it isn't acceptable. This is one origin of try markers.

The six types of initial noun phrases, each modifiable by a try marker, are therefore devices that enable speakers to deal with these three constraints and yet minimize collaborative effort.

The devices used in refashioning are also designed to minimize collaborative effort. Take repair. As Schegloff et al. (1977) noted, repairs are subject to two strong preferences: speakers prefer to repair their own utterances rather than let interlocutors do it; and speakers prefer to initiate their own repairs rather than let interlocutors prompt them to do it. These preferences have several consequences. One is that speakers repair their own utterances as soon as they detect problems (Levelt 1983). This way they minimize the time a potential misunderstanding is on the floor. Speakers also avert potential exchanges as the interlocutor tries to correct the misunderstanding. That minimizes the number of exchanges needed before mutual acceptance. Together, the two preferences help minimize collaborative effort.

Or take expansion and replacement. As with repairs, speakers prefer to make their own expansions unprompted, as in provisional noun phrases and continuations of episodic noun phrases. As for the addressees, they could in principle respond to every noun phrase they didn't understand with *What?* but that wouldn't be very informative. For collaborative efficiency they try to pinpoint their problem. When possible, they prompt specific expansions (e.g., *Putting a shoe on?*), offer their own expansions (e.g., *kind of standing up?*), or offer replacements (e.g., *The guy that's pointing to the left again?*). They also answer speakers' queries. So addressees minimize collaborative effort by indicating quickly and informatively what is needed for mutual acceptance.

The canonical reference is also predicted by least collaborative effort. In it speakers present an elementary noun phrase and addressees presuppose their acceptance. That is, it consists of a minimal noun phrase (not complex enough to warrant installments) and no extra exchanges. So the canonical reference is preferred because it minimizes effort by both parties.

The principles of least effort and of least collaborative effort, therefore, make very different predictions. Least effort predicts that every reference is made with (a) a standard (literary) noun phrase that (b) is as short as possible and yet (c) specifies the referent uniquely in that context. Least collaborative effort predicts that references can be made with (a) nonstandard, nonliterary noun phrases, (b) with ones the speaker believes are *not* adequate in context, and (c) with devices that draw addressees into the process. In particular, it predicts tradeoffs between effort in initial noun phrases and effort in refashioning. It predicts preferences for self-repair and self-initiated repair. It predicts expansions and replacements, and informative requests for expansion. And it predicts a preference for canonical references. On all these counts the evidence favors least collaborative effort.

5 Perspective and Change in Perspective

So far we have outlined the *how* of referring. We have argued that it is an acceptance process in which the two partners establish the mutual belief that the listener has understood the speaker's reference.

But we also have evidence for the *what* of referring—what the two partners mutually accept in the referential process. Recall the director on Trial 1 who described figure I this way: *All right, the next one looks like a person who's ice skating, except they're sticking two arms out in front.* In so doing he took a particular *perspective* on the figure—that it looks like a person, that the person is ice skating, that the person is sticking his arms out—and got the matcher to accept it. But he couldn't have got the matcher to accept just any perspective he happened to think of. He assumed some perspectives should be easy to establish, and others difficult. And by Trial 6 the same director had simplified this perspective to *the ice skater* (cf. Carroll 1980). Why?

Our proposal is that the perspectives people mutually accept, and the way these change over time, are also constrained by the push to minimize collaborative effort. Our evidence, though limited to the Tangram task, supports several qualitative predictions.

Establishing a Common Perspective

When should a speaker initiate a definite reference? Very roughly, he must believe that the referent is mutually identifiable to him and his addressee from their common ground (Chapter 1, this volume; Hawkins 1978). In principle, then, the director just cited could have initiated a definite reference on Trial 1 by saying *All right, the next one* IS THE ONE THAT *looks like a person who's ice skating, except they're sticking two arms out in front.* After all, he knew the two sets of figures were identical and common ground. In a pilot experiment with pictures of six common animals, many directors did just that, as with *Number 4 is the zebra* and *Number 5 is the bear.* The director just cited, however, did not, nor did any of the others. Why not?

In each referential process the director and matcher must find a perspective they can mutually accept for current purposes. Should they view figure I as an ice skater, a ballerina, a person leaning left with a tail, or a person with a leg sticking out back, each of which occurred in our transcripts? Although they can presuppose common, general purpose perspectives for such everyday objects as tables, dogs, and ants, they cannot for our Tangram figures. For each of these they need to take special steps at the first mention to establish a common perspective. If that takes more collaborative effort than the director believes possible on Trial 1, he shouldn't *refer* to the figures but try first to establish a common perspective. That is precisely what the directors did.

On Trial 1 the directors always *described* the figures. The descriptions were of four main types, as exemplified here (the critical features in italics):

1. **Resemblance.** Okay, um, number 7 kind of *looks like* a, a fat person, sitting down, uh, with his legs or knees to his right. [figure H]

2. **Categorization.** Okay, the next one, uh, *is* a diamond on top with, um, a thing that looks like a ripped up square. [figure J]

3. **Attribution.** And the second one *has* a triangle pointing to the left, in the bottom left-hand corner, ... [figure B]

4. **Action.** Okay, the next one *is pointing right*. [figure J]

So on Trial 1, in effect, the two partners reached mutual acceptance on how each figure was to be viewed.

After Trial 1, by contrast, they used identificational statements with definite references on 89% of the initial utterances for each figure, as in *Um, the next one's the person ice skating that has two arms?* Only seven times (five on Trial 2 and one each on Trials 3 and 6) did they categorize a figure (*is an X*) where they might be expected to identify it (*is the X*). There were good reasons for each, such as being in error the trial before, changing perspective, and not having been described before.

So on Trial 1, we suggest, the directors described the Tangram figures because they couldn't count on a common perspective, and to presuppose one in making a definite reference would have cost too much in collaborative effort.

Bases for Reference

When the director cited earlier got the matcher to accept that figure I "looks like a person who's ice skating, except they're sticking two arms out in front," he established a possible basis for later references whether he intended to or not. On Trial 2, indeed, he exploited the previous acceptance in presenting *the person ice skating that has two arms?* Yet on Trial 1 he established other possible bases as well, since on Trial 2 he could have offered *the figure that was number 3 last time*.

These two bases correspond to two main categories of definite descriptions in our transcripts. The references in the first category were based on previously established perspectives, as in *the rabbit* [figure E], *the person with his arms up* [figure C], and even *your monk and my machine-gun* [figure D] when the two partners hadn't come to a common perspective (see Perrault and Cohen 1981). The references in the second category were based on procedures associated with the making of the previous reference, such as mistakes (*the one we got confused on last time*), failures to find satisfactory perspectives (*the one that doesn't look like anything*), and position on the list (*the first one from last time*).

Which basis for reference should be preferred? Most objects have both *permanent* or enduring properties, such as shape, color, and personal identity, and *temporary* properties, such as location, orientation, and time of first notice. With a definite reference the speaker is usually trying to get the addressee to reidentify an object as the same as one he had identified before (see Strawson 1965). For this, the permanent properties ought to be more effective. They are salient, distinctive of each figure, a highly recognizable part of common ground, and therefore easy to exploit in reaching mutual acceptance. In contrast, temporary properties are susceptible to change from one act of identification to the next and so may be easily confused (see also Glucksberg et al. 1975). If the two partners are trying to minimize collaborative effort on a reference, they should prefer permanent properties.

Our transcripts bear out this prediction. Overall, 90% of the references were based solely on such permanent properties as shape and appearance; 2% were based solely on more temporary procedural experiences like position on list, mistakes, and failures; and 7% involved some combination of these. Procedural experiences were resorted to only when more permanent properties weren't readily available.

Literal and Analogical Perspectives

Another prediction from minimizing collaborative effort is that people should prefer certain perspectives to others as bases for their references. An object (such as a bed) can usually be viewed either as a whole or as a juxtaposition of parts (a headboard, foot, mattress, pillow, etc.). Getting a definite description (and the perspective it imposes) accepted should take less collaborative effort if the common perspective the partners try to establish is *holistic*, in which the object is conceived of as a whole, than if it is *segmental*, in which the object is conceived of as segments that happen to be juxtaposed. Accepting a perspective on the whole establishes perspectives on each part, but not vice versa. All other things being equal, the partners should prefer holistic to segmental perspectives.

The perspectives actually taken on our Tangram figures are consistent with this prediction. They were of two quite different kinds. The *analogical* perspectives focused on the resemblances of the figures to natural objects, as in these three examples:

Number 2 is, uh, it looks like a person, uh, sitting with his legs under him.

Number 5 looks like a girl dancing sort of.

The next one looks like a person meditating.

Of these, 84% were introduced with *looks like* or *resembles*, and, as befits their character, 42% were hedged with *sort of*, *kind of*, or *something like*. The *literal* perspectives focused on the literal features of the figures, their geometric parts and relations, as in these two examples:

> Um, it's a, oh, hexagonic shape, and then on the bottom right side it has this diamond.

> Number 1 has a diamond on the top and a square. The left side is, um, like a rectangle shape, and the right side is cut off.

Fully 89% of these were introduced with *is* or *has*, and only 4% carried hedges.

The analogical perspectives tended to be holistic, and the literal ones segmental. In the analogical perspectives the pieces of the figure were tied together with concepts like *person meditating* or *person sitting with his legs under him*, whereas in the literal perspectives the geometric pieces were merely juxtaposed. If there is a preference for holistic over segmental perspectives, analogical perspectives should be given priority, and they were.

The strategy most often adopted on Trial 1 was to introduce an analogical perspective, as if that was the way the director saw the figure, and then, so the matcher could identify the right figure, to add a literal perspective, as here:

> Okay. All right. The next one looks kind of like, um, a candle that's burning? It's got a diamond for the top, except it's got something sticking out of it to the side. It's got just a diamond sticking up at the top and then one long column that has something sticking out to the left. [figure D]

Of the eighty times an analogical perspective was introduced on Trial 1, it came first or alone 93% of the time; when there were parts (fifty-four of eighty references), whether analogical or geometric, they came afterward 89% of the time. On Trial 1, 42% of the figures were described from both perspectives, but by Trial 6, 77% of the definite references were built on analogical perspectives alone, and only 19% contained literal elements. Overall, only seventeen of our 576 figure placements didn't carry some form of analogical depiction (see Cohen 1985 for similar examples). The push toward holistic perspectives was very strong indeed.

Changes in Perspective

If the two partners are trying to minimize collaborative effort, they should refine perspectives in predictable ways. For the director cited earlier, the perspective first taken on figure I, that it *looks like a person who's ice skating, except they're sticking two arms out in front*, got simplified by Trial 6 to *ice skater*.

The refinements in perspective in our transcripts were of two main types—*simplification* and, less often, *narrowing*. With simplification, certain details were omitted, as in these successive references to figure C:

1. Okay, the number 7 looks like, sort of like an angel flying away or something. It's got two arms.
2. Okay, the seventh one, um, looks like someone, looks like the angel flying away, or that's what I said last time.
3. Fourth one is the, uh, flying one.
4. Fifth one is the one that looks like an angel.
5. Um, the second one is the angel one.
6. Sixth one's the angel.

The first thing omitted was mention of the arms, followed by mention of its being an angel, which was then reintroduced with no more mention of it flying. With narrowing, the focus of a perspective was narrowed to just one part of a figure. The focus could move onto a central part (corresponding to the head noun in the previous description), as when *Number 3's the graduate at the podium* was refined to *Number 11's the graduate*. Or it could move onto a peripheral, but distinctive part, as when *Okay, the first one's the guy in a sleeping bag* was refined to *Sleeping bag* (cf. Carroll 1980).

Now a holistic perspective on an object may still reflect either complex or simple categories. Figure I was categorized in our transcripts by one director (a) as a *person with a leg sticking out back*, and by another (b) as a *ballerina*. Although both categories are holistic, the first is specified with several concepts—being a person, having a leg stick out, and having it stick out back—whereas the second is specified with a single encompassing concept—being a ballerina. The first one will be called a multinary category, and the second a unitary category.

All other things being equal, mutual acceptance should take fewer steps on one concept than on many, so the two partners should prefer unitary categories to multinary categories. They did. With simplification, multinary concepts like *angel flying away with two arms* were refined to unitary ones like *angel*, or at least to less complex multinary ones. The same happened with narrowing. These two refinements, of course, also lead to the shortening of noun phrases. Here, then, is another major source for the shortening in this and previous studies of repeated references.

In summary, the changes in repeated references can be viewed in part as an outgrowth of the collaborative process. Trying to minimize collaborative effort, the director shunned definite references for mere descriptions on Trial 1. Likewise, in initiating references on Trials 2 through 6, he tended to opt for holistic over segmental perspectives, for permanent over temporary features, and for unitary over multinary categories.

6 Speaking Generally

Participants in conversation, we have demonstrated, work together even in such a basic process as the making of a definite reference. Our proposal, more generally, is that they take for granted this principle:

Principle of mutual responsibility. The participants in a conversation try to establish, roughly by the initiation of each new contribution, the mutual belief that the listeners have understood what the speaker meant in the last utterance to a criterion sufficient for current purposes.

With definite reference their attempts take the form of an acceptance process. The speaker initiates the process by presenting one of at least five types of noun phrases or by inviting a sixth. Both speaker and addressees may repair, expand on, or replace this noun phrase in iterative fashion until they arrive at a version they mutually accept. In this process they try to minimize collaborative effort, presenting and refashioning these noun phrases as efficiently as possible. One result is that the preferred form of reference is the one in which the speaker presents an elementary noun phrase and the addressees presuppose their acceptance of it without taking an extra turn.

The principle of mutual responsibility, however, places two important caveats on this process. The mutual belief is to be established "roughly by the initiation of each new contribution" and "to a criterion sufficient for current purposes." Although our findings don't bear directly on these caveats, we think they are crucial.

The Criterion Problem

In our proposal the participants aren't trying to assure perfect understanding of each utterance but only understanding "to a criterion sufficient for current purposes." What are these purposes, and how much is sufficient?

Some conversational purposes are broad and dictate a generally high or low criterion for understanding. Suppose A is telling B where he lives. If B's purpose is to be able to get to his house, she will set her criterion high. If it is merely to break the ice at a party, she will set it low. We have all endured, at a low criterion, people who have talked about each of six children and their families, none of whom we care a whit about. The speaker and addressee may even set discrepant criteria, as when a parent talks to a child. In our task the two partners presumably both set their criteria high, since they were trying to get each figure placed without error before going on. That is one reason they were so diligent in reaching acceptances, often explicit ones.

Even in situations of low or discrepant criteria, however, the ground rules of mutual responsibility are still in force. The participants mutually accept each contribution, at least tacitly, before going on to the next. Granted, they may often be play-acting their parts. Yet even in these conversations we should find coordinating signals such as back-channel responses and try markers (though perhaps distributed more unevenly), however insincere they may be. And speakers should feel they are being understood well enough even when they are not.

Many purposes in conversation, however, change moment by moment as the two people tolerate more or less uncertainty about the listener's understanding of the speaker's references. The heavier burden usually falls on the listener, since she is in the best position to assess her own comprehension. When the speaker utters *I just found the keys*, marking the noun phrase as an elementary (rather than a provisional or trial) presentation, the listener is under strong pressure to accept it. After all, the speaker marked it as elementary, so he must believe it to be adequate for current purposes. If she rejects it, she risks offending him by indicating that it wasn't adequate. She also risks revealing her own incompetence if indeed it should have been adequate. Finally, like the speaker, the listener wants to minimize collaborative effort to avoid extra steps in the acceptance process—and that, too, puts pressure on her to accept. All this encourages her to tolerate a certain lack of understanding, even to feign understanding when it is not justified. She may do this trusting that the holes will be filled in later, or that they won't have serious consequences.

The listener must tolerate uncertainty anyway. Although the two parties might like to mutually accept each element second by second as they proceed, this ideal is impractical. Certain definite references, for example, cannot be understood until the speaker has completed his utterance. In *Although he doesn't know it yet, we are buying a new bicycle for Harry*, the referents for *he* and *it* cannot be identified until *Harry* has been uttered. It would be premature of the addressee to ask *Who doesn't know what?* after the first clause. The natural place to ask such questions is immediately after the utterance is complete.

In this view the two partners assume a unit of conversation we have called the *contribution*. It consists, minimally, of the utterance of one sentence on the topic of conversation, where the sentence can be full or elliptical, or even a quasi-sentence like *Coffee, please*. But to become a contribution the utterance has to be mutually accepted before the initiation of the next contribution, and that process may require repairs, expansions, and replacements of all or part of the initial presentation. Indeed, as Schegloff et al. (1977) have shown, speakers are usually allowed to present utterances without being interrupted. The place their partners initiate most repairs and expansions and offer most replacements is immediately after the presentation and before the next contribution is initiated. It is for this reason that allowing a new contribution to proceed is tantamount to a mutual acceptance of the old one.

Modes of Language Use

Conversation, though fundamental, isn't the only site of language use. There are novels, newspapers, and letters—literary uses—as well as radio and television broadcasts, sermons, tape-recorded messages, large lectures, and many others. In these circumstances the participants may not have full access to one another and hence cannot adhere to the principle of mutual responsibility as it has evolved for conversation. The principle may get weakened or modified in various ways. Precisely how it is weakened or modified defines a family of *language modes*. In this paper we have described one such mode, the collaborative mode, but there are many others. We shall mention just a few.

In many circumstances, as in literary forms, lectures, and radio broadcasts, writers and speakers are distant from their addressees in place, time, or both. They might be assumed to adhere to a weakened version of mutual responsibility:

Principle of distant responsibility. The speaker or writer tries to make sure, roughly by the initiation of each new contribution, that the addressees should have been able to understand his meaning in the last utterance to a criterion sufficient for current purposes.

How people adhere to the principle should depend on whether they are speaking or writing, and whether the product is extemporaneous or planned.

In spontaneous speech without concurrent listeners, speakers still monitor what they say (Levelt 1983) and can therefore change course in the process of making a reference. If so, they should still (a) initiate the process with elementary, episodic, provisional, and dummy noun phrases and (b) repair, expand, and even replace their initial noun phrases. It is just that they do all this without feedback from listeners. In a study by Levelt (1983), people were asked to describe complex spatial networks into a tape recorder. As expected, they produced large numbers of what we have called repairs, expansions, and replacements. This is typical of such monologues (see also Goffman 1981; Maclay and Osgood 1959). On the other hand, people don't shorten their repeated references as much when speaking into a tape recorder (Krauss and Weinheimer 1966).

Writers with time to plan, edit, and rewrite, however, should satisfy their responsibilities to readers by eliminating everything but elementary proposals, and many writers do. Others retain a sprinkling of provisional noun phrases, repairs, expansions, and replacements apparently to affect a spontaneous style or for other rhetorical effects. So here are two noncollaborative modes, one spontaneous and one planned, both the result of adhering to the principle of distant responsibility.

There may be several collaborative modes. In a study by Cohen (1985), pairs of people were recorded as they (a) spoke over a telephone hookup or (b) typed messages that were simultaneously displayed on both their own and their partner's computer terminals. The task was for one partner to instruct the other in how to assemble a water pump. In both environments the two partners used methods we have argued are part of the acceptance process. But, as Cohen demonstrated, the partners with spoken access used much finer-grained methods than those in the keyboard condition. An instructor on the telephone, for example, was more likely to ask his or her partner explicitly to identify a referent before they went on. On the keyboard, the two partners couldn't go as quickly, use nuances of intonation, or interrupt each other with such precise timing, so they apparently adapted their collaborative techniques to fit the limitations. How people adapt to such constraints in general is an open question.

Social factors also govern the collaborative mode. An army private being dressed down by a commanding officer is simply not allowed to interrupt or offer the feedback usually found among equals. Yet the officer can interrupt the private, request confirmations, offer replacements, and do much else. In a study by Ragan (1983), interviewers of job applicants initiated many side sequences, whereas the applicants never did. Further, applicants were much more likely than interviewers to qualify statements, revealing uncertainty about the adequacy of their presentations, and to seek acceptance with *you know*. So the form that collaboration takes is also adapted to certain social constraints. How the participants make these adaptations has yet to be established.

Participants in a conversation, we have argued, are mutually responsible for establishing what the speaker meant. Definite reference is only one part of that process. They must collaborate, in one way or another, on most or perhaps all other parts of speaker's meaning as well. Collaboration may take one form for word denotation, another for demonstrative reference, a third for assertions, and so on, yet there should be commonalities. The techniques documented for definite reference are likely useful for other parts of the speaker's meaning, too.

5

Contributing to Discourse

WITH EDWARD F. SCHAEFER

For people to contribute to discourse, they must do more than utter the right sentence at the right time. The basic requirement is that they add to their common ground in an orderly way. To do this, we argue, they try to establish for each utterance the mutual belief that the addressees have understood what the speaker meant well enough for current purposes. This is accomplished by the collective actions of the current contributor and his or her partners, and these result in units of conversations called contributions. We present a model of contributions and show how it accounts for a variety of features of everyday conversations.

People take part in conversation in order to plan, debate, discuss, gossip, and carry out other social processes. When they do take part, they could be said to *contribute* to the discourse. But how do they contribute? At first the answer seems obvious. A discourse is a sequence of utterances produced as the participants proceed turn by turn. All that participants have to do to contribute is utter the right sentence at the right time. They may make errors, but once they have corrected them, they are done. The other participants have merely to listen and understand. This is the view subscribed to in most discourse theories in psychology, linguistics, philosophy, and artificial intelligence.

A closer look at actual conversations, however, suggests that they are much more than sequences of utterances produced turn by turn. They are highly coordinated activities in which the current speaker tries to make sure he or she is being attended to, heard, and understood by the other participants, and they in turn try to let the speaker know when he or she has succeeded. Contributing to a discourse, then, appears to require more than just uttering the right words at the right time. It seems to consist of collective acts performed by the participants working together.

In this chapter we describe a model of contributions as parts of collective acts. We first describe the need for such a model, next present the model itself, and then show how it accounts for the commonest devices people use in contributing to conversations. As evidence for the model, we appeal to a large corpus of everyday conversations called the London-Lund corpus (Svartvik and Quirk 1980). The empirical claim is that the model accounts for the bulk of the successful talk in these conversations.

1   The Course of Discourse

Models of discourse differ greatly depending on whether they originate in philosophy (e.g., Kamp 1981; Lewis 1979; Stalnaker 1978), linguistics (Heim 1983), artificial intelligence (Grosz and Sidner 1986; Reichman 1978; Polanyi and Scha 1985), or psychology (Clark and Haviland 1977; Johnson-Laird 1983; van Dijk and Kintsch 1983). Still, in one way or another, most of them make three assumptions.

Common ground.   The participants in a discourse presuppose a certain common ground.

Accumulation.   In the course of a discourse, the participants try to add to their common ground.

Unilateral action.   The principal means by which the participants add to their common ground is by the speaker uttering the right sentence at the right time.

To take Kamp's proposal as an example, the content of a discourse is accumulated in a Discourse Representation Model, or DRM, which is tacitly assumed to be common ground for the participants. With each new utterance, new structures get added to the DRM. These structures are simply assumed to be what the speaker intended; there are no special provisions for making certain they are. The first two assumptions, we will argue with certain qualifications, are necessary for any model of discourse. The third, however, is insufficient to handle a broad class of discourse phenomena that have been systematically excluded from consideration.

When people take part in a conversation, they bring with them a certain amount of baggage—prior beliefs, assumptions, and other information. Part of that baggage is their *common ground*, which Stalnaker (1978) described this way: "Roughly speaking, the presuppositions of a speaker are the propositions whose truth he takes for granted as part

of the background of the conversation ... Presuppositions are what is
taken by the speaker to be the *common ground* of the participants in
the conversation, what is treated as their *common knowledge* or *mutual knowledge*" (320, Stalnaker's emphases).[1] Each participant in a
conversation, of course, makes his or her own presuppositions. But as
Stalnaker noted, "it is part of the concept of presupposition that the
speaker assumes that the members of his audience presuppose everything that he presupposes" (321). In actual conversations, the presuppositions vary from one participant to the next, though usually not too
drastically.

The common ground of the participants in a conversation changes
as the conversation proceeds. As Lewis put it, "Presuppositions can
be created or destroyed in the course of a conversation. This change
is rule-governed, at least up to a point. The presuppositions at time t'
depend, in a way about which at least some general principles can be
laid down, on the presuppositions at an earlier time t and on the course
of the conversation (and nearby events) between t and t'" (1979, 339).
But even when presuppositions are destroyed, the participants know
they have been destroyed, and that knowledge itself becomes part of
their common ground. So we can say that the common ground of the
participants *accumulates* in the course of a conversation.

Assertions offer an example of how common ground accumulates.
Suppose Ann tells Bob she is leaving. As Stalnaker argued, "the essential effect of an assertion is to change the presuppositions of the participants in the conversation by adding the content of what is asserted
to what is presupposed. This effect is avoided only if the assertion is
rejected" (323). Initially, Ann takes it *not* to be common ground that
she is leaving. So as she makes her assertion, Ann and Bob accumulate
one more piece of common ground.

Other speech acts add to common ground in other ways. When Ann
asks Bob what he is doing, the effect is to add the proposition that she
wants him to tell her what he is doing. When Ann promises Bob to hire
him, the effect is to add her commitment to hire him. Many things Ann
tells Bob require presuppositions for them to be acceptable. In saying,
Even Connie has read Ulysses. Ann takes it for granted that people
other than Connie have read Joyce, and that Connie wasn't expected
to have. What if those presuppositions are lacking? As Lewis noted,
"Say something that requires a missing presupposition, and straight-

---

[1] Here Stalnaker refers explicitly to the technical notions or common and mutual
knowledge proposed by Lewis (1969) and Schiffer (1972); for more on the need for
this criterion, see Chapter 1, this volume, and Cohen (1978).

way that presupposition springs into existence, making what you said acceptable after all" (339). So Ann adds to their common ground not only that Connie has read the novel, but also that other people have and that Connie wasn't expected to have. Adding these extra presuppositions has been called *bridging* (Clark and Haviland 1974, 1977) and *accommodation* (Lewis 1979). This process is ubiquitous.

But the models of discourse mentioned so far all skirt an essential requirement for the accumulation of common ground—namely, that the participants establish that each utterance has been understood as intended. Suppose that Ann utters *She's leaving* in trying to assert that Connie is leaving her job. That act doesn't automatically add the content of what is asserted to what is presupposed. What if Bob is distracted and doesn't hear Ann? What if he thinks she has uttered *She's sleeping*? What if he thinks she is referring to Diane and not Connie? What if he thinks Connie's leaving her husband and not her job? In these and other cases, Ann's beliefs about their common ground will change in one direction, and Bob's in another. Instead of accumulating, their beliefs will diverge, setting the stage for further divergences. Ann and Bob must take positive steps to see that the content of her assertion is added to common ground.

Most models of discourse deal with this issue via the following tacit idealization: Each participant assumes that the content of each utterance is automatically added to common ground. Once Ann has uttered *She's leaving* in the right context, she and Bob are done. He will have understood it as intended, and the two of them can mutually believe this. A few models (e.g., Grosz and Sidner 1986; Litman and Allen 1987; Stalnaker 1978) tacitly make a weaker, conditional idealization: Each participant assumes that the content of an utterance is added to common ground *unless there is evidence to the contrary*. Ann and Bob repair any troubles they encounter with Ann's utterance, and once they have done that, they add its contents to common ground. They don't require or offer *positive* evidence of understanding.

These two idealizations, of course, are just that—idealizations—and in detail incorrect. They work only for conversations with certain features removed.[2] But, as we will argue, many of these features are essential to the process by which common ground actually accumulates. Excluding them misrepresents not only the process of accumulation, but also, ultimately, such phenomena as illocutionary acts, definite ref-

---

[2]Many models of discourse are designed around entirely artificial examples, and the rest, around natural examples sanitized in various ways. The question is how sanitized. The London-Lund transcripts, too, fail to represent certain features, but they include more than most.

erence, repairs, and certain processes of producing and understanding utterances.

What Ann and Bob need are systematic procedures for establishing the mutual belief that Bob has understood what Ann meant. Our proposal is that they do this via a collective process we call *contributing* to discourse (Clark and Schaefer 1987; Chapter 4, this volume; Isaacs and Clark 1987; Wilkes-Gibbs 1986).

2 Contributions to Discourse

Suppose that one person, a *contributor*, wants to contribute something to a conversation with other participants, his or her *partners*. By our proposal, making such a contribution requires two things. One is that the contributor try to specify the content of his or her contribution, and the partners try to register that content. Ann tries to tell Bob that Connie is leaving, and he tries to register that information. This process we will call *content specification*. The second requirement is that the contributor and partners together try to reach the following criterion:

Grounding criterion. The contributor and the partners mutually believe that the partners have understood what the contributor meant, to a criterion sufficient for current purposes.

Ann and Bob try to establish the mutual belief that he has understood that she believes Connie is leaving. This process we will call content grounding or, simply, *grounding*. It is this process, we propose, that enables common ground to accumulate in an orderly way. It satisfies the common ground and accumulation assumptions and replaces the tacit idealization that is otherwise needed. Together these two processes¡ create a unit of conversation we will call a *contribution*.

What type of unit is a contribution? Traditionally, intentional acts have come in at least two types—*individual* acts and *collective* acts (Chapter 7, this volume; Grosz and Sidner 1989; Searle 1989). When Ann shakes a stick, plays the piano, or paddles a kayak, she is performing an individual act—an act performed by an individual. When Ann and Bob shake hands, play a duet, or paddle a canoe together, the pair of them are performing a collective act—an act done by a collective, two or more people acting in ensemble. Yet in the hand shake, we can identify three distinct acts:

   (a) the collective act of Ann and Bob shaking hands;

   (b) Ann's individual act as part of (a);

   (c) Bob's individual act as part of (a).

The individual acts in (b) and (c), however, are of a special type. When Ann shakes a stick, her act is *autonomous*, something she could do without coordinating with anyone else. But when she shakes Bob's hand as *part of* (a), her act is something she can achieve only as part of the collective act of shaking hands. What she does just isn't the same as pumping Bob's hand when he is unconscious or not cooperating. The first requires Bob to do his part, and the second doesn't. We can therefore distinguish two types of individual acts: *participatory acts* are those that an agent performs as parts of collective acts; and *autonomous acts* are those that an agent performs on his or her own. Every collective act is performed by means of participatory acts.

The proposal here is that contributions are participatory acts. When Ann tells Bob that she is busy, she is performing an individual act: She is contributing an assertion to the discourse. But this is something she can only do as part of a collective act in which Bob also does his part. Again we can identify three acts:

(a) the collective act of Ann and Bob adding what Ann meant to their common ground;

(b) Ann's individual act of contributing to the discourse as part of (a);

(c) Bob's individual act of registering Ann's contribution as part of (a).

Many units of conversation—words, phrases, clauses, sentences, tone units, and the like—are created by a speaker acting autonomously. But contributions are created by the participants acting collectively. They emerge only as the contributor and partners coordinate actions in just the right way. We will use the term "contribution" to refer both to Ann's participatory act and to the collective unit of conversation formed by it.

An Example

Consider this attempt by one man, A, to ask another, B, how much time Norman gets off (from the London-Lund corpus):[3]

A. is it . how much does Norman get off - -
B. pardon

---

[3]In our examples we will retain the following symbols from the London-Lund notation: "." for a brief pause (of one light syllable); "-" for a unit pause (of one stress unit or foot); "," for the end of tone unit, which we mark only if it comes mid-turn; "(laughs)" or single parentheses for contextual comments; "((words))" or double parentheses for incomprehensible words; and "*yes*" or asterisks for paired instances of simultaneous talk.

A. how much does Norman get off
B. oh, only Friday and Monday
A. m
B. [continues]

Traditionally, one would describe A as having asked B his question by uttering the sentence *How much does Norman get off*. But that description won't do. Although A utters this sentence, he clearly recognizes that he hasn't *succeeded* in asking B his question. Our interest is in how A succeeds.

The process is initiated when A issues the utterance *how much does Norman get off*. The trouble is, B apparently doesn't hear it, so he says *pardon* to get A to re-present it, and this A does. This time B responds *oh*. In doing so, he asserts his new awareness of what A is doing. He then proceeds to answer A's question by uttering *only Friday and Monday*. Note that this answer gives further evidence of B's understanding. If he had replied *about six hundred pounds a month*, he would have displayed a misunderstanding, and that would have taken him and A several turns to clear up before going on. As it is, A accepts B's reply with *m*, what Schegloff (1982) has called a *continuer*, and that conversation goes on.

What A tries to contribute is a question. For it to be a genuine contribution, A must do more than *try* to ask it: He must believe that he has *succeeded* in asking it. That requires A and B to mutually believe that B has understood it. More precisely, A must come to believe he and B have satisfied the grounding criterion, and so must B. At what point does this occur? Clearly not after A's first *is it . how much does Norman get off*, for B has to ask A for a repeat. Nor is it right after A's second *how much does Norman get off*. Apparently, B thinks he has understood by that point, but feels the need to let A know by saying *oh*. In making this claim public, B establishes the mutual belief that *he* thinks he has understood. But that isn't enough to satisfy the grounding criterion, for A might not accept B's claim. Here, however, A does accept it, for he lets B give his answer. He could still have rejected B's claim of understanding by saying that B's answer was inappropriate, but he doesn't. So A and B reach the mutual belief in B's understanding only with the completion of B's answer, *only Friday and Monday*. A's contribution takes A and B four turns and five moves to complete.

This process makes essential use of all the mechanisms available for repair in conversation. As Schegloff, Jefferson, and Sacks (1977) have argued, repairs are organized according to the participants' opportunities for making them. In our example, the first opportunity comes within A's first turn, where the repair would ordinarily be initiated and made by A. As it happens, A makes such a repair. He begins with *is it*, interrupts himself, and starts anew with, *how much does Norman get off*. The second opportunity comes in the space immediately after A's turn, where the repair would ordinarily be initiated by B and made by A. In our example there is a repair here too. It is initiated by *pardon* and ends with *oh*. The third opportunity comes after B's response to A's question—after *only Friday and Monday*—where A could initiate and make the repair, but A doesn't do this.

The model of contributions we are proposing cannot be reduced simply to a system of repairs. The main reason is that the model relies not only on evidence of troubles that need repairing, but on positive evidence of understanding. One of the participants' goals is to reach the grounding criterion, and to do that, they must not only repair any troubles they encounter, but take positive steps to establish understanding and avoid trouble in the first place. Repairs are a necessary ingredient in the model, but they are not sufficient. We will here take for granted what is known about repairs.

Presentation and Acceptance

How do A and B achieve A's contribution to discourse? That is dictated in part by their joint goal—reaching the mutual belief that B has understood A well enough for current purposes. Most contributions begin with an action by A, the contributor. After all, he is the one who will be held responsible for asking the question, so it is usually up to him to initiate it. What happens next depends on both A and B, because they have to arrive at a mutually satisfactory interpretation of that action. The process of contributing divides conceptually into two phases.

Presentation Phase: A presents utterance *u* for B to consider. He does so on the assumption that, if B gives evidence *e* or stronger, he can believe that B understands what A means by *u*.

Acceptance Phase: B accepts utterance *u* by giving evidence *e'* that he believes he understands what A means by *u*. He does so on the assumption that, once A registers evidence *e'*, he will also believe that B understands.

We will speak of A *presenting* an action for B to consider, and of B *accepting* that action as having been understood. If these two steps are done right, A and B will each believe they have arrived at the mutual belief that B understands what A meant by his action. That, in turn, is what it takes for A to contribute to the discourse.

Ordinarily, the presentation and acceptance phases are identified with particular moves by A and B in the conversation. In our example, they are as follows:

Presentation Phase:

A. is it . how much does Norman get off –

Acceptance Phase:

B. pardon

A. how much does Norman get off

B. oh

The presentation phase is completed with A uttering *how much does Norman get off*, and the acceptance phase with B's *oh*. The way we will view it, A's contribution ends with the initiation of B's answer, *only Friday and Monday*. This, however, is something A and B can determine only retrospectively—after B has given his answer without A's objection. Only then can A and B think back and say, *Ah, that was the point at which we completed A's question and B initiated his answer*.

In the simplest cases, the presentation phase consists of A uttering a full or elliptical sentence (like *how much does Norman get off*) or just a word or phrase (like *pardon* or *only Friday and Monday*). In more complex cases, as we will see, it may consist of two or more contributions, which creates a hierarchy of contributions. In our scheme, every signal that one person directs toward another, whether verbal or nonverbal, is presented for the other person to consider.[4] This way, every utterance and every non-verbal signal belongs to the presentation phase of some contribution.

A should try in this phase to present an utterance that B can understand, and that isn't easy. The main problem is that A has to do this in real time, which often leads to mischosen words, premature commitments, and other errors. To be comprehensible, A has to detect and repair these errors as soon as possible (Schegloff et al. 1977). The result is often a convoluted presentation, such as A's here:

A. I I'm . we're not prepared, to go on being part, I'm not prepared to go on being part of Yiddish literature

B. yeah

A. we must ha- we're . big enough to stand on our own feet now

B. yes

---

[4]By signal, we mean any act by which the speaker means something in Grice's (1957) sense of nonnatural meaning; that is, it must involve what Grice called m-intentions.

A's self-repairs must themselves make clear what is being revised and how, and that also takes care. As Levelt (1983) has shown, speakers make self-repairs as soon as they detect a problem, and they almost always succeed in making them structurally unambiguous. The point is, a presentation is more than the uttering of a sentence. It is the creation in real time of a spoken structure from which the partner can identify the words, phrases, and sentences that the contributor intended as final.

Still, the acceptance phase is where most complications arise. It is generally initiated by the partner B indicating his state of understanding at that moment. There are two main cases to consider—when B indicates understanding, and when he indicates trouble understanding.

Evidence of Understanding

The acceptance phase is usually initiated by B giving A evidence that he believes he understands what A meant by *u*. B's evidence can be of several types. He can say that he understands, as with *I see* or *uh huh*. Or he can *demonstrate* that he understands. One way is by showing what it is he understands, as with a paraphrase, or what it is he heard, as with a verbatim repetition. Another is by showing his willingness to go on. The least obvious way is by showing continued attention. When B reveals no change in his attentive demeanor or eye contact, he implies that he hasn't detected any problems—that he believes he is understanding well enough for current purposes. The five main types of evidence then, are these;

1. **Continued attention.** B shows he is continuing to attend and therefore remains satisfied with A's presentation.
2. **Initiation of the relevant next contribution.** B starts in on the next contribution that would be relevant at a level as high as the current one.
3. **Acknowledgment.** B nods or says *uh huh*, *yeah*, or the like.
4. **Demonstration.** B demonstrates all or part of what he has understood A to mean.
5. **Display.** B displays verbatim all or part of A's presentation.

These types are graded roughly from weakest to strongest.

But what type of evidence *should* B present? Most presentations carry some indication of the strength of evidence A expects in order to convince him that B has understood. The presentation of a telephone number may project a verbatim display of that number (Clark and Schaefer 1987). Other presentations may project an acknowledgment like *uh huh*. Still others may project merely continued attention. Generally, the more complicated A's presentation, or the more demanding the current purpose, the more evidence should be needed to convince A that B has understood. What evidence is needed for which presentations is an empirical issue that we will examine.

Note that the acceptance process is recursive. B's evidence in response to A's presentation is itself a presentation that needs to be accepted. But where does the recursion stop? Suppose A presents *I'm leaving tomorrow.* Why isn't it possible for B to accept that by presenting m, which A accepts by presenting m, which B accepts by presenting m, and so on ad infinitum? What keeps the process from spinning out indefinitely? The answer, we propose, is this:

Strength of evidence principle. The participants expect that, if evidence e_0 is needed for accepting presentation u_0, and e_1 for accepting the presentation of e_0, then e_1 will be weaker than e_0.

B may accept A's presentation by uttering "m," but they expect something weaker to be able to accept that "m." The upshot is that every acceptance phase should end in continued attention or initiation of the next turn, the weakest evidence available.

If this rule is correct, recursion should rarely go beyond two or three cycles, and it rarely does. Here is an acceptance phase with three cycles (again from the London-Lund corpus):

A. F . six two
B. F six two
A. yes
B. thanks very much

A presents a book identification number *F six two.* B accepts the number by displaying it verbatim. A in turn accepts the display by the weaker evidence of *yes.* Finally, B accepts the *yes* by proceeding to the next contribution (see Clark and Schaefer 1987). The final step completes the acceptance phase of A's original contribution.

Evidence of Trouble in Understanding

There will be times, of course, when B doesn't hear or understand A's presentation entirely, as in the Norman example, and then B should initiate the acceptance phase by giving evidence of that trouble. Now, for any u' that is part of A's presentation, B could believe he is in any one of four successively stronger states of understanding (Clark and Schaefer 1987):

State 0. B didn't notice that A uttered any u'.
State 1. B noticed that A uttered some u' (but wasn't in State 2).

State 2. B correctly heard u' (but wasn't in State 3).

State 3. B understood what A meant by u'.

Ordinarily, State 3 presupposes State 2, which presupposes State 1, though B may sometimes believe he understands what A meant without knowing precisely what A presented. And, of course, B may be in different states for different parts of A's presentation. A and B's goal is to reach the mutual belief that B is in State 3 for the entire presentation.

The route by which A and B reach that goal depends on the partner's initial assessment of his understanding. In the Norman example, B indicates (with *pardon*) that he is in State 1 for A's entire initial presentation, and that leads A to repeat it. After the repeat, B indicates (with *oh*) that he is in State 3, and that allows him to go on to his answer. If B had initially indicated something else—for example, *Norman who?*—the acceptance phase would have taken a different course (see Clark and Schaefer 1987). As with positive evidence, each part of the acceptance phase is itself a contribution. B's *pardon* is the presentation phase of a request; A's repeat of *how much does Norman get off* is the presentation phase of a response to it; and B's *oh* is the presentation phase of a type of assertion. Each of these utterances initiates a contribution that is hierarchically subordinate to A's original contribution—his question.

One assumption of the model is the Principle of Least Collaborative Effort (Chapter 4, this volume). The idea is that the participants in a contribution try to minimize the total effort spent on that contribution—in both the presentation and the acceptance phases. Each time A initiates a contribution, he tries to anticipate how much effort it will take him and B, and he designs his presentation to minimize it. That means, for example, that A should repair his own errors as he goes along rather than leave them for B to deal with. Self-repairs by A usually take less total effort than repairs initiated by B. Empirically, indeed, self-repairs are preferred to repairs initiated by others (Schegloff et al. 1977). Generally, the more effort spent on designing the right presentation, the less effort is needed for acceptance. The problem is how to distribute the effort in order to minimize it, and that depends on both systematic and accidental features of the situation.

Patterns of Contributing

The model of contributions proposed here is mainly a logic for the process of adding to a discourse. How the process actually gets played out should depend on several factors. One is the evidential devices available. Face to face, people can nod, smile, and display mutual gaze;

on the telephone, they cannot. Face to face and on the telephone, people can exploit the precise timing of their utterances, as with brief interruptions (Jefferson 1973); on computer terminal hookups, they cannot (Cohen 1984). The course that contributions take should depend on the availability, effectiveness, and efficiency of devices such as these. It should also depend on the nature of the discourse at hand. Task-oriented dialogues, for example, may require stronger evidence of understanding on average than casual discussions (Chapter 4, this volume; Cohen 1984). In telephone calls to directory enquiries, for example, the caller and operator set a high criterion to establish precise names, addresses, and telephone numbers (Clark and Schaefer 1987). Other factors should be important, too.

Still, the model of contributions leads to three general predictions. First, if contributions are necessary for successful conversations, their presentation and acceptance phases should be identifiable in such conversations. Second, the forms the two phases take should depend on the evidential devices available and the requirements placed on that evidence. And third, presentation and acceptance phases should emerge as hierarchical structures reflecting the recursive process by which they are created. For evidence, we will look to the London-Lund corpus, including previous studies of the corpus by Oreström (1983), Stenström (1984), and Thavenius (1983). This corpus is a vast collection of casual British conversations surreptitiously tape recorded in and around university settings. The transcripts are marked for pauses, overlapping speech, intonation, and loudness, but not for gestures or eye contact. Since we cannot test for the use of continued attention or eye gaze (see Goodwin 1981), our analyses must remain incomplete in this respect. All of the examples cited in this paper are taken from this corpus.

Two patterns of contributions dominate this corpus. One occurs every time there is a relevant, orderly change in turns, and the other, every time a partner adds a *yes* or *uh huh* or *m* in the background. We will examine the logic behind these two patterns first. Yet the less common patterns of contributing are important in their own right, so we will examine some of those as well. We will argue that these patterns, taken together, account for most though not all patterns that occur in everyday conversation.

3 Contributions by Turns

The commonest form of contribution coincides with the turn. Almost every time a speaker starts a new turn, he or she either (a) accepts what the last speaker has just said or (b) initiates a repair of the problem they ran into in accepting it. In this way, a new contribution is initiated with each relevant change in turn. The question is, how is this done?

Many turns in conversation are organized in adjacency pairs (Schegloff and Sacks 1973). The prototype is the question–answer pair, as in the first two turns of this example:

A. how far is it from Huddersfield to Coventry .
B. um . about um a hundred miles -
A. so, in fact, if you were . living in London during that
   period, . you would be closer - .

Adjacency pairs consist of two ordered utterances, the first and second pair parts, produced by two different speakers. The two parts (here, the question and answer) come in types that specify which is to come first and which second; the form and content of the second part (here, the answer) depends on the type of the first part (the question). One crucial property is conditional relevance. Given a first pair part, a second pair part is conditionally relevant, that is, relevant and expectable, as the next utterance. Once A has asked the question, it is relevant and expectable for B to answer it in the next turn. Other types of adjacency pairs are illustrated in Table 1.

Conditional Relevance

These features of adjacency pairs are systematically exploited by people contributing to discourse. Take A's question, which he initiates by presenting, *How far is it from Huddersfield to Coventry?* How should B initiate the acceptance phase? If she thinks she understands A's presentation, she can reach her goal most efficiently by initiating her answer immediately. In doing that, she gives three types of evidence of understanding at once: (1) By passing up the chance to ask A for a repair, she indicates that she believes she has understood A's contribution. (2) By initiating an answer, a second pair part, she shows that she recognizes that A has asked a question, a first pair part. She does this by exploiting the conditional relevance of a second pair part given the first. (3) By formulating the answer she does, she displays part of her understanding of what particular question was asked. Her *Um about um a hundred miles* is consistent with A having asked a WH-question about distance. So when A accepts B's answer as an appropriate one, he also accepts 1, 2, and 3, B's evidence that he has understood what A meant. The crucial point is this: Giving an answer can be used to accept the presentation of a question by virtue

TABLE 1
Types of Adjacency Pairs

Types of Adjacency Pairs		Example	
First Part	Second Part	A's Utterance	B's Response
Question	Answer	Where is Connie?	At the store.
Request	Compliance/ Refusal	Please pass the horseradish.	[B passes the horseradish.]
Request	Acceptance/ Rejection	Please pass the horseradish.	Okay.
Proposal	Acceptance/ Rejection	Here is your change.	[B takes it.]
Offer	Acceptance/ Rejection	Would you like some coffee?	Yes, thanks.
Invitation	Acceptance/ Rejection	Come to dinner Sunday.	Okay.
Apology	Acceptance/ Rejection	Sorry.	Oh, that's all right.
Thanks	Acceptance/ Rejection	Thank you.	You're welcome.
Assessment	Agreement/ Disagreement	That film was terrible.	Yes, it was.
Compliment	Agreement/ Disagreement	Your new coat is beautiful.	Yes, it's nice.
Summons	Answer	Hey, Ben	Yes?
Greetings	Greetings	Hi, Ben.	Hi, Ann.
Farewell	Farewell	Goodbye.	Goodbye.

of its conditional relevance. That holds for the second part of any adjacency pair.

Answers, of course, are also contributions, so they, too, should have presentation and acceptance phases. The commonest way to accept an utterance as an answer is to exploit a slightly different form of conditional relevance. Take B's answer that it is about a hundred miles from Huddersfield to Coventry. This is not the first pair part of an adjacency pair. And yet, once it is on record, it is relevant and expectable that A will proceed to the use he wants to make of that information. That is, after the second part of an adjacency pair, it is conditionally relevant immediately to initiate the next contribution at the same level as those two parts.

We can see how this works in our example. Once B has uttered, *Um about um a hundred miles*, it is conditionally relevant for A to use this information, and he does. He initiates his acceptance by proceeding to the next contribution at the same level as B's answer, *So in fact if you were living in London during that period you would be closer*. In

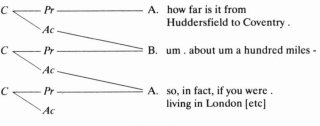

FIGURE 1

this way, A gives the same three types of evidence that B did with her answer: (1) he passes up the opportunity to ask B for a repair on her utterance; (2) he shows his recognition that B has answered his question; and (3) he displays part of his understanding of B's answer (by drawing a reasonable conclusion from it). As Sacks et al. (1974, 728) noted, "Regularly, then, a turn's talk will display its speaker's understanding of a prior turn's talk, or whatever other talk it marks itself as directed to" (see also Goffman 1976). So A accepts the presentation of B's answer via much the same rationale as B uses in accepting the presentation of A's question.

Contributions like A's question, B's answer, and A's next question can be represented in what we will call *contribution trees*. The tree for this example, shown in Figure 1, illustrates several features of contributions. First, every contribution (C) has a presentation phase (Pr) and an acceptance phase (Ac). Second, every utterance belongs to the presentation phase of some contribution. Third, as a result, most contributions are ultimately completed by the partner initiating some next contribution. (The rest are completed by evidence of continued attention.) We have denoted this by drawing a slanting line from Ac of the first contribution to the presentation of the next. And fourth, a contribution C_2 belongs to the acceptance phase of a previous contribution C_1 only if it directly addresses the hearing or understanding of Pr of C_1. Although Figure 1 has no embedded contributions, we will present other trees that do.

A word of caution. Contribution trees are not fixed beforehand. They emerge piece by piece as participants construct them in collaboration. They are often revised en route, and the function of certain utterances is determined only retrospectively. Revisions and retrospective identifications are impossible to capture in static trees. Yet we have tried to represent some of the emergent properties by placing on each line the contribution, presentation, or acceptance that the

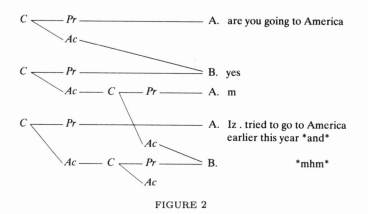

FIGURE 2

current speaker believes he or she is working on at the moment. We cannot always be sure even of these beliefs, and in some trees they have plausible alternatives.

Another way to initiate the acceptance phase of an answer, or of the second part of most adjacency pairs, is by explicit assertions of understanding. Take this example:

A. are you going to America
B. yes
A. m
A. Iz . tried to go to America earlier this year [continues]

A initiates his acceptance of B's answer by uttering *m*, explicitly asserting that he believes he has understood it, and then immediately goes on. Stenström (1984) has called these moves *follow-ups*. In her analysis of questions and answers in the London-Lund corpus, answers had follow-ups 41% of the time—36% of the time in face-to-face conversations and 50% of the time in telephone conversations—so they are common. The contribution tree for this example is shown in Figure 2.

On occasion, however, the questioner will understand an answer but reject it as inappropriate because it reveals a misunderstanding of the question, as in this example:

B. k who evaluates the property - - -
A. uh whoever you ask((ed)), . the surveyor for the building society
B. no, I meant who decides what price it'll go on the market -
A. (- snorts) . whatever people will pay - -
B. but why was Chetwynd Road so cheap - - -

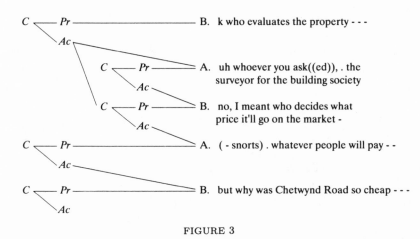

FIGURE 3

A's answer in line 2, *uh whoever you asked - - the surveyor for the building society*, shows B that she has misinterpreted the word *evaluates*. So B rejects her acceptance with *no* and rephrases what he meant, *who decides what price it'll go on the market*. This time A presents as her answer *whatever people will pay*, which B accepts by going on. B's *no, I meant . . .* is often called a third turn repair.

Consider the acceptance phase of B's question. Ordinarily, two partners treat the initiation of an appropriate answer as completing the acceptance of the question. But, as we said, they can only do that retrospectively, since they have to wait on the questioner accepting the answer as evidence of correct understanding. In this example, B rejects A's first answer as inappropriate. So A's answer, instead of initiating the next contribution, is now treated as the first move in the acceptance phase of B's question. The acceptance phase gets completed only with the initiation of A's second answer, *whatever people will pay*, which B does accept. The contribution tree that results is shown in Figure 3. It shows how A first accepts B's question by trying to answer it, but when B rejects A's interpretation of the question, the two of them leave A's answer high and dry, abandoning it altogether.

On still other occasions, a participant's attempt to contribute will fail when his or her presentation is ignored altogether. Consider this example:

C. well . I've got um . a boy ex Gordonstoun -
B. I say
C. who sticks out like a *sore thumb*

B. *what* what's his name then Charlie - -
C. and I've got . several flower people
B. ooh uh tha- that's nice.
C. oh it isn't actually, cos I've been giving them dictation - in English, . because their spelling's hopeless, their punctuation's worse you know
B. yeah

When B says *What's his name then Charlie?*, he appears to initiate a contribution asking C for the name of the ex-Gordonstoun boy. As it happens, C ignores B's presentation, and B lets it drop. So although B tried to ask a question, there is no evidence that he succeeded. He simply failed to contribute to the discourse. The conclusion is important: Acceptance requires more than just going on to a next contribution. It must be a *relevant* next contribution—such as an answer.

So far, then, we have two powerful methods for accepting presentations. Partners can accept a presentation—almost any presentation— by proceeding to a relevant next contribution at the same level as the current one. Or they can explicitly assert that they understand with a *yes*, *right*, or *I see*.

Side Sequences

In adjacency pairs, when one partner doesn't accept the first pair part, he or she will usually initiate a repair sequence, as here:

A. ((where *are* you))
  B. m?
  A. where *are* you .
B. well I'm still at college .
A. [continues]

B apparently doesn't hear A's question and asks for a repeat. Or consider this example:

A. well wo uh what shall we do about uh *this* boy then
  B. Duveen?
  A. m
B. well I propose to *write*, uh saying . I'm very sorry I cannot, uh teach . at the *institute* . [continues]

B seems unclear about A's reference—which boy?—and initiates a repair to clear it up. In both examples, A and B step aside for two turns (the indented ones) to clear up the problem before B initiates his answer.

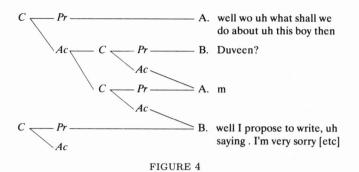

		A.	well wo uh what shall we do about uh this boy then
		B.	Duveen?
		A.	m
		B.	well I propose to write, uh saying . I'm very sorry [etc]

FIGURE 4

The device A and B use in the two indented turns are *side sequences* (Jefferson 1972).[5] Once A has presented *Well wo uh what shall we do about uh this boy then?*, B initiates the acceptance phase by opening up a side sequence to clear up A's reference to the boy. He asks a question (with *Duveen?*), which A tries to answer (with *m*). But that doesn't complete the acceptance phase of A's question. B needs to accept both A's original presentation and A's *m*. A and B, however, each recognize that, once the side sequence is completed, it is again conditionally relevant for B to answer A's question. So B can complete his acceptance of A's question by initiating that answer, *Well I propose to write uh saying I'm very sorry I cannot teach at the institute.* In doing this, he also gives evidence he has understood A's *m*, closing the side sequence. Unless A rejects B's answer, A's contribution is complete. The tree that results is shown in Figure 4.

Side sequences can be initiated not just after first pair parts, but after almost any presentation. What makes them so useful is that they allow the partners to focus on precisely those features of a presentation that are troublesome. They can focus on general hearing, as with *What?*, or on highly specific information, as with *Duveen?* (see Clark and Schaefer 1987; Schegloff et al. 1977). Also, side sequences can be extended until the problem is cleared up, as in this five-turn side sequence:

A. what film have you been to see .
B. film .
A. I thought you went . you were going to the National - Theatre - National Film Theatre

---

[5]Specialized types of side sequences have been studied under the terms insertion sequence by Schegloff (1972), clarification and correction subdialogues by Litman and Allen (1981) and debugging explanations by Grosz and Sidner (1986).

  B. no no, . um . that was at the weekend, - .
    ((we were discussing)) the weekend, remember
  A. *oh yes* - . yes . yes
 B. I'm going to see it's uh - - (- sighs) ((it's called)) il Posto - it's
   uh - . Olmi ((I think))

Side sequences like these are closed by the participants proceeding on to the next contribution at a level as high as the contribution of which they are a part. They are one of the commonest and most versatile grounding devices available.

 All this leads to a fundamental generalization about contributions: *A new contribution is initiated with every cooperative change in turns.* Such a contribution closes the current one when it is relevant and at a level as high as the current one—subject to a veto by the current contributor. Or it opens a side sequence that is closed when a relevant new contribution is initiated at a level above the side sequence. Although contributions created this way can be of any length, they tend not to go on too long. In Oreström's (1983) analysis of the London-Lund conversations, there was a new turn after a median interval of thirteen words; two-thirds of all turns were less than twenty words long. So contributions formed this way are of a practical length. They are long enough for a contributor to perform complete illocutionary acts like assertions, questions, and offers. They are also short enough to lie within the participants' memory limitations and allow troubles to get repaired before they snowball.

4 Contributions within Turns

When a speaker takes an extended turn—as in an anecdote, long description, or involved instruction—the partners ordinarily accept separate portions of it by means of what we will call *acknowledgments.* These are expressions such as *mhm, yes,* and *quite* that are spoken in the background, or gestures such as head nods and smiles. Consider this example:

 B. but you daren't set synthesis again you see, . you set analysis,
   and you can put the answers down, and your assistant
   examiners will work them,
 A. *yes quite, yes, yes*
 B. but if you give them a give n them a free hand on synthesis,
   and they'd be marking all sorts of stuff, because they can't do
   the stuff *themselves,*
 A.   *quite m*
 B. I must watch [continues]

As B comes to the end of certain thoughts, A acknowledges them with *yes*, *quite*, and *m* in various combinations. How do these work?

Acknowledgments fall into two major categories—*continuers* and *assessments*. People use continuers such as *m*, *yes*, *quite*, and *I see*, according to Schegloff (1982), to display continued attention and to indicate they recognize that the primary speaker is in the middle of an extended unit of speech. They use them to signal that they are passing up the opportunity to initiate a repair on the turn so far and, by implication, that they believe they have understood it so far. Continuers are signals for the primary speaker to continue. With assessments such as *gosh, really?*, *oh*, and *good God*, people do all this as well as offer brief assessments of what is said. Acknowledgments generally do *not* constitute turns. When A says, *yes quite, yes, yes*, he is speaking without taking the floor (Schegloff 1982).

Acknowledgments are generally placed at or near the ends of major grammatical constituents. In the London-Lund corpus, continuers occur right at grammatical boundaries 77% of the time and near such boundaries most of the rest of the time (Oreström 1983). And they tend to overlap with the primary speaker's talk. In the London-Lund corpus, they do so 45% of the time overall—and even 33% of the time when they occur right at grammatical boundaries (Oreström 1983). Assessments, which are much rarer, also tend to occur at or near grammatical boundaries, though they are generally engineered to occur without overlap (Goodwin 1986).

Acknowledgments are placed where they are in order to mark the scope of their acceptance. In our example, A places *yes quite, yes, yes* over the last phrase of B's utterance to indicate acceptance of B's presentation up through that phrase. He places *quite m* over the last phrase of B's next utterance to indicate acceptance of everything from the last acknowledgment through this phrase. Each acknowledgment marks the final boundary of his scope, though not always with the precision shown in our example.

But an acknowledgment must itself be understood and accepted as evidence of understanding of the material in its scope. B can mishear or misunderstand it—*Pardon me?* or *What?* Even if he understands it, he may reject the claim A is making with it—that he has understood B's presentation. B might respond, *Are you really listening?* or *Do you understand?* (Think of half-listening spouses or children.) A has to understand B's acknowledgment and accept it as adequate evidence.

This may be a problem in principle, but it is rarely a problem in practice. Partners generally use acknowledgments only when they are

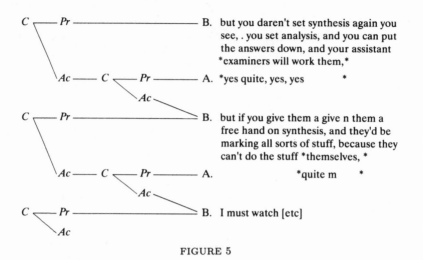

FIGURE 5

quite confident that they understand and that the contributor isn't expecting strong evidence. That helps explain why acknowledgments are so brief and are reduced in loudness and lower in pitch (Oreström 1983): The partners don't expect them to need or be given much consideration. The contributors, in turn, should find them easy to understand and accept. All they need to do to accept them is show continued attention and proceed without a break to the next contribution at the same level as their last one. The contribution tree for our example is shown in Figure 5.

Acknowledgments such as *yes*, *quite*, or *m*, therefore, divide extended turns into units that are practical for establishing understanding and correcting misunderstandings. The participants complete a contribution at the end of every major grammatical unit in which the partner offers an acknowledgment. In Oreström's (1983) analysis of turns thirty words or longer in the London-Lund conversations, there was an acknowledgment after a median interval of only nine words; 80% of the time there was at least one acknowledgment every fifteen words. And since these conversations were face-to-face, there were probably also head nods, smiles, and other non-verbal acknowledgments. The contributions created this way are about the same size as those created by turns.

Acknowledgments, in brief, are backgrounded attempts by partners to create contributions from extended turns, and they almost always succeed.

5 Contributions via Sentence Parts

Most of the contributions discussed so far have been associated with sentences. The contributor presents a full or elliptical sentence, like *how much does Norman get off* or *who evaluates the property* or *oh*, and it is accepted as a whole. These contributions are used for asking questions, making assertions, making requests—that is, for performing illocutionary acts á la Austin (1962). When we think of contributions, this is what we normally think of—people contributing to conversation by means of questions, assertions, requests, and other illocutionary acts.

Many contributions, however, are associated with only parts of sentences—usually single words or phrases. With these, contributors perform only parts of illocutionary acts—such propositional acts as referring, naming, denoting, and predicating (Searle 1969). But why contribute anything so small as that? There is usually a special reason. The contributor is uncertain about some piece of information, or needs help on some item, or wants to present an utterance too complex to be understood in one piece. In this way, contributions via sentence parts appear to be less preferred than contributions one or more sentences in size. Still, they are common enough. We will examine only three types of such contributions—installment contributions, trial constituents, and collaborative completions.

Installment Contributions

When speakers have complicated information to present, they often take more explicit steps to make sure they are being understood. One way is by presenting the information in *installments*. In this example, A has just asked B on the telephone, *could you possibly tell me what Sir Humphrey Davy's address is—Professor Worth thought you might know*, and B is answering:

B. Banque Nationale de Liban - - -
  A. yes
B. nine to thirteen.
  A. sorry
  B. nine . to . thirteen
  A. yeah .
B. King Edward Street - -
  A. yeah -
B. London .
  A. yes
B. NE two P -

    A. yes -
  B. four AF -
    A. F -
    B. yes
  A. thanks very much .

What precisely is going on here?

B's answer is accomplished in six *installments*, each taking the form of a contribution, with a presentation and an acceptance phase. B divides her presentation into six parts, first *Bank Nationale de Liban*, then *nine to thirteen*, and on through *four AF*. Furthermore, she pronounces these as items in a list, placing a rising or fall–rise intonation on the first five installments and a falling intonation on the last. So when B pronounces *Liban* with a rising intonation and then pauses, she indicates that this is only the first segment of her presentation and invites A to indicate his understanding of it. A accepts that presentation with *yes*. As for the second segment, A doesn't understand it the first time around, so B re-presents it, this time with pauses between the words. The contribution looks like this:

Presentation Phase:
  B. nine to thirteen .

Acceptance Phase:
  A. sorry
  B. nine . to . thirteen
  A. yeah .

The remaining four installments are accepted separately as well.

These six contributions are themselves parts of a more inclusive contribution, which has its own presentation and acceptance phases. Its presentation consists of the six installment contributions, and its acceptance is achieved by A initiating the next contribution at the same level, *thank you very much*. The contribution tree for B's entire answer is shown in Figure 6 (see also Clark and Schaefer 1987). So dividing a presentation into installments creates hierarchical structure in the presentation phase of a contribution.

Why use installment presentations? One reason is to enable the partners to register the presented information verbatim, perhaps to write it down, as with addresses, telephone numbers, and recipes (see Clark and Schaefer 1987; Goldberg 1975). Another reason is to make sure, in instructing addressees, that they have understood each step before going on (Cohen 1984; Chapter 4, this volume). But installment presentations also crop up in quite ordinary descriptions, as here:

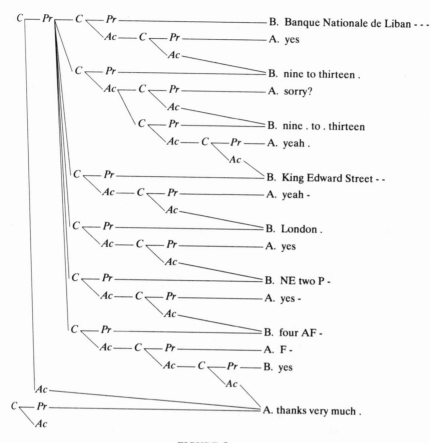

B. Banque Nationale de Liban - - -
A. yes
B. nine to thirteen .
A. sorry?
B. nine . to . thirteen
A. yeah .
B. King Edward Street - -
A. yeah -
B. London .
A. yes
B. NE two P -
A. yes -
B. four AF -
A. F -
B. yes
A. thanks very much .

FIGURE 6

B. how how was the wedding -
A. oh it was it was really good, it was uh it was a lovely day
B. yes
A. and . it was a super place, . to have it . of course
B. yes -
A. and we went and sat on sat in an orchard, at Grantchester,
and had a huge tea *afterwards (laughs -)*
B. *(laughs - -)*.
A. **uh**
B. **it does** sound, very nice indeed

By presenting her description in installments, A gets B to help her
complete her extended answer without interruption (Schegloff 1982).

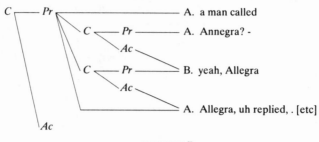

FIGURE 7

Trial Constituents

Another way of grounding mid-presentation is with *trial constituents*. Sometimes speakers find themselves about to present a name or description that they aren't sure is factually correct or entirely comprehensible. They can present that constituent—usually a name or description—with what Sacks and Schegloff (1979) have called a *try marker*, a rising intonation followed by a slight pause, and get their partners to confirm or correct it before completing the presentation. Consider this example:

A. so I wrote off to . Bill, . uh who ((had)) presumably
   disappeared by this time, certainly, a man called Annegra? -
B. yeah, Allegra
A. Allegra, uh replied, . uh and I . put . two other people, who'd
   been in for . the BBST job . with me [continues]

Apparently, A is trying to assert, *A man called Annegra replied, and I ...*, but he becomes uncertain about the name Annegra. He therefore presents *Annegra* as a trial constituent with rising intonation and a slight pause. B responds *yeah* to confirm that she knows who he is trying to refer to, and then corrects the name to *Allegra*. A then accepts the correction by representing *Allegra* and continuing on. The entire correction is made swiftly and efficiently. What we have is a local contribution, complete with its own presentation and acceptance phases, as follows:

Presentation Phase:
A. Annegra? -
Acceptance Phase:
B. yeah, Allegra

This is embedded within A's larger presentation of *a man called Allegra replied*, as shown in the contribution tree in Figure 7.

Completions

In initiating a contribution, speakers usually present an utterance for their partners' consideration. Sometimes, however, that utterance is completed by the partners, as here:

A. um the problem is a that you((′ve)) got to get planning consent -
B. before you start -
A. before you start on that part, yes
A. you can do anything internally, you wish
B. but the big stuff is, the external stuff [continues]

A begins, *um the problem is that you've got to get planning consent*, and pauses, perhaps searching for a way to express what she wants to say next. This leads B to offer a plausible completion, *before you start*. Is the completion appropriate? That is up to A, and indeed she accepts it by repeating *before you start*, amending it with *on that part*, and asserting acceptance with *yes*. Once that is completed A continues with her turn. As Wilkes-Gibbs (1986; see also Lerner 1987) has argued from an extensive corpus of completions, they tend to follow these steps:

1. A presents a sentence fragment.
2. A may indicate she is having trouble completing it.
3. B offers a completion, often with a questioning intonation.
4a. A may explicitly accept B's completion (*yes*) or reject it (*no*).
4b. B may repeat A's completion verbatim, or B represents it correctly.
5. The conversation continues.

Explicit rejections at step 4a tend to precede the correction at step 4b, but explicit acceptances tend to follow the repetition, yielding 4b then 4a. And when these two steps don't occur, the completion gets accepted in some other way. In our example, we find at least five of these six steps. Collaborative completions are surprisingly common in everyday conversation.

If B has completed A's sentence, then whose assertion, whose contribution, is it? Actually, there are two contributions. One is A's when she asserts, *the problem is that you've got to get planning consent before you start on that part*. Even if she hadn't repeated *before you start*, she would have been held accountable for having made this claim; she would have produced the first fragment and accepted B's version of the rest of it. But B has also made a contribution with his completion.

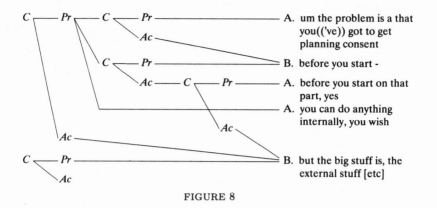

FIGURE 8

.In offering it, he accepts her first fragment and helps complete it. B's contribution takes this form:

Presentation Phase:

  B. before you start -

Acceptance Phase:

  A. before you start on that part, yes

But this is part of A's whole contribution, as shown in Figure 8.

Completions may become much more extended as the primary speaker and partner search explicitly for a name, as here:

  C. and we went to Bridport, and we went to Weymouth one day, um we went to um - . what was it called .
  A. you didn't go inland -
  C. um not very much, - - . oh what's that -
  A. *((3 sylls))*
  C. *really* lovely place, along the coast, where th- where the swannery is
  A. oh um - - Abbot something
  C. yes -
  A. Abbot Newton -* - Abbotsbury*
  C. *no, Abbotsbury,* that's right -
  C. it was lovely

C requests completions with the pleas *what was it called, oh what's that, where th- where the swannery is,* and A does his best to help out. They finally make it when C says, *Abbotsbury that's right,* and goes on. So although the acceptance phase runs quite a complicated course, it has essentially the same structure as the simpler example.

TABLE 2
Typical Forms of Evidence Elicited by Presentations

PRESENTATION OF UTTERANCE u	ACCEPTANCE OF EVIDENCE e
Acknowledgment	Continued attention
Completed turn	Initiation of next relevant turn
Portion of continuing turn	Acknowledgment, often overlapping
Installment of extended turn	Acknowledgment during pause
Installment for rote memory	Verbatim display
Trial constituent	Explicit answer
Incomplete utterance	Completion
Completion	Repeat plus assent

6 Conclusions

When people participate in a discourse, they generally try to make a success of it. According to most theories, all they have to do to achieve success is utter the right sentence at the right time. But this leaves too much to chance. Was the utterance heard correctly? Was it interpreted correctly? Do all the participants believe it was interpreted correctly? In actual conversations, we have argued, people hold out for a higher criterion. They try to ground what is said—to reach the mutual belief that what the speaker meant has been understood by everyone well enough for current purposes. In doing this, they create units of discourse called contributions.

Shapes of Contributions

Contributions take the shape they do, we have argued, because they are constructed in two phases. In the presentation phase, the contributor, say Ann, typically presents an utterance u for her partner, say Bob, to consider. In the acceptance phase, Bob then provides her with evidence e that he believes he understands what Ann means by u, evidence she then accepts. But these two phases admit so many options and complications that they take a variety of shapes. Here are some of them.

Ann's presentation can take any of the forms in the left hand column of Table 2 and many other forms as well. It may also contain subordinate contributions. A difficult instruction, for example, can be divided up and presented in installments, each with its own presentation and acceptance phases, and yet the entire instruction is treated as a presentation that requires an acceptance phase. This is one source of embedding in contributions.

In the acceptance phase, the evidence that Bob offers depends in part on the type of presentation it is in response to. The right hand column in Table 2 lists the typical form of evidence elicited in our corpus for each type of presentation. Since we had no access to eye contact, head nods, or other gestures, we can only assume that acknowledgments were accepted with continued attention. The other presentation types were accepted with linguistic acts. These acts, of course, are themselves contributions, with presentation and acceptance phases, and that makes the acceptance phase inherently recursive. This recursion stops, however, once Ann and Bob reach the weakest type of positive evidence—namely, continued attention—and that generally occurs in one or two cycles. So this is a second source of embedding in contributions.

The acceptance phase takes a different course whenever Bob has had trouble understanding. In that case he ordinarily initiates the acceptance phase by indicating what the trouble is—*Duveen?* or *pardon* or *m?*—and the rest of the acceptance phase is spent clearing it up. Different devices are available for indicating different types of trouble (Clark and Schaefer 1987; Schegloff et al. 1977), and we have illustrated only a few. This is a third source of embedding in contributions. The important point is that these devices help define what constitutes positive evidence of understanding. Offering a continuer like *uh huh* and initiating the next relevant turn are effective as positive evidence in part because they show that the partner is choosing not to initiate a repair.

Size of Contributions

Contributions come in many sizes. Some are initiated by single words or phrases, and others by clauses, full sentences, or whole turns. What determines the size? If the participants stopped to ground every word, it would take too long to say anything, and yet if they didn't stop often enough, misunderstandings could snowball before they could be repaired. The participants should generally settle for something in between. Indeed, the two commonest devices for completing contributions—new turns and acknowledgments—resulted in contributions with median lengths of 9 to 13 words.

But participants systematically vary the size and make-up of their contributions to suit current purposes. According to the contribution model, Bob is to understand Ann to a criterion sufficient for current purposes. If either of them anticipates that Bob will find some word, phrase, or clause especially difficult or want to register some information verbatim, they can divide the discourse into contributions of the corresponding size. We saw in Figure 6 how a complicated address to be registered verbatim was divided into installments (see also Clark and Schaefer 1987). Likewise, if it is anticipated that Bob will understand everything easily, they can make their contributions longer. Figure 5 shows how an extended description that was easy to understand was divided into presentations several clauses long. Generally, the more difficult it is anticipated a unit will be to understand well enough for current purposes, the more contributions it will be divided into.

The preferred contribution, nevertheless, appears to be the length of a simple or complex sentence. Most contributions are initiated by uttering a full sentence (e.g., *how far is it from Huddersfield to Coventry*), an elliptical sentence (e.g., *about a hundred miles*), a phrasal sentence (e.g., *sorry*), or an atomic sentence (e.g., *yes* or *oh* or *m*). Many of these are accomplished as complete turns and therefore count as complete contributions. And when a turn consists of more than one sentence, it is often broken up by acknowledgments into contributions the size of single sentences.

Our conjecture is that the preferred contribution is one or more illocutionary acts á la Austin (1962). When Ann initiates a contribution by uttering a full sentence, she is trying to make an assertion, ask a question, or make an apology, or do more than one of these at a time. Not that she cannot contribute a single propositional act instead, but she will do that only for special reasons. In the first installment in Figure 6, B contributed only a reference (*Banque Nationale de Liban*) because it was crucial for A to get the reference verbatim. Even then, the reference was part of a larger contribution in which B was making an assertion (see Cohen 1984). The same is true of trial constituents and completions. And these are not the only forms contributions can take.

The process of contributing cannot be fixed beforehand because it is subject to accidental features of the situation. Suppose Ann wants to contribute an assertion to the on-going social process. Although she may begin expecting to do this in one unbroken action, she may discover along the way that she can't. It may happen that Bob gets distracted and mishears her, or she cannot retrieve a name quickly enough, or she misjudges how much he knows about a referent. Any accident like this can force Ann and Bob into a complex acceptance process that may bring in any of the devices we have mentioned. In conversations there are no crystal balls. Unforeseen circumstances can take contributions off in entirely unexpected directions.

Contributions, therefore, are different from most standard linguistic units. They are not formulated autonomously by the speaker according to some prior plan, but emerge as the contributor and partner act collectively. Success depends on the coordinated actions by the two of them. We have tried to show what these actions look like and why.

6

Understanding by Addressees and Overhearers

WITH MICHAEL F. SCHOBER

In conversation speakers design their utterances to be understood against the common ground they share with their addressees—their common experience, expertise, dialect, and culture. That ordinarily gives addressees an advantage over overhearers in understanding. Addressees have an additional advantage, we propose, because they can actively collaborate with speakers in reaching the mutual belief that they have understood what was said, whereas overhearers cannot. As evidence for the proposal, we looked at triples of people in which one person told another person in conversation how to arrange twelve complex figures while an overhearer tried to arrange them, too. All three began as strangers with the same background information. As predicted, addressees were more accurate at arranging the figures than overhearers even when the overhearers heard every word. Other evidence suggests that the very process of understanding is different for addressees and overhearers.

People understand each other in conversations by gathering evidence about each other's intentions. How do they do that? The traditional view, which we will call the *autonomous view*, is that they listen to the words uttered, decode them, and interpret them against what they take to be the common ground of the participants in the conversation (e.g., Anderson 1985; Clark and Haviland 1977; Fodor 1983; Johnson-Laird 1983; Sperber and Wilson 1986; van Dijk and Kintsch 1983; see also Chapter 5, this volume). An alternative view, the *collaborative view*, is that speakers and their addressees go beyond these autonomous actions and collaborate with each other moment by moment to try to ensure that what is said is also understood. Collaboration

176

takes extra processes and may require extra steps in the conversation (Chapter 4, this volume; Garrod and Anderson 1987; Goodwin 1981; Kraut, Lewis, and Swezey 1982; Schegloff 1982; Schegloff, Jefferson, and Sacks 1977).

These two views contrast in the way addressees and overhearers understand. Addressees are participants in the conversation at the moment, and overhearers are not (Goffman 1976; McGregor 1986). Speakers are responsible for making themselves understood to the other participants, but not to overhearers. Indeed, speakers can take one of several attitudes toward overhearers (Chapters 7 and 9, this volume). They may try to disclose, conceal, or disguise what they say, or they may be indifferent toward them. We will limit ourselves to the case of indifference. On the autonomous view, overhearers should do as well as addressees in understanding utterances in conversation whenever they have the same background as the addressees. They might even do better because they do not have to worry about what to say next, which can only interfere with the process of understanding. On the collaborative view, however, overhearers should be at a disadvantage even if they have all the right background. Let us see why.

In conversation, the participants accumulate information as part of their common ground—their mutual knowledge, beliefs, and assumptions (Clark 1985; Gazdar 1979; Lewis 1979; Stalnaker 1978). If Susan and Evan know each other, they begin each conversation with a good deal of common ground, and, as they talk, they add to it. They design their utterances to be understood against their accumulating common ground. When Susan tells Evan *He's here*, she intends him to identify who she is referring to by consulting their common ground. Its source may be their conversation so far (Steve was just mentioned), their shared perceptual surroundings (Ed just walked in), previous joint experiences (Susan and Evan had arranged to meet Scott at that time), information universally known or believed in one of the cultural communities to which Susan and Evan know they both belong (the Pope is visiting that day), or some combination of these (Chapter 1, this volume).

On both views of understanding, overhearers should be at a disadvantage whenever they are ignorant of critical parts of the participants' common ground. Suppose Liz is overhearing Susan speak to Evan. She should have trouble if she has not caught the first part of the conversation, or if Susan and Evan are old friends, or if Susan and Evan are members of a culture she does not belong to. Her difficulties should occur on just those parts of Susan's meaning that depend on common ground to which Liz is not privy (Chapter 9, this volume). By the autonomous view, however, Liz should do as well as Evan whenever three conditions hold: (1) Susan, Evan, and Liz are from the same cultures, (2) they do not know each other in advance, and (3) Liz has listened in on the conversation from the start.

On the collaborative view, overhearers should be at a disadvantage even when all three conditions hold. The idea is that the participants in a conversation try to establish the mutual belief that the listeners have understood what the speaker meant to a criterion sufficient for current purposes. This is a collaborative process, called *grounding*, that requires actions by both speakers and their addressees (Clark and Schaefer 1987). A reference or a question, for example, is not considered complete until both speaker and addressees have acknowledged that they have established the mutual belief that it has been understood. Consider this attested example (Svartvik and Quirk 1980):

A: well wo uh what shall we do about uh this boy then -
B: Duveen?
A: m
B: well I propose to write uh saying . I'm very sorry I cannot - uh teach . at the institute

Although A tries to ask B what should be done about Duveen, A and B don't consider the question complete until A has cleared up B's problem well enough for B to answer *well I propose to write*, etc. It takes three turns for A's question to become complete (see Chapter 5, this volume).

Overhearers should be at a disadvantage just because they don't have grounding as a resource. Suppose C overhears the first utterance, and B understands who *this boy* refers to but C does not. B won't have to ask *Duveen?*, but C, not being a participant in the conversation, has no way of asking for such a confirmation. A and B will continue in the mutual belief that B has understood A's assertion, whereas C cannot be sure she has understood it. That puts her at a disadvantage.

To make the argument concrete, let us define four time points in the understanding of a speech act such as an assertion or question.

1. **Initiation point.** This is the point at which a speaker initiates the speech act of interest. In our example, the initiation point of A's question is at the word *well*.

2. **Completion point.** This is the point at which the participants deem the grounding of that speech act to be complete. In our example, the completion point of A's question is at the end of the sound *m*.

3. Recognition point. This is the point at which the addressee believes that he or she has grasped what the speaker meant. In our example, that presumably coincides with the completion point.

4. Conjecture point. This is the point at which the overhearer conjectures that he or she has grasped what the speaker meant.

Suppose two listeners B and C have the same background knowledge, but B is a participant in the conversation and C is an overhearer. On the average, B's recognition point and C's conjecture point will be the same. Suppose further, however, that these two points will vary from one occasion to the next, and these variances are not completely correlated. On one occasion, B's recognition point may precede C's conjecture point, and on another occasion, it may follow it.

Because of the grounding process, B's recognition point will ordinarily be identical to A and B's completion point. In our example, the completion point was collaboratively determined by A and B based on B's belief that he understood what A was asserting. Ideally, it should never come *before* B's recognition point, because B should always accept that he has understood. Suppose that B and C have the same mean speed of understanding, but these speeds have partly independent variances. Then C's conjecture point should precede the completion point roughly 50% of the time and follow it the other 50%. Whenever C understands before the completion point, she is in the clear, though she still cannot check on her understanding. But whenever her conjecture comes *after* the completion point, she is at a disadvantage, and for two reasons. First, she is receiving no more information to help her understand. And second, she has to continue processing the last utterance while trying simultaneously to listen to the next one. This should interfere and lead to mistakes on both the last and the current utterances.

The collaborative model leads to several predictions. First, overhearers should have greater difficulties understanding than addressees even when they are equal in background knowledge. The autonomous view predicts no difference. Second, misunderstandings by overhearers should increase dramatically whenever their conjecture point comes after the completion point. About this the autonomous view makes no obvious prediction. And third, overhearers should have even more difficulties understanding when they do not share all the background knowledge of the participants. The autonomous view makes the same prediction. There is also a possible fourth prediction, consistent with both views. Overhearers who have some control over the pacing of the conversation (e.g., they are listening to a tape recording of the conversation and can stop it whenever they want) should have less trouble understanding than overhearers who have no control over the pacing. Those with control will have more time to process the critical information without interference from having to listen simultaneously to the next utterances. Experiment 1 was designed to test these predictions.

1 Experiment 1

Method

The experiment divided into two parts. In the first, ten pairs of students who were not acquainted with each other carried out a task in which one of them, the *director*, talked with the other, the *matcher*, in order to get the matcher to arrange twelve figures in a particular order. Each pair repeated this task for six trials. In the second part, tape recordings of these conversations were presented to forty overhearing matchers (from here on, *overhearers*), who were to arrange the same twelve figures just as the matchers had done. Half of the overhearers listened to the conversations from Trial 1 on, and the other half, only from Trial 3 on. Half of each of these groups were allowed to use the "pause" button to stop the tape whenever they wanted, and the other half were not. The two principal measures of understanding were accuracy and time of placement of the correct figure.

The task in the first part was a version of a communication task originally devised by Krauss and Glucksberg (Krauss and Weinheimer 1964, 1966, 1967; Krauss and Glucksberg 1969, 1977; Glucksberg, Krauss, and Higgins 1975; see also Asher 1979; Chapter 4, this volume). In our version, the two students were seated at tables on either side of a barrier so that they could not see each other. (Although both sexes took part in all roles in the experiment, we will refer to the director as female, the matcher as male, and the overhearers as female). In front of the matcher on the table was a set of sixteen cardboard cards, each displaying a different figure on it (see Figure 1); the figures were black paper cutouts of Tangram figures (Elffers 1976) or altered versions of Tangram figures. Also in front of the matcher was a cardboard sorting frame with twelve spaces numbered from one to twelve. In front of the director was a sheet of paper with the matcher's same sixteen figures photocopied onto it in a random order. The first twelve of the sixteen figures on the director's sheet were numbered from one to twelve.

The students were told that the director's job was to get the matcher to place his cards on the sorting frame in the correct order—the director's order—as quickly and as accurately as possible. They

FIGURE 1 The Tangram Figures

could talk with each other as much as they wanted. The director was to go through the positions sequentially, starting with figure number one and ending with figure number twelve. Only twelve out of sixteen figures were used on a trial so that the director and matcher could not use process of elimination to arrange the last few on any given trial. Each pair played the game six times. The same figures were used in each trial, but the target matrix was in a different random order each time. During each trial, the students were timed and tape recorded. We noted the order in which the matcher put down the cards. The director and matcher were told that other students would listen to the tape recording, but they were not told why. There were ten male and ten female participants, with six mixed-sex pairs and two same-sex pairs for each sex.

In the second part of the experiment, forty overhearers listened to all or part of one of the tape recorded conversations, and performed the matcher's task, sorting the cards, while listening to it. There were four overhearing groups. Half the overhearers heard the entire conversation, and the other half only heard Trials 3 through 6. In each of these groups, half were allowed to press a pause button on the tape recorder, and half were not. Each of the ten conversations was heard by four different students, one in each of the four overhearing groups. As with the matchers, we noted the order in which the overhearers put down their cards, but we also noted whenever they put down a card noticeably before or after the speakers on the tape had verbally completed their placement. We tape recorded these sessions to be able to study the patterns and lengths of pauses. Of the forty overhearers, twenty-two were female and eighteen were male.

All participants were Stanford students, native speakers of American English, all but one of whom received Psychology 1 course credit. None of the directors and matchers knew each other before the beginning of the experiment. Only one of the forty overhearers recognized either of the voices on the tape, so we can assume that the overhearers were not privy to any common ground beyond that which accumulated during the experiment.

Results

Collaboration

Speakers in the first task followed the pattern of collaboration that Clark and Wilkes-Gibbs (Chapter 4, this volume) observed. The first time that figures appeared on the directors' sheets, the directors *described* them; from then on, they *referred* to them with definite descriptions, which got shorter and shorter as the trials progressed. On Trial 1, the two of them also tended to negotiate for several turns in placing each figure, but by Trial 6, they were down to one turn each. For example, the first time one pair saw one of the figures (second on the second row in Figure 1), the two of them had this exchange:[1]

D: Then number 12 . is (laughs) looks like a, a dancer
    or something really weird. Um . and, has a square
    head . and um, there's like, there's uh the kinda this um .
M: Which way is the head tilted?
D: The head is . eh- towards the left, and then th- an arm
    could be like up towards the right?
M: Mm-hm,
D: *And . It's- *
M: *an- . a big* fat leg? *You know that one?*
D: *Yeah, a big* fat leg.

---

[1] Overlapping speech in adjacent turns is enclosed in asterisks (see Svartvik and Quirk 1980).

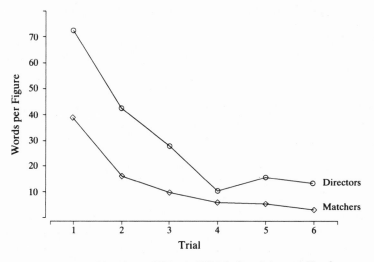

FIGURE 2 Number of Words Which Participants Used
to Come to Agreement about a Figure's Identity

M: and a little leg.
D: Right.
M: Okay.
D: Okay?
M: Yeah.

By the last trial, the reference was more compact, and the two of them took only one turn each:

D: Um, 12 . the dancer with the big fat leg?
M: Okay.

This final reference combines the perspectives offered by both the director and the matcher. In general, the perspectives that speakers ended up agreeing on ranged widely. By the last trial, the figure at the bottom left in Figure 1 was variously referred to as *the rice bag, the whale, the complacent one, the stretched-out stop sign*, and *the baby in a straitjacket*.

These patterns of collaboration were supported by the statistics. Figure 2 shows that the director and matcher each took fewer and fewer words over trials coming to agreement about each reference. Directors, who in their role spoke more, started at about seventy-three words per figure and ended at about thirteen; linear trend: $F(1,45) = 159.77$, $p < .001$. Matchers began with about thirty-nine per figure and ended up at only about three; linear trend: $F(1,45) = 98.54$, $p < .001$.

The average number of turns the director spent discussing each figure decreased from 7.8 to 1.1 over the six trials; linear trend: $F(1,45) = 125.83$, $p < .001$. And the amount of time spent per figure, which is highly correlated with number of words spoken, dropped from about thirty-nine seconds per position on Trial 1 to about six seconds per position on Trial 6; linear trend: $F(1,45) = 179.15$, $p < .001$. These results corroborate Krauss and Weinheimer's (1964, 1966, 1967) classic observations on repeated references.

Accuracy of Understanding

Our principal test of the autonomous and collaborative views of understanding was based on accuracy, the percentage of figures placed correctly. By both views, overhearers who entered on Trial 1, whom we will call *early* overhearers, should be more accurate over all trials than those who entered on Trial 3 (*late* overhearers), and they were, 88 to 68%; $F(1,38) = 20.26$, $p < .001$. Even after four trials the late overhearers were not as accurate as early overhearers, $F(1,38) = 15.83$, $p < .001$. By the collaborative model, however, the matchers should do better than the early overhearers even though these overhearers heard every word uttered by the speakers. This is precisely what occurred, 99 to 88%; $F(1,28) = 10.51$, $p < .005$. That is, being witness to the buildup of common ground did not seem to provide all the necessary information for overhearers to understand the references as well as addressees. This is direct evidence against the autonomous view of understanding.

Both matchers and overhearers got more accurate as they went along; linear trend: $F(1,135) = 4.69$, $p < .025$. Figure 3 plots percentage correct in each condition on each trial. As the figure shows, the matchers were very accurate from the outset. They averaged 93% correct on Trial 1 and were perfect from Trial 4 on; linear trend: $F(1,45) = 20.44$, $p < .001$. In contrast, early overhearers began at 81% correct and by Trial 6 increased to only 95%, linear trend: $F(1,95) = 17.13$, $p < .001$. Late overhearers also improved from 55 to 73%; linear trend: $F(1,57) = 15.41$, $p < .001$. Over the last four trials, they improved at a faster rate than the early overhearers; linear trend: $F(1,114) = 8.58$, $p < .01$. There are several possible reasons why they improved more quickly, but we have no evidence to choose among them.

Every overhearer given the opportunity to pause *did* pause at least once during the course of the experiment. They paused from zero to seven times during a trial, and their pauses ranged from two to seventy-nine seconds in length. Still, all this pausing did not help. The pause and no pause conditions yielded 89 and 88% correct responses for the

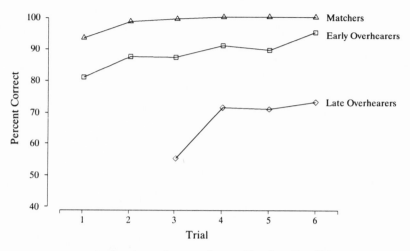

FIGURE 3   Accuracy Averaged over Pausing Conditions

early overhearers, and 73 and 68% for the late overhearers; these differences were not significant. After the experiment, most overhearers thought the opportunity to pause had helped (even though it had not). In some cases, pausing actually seemed to hurt, because when the conversation became very quick, it was easy for the overhearer to lose her place on the sorting board, and end up missing descriptions. Because the overhearers' performance did not improve even when they had unlimited time to think about the speakers' words, we know that they did not do poorly simply because they had not happened to find a card soon enough whose identity they were already sure about.

Procedural Differences

In interpreting this task, we assume that the moment at which the matcher or overhearer placed a card corresponds more or less to their recognition or conjecture points—the points at which they believed they had identified the referent. The assumption, of course, is not quite right, because different people surely have different strategies for marking their beliefs and different criteria for making their guesses. The assumption is probably even too strong, because overhearers may put down cards with less confidence than addressees. If anything, however, this works against predictions of the collaborative model.

By the collaborative model, overhearers should put some of their cards down considerably before matchers, and some considerably after, and they did. Table 1 shows that overhearers placed only 63% of their cards down by the speakers' verbal completion points, as compared

TABLE 1
Time and Accuracy of Placements Relative to
Speakers' Completion Points

	EARLY	ON TIME	LATE	VERY LATE	BLANK	TOTAL
Percent placements in each time period						
Matchers	0	99	0.4	0.6	0	100
Early overhearers	15	56	20	7	2	100
Late overhearers	6	49	25	10	10	100
Probability of error in each time period						
Matchers	–	.02	.00	.20		
Early overhearers	.03	.05	.16	.35		
Late overhearers	.11	.20	.31	.55		

with the matchers' 99%; $t(94) = 6.76$, $p < .001$. Overhearers made their placements during the director's description of the next figure (*late*) or even after that (*very late*) 31% of the time, as compared with the matchers' rate of 1%; $t(94) = 5.63$, $p < .001$. And they left blanks in their frames 6% of the time, whereas matchers never did. Early overhearers gave more *early* or *on time* responses than late overhearers, 71 to 55%; $t(94) = 3.36$, $p < .002$.

For the collaborative model, the important prediction is that late placements are more likely to be incorrect. That prediction was confirmed. As Table 1 shows, overhearers were more likely to make an error when they placed a card *after* the speaker's completion point than before it, 28 to 12%; $t(47) = 7.38$, $p < .001$. (The seemingly high *very late* error rate of 20% among the addressees represents one error in only five card placements.)

The matchers and overhearers also sometimes changed the cards they put down. They would place a card in the sorting frame and later replace it with another, indicating they had changed their choice for the correct referent. On the collaborative view, overhearers should do this more often than matchers, simply because overhearers cannot verbally test out their hypotheses; and they did, 5.1 to 1.6% of the time; $t(38) = 4.26$, $p < .0001$. The matchers' changes were always to correct an error, but only 56% of the overhearers' changes were to the correct referent. Still, among the answers they did get right, both matchers and overhearers overwhelmingly got them right on the first try (as opposed to changing their answers from incorrect ones): 97% for participants, and 96% for overhearers. For the responses that overhearers ultimately got wrong, the rate of changing, 32%, was much higher than their overall rate of 5.1%.

Overhearers distributed their errors fairly evenly among positions on the sorting frame within trials, so they did not have more trouble within a trial as it proceeded, linear trend: $F(1,429) = 0.49$, *n.s.* Getting behind early on did not cause them to do worse on later positions; rather, they tended to try to concentrate on the current reference, only going back to previously missed references when they could. And as expected, some figures were harder for overhearers than others. The percentage of errors ranged from 3.3% on the second Tangram on the bottom row of Figure 1 to 29% for each of the middle two figures on the second row. The differences among figures were significant; $F(15,630) = 5.96$, $p < .001$, but could have arisen for any number of reasons.

Subjective Commentary

Overhearers often muttered to themselves during trials and made comments to the experimenter between trials. During pauses, several of them repeated the descriptions that the directors had just made, for example, *Triangular shape to the right with rabbit ears ... triangular shape to the right with rabbit ears ...*, or *Facing right ... foot facing right.* They demonstrated verbally what we already knew from their changes, that they kept descriptions they had not understood in mind and went back to work on them when they had a chance. One overhearer paused during the description of the 12th position and muttered *What kind of an animal?* repeating the description of the 7th position, which she had left blank. Another overhearer, who had had trouble with *the Number One*, exclaimed when she finally figured it out *So that's the Number One thing!*

Overhearers clearly realized they did not understand some references. One said *I have trouble with this one* when she heard a rather obscure description for the second time. Another paused the tape after an unusual description, muttering, *Wait, Hoover Tower figure, with the tray on the left ... Geez, I dunno.* When the same figure was described in a later trial, she announced in annoyed tones *I don't know the Hoover Tower figure!* Another expressed dismay at not understanding a reference: *I don't know which one—monk they're talking about.* Several overhearers wanted to rewind the tape to remind themselves of descriptions they had forgotten. The point is, if these listeners had been addressees, they would have cleared up these failures before the conversation went on. As overhearers without the opportunity to collaborate, they could not.

One overhearer assumed that over time she would be able to understand the conversation fully, but found that she was not: *It's harder—I thought it'd be easier, 'cuz they just say, y'know, 'this one'.* Another overhearer got right to the point in explaining why he was having trouble: *I think if—it's like if I was more a part of the thing, then it would be ... They're just talking to each other, and using their definitions.*

Discussion

Our results so far are clear. Overhearers who did not witness the buildup of common ground between conversational participants understood fewer references than the participants themselves. But so did overhearers who *did* witness the buildup (for similar findings, see Kraut et al. 1982). Nor did it help overhearers to be able to control the pacing of the conversation by pausing the tape. Overhearers appeared to use their time differently from participants. They made more guesses, and they made these over a broader distribution of time. Although the first of our results is consistent with the autonomous view of understanding, the remainder are not. All these results are consistent with the collaborative model.

Still, we were not entirely satisfied with Experiment 1. First, there was an alternative explanation for why the overhearers did so badly in Experiment 1. Listening to a tape recording of a conversation just is not as vivid, as engaging, as easy as listening to the conversation live. That might have been the reason overhearers were worse off. Second, we had only a crude test of the timing predictions of the collaborative model. In Experiment 1, we were able to classify the matchers' and overhearers' responses only as early, on time, late, very late, or missing. That did not allow a very sensitive test of these predictions. Experiment 2 was designed to overcome both of these problems. We had overhearers listen to live conversations, and we videotaped and later timed the matcher and overhearer as they placed their cards in the sorting frames.

2 Experiment 2

Methods

The task was the same as in Experiment 1. Fourteen pairs of students played the Tangram-matching game six times with the figures in a different random order each time. Once again, only twelve out of sixteen figures were used on each trial. This time an overhearer was present in the room along with the director and matcher, all separated by visual barriers. A single hidden video camera was trained on the sorting boards in front of the matcher and overhearer and recorded the movements of their hands and the cards. And once again, the director, matcher, and overhearer began as strangers.

Running the experiment with all three people in the room caused a logistics problem. We had to ensure that the director and matcher, who knew there was another person in the room, would be indifferent to her in the design of their utterances. The excuse we fashioned was that she was a coder present to reduce experimental bias. We explained this to the director and matcher when we read them the instructions. The overhearers, therefore, had to come early to hear their instructions. This meant that they also listened to all the instructions given to the director and matcher. This gave them more time to think about the task, but any possible advantage this gave them would work against our hypothesis. The matcher and overhearer sat at exactly the same distance from the director, and their cards, apparatus, and surroundings were otherwise identical.

After the experiment, all three students filled out questionnaires. They were asked whether they had previously known any of the other students in the room, how difficult they had found the task and why, and what they thought the experiment was testing. The last question was designed to determine whether the director and matcher had been aware of the overhearer's role, and none had. The students were members of the Stanford community, all native speakers of English, who were either paid or received experimental credit for participating. One triple of students was eliminated because they had known each other before the experiment, another because they failed to follow directions, and two more because the director and matcher were still making two or more errors out of twelve on the sixth trial. These last two triples are highly unusual for experiments of this kind, where matchers typically make no errors by the sixth trial (see Experiment 1; Chapter 4, this volume; Isaacs and Clark 1987; Chapter 9, this volume). Removing these two triples, however, does not alter the main results. The main results, then, are based on ten triples.

Results

Accuracy

By the collaborative model, the matchers should be more accurate than the overhearers, and they were, 98 to 85% correct; $F(1,18) = 10.83$, $p < .005$. (When we included the two error-prone triples, the matchers were still more accurate, 95 to 85% correct; $F(1,22) = 7.00$, $p < .015$.) Matchers started out with 95% correct on Trial 1, and, by Trial 6, they all matched every reference correctly. In contrast, overhearers started out with only 78% correct and only improved to 89% by the last trial. (With the two error-prone triples included, overhearers started out with 80% correct and ended up at 91% by the last trial). Both matchers

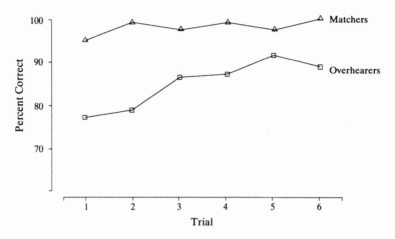

FIGURE 4 Accuracy on the Matching Test

and overhearers improved over the course of the trials; linear trend: $F(1,90) = 10.89$, $p < .01$, but overhearers improved a bit more than the participants; linear trend: $F(1,90) = 7.01$, $p < .01$, perhaps because the participants started out so well. Figure 4 summarizes these results. As in Experiment 1, overhearers changed their minds about the cards they put down more often than matchers, 4.2 to 1.3% of the time; $t(9) = 3.99$, $p < .005$. In short, it did not help overhearers to listen to the conversations live. They still did not do as well as the matcher. This is decisive evidence against the autonomous view of understanding in conversation.

Placement Times

The director and matcher engaged in the same collaborative strategies as in Experiment 1, at first describing figures and then referring to them with increasingly abbreviated references. Because we videotaped the matchers and overhearers, we were able to time the initiation points, completion points, and card placements to the nearest tenth of a second. The first measure we calculated was what we will call *placement times*. The placement time for a matcher or overhearer on a figure was the time duration from the initiation point for that figure (the moment the director began talking about it) to the placement point (the moment the matcher or overhearer put his or her final card choice down). As in Experiment 1, the average placement time per figure got shorter and shorter over the six trials; linear trend: $F(1,45) = 97.38$, $p < .001$. Nevertheless, the placement times were almost the same for overhearers as for matchers; $F(1,9) = 0.16$, *n.s.* On Trial 1, the mean

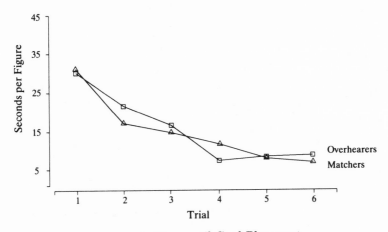

FIGURE 5 Time until Card Placement

placement time per figure was 31.1 seconds for matchers and 30.2 seconds for overhearers. By Trial 6, these times were down to 6.3 and 8.3 seconds (see Figure 5). Nor were there reliable differences between matchers and overhearers in the *median* placement times per figure.

Next we compared each placement point (the moment a matcher or overhearer made his or her final card placement) relative to the completion point (the point at which the director and matcher made it clear verbally that they were ready to go on to the next figure). By the collaborative model, the matcher's placement points should ordinarily come just before the completion points, and on the average they did, by 0.5 seconds. The matcher and director should not be willing to go on until the matcher had signaled he was able to put down his card. But on the average the overhearer's placement points also came just before the completion points, by 1.2 seconds. These two differences are not reliably different.

The story was very different, however, for the standard deviation of these placement-completion intervals. As predicted, overhearers placed their cards down both much earlier *and* much later than matchers. So while the mean placement-completion intervals were the same for matchers and overhearers, the standard deviation was about five times larger for overhearers than for matchers, $F(1,18) = 12.64$, $p < .005$. The average standard deviations of these intervals for matchers and overhearers are plotted over trials in Figure 6. The difference between the two standard deviations held up even when we removed null responses (to which we had assigned a time corresponding to the end of

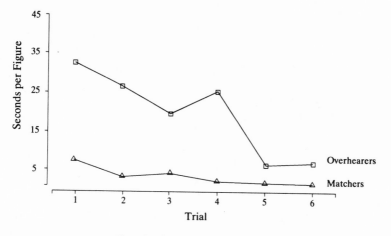

FIGURE 6 Standard Deviations of Card Placements

the entire trial); $F(1,18) = 9.26$, $p < .007$. Another way of looking at the placement-completion interval is to correlate the placement time for each figure on each trial with the corresponding completion time. On the average, this correlation was .96 for matchers but only .68 for overhearers; $t(11.5) = 3.21$, $p < .01$. This means that matchers tended to put their cards down at about the same time as they finished establishing each reference with their partners, while overhearers did not track the participants' completion points so closely.

Pacing and Accuracy

By the collaborative model, pacing should have direct effects on the overhearers' accuracy. Overhearers who have understood a reference before the completion point will be prepared for the next reference, whereas those who have not will have to contend with the next reference while trying to complete understanding of the last one. One prediction, then, is this: Overhearers are more likely to be incorrect on those placements that follow the completion point than on those that precede it. And this was the case. They made errors 9.6% of the time on placements before the completion point, but 21% of the time on placements after the completion point; $F(1,9) = 15.06$, $p < .005$.

For more detailed evidence for this prediction, we ranked all one hundred and twenty overhearer placements within Trial 1 from earliest to latest relative to the completion points. We have plotted these by deciles in Figure 7. As the figure shows, overhearers were very accurate (100% correct) when their placements were very early rel-

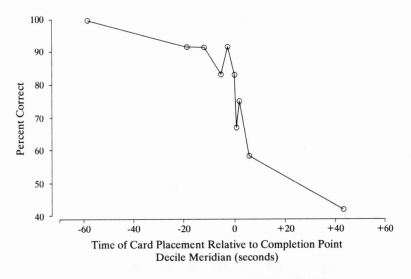

FIGURE 7 Overhearers' Accuracy, Trial 1, Relative to
Conversational Partners' Completion Points

ative to the completion points. They became a bit less accurate as
their placements approached the completion points, but their accuracy
dropped precipitously once their placements came after the completion
points. They were correct on only 42% of their placements in the latest decile. This, then, is further striking evidence for the collaborative
model.

Another possible consequence of the collaborative view is that a
late placement will compete specifically with the very next placement.
We looked to see whether overhearers would do worse for placements
that directly followed late placements than for those following early
or on-time placements, and we found no difference in accuracy at all,
86 to 85%, *n.s.* As we noted in the first study, overhearers tended
to concentrate on the reference currently under discussion and went
back to a previous figure only when they had understood the current one.

Directors, matchers, and overhearers, of course, should differ in
their effectiveness in communicating. Some pairs of directors and
matchers should be more effective as conversational partners than others, and their choice of perspectives and their pacing should be right
for some overhearers and confusing for others. By the collaborative
model, these variations should affect the overhearers' accuracy. The
speedier a director and matcher are compared to the average director

and matcher, the less time they give an overhearer to grasp each reference, the more likely she is to make her placement late, and the more likely she is to make an error. This was in fact borne out. On Trial 1, the matcher's mean time of card placement correlated -.78 with the median difference between the overhearer's and matcher's placement times; $t(8) = 3.54$, $p < .005$, one-tailed. The overhearer's number of errors on Trial 1 also correlated .58 with the median difference between the overhearer's and matcher's placement times; $t(8) = 2.01$, $p < .05$, one-tailed.

Subjective Comments

On the questionnaires, directors, matchers, and overhearers alike commented on the collaborative nature of the task. Many directors and matchers noted that the task had been difficult until they had established *common names for referring to the figures*, a *'vocabulary' for the figures, familiar ideas about what they [the shapes] could represent*, or *'names' coding the figures*, or until they *were on the same wavelength, spoke a common descriptor-language*. It was precisely this vocabulary that overhearers often complained about. They noted that the director and matcher sometimes *had a name for a figure which I didn't remember or which described it in a way not clear for me*, or *agreed on terms that I didn't quite catch*, or *developed their own terms and it took a while to catch on to their terminology*. They realized they were at a disadvantage because they *couldn't communicate with the players, couldn't ask questions to clarify some of the shapes*, and *disagreed with a few of the interpretations given for the symbols and I kept wanting to add my input!*

Overhearers were also aware that pacing was a problem. One was *forced to rush on to the next figure whether or not I'd gotten the previous one*. Another found it *difficult to keep up with the other two ... occasionally I would fall behind and forget what needed to be filled in*. For another, *sometimes the matcher found her shape before I found mine and I missed some of the next description*. Another overhearer claimed that *at the end I knew the terms but they went very quickly*. One described it succinctly: *it went too fast*.

Many directors, matchers, and overhearers, then, recognized the very processes predicted by the collaborative model. Most overhearers realized that they were at a disadvantage because they were not part of the grounding process or in control of the pacing. But not all of them. One argued that *on the whole ... it was good that I just listened instead of trying to describe* and *discern at the same time*. She seemed to be echoing the autonomous view of understanding, suggesting that overhearers should understand at least as well as the participants. The data do not, of course, bear her out.

3 Conclusions

Our results suggest that the *social* process of interacting in conversation plays a central role in the *cognitive* process of understanding. Listeners who participate in a conversational interaction go about understanding very differently from those who are excluded from it. It is because of these differences that addressees understand faster and more accurately than overhearers. If understanding in conversation were an autonomous process, there should be no such differences. The conclusion, then, is that understanding is part of a collaborative process (see also Kraut et al. 1982).

Our findings show that the process of understanding differs for addressees and overhearers in several ways. Consider speaker A, addressee B, and overhearer C.

1. **Collaboration.** B ordinarily collaborates with A as he tries to understand her, whereas C does not. One thing it means for B to collaborate with A is for B to monitor his understanding and keep A informed of the state of his understanding. If all goes well, B need only say *Okay* or *Yeah*—he has understood. But when he gets into trouble, he has to identify the trouble, describe it to A, and resolve it. C monitors *her* understanding as well, but she does not have to describe her troubles to anyone nor does she have the opportunity to enlist anyone's help. The only way she can resolve her problems is via conjectures based on her beliefs about A and B's common ground and what A said. So B reaches his final state of understanding in collaboration with A, whereas C has to do it all by conjecture.

2. **Criterion for understanding.** B's criterion for understanding is the belief that he and A mutually believe he has understood her well enough for current purposes. He can work until he has understood as well as he wants. C's criterion is a different matter. She can only reach the belief that she has understood as well as she *could*. She has no way of working until she has understood as well as she wants.

3. **Perspective.** Part of what B does in collaboration with A is search for a common perspective, a perspective shared with A on what A is trying to say. In our task that meant searching for a shared way of conceiving each figure—for example, as a rice bag, a whale, a stretched-out stop sign, a baby in a straitjacket, or a com-

placent one. B can even introduce his own perspective, as long as he gets A to agree to it. C, in contrast, is forced to accept whatever perspective A and B throw her way. If it is not a perspective she can grasp, that is her tough luck.

The two types of listeners in our experiments reflected these differences. As for collaboration, the matchers did not sit idly by as the directors described the figures. They actively collaborated with them from the very start. The process was lengthy at first, but soon became very efficient. As for the criterion of understanding, the matchers almost always committed themselves by placing their cards right at the completion points of the directors' assertions. They worked until they were satisfied they understood, and they were almost always right. The points at which the overhearers placed their cards were not so closely tied to the completion points, and their criteria for placing cards were lower. They often changed their minds, and they were often wrong. They were forced to accept a lower criterion simply because the crucial resource—the grounding process—was not available to them. Finally, the matchers worked hard to find perspectives they could share with the directors. Ironically, these were often the same perspectives that the overhearers complained that they could not grasp and that kept them from identifying the right figures.

Why does collaboration leave overhearers at a disadvantage? It is known that speakers accommodate to their particular interlocutors in everything from loudness and speed, to dialect and pronunciation (Bell 1984; Giles, Mulac, Bradac, and Johnson 1987; Street and Giles 1982; Thakerar, Giles, and Cheshire 1982). But factors like these do not seem able to account for our findings. Speakers also adjust to the expertise of their interlocutors, often supplying them with or acquiring from them the needed expertise as they talk (Isaacs and Clark 1987). Discrepancies in expertise per se do not offer a plausible account of our findings either since our matchers and overhearers began on a par in expertise. We must look instead at the heart of collaboration, the process of grounding.

Grounding is really an opportunistic process. It succeeds in part by exploiting adventitious commonalities between speakers and addressees. In our task, A offers one way of viewing a figure—say, as a whale—and if B happens to be able to see it that way, he accepts it, and they go on. If he cannot see it that way, the two of them try another perspective. The process is opportunistic in that it takes advantage of the first perspective A and B find they can agree on. If it is a perspective C can grasp, she is in luck, but if it is not, she is likely to fail. Her state of understanding plays no role in A and B's decision to stop or go on. With an opportunistic process like this, C is at a disadvantage, and the damage may accumulate.

Do these findings apply to other types of conversation? In their essential features, the answer must be yes. Grounding has been documented to be a central process in ordinary English conversation (Chapter 5, this volume), telephone calls to directory enquiries (Clark and Schaefer, 1987), and a variety of task-oriented conversations (Chapter 4, this volume; Garrod and Anderson 1987; Isaacs and Clark 1987). What we have demonstrated is that listeners who participate in grounding have an advantage over those who do not. So wherever grounding occurs, addressees should have an advantage over overhearers, all else being equal. In real conversations, particular speakers always bring particular perspectives to bear upon particular topics. Understanding can only be guaranteed for listeners who actively participate in establishing these perspectives.

Understanding by addressees is rarely studied in experiments on comprehension, because in most of them the participants are treated as if they were overhearers. First, the participants are made to listen to tape-recorded speech in isolation from the speaker. They have no way of influencing the pace or form of the speaker's utterances, as addressees normally do. They do not have to prepare to speak while listening, or identify and make their misunderstandings known to the speaker. Second, the speech they hear is sanitized. Rarely does it have repeats, *uhs*, interruptions, mistimings, or self-corrections, all of which change the very nature of parsing. At the same time, it does not make these features available for the participants to exploit in the grounding process, as addressees normally do (see Chapter 5, this volume). And third, because there is no interaction between speaker and listener, the grounding criterion is not even definable. The participants have to be satisfied with a lower, and different, standard of understanding.

Understanding, in short, can never be fully captured in traditional theories of understanding. These theories, like the experiments they depend on, assume that listeners do what they do autonomously—that is, without direct collaboration with the speaker. If we are right, these theories will have to be revised to deal with the grounding process. Just how radical the revisions must be remains to be seen.

Part III

Audience Design in Language Use

Introduction to Part III

When we talk, we design our utterances for the people we believe are or may be listening—our addressees, the other participants in the conversation, and even overhearers. We make sure the other participants in the conversation can readily understand what we mean. We also deal with overhearers—bystanders and potential eavesdroppers—depending on the attitude we take toward them. The term Thomas Carlson and I coined for this feature of utterances is *audience design*.[1] It has obvious roots in Harold Garfinkel's (1967) "recipient design," which Harvey Sacks, Emanuel Schegloff, and Gail Jefferson (1974) described this way: "By 'recipient design' we refer to a multitude of respects in which the talk by a party in a conversation is constructed or designed in ways which display an orientation and sensitivity to the particular other(s) who are the co-participants." The term *audience design* covers overhearers as well as co-participants. For us, overhearers represent an important test case in the design of utterances.

My interest in audience design came about rather by accident. From the early 70s on, I had investigated illocutionary acts such as requests, questions, assertions, and offers. I was especially interested in how people understood so-called indirect illocutionary acts (see Clark 1979). Imagine a friend asking you *Do you know what time it is?* as an indirect way of reminding you of a dentist appointment. To understand her, you must appeal to information in your common ground with her about the dentist appointment. Overhearers may not be privy to the information they need to understand her—for example, the information about the dentist appointment—and they know it. All they can see—if that— is that your friend is asking if you know what time it is. They may

---

[1] Gregory Murphy and I also used the term in papers in 1982 and 1983. So did Bell in 1984, but with a more restricted meaning.

suspect she is doing something more, but about that they can only guess.[2]

The problem is that most theories of understanding—now as much as then—take for granted that understanding works the same regardless of the listener's status. So in the late 70's, I began work on a notion I called "modes of understanding." The idea was that listeners fall into distinct types. These are: (a) the speaker monitoring him- or herself, (b) the addressees, (c) other participants in the conversation that I came to call *side participants*, (d) bystanders, and (e) eavesdroppers. These listener types are logically distinct by virtue of the information they can appeal to in understanding what the speaker means. Each type of listener therefore proceeds according to a different "mode" of understanding. These modes have their rationale in Grice's notion of speaker's meaning: Addressees can recognize what the speaker means because they are intended to; other listeners can only guess at it.

But in working out these modes, I came to an impasse. I had no rationale for how side participants should reason. Grice's notion of speaker's meaning applied to addressees, but not to side participants. The same was true of every theory of illocutionary acts from Austin's on. Yet, when I talk to two people and ask one of them a question, I surely intend the other one, the side participant, to understand what I am asking the first, the addressee. But how?

That was in the autumn of 1979, Eve Clark and I had just had a son, and there was the issue of who was to do what in his daily care. One night, she was changing his diapers and I was looking on when she said to him, *Damon, don't you think Herb should change your diapers next time.* Voilà, I thought. She has indirectly asked me to change his diapers but without addressing me. She could only do that if she was "informing" me of what she is telling him, and her "informing" me must also an illocutionary act. I took the idea to Carlson, and we applied it to the more general issue: What speech acts does a speaker perform in talking to two or more people at a time—whether some are side participants, or all are addressees? We reported our solution in "Hearers and speech acts" in *Language* in 1982. That paper appears here, slightly abridged, as Chapter 7.[3]

After Carlson and I finished that paper, I returned to modes of understanding, but this time came to an impasse with overhearers. As

[2]I first discussed these notions in an invited address to the American Psychological Association meetings in 1980.

[3]We reported related arguments in "Speech acts and hearers' beliefs" at a Conference on Mutual Knowledge at the University of Essex in 1980, published in *Mutual Knowledge*, 1982, edited by Neil Smith.

Carlson and I had noted in passing, speakers can take several distinct attitudes toward overhearers. They may choose to disclose, conceal, or disguise what they mean for overhearers, or simply be indifferent to them. Depending on their choice, they will design very different utterances. Speakers, for example, can conceal what they say from overhearers and still remain comprehensible to their addressees. But how do they do this? And how *do* speakers design their utterances to disclose, disguise, or be indifferent.

Edward Schaefer and I investigated the issue in several ways. Our first tack was to develop a general schema for the attitudes of disclosure, concealment, disguisement, and indifference. The schema we arrived at is described in "Dealing with overhearers," which appears in this volume for the first time. Our second tack was to test the concealment part of our schema experimentally. In our experiment, we had pairs of students try to conceal what they were referring to from a third student who was sitting nearby. We reported the results in "Concealing one's meaning from overhearers," published in the *Journal of Language and Memory* in 1987. It appears here as Chapter 9. Unfortunately, there are some redundancies between Chapters 7, 8, and 9. All I can do is ask you to ignore them.

When I return again to modes of understanding, I trust I won't run into any more such impasses.

7

Hearers and Speech Acts

WITH THOMAS B. CARLSON

In conversations involving more than two people, most utterances are intended to be understood not only by the people being addressed, but also by the others. These utterances cannot be accounted for in current theories of speech acts unless several basic changes are made. In our proposal, the speaker performs two types of illocutionary act with each utterance. One is the traditional kind, such as an assertion, promise, or apology; this is directed at the addressees. The other, called an informative, is directed at all the participants in the conversation—the addressees and third parties alike. It is intended to inform all of them jointly of the assertion, promise, or apology being directed at the addressees. We present evidence that every traditional illocutionary act is performed by means of an informative.

Although hearers play an essential role in speech acts, that role has never been fully examined. Consider requests, such as this one from "Othello".

(1)   Othello, to Desdemona, in front of Iago and Roderigo: *Come, Desdemona.*

In Searle's 1969 theory and its descendants—the *standard theories* as we will call them—Othello's request "counts as an attempt to get H to do A". It is an attempt by Othello to get the "hearer" H to go with him. This, of course, is incorrect: by "hearer", Searle really means *addressee*.[1] Although Othello has an audience of three "hearers"—

---

[1] Searle is in good company. Austin 1962, Bach and Harnish 1979, Bennett 1973, Chomsky 1975, Davison 1975, Fraser 1975, Garner 1975, Gordon and Lakoff 1971, Kempson 1975, 1977, Lewis 1969, and Morgan 1977 all use "hearer" for *addressee*.

Desdemona, Iago, and Roderigo—he isn't trying to get all three of them to go with him. His request is for Desdemona alone. She is an addressee, not just a hearer. The standard theories are theories about illocutionary acts directed at addressees.

Are there illocutionary acts directed at hearers such as Iago and Roderigo? The standard theories, by their silence on the question, appear to assume the answer is no.[2] This, too, seems incorrect. Although Othello isn't addressing Iago and Roderigo, he intends them to understand what he is saying. Indeed, he intends them to understand in the same way that he intends Desdemona to understand—by means of their recognition of his intentions, just as theories of illocutionary acts require. The difference is that what Iago and Roderigo are to understand is not that they are to go with Othello, but that he is requesting Desdemona to go with him. As a first conjecture, then, Othello is performing illocutionary acts directed at all three hearers. However, the ones he is directing at Iago and Roderigo aren't the same as the ones he is directing at Desdemona.

In this paper, we argue that this conjecture is correct: Speakers perform illocutionary acts not only toward addressees, but also toward certain other hearers. We define a type of hearer we call a *participant*, whose role as hearer is distinct from the roles of both addressee and overhearer. In example 1, Iago, Roderigo, and Desdemona are participants; Desdemona is also the addressee. Then we take up three hypotheses:

The Participant Hypothesis. Certain illocutionary acts are directed at hearers in their roles as addressees, and others are directed at hearers in their roles as participants.

The first class, called *addressee-directed illocutionary acts*, includes all the familiar illocutionary acts such as assertions, requests, promises, and apologies. It is the second class, called *participant-directed illocutionary acts*, that is new.

The Informative Hypothesis. The fundamental kind of participant-directed illocutionary act is one by which the speaker jointly

Donnellan 1968 and Grice 1968 refer to an undifferentiated "audience". Others, including Fillmore 1972, Green 1975, and Katz 1977, have used "addressee"—though still others, such as R. Lakoff 1972 and Ervin-Tripp 1976, have used this interchangeably with "hearer".

[2]Allusions have been made to the effect of a third party on the significance of a speaker's utterance to an addressee (Bird 1975; Rubin 1978; Verschueren 1978), but no discussion of illocutionary acts toward these third parties has taken place (see also footnotes 9 and 10, below).

informs all the participants fully of the illocutionary act that he is simultaneously performing toward the addressee or addressees.

These illocutionary acts will be called *informatives*. This leads to the third hypothesis:

The Informative-First Hypothesis. All addressee-directed illocutionary acts are performed by means of informatives.

By this hypothesis, Othello makes his request of Desdemona by means of an informative directed at Iago, Roderigo, *and* Desdemona.[3]

This proposal has far-reaching consequences for speech-act theories. Ever since Austin 1962, the act of speaking has been divided by levels into component acts that are causally related: phonetic acts, locutionary acts, illocutionary acts, and perlocutionary acts, among others.[4] Our proposal is to add a new level—a new component act—to this causal chain. Consider an analogy (cf. Austin, 107); in shooting a gun, a person tenses certain muscles, by means of which he crooks his right index finger, by means of which he pulls the trigger, by means of which he shoots the gun. If no one had described the act of crooking the right index finger, which is a necessary component of this causal chain, then the theory of gun-shooting would be incomplete. For speech acts, since no one has described the act of informing participants, which is just as necessary a component of speaking, speech-act theories are likewise incomplete. They need to be amended by a new level of component acts, the informatives.

We take up the hypotheses roughly in order. In Section 1, we describe situations that appear to require participant-directed illocutionary acts. In Section 2, we describe these situations more completely. In Section 3, we argue that informatives are a type of illocutionary act. In Section 4, we lay out the evidence for the informative-first hypothesis. In Section 5, we show how this analysis accounts for two kinds of indirect illocutionary acts.

1 Five Problems

Are hearers like Iago and Roderigo truly the targets of illocutionary acts? We will describe five problems for the standard theories that appear to be resolved only if the answer is yes. For each problem, we will consider examples in which the speaker performs a traditional

---

[3] Note that the third hypothesis presupposes the second, which in turn presupposes the first. So it is possible to accept the first hypothesis alone, the first two alone, or all three.

[4] By a "causal" relation, we mean a "by-means-of" relation. For discussion, see Austin 1962, Grice 1968, Goldman 1970, and our Section 5.

illocutionary act toward one hearer, and must be assumed at the same time and with the same utterance to be informing other hearers of that act. These other hearers will be called *side-participants*, and the acts of informing them *informatives*.

Conversations

In ordinary conversations, the information that the parties acquire accumulates in a principled way (see Gazdar 1979, Stalnaker 1978). Imagine Ann, Barbara, and Charles in a conversation. When Ann asks Barbara a question, Charles is expected to keep track of that question, even though he is not being addressed. And when Ann asks *him* a question, he is expected to keep track of the fact that Barbara—and Ann—are keeping track of this question, too. That is, the parties to a conversation generally adhere to a *Principle of Responsibility*: Each is responsible at all times for keeping track of what is being said, and for enabling everyone else to keep track of what is being said. Each party keeps a cumulative record that becomes part of everyone's *common ground*, in the technical sense of Karttunen & Peters 1975, Stalnaker 1978, and Chapter 2, this volume. With each contribution to the conversation, the current speaker presupposes the common ground already established; and all the parties, the speaker included, add what is new in that contribution to their common ground,

The problem this poses for the standard theories is that speakers cannot fulfill this responsibility without the use of informatives. Consider this example:

(2)   Charles, to Ann and Barbara: *What did the two of you do today?*
       Ann, to Charles, in front of Barbara: *We went to the museum.*
       Barbara, to Charles, in front of Ann: *Before that, we went to the theater.*

Here Ann and Barbara take turns telling Charles what they did together. When Ann asserts that they went to the museum, she is addressing Charles. She can't be addressing Barbara, since she would be telling her something it was obvious to the two of them that Barbara already knew (cf. Searle 1969, Stalnaker 1978). Yet if the conversation is to accumulate, Ann must let Barbara know what she is telling Charles. Otherwise, Barbara cannot keep track of what is being said; she may repeat things Ann has already said. So Ann must inform Barbara that she is telling Charles that they went to the museum. Barbara presupposes just that when she says *Before that, we went to the theater.*

If Barbara understands English, how could Ann fail to let her know what she was telling Charles? There are many ways. Ann could have told Charles *We went to the place you recommended to me this morning*, knowing that Barbara had no idea he had recommended the museum. In that case, Ann would have good reason for believing that Barbara could *not* determine what she was telling Charles and therefore would not be able to build on what she had just said: Barbara might mistakenly go on *And then we went to the museum*, duplicating Ann's contribution. So, to fulfill her responsibility, Ann must do more than tell Charles they went to the museum. She must tell him in such a way that she simultaneously informs Barbara of what she is telling him.

The need for informatives is especially clear for certain types of ellipsis in conversation; e.g.,

(3)　Charles, to Ann, in front of Barbara: *Did you like the museum?*
　　　Ann, to Charles, in front of Barbara: *Yes, I did.*
　　　Charles, to Barbara, in front of Ann: *What about you?*
　　　Barbara, to Charles, in front of Ann: *I liked it, too.*

When Charles asks Ann his question, he must also be informing Barbara what he is asking Ann. Otherwise, he cannot be certain that Barbara will understand his highly elliptical question, *What about you?* Imagine instead that Charles had asked Ann *Did you like the place I recommended this morning?*, knowing that Barbara was not privy to that conversation: he couldn't then expect her to understand *What about you?* So Charles must do two things in uttering *Did you like the museum?*: (a) ask Ann whether she liked the museum, and (b) inform Barbara that he is asking Ann this. Only then will his next elliptical question be felicitous.

The necessity for informatives is also obvious whenever there is a change of addressee in the middle of an utterance. This often occurs with tag questions, as in this example from Graham Greene's *The Human Factor*:

(4)　Hargreaves, to Percival, in front of Daintry: *Daintry began his check with those, [turning to Daintry] didn't you?*

In the first half, Hargreaves is making an assertion to Percival. Yet he must also be informing Daintry of that assertion; otherwise, he couldn't turn to Daintry and ask him to confirm it. Daintry, for example, must understand what *his check* and *those* refer to. With the tag question, there is a similar problem. As Millar and Brown (1979, 44) point out for similar Scots examples: "The speaker is not seeking confirmation of his proposition for his own sake—he is not uncertain of the truth of his proposition—but for the sake of the third party." With his tag question, Hargreaves' main aim is not to ask Daintry the question, but to inform *Percival* that he is asking Daintry that question. Informatives are essential in both halves of his utterance.

Indirect Illocutionary Acts

In the standard theories, the speaker can perform one illocutionary act toward an addressee and thereby perform another toward the same addressee. The first is called a direct illocutionary act; the second, an indirect illocutionary acts (Bach and Harnish 1979; Morgan 1978; Searle 1975). Take this example:

(5)   Ann, to Barbara, in front of Charles: *Barbara, I insist that you tell Charles who we met at the museum today.*

Ann is directly asserting that she insists that Barbara tell Charles something, and she is indirectly requesting Barbara to do this. Both the assertion and the request are addressed to Barbara. Now consider this:

(6)   Ann, to Charles, in front of Barbara: *Charles, I insist that Barbara tell you who we met at the museum today.*

Again Ann is directly asserting that she insists that Barbara tell Charles something, and she is indirectly requesting Barbara to do this. In this case, however, the assertion is addressed to Charles, and the request to Barbara. Thus, there are two distinct types of indirect illocutionary acts: those like (5), in which the direct and indirect addressees are the same; and those like (6), in which they are different. These two types will be called *linear* and *lateral* indirect illocutionary acts, respectively. The indirect addressees in the two types will be called *linear* and *lateral* addressees, respectively.

Lateral indirect illocutionary acts pose a problem for the standard theories. In (6), the standard theories say that Ann's only direct illocutionary act is the assertion to Charles. But if she isn't performing any illocutionary act toward Barbara, how is it possible for her to perform an *indirect* illocutionary act toward Barbara—the indirect request? In the standard theories, all indirect illocutionary acts are performed by means of direct ones aimed at the same hearer. These theories predict that the lateral request in (6) is not possible.

One solution is to deny that Ann's request in (6) is indirect. Instead, one would say that she is performing two *direct* illocutionary acts—an assertion toward Charles, and a request of Barbara. There are two drawbacks to this. One is that, in (6), Ann is clearly addressing Charles, not Barbara. She uses the vocative *Charles*; and she speaks of Charles as *you*, but of Barbara in the third person. This solution would require a drastic revision of the notion of addressee. This solution also obliterates the parallels between (5) and (6): in (5), Ann's request is clearly indirect; in (6), it should be indirect for the same reasons.

A second solution is to drop the "indirect performance criterion" that indirect illocutionary acts must be performed by means of direct illocutionary acts addressed to the same hearer or hearers. This move, however, would be self-defeating. In Searle's 1975 theory, it is this criterion that makes an illocutionary act indirect.[5] If it were dropped, indirect acts would become formally indistinguishable from direct acts, and much of the motivation for the theory would disappear.

A third solution is to bring in informatives. In uttering (6), Ann is informing Barbara of her assertion to Charles, and she is thereby making her indirect request of Barbara. This solution retains the idea that Ann's request of Barbara is indirect. It also retains the indirect performance criterion, since Ann's indirect request is performed by means of a direct informative to the same hearer. The analysis which we will offer later differs from this solution only in some details.

Lateral indirect illocutionary acts must be contended with because they are so common: e.g.,

(7)   Charles, to Ann, in front of Barbara: *Ann, what's playing at the theater next week?*
        Ann, to Charles, in front of Barbara: *Sorry, I don't know. But Barbara does.*
        Barbara, to Charles, in front of Ann: *"Much Ado About Nothing".*

In telling Charles that Barbara knows what's playing, Ann is indirectly and laterally asking Barbara to answer Charles' question. Again:

(8)   Father, to son, in front of daughter Julia: *Ned, go do your homework.*
        Ned, to father, in front of Julia: *I can't. Julia stole all my pencils.*
        Julia, to father, in front of Ned: *No, Papa, I did not.*

When Ned addresses his father, he is laterally charging his sister with stealing his pencils, a charge she then laterally denies. Lateral indirectness like this is quite an ordinary part of conversations.[6]

---

[5] Cf. the inclusion principle discussed in Section 4, below.

[6] Evidently the use of lateral indirectness is acquired quite early. Sully (1896: 474–5) gave several illustrations from the study of C., a somewhat precocious five-year-old:

One day (the end of the seventh month) he was playing on the Heath under the eye of his mother. He had put on one of the seats a lot of grass and sand as fodder for his wooden horse. While he went away for a minute a strange nurse and children arrived, making a perfectly legitimate use of the bench by seating themselves on it, and in order

In talking laterally, the speaker doesn't appear to be speaking to the indirect addressee, but to someone else, and this appearance is often useful. One example is what Greenburg 1964 has called the "third person invisible". Imagine that a grown son has brought home a female friend for his mother's approval:

(9)   Mother, to son, in front of his friend: *Does she want another cup of coffee?*

In asking her son this, the mother is really telling the woman indirectly that she is refusing to speak to her. If the mother had said directly *I refuse to speak to you*, she would be belying her own words. She can accomplish what she wants only indirectly *and* laterally, e.g., by telling her son *I refuse to speak to that woman*, or as in (9).

In other examples, the speaker makes a pretense of speaking linearly when the primary illocutionary act is lateral and indirect; e.g.,

(10)   Mother, to three-month-old, in front of father: *Don't you think your father should change your diapers?*

(11)   Father, to dog, in front of son: *Lassie, Daniel is about to take you for a walk.*

(12)   Mechanic, to automobile, in front of co-worker: *Damn it, car, I need two more hands to help me bolt your fender back on.*

In (10), the mother is laterally and indirectly asking father to change the baby's diapers; in (11), the father is ordering the son to take the dog for a walk; and in (12) the mechanic is asking his co-worker for help. The pretenses are clear, because the direct illocutionary acts are aimed at things that couldn't be real targets of what the speakers are saying.

An extreme form of lateral indirectness is required when direct illocutionary acts are precluded by taboo. Certain Australian groups have "mother-in-law languages" for talking in the presence of relatives with whom it is forbidden to speak (Dixon 1972; Thomson 1935). However, when a woman wants to communicate with her son-in-law, whom she cannot address directly, she can address a nearby dog or child. Thomson (485) describes how a Wik Monkan woman can ask her son-in-law for tobacco:

She may not use direct talk (*wik koi'um*) which is: *ŋ aindäŋŋ aiya mai ken ya'a*, "Son-in-law I tobacco nothing," but in *ŋonk wonk tonn* [the avoid-

---

to get room brushing away the precious result of his forging expedition. On coming back and seeing what had happened he turned to his mother and swelling with indignation exclaimed loudly: *'What do you mean by it, letting these children move away my things?* Of course this was intended to intimidate the real culprits, the children.

ance language], speaking to her daughter's dog: *kemiäŋmampi θaiya koṇ katụme*. "Daughter's son (i.e., the dog is the child of her *tuwa* [child]), I tobacco nothing." If he has none, instead of replying directly *ŋ aiya ya'a*, he again addresses the dog: *ŋ aindäŋŋ aiya katụm*, "Son (to his dog), I (have) nothing," or if he has a small piece only he may say *inwé ŋ ainda wettä*, "Here (is) son no good." Freely rendered "Son, here is a little no good piece."

Interestingly, the Wị̄k Monkan term for the avoidance language is *ŋoṇk woṇk toṇn*, literally "speech side another", which Thomson glosses as "one side talk". The woman is speaking "one side" to her son-in-law. This is contrasted with *wị̄k koị'ụm* or "straight talk", i.e. speech to linear addressees.

So lateral indirect illocutionary acts, though ubiquitous, cannot be accounted for by the standard theories. They appear to require the recognition of informatives.

Designating Addressees

In conversations with three or more parties, one person can "speak to" the others without knowing which of them he is addressing; for instance,

(13)   Charles, to Ann and Barbara: *Please return my map, whichever of you has it.*

Imagine that Ann and Barbara know that Ann has the map, and that Charles has no idea which one of them has it. So Charles is making a request of Ann, but he doesn't know this. As far as he is concerned, he is aiming what he is saying as much at Barbara as at Ann.

The standard theories aren't equipped to handle (13); they presuppose that the speaker knows to whom he is addressing each illocutionary act. A request, says Searle (1969, 57), is "an attempt to get H to do A", where H is "the hearer" "in the presence of whom the sentence is uttered." Charles, however, isn't trying to get both Ann and Barbara to return his map. The person he is trying to get to return the map is the one who has it, whichever one that may be,

Charles makes this explicit with his vocative, *whichever of you has it*. The problem is that Charles's intentions toward Ann and Barbara are identical. So if he is performing an illocutionary act toward, say, Ann—which he must be, if he is making a request—then he must also be performing an illocutionary act toward Barbara.

One solution is to assume that Charles is performing two illocutionary acts simultaneously. He is making a request of the person with the map, and he is informing the other person of that request. He lets the situation sort out which person is which. In this way, Charles is treating Ann and Barbara in virtually the same way. Later, we will return to such examples and offer a solution in which Charles treats Ann and Barbara entirely symmetrically. The point for now is that examples like (13) also appear to require informatives.

Public Side-Participants

On many occasions, government officials, television newsmen, and others are ostensibly addressing certain hearers, but their primary aim is to inform the on-looking public of what they are saying to these hearers. Consider, first, a television interview between, say, Crothers and Senator Smyth. In private, their talk might go like this:

(14)   Crothers, to Senator Smyth: *Well, Joe, what do you think of the New Hampshire stink?*
       Smyth, to Crothers: *It's a goddam mess. If Bill doesn't watch his ass, Bert may take away all his marbles.*

Before the television camera, however, Crothers and Smyth treat the unseen viewers as side-participants, and their utterances change radically:

(15)   Crothers, to Smyth: *Senator Smyth, what do you think of Jones's controversial remarks in the New Hampshire election campaign last week?*
       Smyth, to Crothers: *They were unfortunate. If Senator Jones doesn't watch his step, Bert Appleman may get impatient with him and cut off all his campaign funds.*
       Crothers, to Smyth: *You're speaking of Bert Appleman, the Democratic Party National Chairman, aren't you?*
       Smyth, to Crothers: *Yes, I am.*

The features that Crothers and Smyth add to accommodate the side-participants are of three types. First, the private references to Joe, to *the New Hampshire stink*, to Bill, to Bert, and to *marbles* are filled out so that the television audience can understand them, too. Second, when Smyth doesn't fill out his references enough, as with the mention of Bert Appleman, Crothers requests clarification, even though he himself knows perfectly well who is being referred to. Third, both men move into a register appropriate for their public personae: they avoid informality and offensive expletives.

Consider, next, open letters addressed to *the President* or *the oil companies* or *Members of Congress*, which are published as political advertisements in newspapers and magazines, or *letters to the editor*, which are expressly written for possible publication in the editor's newspaper or magazine. Although these letters are addressed to the President, the oil companies, etc., their main targets are the newspaper and magazine readers who are the side-participants in these public acts. Without informatives to these readers, the purpose of these public acts would be lost.

On other occasions, side-participants are desirable but not necessary. Consider public expressions of thanks, congratulations, apologies, and condolences:

(16)   Mayor, to fireman: *On behalf of the citizens of San Francisco, I thank you for saving three lives in last Thursday's fire, and in appreciation I give you this medal.*

(17)   Duchess of Kent, to Billy Jean King on winning the women's finals at Wimbledon: *Congratulations on your fine performance. Here is the winner's cup.*

(18)   The President, to Queen Elizabeth, as she steps out of an airplane in Washington: *Welcome to the United States.*

In all three cases, the main point is to express a politically important feeling in public. The public is intended to bear witness to these feelings. Although these speakers could have expressed these feelings without any guests present, it is ordinarily the public participation in the expression of the feelings that counts.

With certain public acts, therefore, it is the informatives—the acts of informing the side-participants of what is being said—that fulfill the main purpose of what is being said.

Institutional Witnesses

In Austin's classic work, the first three illocutionary acts mentioned are the marriage vow *I do*, the christening *I name this ship the Queen Elizabeth*, and the bequest *I give and bequeath my watch to my brother*. These attracted his attention because they are parts of "accepted conventional procedures" in the church and the law; so it is easy to see when they are mis-invoked, mis-applied, or mis-executed—i.e., when they are infelicitous. As it happens, many such procedures also appear to require informatives for felicitous performance.

Consider the questioning of the defendant at a murder trial by the prosecuting attorney:

(19)   Attorney, to defendant, in front of judge, jury, and court officials: *When did you arrive at the bank?*

The attorney is asking the defendant (the addressee) a question. But if this is to count as an official question, as a part of the official trial, then he must also be informing the judge, jury, and other court officials that he is asking the defendant that question. The informatives directed at these institutional witnesses are mandatory.

To see this, consider several ways in which the attorney could succeed in asking the defendant the right question, but without properly informing the institutional witnesses. He could speak in too low a voice; in that case, the judge would ask him to repeat the question so all could hear. Or he could leave the question ambiguous for the judge and jury between two interpretations of *bank*; in that case, the judge would ask him to clarify the question. More subtly, he could phrase the question *When did you arrive at the place where Mary works?*, knowing that the suspect would understand that he was referring to the bank, but that the judge and jury couldn't (since they don't know of Mary or where she works). In that case, the defense attorney could object, and the judge would ask for a rewording. As in ordinary conversations, it isn't enough for the attorney to ask the witness a question that the witness fully understands. With his utterance, he must also properly inform the institutional witnesses of that question.

In many legal settings, the institutional witnesses sign documents affirming that they witnessed the appropriate illocutionary acts toward the addressees and accept these as felicitous—as not being false, or fraudulent, or insincere. This includes wills, contracts, and passport applications, as well as most actions in court. With a will, for example, it isn't legally sufficient for a person to make a bequest sincerely and in sound mind: he must properly inform two witnesses that he is doing so, and they must attest to this by signing the will. There is even a person specially designated as a legally certified side-participant to such acts: the notary public.

Consider, finally, the marriage vow made by the groom to the bride, as prescribed by the *Book of Common Prayer*:

(20)   Groom, to bride, in front of minister and wedding company: *In the Name of God, I, John, take you, Mary, to be my wife, to have and to hold from this day forward [etc.]*

John could make this vow to Mary sincerely without anyone else around. But for it to count as a *marriage* vow, he must also inform the minister and the wedding company that he is making this vow. As the *Book of Common Prayer* prescribes, "it is required ... that the ceremony be attested by at least two witnesses." What these witnesses must apparently attest to is not merely that John said the right words, but that he meant what he said. Before the ceremony, the witnesses are asked, *If any of you can show just cause why they [the bride and groom] may not lawfully be married, speak now; or forever hold your peace.* If the witnesses believed that John's intentions were in any way insincere—e.g. that he planned to abandon Mary for another woman after the ceremony—they could not in good conscience attest to his marriage vow.[7]

The problem raised by these examples is the same as before: the standard theories say nothing about illocutionary acts directed at hearers other than the addressees. Yet for an attorney's question to be official, for a will to be legal, or for a marriage vow to be proper, the speaker must act toward the institutional witnesses as well as toward his addressees. He must fully inform the witnesses of what he is doing to his addressees. Without informatives, these institutional procedures would collapse.

2 Audience Design

If speakers relied solely on conventional linguistic devices to convey what they meant, everyone who knew the language should have equal ability to understand them. But the examples we have offered suggest quite the opposite. when the speakers design their utterances, they assign different hearers to different roles; and then they decide how to say what they say on the basis of what they know, believe, and suppose that these hearers, in their assigned roles, know, believe, and suppose. That is, a fundamental property of utterances is one that we will call *audience design*. To characterize informatives properly, we must first characterize the roles to which these hearers are assigned, and the ways in which speakers design their utterances with these hearers in mind.

Hearer Roles

Conversations consist, very roughly, of sequences of utterances among two or more people; with each utterance, the speaker performs one or more illocutionary acts directed at addressees. Consider one of these utterances:

---

[7]Marriage appears to be the only Christian sacrament that requires official witnesses (aside from God—who, when not the addressee, is a side-participant in most sacramental speech acts). In a Roman Catholic marriage, witnesses may not have to be full side-participants in the sense we mean it, even though they ordinarily will. According to one Roman Catholic handbook (Jone 1959, 523), "Witnesses need not have the explicit intention of acting as witnesses to a marriage. It is sufficient if they do so accidentally, even though the contractants are not aware of this ... Marriage is also valid if the witnesses are forced to assist by violence, fear or deception." We are indebted to A. P. Martinich for bringing these points to our attention. For a discussion of sacramental speech acts but without mention of witnesses, see Martinich 1975.

(21)   Ann, to Barbara, in front of Charles, with David eavesdropping:
        Barbara, when did the two of you arrive last night?

For every addressee-directed illocutionary act such as Ann's question to Barbara, we can identify four basic roles:

Speaker (agent of the illocutionary act). This is the person who performs the illocutionary act: in (21), the role is filled by Ann.[8]

Participants in the addressee-directed illocutionary act. These are the hearers who the speaker intends to "take part in" the illocutionary act that is directed at the addressees. In (21), the participants include Barbara and Charles, but not David. What it means to "take part in" an illocutionary act will be spelled out below.

Addressees of the addressee-directed illocutionary act. Certain of the participants are intended to take on additional roles as addressees of the illocutionary act. In (21), Barbara is the addressee. The addressees are the participants who are, or could be, designated vocatively in the utterance, as Barbara is named in (21). They need not coincide with the set of hearers referred to by *you*, but need only be a subset of those hearers: in (21), *you* refers to both Barbara and Charles, whereas the only addressee is Barbara. The participants, then, divide into two subsets: those who are also addressees, like Barbara, and those who are not, like Charles. It is convenient to call the latter participants *side-participants*, the term we have already been using for these hearers.

Overhearers of the addressee-directed illocutionary act. These are the hearers who are not intended by the speaker to "take part in" the illocutionary act, in the favored sense of "take part in,"

---

[8] Just as the notion of hearer can be differentiated into various roles, so can that of speaker. Goffman 1979 distinguishes between the "animator" of an utterance (the person uttering the words), the "author" of the utterance ("the person who has selected the sentiments that are being expressed and the words in which they are encoded"), and the "principal" (the person who is "committed to what the words say"). Suppose that George (standing with Jane) says to Julia, in front of Margaret, *Julia, Jane and I congratulate you on your new discovery.* Although George is the animator and the author of the utterance, he is merely the spokesman for the congratulations, for which he and Jane together are the principals. Informatives may aid in these distinctions. In George's utterance, George himself is informing Julia and Margaret of something; but what he is informing them of is the congratulations that he and Jane are jointly performing. George is the sole agent of the informative, but George and Jane jointly are the agents of the congratulations. Informatives would enable us to distinguish between the agents of the two illocutionary acts. In other ways, too, this analysis would fit nicely into the informative analysis proposed in Section 4, below.

but who are nevertheless listening in. In (21), David is an over-hearer.[9]

These four roles are defined by the speaker. He defines his own role as speaker; he defines who is to "take part in" his illocutionary act, separating the participants from the overhearers; and he defines who among the participants are to be addressees. He makes these role assignments by the way he designs his utterance, and by the way he positions himself with respect to the audience. We will take up these methods in our discussion of audience design and role assignment. On any occasion, the speaker may not succeed in getting his hearers to recognize the roles to which they are being assigned, despite a flawless performance on his part; hearers do make mistakes. For our purposes, however, these cases are irrelevant. What is relevant are the speaker's intentions about who is to assume which roles. It is these intended roles that are being designated as speaker, addressee, participant, and overhearer.

Types of Audience Design

The speaker designs his utterance with these roles in mind. In this way, audience design can be divided roughly into participant design, addressee design, and overhearer design.[10] The basic design, as we will present it, is for participants. Addressees and overhearers are taken care of in modulations on the basic design.

The basic design is characterized by the Principle of Responsibility proposed earlier. By this principle, the speaker is responsible for designing his utterance so that all the parties to the conversation can

---

[9]These distinctions aren't altogether new. Virtually the same ones have been made in studies of the sequential organization of conversation (see footnote 10), although not with respect to the speaker's illocutionary intentions. Goffman's distinctions (1975, 260: see also 1978, 1979) are very close to ours:

Observe now that, broadly speaking, there are three kinds of listeners to talk; those who overhear, whether or not their unratified participation is inadvertent and whether or not it has been encouraged; those who are ratified participants but (in the case of more than two-person talk) are not specifically addressed by the speaker; and those ratified participants who are addressed, that is, oriented to by the speaker in a manner to suggest that his words are particularly for them, and that some answer is therefore anticipated from them, more so than from the other ratified participants.

[10]Our concept of audience design has obvious roots in the notion of "recipient design" used in studies of the sequential organization of conversation (cf. Sudnow 1972, Psathas 1979). Sacks et al. 1974, who attribute the concept to Garfinkel 1967, describe it as follows: "By 'recipient design' we refer to a multitude of respects in which the talk by a party in a conversation is constructed or designed in ways which display an orientation and sensitivity to the particular other(s) who are the co-participants." Our notion of audience design encompasses overhearers as well as addressees and "co-participants."

keep track of what he is saying. This defines what might be called a *canonical conversation*. With each contribution, the speaker assigns to every other party in the conversation the role of participant. The conversation can therefore accumulate as a whole, and the common ground that accrues is easy for everyone to keep track of.

In non-canonical conversations, this simplicity is lost. Imagine A talking with B, C, and D. If the conversation isn't canonical, A must keep track separately of his common ground with B, with C, and with D. If he knows B well, C moderately, and D very little, then there will be large disparities in common ground to begin with. If he informs B, C, and D of different things during the conversation, and if he is informed by them of different things, these disparities can only grow and become even more difficult to keep track of. The speaker's task is therefore greatly simplified in that most conversations, or most parts of conversations, are assumed to be canonical by all parties. The parties accomplish this by always assigning all other parties to the role of participant.

Although most conversations, or parts of conversations, are canonical, speakers can and do deal with disparities in common ground when they must. They exploit these disparities to say one thing to one group of participants while saying something else to another, or to carry out elaborate deceptions. We will return to these possibilities later.

The addressees are the ostensible targets of what is being said. Ordinarily, they are the participants for whom the speaker has the most direct and obvious goals in designing his utterances. In (2), when Ann tells Charles *We went to the museum*, she is making sure both Barbara and Charles understand what she is doing, but she has designed her utterance with Charles in particular in mind: she wants to get him to believe that they went to the museum. As a preparatory condition, then, she must assume, very roughly, that Charles doesn't already believe what she is asserting. She doesn't have to assume this for Barbara; indeed, Ann thinks that Barbara already does believe the proposition that she is asserting. Most of Searle's "felicity conditions" for speech acts are satisfied as part of addressee design, not merely participant design.

Speakers also design their utterances with overhearers in mind. Although they don't intend the overhearers to "take part in" what they are saying—in the favored sense of "take part in"—they realize that the overhearers can nevertheless form conjectures or hypotheses about what they mean. The purpose of overhearer design is to deal with these hypotheses. By designing their utterances just right, speakers can lead overhearers to form correct hypotheses, incorrect hypotheses, or even no coherent hypotheses at all. If they know their overhearers, they can even design what they say to fit them in particular. These we will call *known overhearers*. Yet speakers also recognize the possibility of *unknown overhearers*, and they can design what they say with them in mind, too. That is, speakers can harbor intentions toward both known and unknown overhearers, and can design their utterances accordingly. These intentions, however, are different from those that speakers have toward the participants, as we will argue, in that they are not intended to be recognized as intended to be recognized.[11]

In the most obvious examples of overhearer design, speakers try to prevent overhearers from correctly guessing what they are saying. For example, there is the secrets-in-a-crowd scenario:

(22)   Ann, to Barbara, on crowded bus: *Do you remember that thing about you-know-who that we were talking about last week? Well, it happened.*

Ann's references are designed to be opaque to everyone but Barbara, who is the only one for whom the last week's conversation is common ground. Similarly, there is the spelling ploy used by parents in front of children:

(23)   Father, to mother, in front of Johnnie: *What did you think of the b-i-c-y-c-l-e we saw in the store?*

With spies, this sort of prevention is a sine qua non of communication. One strategy is to switch to a language not known to potential overhearers, namely a spy code.[12] Another is to switch to a code that masquerades as a genuine language, and thus leads overhearers to the wrong hypotheses.[13]

---

[11] Consider what Goffman 1978 has called "response cries," as when a man, walking alone down the street and slipping on some ice, says *Oops* loud enough for the people who happen to be watching to hear. As Goffman argues, the man intends these self-imprecations to be heard by people nearby, in order to let them know he is aware of what befell him and is in full control. Yet he isn't addressing those people. He intends his *Oops* to appear to be a self-imprecation that they just happen to overhear. In our terms, he intends them to recognize what he meant, but not by means of their recognition of his intention that they do so.

[12] Kahn 1967 gives the following example of a telegram from President Lincoln to Colonel Ludlow during the Civil War: *Guard adam they at wayland brown for kissing venus correspondents at neptune are off nelly turning up can get shy detained tribune and times richardson the are ascertain and you fills belly this if detained please odor of ludlow commissioner.* Translation: *For Colonel Ludlow. Richardson and Brown, correspondents of the* Tribune, *captured at Vicksburg, are detained at Richmond. Please ascertain why they are detained and get them off if you can. The President.*

[13] As in this World War II conversation between Kurusu, the Japanese Ambassador to the US, and Yamamoto, the Foreign Office American Division Chief, shortly

Overhearers are generally not meant to realize how utterances have been designed for them. The deception may be benign, as when a worker sings the praises of his boss while knowing that the boss may be overhearing. It is less benign when the same worker winks broadly at his co-workers to indicate the irony of his remarks. Other times, the design may have more serious ends, as when Hamlet, in Act III, Scene 1, plays the madman in talking to Ophelia—apparently to draw two known overhearers, the King and Polonius, into thinking that he is going mad. In these examples, the conjectures to which the overhearers are led are sometimes correct, and sometimes not.

Another element in overhearer design is politeness and register (see Comrie 1976, Levinson 1979). In most societies, certain words are taboo in certain circumstances, in which they may not even be overheard. In urban America, obscenities freely used in locker rooms are often avoided in public places where they may be overheard.[14] The goal is to project the speaker's public persona and to avert overhearer discomfort. Many aspects of speech registers, from the oratorical to the intimate, have related origins, as do the Australian "mother-in-law" languages mentioned above. Because it is forbidden to use ordinary speech in the presence of one's mother-in-law or other specified kin, what has developed is a special register, with its own vocabulary, that is used near a tabooed kin who might possibly overhear.

Role Assignment

As a critical part of audience design, the speaker must designate which hearers are to take which roles. It is essential that the speaker and participants, and the speaker and addressees, mutually recognize which hearers are being designated as participants and which as addressees. How speakers accomplish this is a complicated topic (see Goffman 1979). We will mention only the major devices by which they do this: physical arrangement, conversational history, gestures, manner of speaking, and linguistic content. Most utterances rely on some combination of these five factors.

---

before Pearl Harbor (from Kahn): *But without anything, they want to keep carrying on the matrimonial question [i.e. the negotiations]. They do. In the meantime we're faced with the excitement of having a child born [i.e., we're faced with a crisis]. On top of that Tokugawa [i.e. the army] is really champing at the bit, isn't he?*

[14]Strikingly, it isn't the meaning of a particular expression that is eschewed, but rather its form or sound. As Randolph 1928 has noted, people will use circumlocutions like *She's ready to go* or *The hammer's back* just to avoid saying *The gun's cocked*. The idea is, apparently, that an overhearer might hear only the critical word, and mistake it for an obscenity.

Participants are often distinguished from overhearers by physical arrangement. Hearers in the same group as the speaker can ordinarily assume they are intended to be participants, whereas other hearers cannot. What constitutes a group (a "with", in Goffman's 1971 terminology) is highly constrained by physical arrangement. The people must be near each other relative to the space available—not separated by obvious physical or psychological barriers, and accessible to each other auditorily and visually (see Goffman 1963, 1971).

Participants are also distinguished from overhearers by the history of the ongoing conversation. If certain hearers were participants during the last utterance, and if the speaker gives no indication to the contrary, then they can assume that they are also participants for the current utterance. It may happen that two parties in a group exchange so many remarks that they come to define their own conversation, with the others splitting off into a separate conversation. It can also happen that one party in a group comes to be ignored, and is no longer taken to be a participant in what is being said.

Addressees are generally designated in part by gestures. They can be picked out by eye contact, sometimes accompanied by a hand gesture or nod of the head. Furthermore, certain people in a group can be excluded as addressees or participants by the speaker's turning his back on them. The advantage of gestures is that they are public acts, easily recognized simultaneously by all the parties involved.

Addressees and participants can also be designated by manner of speaking. By whispering, a speaker can select a small group of people as participants or addressees, letting everyone else know they are not participants. By speaking in a markedly loud voice, a speaker can do just the opposite. At a restaurant, Ann might say to her companion *This could do with a little salt*, asking him to pass the salt. By saying this loudly within earshot of the waiter, she could designate the waiter as participant and indicate that he instead was to fulfill her request. By using a high pitch, a speaker can designate children as opposed to adults as participants; by over-articulating, a speaker can likewise designate foreigners.

Finally, of course, addressees, participants, and overhearers are often designated through the content of what is said. Addressees can be defined by vocatives and other devices. Participants can be brought in by prefatory utterances, such as *George and Julia, I want you to hear what I have to say to Edward,* and in other ways. Overhearers can be excluded as participants by similar devices. Later we will take up devices for designating addressees in some detail.

In summary, speakers intend certain hearers to fill certain roles, and they design their utterances accordingly. In particular, they have devices for getting hearers to recognize mutually who is to take which roles. Most of these devices derive not from the content of what is said, but from such factors as the physical arrangement of the hearers, the history of the conversation, gestures, and the manner of speaking. All these factors, whether "linguistic" or not, must be considered part of the means by which the speaker performs illocutionary acts. They are crucial for designating to whom these acts are directed.

3 Informatives

So far our characterization of informatives has been informal. We now consider them more closely, taking up three issues. First, are informatives truly illocutionary acts? Second, to whom are informatives directed? And third, how would informatives be characterized in the standard theories?

Informatives as Illocutionary Acts

Informatives are speech acts—but which type are they? Since they are performed with whole utterances, they cannot be propositional acts such as reference or predication (Searle 1969). The obvious candidates are Austin's locutionary, illocutionary, and perlocutionary acts.

Informatives are clearly not locutionary acts, since these are merely acts of "saying something" (Austin, 94). In (1), Othello's locutionary act consists of saying the imperative sentence *Come, Desdemona* with *come* and *Desdemona* having a certain meaning and reference. Since locutionary acts aren't directed by speakers to specific hearers, Othello's act of informing Iago and Roderigo of his request to Desdemona cannot be a locutionary act. In Austin's scheme, locutionary acts would be used in performing informatives, and so they would be kept conceptually distinct.

Nor are informatives perlocutionary acts. In uttering (1), Othello is trying to get Desdemona to go with him. If she then goes with him, she does so only as a consequence of her understanding what he meant. Ever since Austin, consequences such as this have been called perlocutionary effects. These are distinguished from illocutionary effects, which consist of hearers' understandings of what speakers mean. Imagine, then, that (in uttering (1)) Othello is also trying to get Iago and Roderigo to stay behind. If they do so, that would be another perlocutionary effect of Othello's utterance. But it would be a consequence of their understanding that he was asking Desdemona to go with him. Our interest, however, is not in the consequences of their understanding what he meant, but in the understanding itself. Our interest, therefore, is in illocutionary effects and in the illocutionary acts that produced them.

In the standard theories, illocutionary acts are distinguished from other speech acts at the utterance level by the fact that they require reflexive intentions—Grice's "m-intentions" (Bach and Harnish 1979; Grice 1957, 1968, 1969; Schiffer 1972; Searle 1969; Strawson 1964). What is required, as Searle (47) put it, is that "the speaker S intends to produce an illocutionary effect IE in the hearer H by means of getting H to recognize S's intention to produce IE." So Othello intends to get Desdemona to understand that he wants her to go with him. But according to this criterion, he gets her to understand this by getting her to recognize his intention to get her to understand this. If informatives are illocutionary acts, Othello must intend to get Iago and Roderigo to understand that he is requesting Desdemona to go with him by means of getting them to recognize his intention to get them to understand that he is doing that. Note that Othello could intend some overhearing guard to guess what he means, too. But if he doesn't intend to do so by means of getting the guard to recognize that intention, then he isn't performing an illocutionary act toward that guard. Let us call a communicative intention that is less than an m-intention (like this one) a *partial intention*.

There is good evidence that informatives require m-intentions, not partial intentions. Let us return to our example of a lateral indirect request:

(6)   Ann, to Charles, in front of Barbara: *Charles, I insist that Barbara tell you who we met at the museum today.*

Ann is indirectly asking Barbara to tell Charles who they met. By the standard theories, requests like this, whether direct or indirect, require m-intentions. How does Ann make this request? She can do it, we argued, only by informing Barbara of her assertion to Charles. Suppose that this informative were based on a partial intention; i.e., Ann didn't intend Barbara to understand by means of her recognition of any of Ann's intentions. If so, there would be no way for Ann to get Barbara to recognize her *indirect* intention to get Barbara to tell Charles who they met at the museum; and this recognition is necessary for such a request. Put simply, m-intentions cannot be indirectly conveyed by partial intentions. Ann's informative must involve m-intentions.

Consider another example given above:

(13)   Charles, to Ann and Barbara: *Please return my map, whichever of you has it.*

Charles is requesting one of the women—he doesn't know which—to return his map; and he is informing the other woman of that request. By definition, he has m-intentions toward the first woman. But since he doesn't know which woman that is, he must have m-intentions toward the second woman as well. Since he is only informing the second woman of his request, that informative must involve m-intentions.

Letters to the editor, intended for publication, force the same conclusion. When people write such letters, they write, in all respects but one, as if they were talking to the newspaper readers and not just the editor. They intend the readers to understand them just as if they were writing them directly—as if addressing them as *Dear reader*. So if m-intentions are required for *Dear reader*, then they are also required for *Dear editor*. *Dear editor* is different only in that the writers are simply informing readers of what they are saying to the editor, whom they address as *you*. Their informatives, therefore, must involve m-intentions.

Finally, consider three-way conversations, as in the following two examples:

(24)   Charles, to Barbara, in front of Ann: *Did the two of you go to the museum?*
Barbara, to Charles, in front of Ann: *Yes, we did.*
Charles, to Barbara, in front of Ann: *And then what?*

(25)   Charles, to Ann, in front of Barbara: *Did the two of you go to the museum?*
Ann, to Charles, in front of Barbara: *Yes, we did.*
Charles, to Barbara, in front of Ann: *And then what?*

For Charles to expect Barbara to grasp the ellipsis of *And then what?* in either (24) or (25), he must make sure she understood the prior question—regardless of whether it was addressed to Barbara herself, as in (24), or to Ann, as in (25). How can he make sure? In (24), it is easy, for he has asked Barbara the prior question directly; he therefore has all the proper m-intentions toward her. In (25), he makes sure only by informing Barbara of that prior question. Intuitively, however, the informative in (25) serves as just as good an antecedent as the direct question in (24). If it does, then it too must involve m-intentions.

The case, however, can be made even stronger. Suppose that Ann and Barbara went to both the Tate and the British Museum, and that Barbara had talked with Charles only about going to the Tate; Barbara didn't know, however, what Ann had discussed with Charles—they might have talked about either museum—and she knew that Charles realized this. In (24), Charles could expect Barbara to recognize that the museum to which he was referring was the Tate, since it was the only museum they had discussed together; i.e., he could expect her to pick out the Tate by means of her recognition of his intention. In (25), however, he could *not* expect her to know to which museum he was referring unless he again intended her to understand by means of her recognition of his intention; otherwise, she could equally well assume he was referring to the British Museum, which she could assume he had discussed previously with Ann. So, for the informative in (25) to serve as a proper antecedent for the elliptical question, it requires an m-intention. A partial intention won't do.

If informatives require m-intentions, they must in this sense be a kind of illocutionary act. What distinguishes them is that they are directed not at addressees, but at participants, which may also include hearers other than addressees. So good evidence exists for the participant hypothesis that certain illocutionary acts are directed at addressees, and others are directed at participants.

Our scheme involves a basic contrast between participants and over-hearers. Participants are intended to take part in addressee-directed illocutionary acts, and overhearers aren't. Now we can say what "taking part in" means: Hearers are intended to take part in an addressee-directed illocutionary act whenever they are m-intended to understand it. What distinguishes overhearers from participants, therefore, is that overhearers aren't m-intended to understand.

Speech Acts to Participants

In each of our examples, the speaker informs the side-participants of the illocutionary act which he is directing at the addressee. In (2), when Ann tells Charles *We went to the museum*, she is informing Barbara that she is telling Charles that they went to the museum. That, however, can't be all that Ann is doing. If she is to enable the conversation to accumulate, she must also inform Charles that she is informing Barbara of her assertion. If she doesn't, Charles cannot assume that Barbara can build on what Ann has told him. The same goes for our other examples.

Informatives, then, are directed at all the participants, not just at the side-participants. This is captured in the participant hypothesis, which states that one class of illocutionary acts is directed at addressees, and another at participants. As a first approximation, an informative is an act by the speaker to make it known to the participants what illocutionary act he is performing for the addressees.

This characterization, however, isn't quite right, since it omits an essential aim of informatives—to make it public knowledge among the speaker and participants what the speaker is doing with his utterance. In (21), when Ann asks Barbara in front of Charles, *Barbara, when did the two of you arrive last night?*, she isn't informing Barbara and Charles separately. She intends Barbara to know that Charles knows, to know that he knows she knows, to know that he knows that she knows that he knows, and so on ad infinitum. This is what is technically called *mutual knowledge* between Barbara and Charles (cf. Schiffer). Ann also intends Barbara to know that her question is mutually known by her and Charles, and she intends Charles to know that it is mutually known by her and Barbara, and so on. With these additions, we require what is technically known as *common knowledge* in a group (Lewis 1969).[15] To make it clear that we are using these technical definitions, we will hyphenate them as "common-knowledge", "commonly-known" etc. Thus, in uttering (21), Ann intends to make it commonly-known among Ann, Barbara, and Charles that, in uttering (21), she is asking Barbara when Barbara and Charles arrived the night before.

In the standard theories, each type of illocutionary act, such as informatives, has associated with it a set of felicity conditions—the necessary and sufficient conditions "for the successful and non-defective performance of the act" (Searle 1969).[16] Since informatives are the means by which speakers "tell" participants what they are doing to addressees, they resemble the illocutionary acts which Searle has called "representatives", and which Austin (as well as Bach and Harnish) has called "constatives." This class includes forms of "telling" such as assertions, reports, claims, and allegations. On that model, the felic-

---

[15]Schiffer (131) also considers mutual knowledge within a group, but his formulation is not equivalent to Lewis' common knowledge. For one thing, his definition allows for a proposition to be mutually known within a group without its being mutually known between two members of the group. Bach and Harnish give a similar definition, but without the infinite iterations of either Lewis or Schiffer.

[16]Searle (54) notes that the failure to satisfy only some of these conditions is sufficient "to vitiate the act in its entirety." Thus Bach and Harnish (55) separate "success" conditions—those conditions "that are singly necessary and jointly sufficient for the performance of an act"—from felicity conditions "that are not success conditions but are required for non-defectiveness." We agree with Bach and Harnish that the role of such felicity conditions in a theory of speech acts is unclear. From our point of view, it is the speaker's illocutionary intentions, as captured in Searle's essential condition (which Bach and Harnish consider a success condition) that are definitive for the act in question. As Searle himself notes (69), "In general the essential condition determines the others."

ity conditions for informatives should look something like this (where "x" is the sentence uttered, "S" is the speaker, "A" is the addressee or addressees, "P" is the participant or participants, and "I" is the illocutionary act which S is directing at A):[17]

Preparatory condition. In uttering x, S is performing I addressed to A.

Sincerity condition. S wants it to be commonly-known among S and P that, in uttering x, S is performing I addressed to A.

Propositional content condition. S predicates that, in uttering x, S is performing I addressed to A.

Existential condition. S's uttering x counts as an attempt by S to make it commonly-known among S and P that, in uttering x, S is performing I addressed to A.

A Notation

To express the parallels between addressee- and participant-directed illocutionary acts, we need a notation. Let us return to Othello's utterance: *Come, Desdemona.* His request has three arguments: the speaker (Othello), the addressee (Desdemona), and the requested act that she go with him. This might be represented as a three-place function as follows: Request(O, D, 'D go with O'). Likewise, Othello's informative has three arguments: the speaker (Othello), the participants (Desdemona, Iago, and Roderigo), and the request of which he is informing them. This might be represented as follows:

(26)   Inform(O, D & I & R, I_1)

Here I_1 stands for Request(O, D, 'D go with O'), where I represents "illocutionary act."[18] In (1), therefore, Othello can be said to be performing two illocutionary acts with the same utterance:

(27)   a. Inform(O, D & I & R, I_1)
       b. Request(O, D, 'D go with O') = I_1

This notation makes it easy to express several constraints on the relation between the addressee-directed and participant-directed acts that

---

[17]The informative defined here is a *joint informative* in which the participants are collectively informed. We take this to be the unmarked case. One can also define an *elementary informative*, in which the speaker informs each participant separately, and doesn't intend his addressee-directed illocutionary acts to become common-knowledge among the participants. The situations that require elementary informatives appear to be rare (see Chapter 7, this volume).

[18]This notation doesn't try to capture all the niceties of the logical form of illocutionary acts. It is intended to represent only roughly the content and force the speaker intends and certain relations among them.

can be performed by a single utterance. First, the agents of the two acts must be identical:[19] in (27), Othello is the first argument of both the Inform and the Request. Second, the targets of the one act—the addressees—must be included among the targets of the other—the participants: in (27), the second argument of the Request (Desdemona) is included in the second argument of the Inform (Desdemona, Iago, and Roderigo).[20] Finally, the third argument of the Inform must refer to the addressee-directed illocutionary act: in (27), the third argument of the Inform is the Request. In this analysis, informatives like (27a) always come paired with addressee-directed illocutionary acts like (27b).

4   Informative-First Hypothesis

For each addressee-directed illocutionary act, there is an informative to let the participants know of that act. In (1), along with Othello's request of Desdemona, there is an informative for Desdemona, Iago, and Roderigo:

(28)   a. Informative: $Inform(O, D \& I \& R, I_1)$
       b. Addressee-directed illocutionary act:
          $I_1 = Request(O, D, \text{'D go with O'})$

What is the connection between (28a) and (28b)?

One possibility is that they are performed independently and in parallel. This can be diagrammed as follows, with the arrows indicating the direction of causation:

(29) $Inform(O, D \& I \& R, I_1)$
           $\nearrow$
       Othello's utterance
           $\searrow$
       $Request(O, D, \text{'D go with O'})$

Othello would be uttering *Come, Desdemona* in order to perform the informative and the request independently. This would be comparable to a person's fanning himself in order to cool himself and to exercise his wrist. Since he can cool himself without exercising his wrist, and can exercise his wrist without cooling himself, these two acts are independent. But can Othello inform Desdemona of his request without making that request, or make his request of Desdemona without informing her of it? It appears not. The independence model is inappropriate at the outset.

---

[19]However, see footnote 8 above.
[20]Note that these targets can be designated either referentially, as here, or attributively, as we have discussed in Section 4.

The second and third possibilities are more promising. In the addressee-first model, (28a) is performed by means of (28b), as in this diagram:

(30)   Othello's utterance
         $\searrow$
       Request(O, D, 'D go with O')
         $\searrow$
       Inform(O, D & I & R, I_1)

Othello makes a request of Desdemona; and by doing so under the appropriate conditions, he informs everyone of his request. In the informative-first model, in contrast, (28b) is performed by means of (28a), as in this diagram:

(31)   Othello's utterance
         $\searrow$
       Inform(O, D & I & R, I_1)
         $\searrow$
       Request(O, D, 'D go with O')

Othello informs Desdemona, Iago, and Roderigo that he is making a request of Desdemona, and by doing this, he also makes the request of Desdemona. In both models, one act is performed by means of another—just as, in shooting a gun, the act of pulling the trigger is performed by means of the act of crooking the right index finger.

The natural place to compare these two models is in speech situations with more than one hearer, where the speaker can have different targets for his informatives and his addressee-directed illocutionary acts. There he must often distinguish addressees from participants. As we noted earlier, he has many ways of getting the participants to recognize who the addressees are; but the principal way is with vocatives. Most vocatives studied so far in linguistics have been the canonical kind: proper names of single individuals, as in *Come, Desdemona*. But they also occur in many other forms, and these provide a surprising line of evidence for distinguishing the addressee-first and the informative-first models.

The Inclusion Principle

The basic function of vocatives is to designate addressees. They generally do this by distinguishing the addressees from the other participants. In (1), there are two "audiences": the participants (Desdemona, Iago, and Roderigo); and the addressee (Desdemona). Let us call these two sets of hearers "Set 1" and "Set 2." In using the vocative, Othello is indicating to Set 1 that he is assigning the role of addressee for this particular request to Desdemona (Set 2) and not to Iago and Roderigo (Set 2'). He is directing his vocative at Set 1 as a means of getting them to recognize Set 2 as distinct from Set 2'. Since performing the vocative is an integral part of performing both the informative and the request, Othello must be performing the informative to Set 1 as a means of making the request to Set 2.[21]

What we will here call the *Inclusion Principle* is one we have met before: when one illocutionary act is used as a means for performing another, the targets of Set 1 must contain the targets of Set 2. This is a basic assumption of Searle's analysis of indirect speech acts. When someone asserts *This soup needs salt* as a means of requesting someone to pass the salt, the addressee of the request must also be an addressee of the assertion. Searle's idea is that the speaker gets the addressee to recognize his request by getting him to recognize the assertion and to see that it isn't sufficient in the circumstances. Without this assumption, Searle's analysis would fall apart.

The Inclusion Principle rules out the addressee-first hypothesis, while leaving the informative-first hypothesis intact. Recall that, in the informative-first hypothesis, Othello performs his informative (one illocutionary act) as a means of performing his request (another illocutionary act). In the addressee-first hypothesis, he does the reverse. So in the informative-first hypothesis, the targets of the first act (Set 1) include the targets of the second (Set 2); but in the addressee-first hypothesis, the targets of the first (Set 2) do not include the targets of the second (Set 1). The Inclusion Principle, therefore, is in direct conflict with the addressee-first model. In plainer words, Othello cannot make a request of Desdemona as a means of informing Iago and Roderigo—since to inform them, he would have to be directing the request at them, too, which he isn't.

This conclusion is a general one. If we accept the Inclusion Principle, then the addressee-first model is ruled out in favor of the informative-first model.

The Equipotentiality Principle

An additional principle applies when vocatives are either attributive (Donnellan 1966, 1968) or indefinite. Consider the attributive vocative here:

---

[21]Consider the request *One of you guys, help yourself to the last beer.* In the vocative, the plural *you guys* requires the targets of the vocative to be more than one guy; but in the request proper, the singular *yourself* requires the target of the request to be exactly one person. The contrast between the two sets of targets is directly indicated in the plural *you* vs. the singular *you.*

(32)   George, to Alistair and Fergus: *The last one of you to leave,
        turn out the lights.*

Suppose that George has no way of knowing who will leave first, Alistair
or Fergus. He cannot direct his vocative at the actual addressee (the
person who is to turn out the lights) since he doesn't know which one
that is. All he can do is direct it at both Alistair and Fergus—and
intend each of them, by recognizing who is picked out, to recognize
which one is the addressee. So, by the Inclusion Principle, George can
only make his request via his informatives, as in this diagram (with
the first causal link from George's utterance omitted):

(33)   Inform(G, A & F, I_1)

   ↘

   Request(G, the last one to leave = X, 'X turn out the lights')

Only in this way is the target of the request (Set 2) included in the
targets of the informative (Set 1).

  The second principle at work here is one we will call the *Equipotentiality Principle.* When a speaker directs what he says at several
hearers at once, not knowing which of them he is actually addressing,
each hearer has an equal potential of being an addressee. So the speaker
must have the same intentions toward all the hearers; he cannot have
special intentions toward any individual hearer. The principle is this:
Whenever the speaker cannot indicate to each of two or more participants whether or not that participant is an addressee, the speaker must
have the same m-intentions toward each of them, regardless of who the
addressees actually are.

  In (32), the only m-intentions that George has equally toward Alistair and Fergus are in his informatives. All George can do directly to
either Alistair or Fergus is inform him of the request he is making of
the person who leaves last. That works out just right, however—since,
by informing each of them of that request, he will automatically make
the request of the right person as well. Suppose that George utters (32)
at noon, and the first person to leave does not do so until midnight.
Although, in one sense, he will have performed both the informatives
and the request at noon, the addressee of the request won't become
specified, and hence the request itself won't become operative, until
midnight. By the Equipotentiality Principle, then, George can make
his request only by means of his informatives.

  The Inclusion and Equipotentiality Principles also apply to indefinite vocatives:

(34)   Schwartz, to history students: *Any of you who needs a syllabus,
        raise your hand.*

Schwartz is directing the vocative *any of you who needs a syllabus* at each of the history students; he is thereby indicating to each of them who are the addressees of his request and who aren't. Since these addressees are a subset of all the history students that he is informing, by the Inclusion Principle, he must be using the informative as a means of making that request, as in this diagram:

(35)   Inform(S, students, I_1)

$$I_1 = \text{Request}(S, X = \text{any student who needs a syllabus,}$$
$$\text{'X raise his hand')}$$

The Equipotentiality Principle leads to the same conclusion. Take the point of view of a student called Margaret. Since Schwartz cannot know whether or not she is an addressee of his request, he must treat her precisely as he is treating all other students. All he can do is inform her that he is making a request of any student who needs a syllabus; but that will do very well. If she happens to be such a student, he will thereby have made a request of her, even though he needn't know that he has done so. If she happens not to be such a student, he will only have informed her that he was making a request of the needy students. To treat Margaret and her fellow students as equally potential addressees of his request, Schwartz must inform each of them of that request, and only by that means make the request of the particular ones who need a syllabus.

It might be objected that vocatives shouldn't be considered a genuine part of the utterances in which they are found: they would be considered separate utterances whose function is to constrain the associated illocutionary acts. Thus Othello would be performing two utterances: with *Desdemona*, he would be "addressing" all three participants in order to designate which one is to be the addressee of his other utterance; with *come*, he would be making a request of the designated addressee. We could then separate the "addressees" of the two utterances—the utterance of *Desdemona* is "addressed" to three people, and the utterance of *come* only to one.

Even if vocatives *were* assumed to be separate utterances, other addressee-specifying devices work the same way. Consider these examples:

(36)   Othello, to Desdemona, in front of Iago and Roderigo: *I want Desdemona to come.*

(37)   George, to Alistair and Fergus: *Would the last one to leave please turn out the lights?*

(38)   Schwartz, to history students: *Any of you who needs a syllabus should raise your hand.*

In these parallels to (1), (32), and (34) respectively, the addressees are specified only through the content of what is requested. The expressions *Desdemona* and *the last one to leave* and *any of you who needs a syllabus* cannot be extirpated and treated as separate utterances.

Even "hidden" vocatives, as in (36)–(38), are unnecessary. Suppose that George is on the roof, out of sight, and is requesting Alistair and Fergus to hand him up certain tools one by one. Further, George doesn't know that Alistair has the saw. George could then say:

(39)   George, in the direction of Alistair and Fergus: *Hand me the saw.*

Alistair and Fergus are both intended to recognize that George is addressing his request to the person with the saw. How? From the fact that George is requesting the saw, and the person who he intends should carry out that request is the one with the saw. We might call this process "addressing by attribution", as if George had said *The one of you with the saw, hand it to me.* He is treating Alistair and Fergus as equally potential addressees, even though he hasn't made that explicit with a vocative or other linguistic device. Here too, therefore, George can make his request only by means of his informatives.

Designating addressees by attribution, as in (39), is commonplace in advertisements. When a television pitchman suggests to his viewers *Treat your child to One-a-Day vitamins*, he is addressing only those viewers with minor children. He intends each viewer to understand what he is suggesting, in order to recognize whether or not he or she is an addressee. The informative must come first.

The Principle of Individual Recognition

Very often, what the speaker is requesting is a coordinated or joint act on the part of two or more addressees:

(40)   Noah, to Shem and Ham: *Begin the trick now.*

Suppose that what Noah is requesting of Shem and Ham is a particularly complicated knife juggling trick that the two of them can only do jointly. It is one of many such tricks they could do; and if either one begins the wrong trick, it could be dangerous. Now Noah isn't asking Shem and Ham to do their parts of the trick separately. He is asking the pair of them to do an act that they can do only as a pair, at least in the way he intends. He is making a collective request. If he had said *Close your eyes*, he would have been making a distributive request, since he would be asking each of them to close his eyes independently.

Collective requests like (40) force us to make explicit a basic assumption of all theories of illocutionary acts. When a speaker performs an illocutionary act, he intends his addressees to recognize certain of his intentions. Now recognition is a mental process that each individual person does on his own: two people may individually recognize the same person, or the same picture, or the same speaker's intention; but it isn't generally assumed that a pair of people, as a collection, jointly recognize that picture, or that person, or that speaker's intention. No one mental system could carry out the single act of recognition; at no one place could that act occur. Speakers, presumably, take this assumption for granted. They adhere to what we will call the *Principle of Individual Recognition* (Clark and Carlson, 1982): Speakers can have m-intentions toward one or more individual hearers at a time, but not toward a collection of hearers.

This principle raises a special problem for collective requests. When Noah asks Shem and Ham to close their eyes in a distributive request, he is in effect making two individual requests, one to Shem and one to Ham. He has m-intentions toward each of them individually and at the same time. Indeed, each can comply without knowing whether the other has been asked to do the same thing. If Noah had said *Do now what I earlier asked you to do*, where neither knew what the other had been told, they could each have recognized his request and complied. All this is not possible with the collective request in (40).

First, Shem and Ham need to be jointly informed of Noah's request. Consider Shem's point of view: by himself, he can recognize that Noah intends him and Ham to begin the trick. But does Ham recognize these intentions? As assurance, Noah must inform Shem that Ham knows about the request, too; otherwise, Shem has no guarantee that he and Ham can coordinate the trick successfully and safely. But Shem realizes that the same reasoning applies for Ham, and so Noah must inform them both equally of the request. What if, for example, Shem thought they were being asked to do knife trick Number 4, while believing that Ham thought it was trick Number 9? Thus Noah cannot request a collective act of Shem and Ham, as in (40), without informing them jointly of that request. The informative is a necessary condition for that request.

With the Principle of Individual Recognition, the informative is more than just a necessary condition. In (40), the target of Noah's request is really the *pair* Shem and Ham. But since Noah cannot intend them as a pair to recognize his intention that the pair of them is to begin the trick now, he cannot make that request directly. The only illocutionary act Noah can direct at Shem individually, or at Ham individually, is the one informing each of them of that collective request. To make the request itself, Noah must intend them to recognize that he is informing them jointly of the request as a means of addressing it to the pair of them. It is through the joint informative, so to speak, that Noah welds Shem and Ham—two otherwise individual recognizers—into a collective recognizer. If we call this collective recognizer Shem-and-Ham, then Noah's illocutionary acts can be diagrammed this way:

(41) $\text{Inform}(N, S \,\&\, H, I_1)$

$\searrow$

   $I_1 = \text{Request}(N, \text{S-\&-H}, \text{'S-\&-H begin trick'})$

Genuine collective requests, therefore, can be performed only by means of informatives to the individual addressees who make up the collection of addressees.

In (40), two hearers were being addressed collectively. The participants can also be treated collectively:

(42)   Adam, to Cain and Abel: *One of you, give me a hand.*

Adam is requesting of either Cain or Abel, but not both, that that person give him a hand. He is leaving it up to them jointly to decide which one is to do it—Cain or Abel. But since he doesn't know which one he is making the request of, he cannot make his request of that person directly. By the Equipotentiality Principle, all he can do is inform them both of that request. When they decide on the addressee, he will thereby have made the request of that person. But Cain and Abel's choice of an addressee must be done jointly; and so they must be jointly informed of the request, just as Shem and Ham had to be jointly informed of Noah's collective request. On both counts, therefore, the request must be performed by means of the informative, and not vice versa.

With distributive requests such as *Close your eyes*, the speaker makes the same request of several addressees at once. He can also make *different* requests of several addressees at once:

(43)   Ann, to Barbara, Charles, and David: *Barbara, Charles, and David, please shake hands with Evelyn, Frank, and George, respectively.*

Barbara is being asked to do one thing, Charles another, and David a third. For Ann to make these separate requests in this way, she can't intend each addressee to understand his own request and nothing more. Barbara, for example, must recognize what all three are being asked to do in order to see which one she is to do. This is even clearer here:

(44) Ann, to Barbara, Charles, and David: *The first three of you to arrive, please shake hands with the next three people to walk in the door, respectively.*

Here each of the addressees must understand how they are distributed across the first three people to walk in the door. In these examples, too, then, it appears that the only way that Ann can make the separate requests of each of them is by informing all three of them of the requests she is making.

Single Nameable Addressees

What about Othello's *Come, Desdemona?* We have already argued that the vocative *Desdemona* is directed not at Desdemona alone, but at Desdemona, Iago, and Roderigo. It therefore isn't part of the request, which is directed only at Desdemona. It must be part of the informative, which is the only illocutionary act directed at all three hearers. We have also argued that the vocative is the means by which Othello designates the addressee of the request. So the informative of which the vocative is a part must also be the means by which Othello performs the request for which the designation of the addressee is required. In short, Othello must be performing the request by means of the informative like this:

(45) Inform(O, D & I & R, I_1)

Request(O, D, 'D go with O')

The informative-first hypothesis is needed on independent grounds for requests like these:

(46) Othello, to Desdemona, Iago, and Roderigo: *Come, Desdemona and anyone else who is interested in coming.*

(47) Othello, to Desdemona, Iago, and Roderigo: *Come, Desdemona and the other one of you who is supposed to come.*

In (46), since the second conjunct of the vocative is indefinite (as in 34), it requires the informative to precede the request; therefore, with the full vocative, the informative must also precede the request. The same logic applies to (47). Now if (1) were claimed to work according to the addressee-first model, and (46)–(47) according to the informative-first model, there would be a glaring inconsistency: one analysis would be claimed for *Come, Desdemona* alone, but quite the opposite for *Come, Desdemona* when it was part of (46)–(47). The three analyses become consistent only when it is assumed that all three requests are performed by means of informatives.

The final case to consider, and the simplest, is one where the speaker addresses a single hearer without any other participants around:

(48)   Othello, to Desdemona: *Come, Desdemona.*

By the standard theories, Othello here is doing only one thing: he is making a request of Desdemona. Yet as at least some have noted (cf. Schiffer), Othello is also informing Desdemona of that request. He must be informing her of it if what he means in (48) is to be distinguished from what he means in (1). In (1) and (48), he is making the identical request of Desdemona. The only difference between (1) and (48) lies in the informative—whether he is informing three participants of that request, or one.

Indeed, in (1), it might be critical for Othello to make clear to Desdemona which informative he intended. If he were informing her alone, his indirect message could be one thing; if he were informing all three jointly, it could be another—that, e.g., he was indirectly asking Iago and Roderigo to stay behind. Thus, for the analyses of (1) and (48) to be consistent, it must be assumed that the request in both is being performed by means of the informative.

This conclusion is also dictated by the logic of the situation. With the informative in (48), Othello can only be making one particular request; yet he can make that very same request with the informative in (1). Logically, therefore, the informative entails the request, but not vice versa. Now in all the analyses in which one illocutionary act is used as a means of performing another, as in indirect speech acts (Searle 1975; Bach and Harnish 1979; Clark 1979), the means entail the ends—given appropriate auxiliary assumptions—and not vice versa. In our examples, therefore, the informatives must be the means, and the addressee-directed illocutionary acts the ends. This is precisely what the informative-first hypothesis claims.

To summarize briefly, we have offered evidence that, regardless of how many addressees or participants there are, and regardless of how the addressees are designated, every addressee-directed illocutionary act must be performed by means of informatives. We will refer to this as the *informative analysis*.

Conditional Requests

Since some of the examples we have offered behave in certain ways like conditional illocutionary acts, one might suggest that they can be handled by what we will call the *conditional analysis of vocatives*. In this analysis, the ordinary request in (32) would be treated as equivalent to the following conditional request:

(49)   George, to Alistair and Fergus: *If you (yourself) are the last to leave, turn out the lights.*

Here both Alistair and Fergus would be addressees, but the request would become operative only for the person who is actually last of leave. Likewise (34) would be equivalent to this:

(50)   Schwartz, to history students: *If you (yourself) are someone who needs a syllabus, raise your hand.*

All the history students would be addressees of the request, but the request would become operative only for the students who need a syllabus (see Rescher 1966).

Plausible as the conditional analysis first appears, it has crippling faults. The first is that it violates the notion of addressee. In this analysis, (1) would be treated as equivalent to the following:

(51)   Othello, to Desdemona, Iago, and Roderigo: *If you are Desdemona, then come.*

All three hearers would be treated as addressees; but since the conditional wouldn't be satisfied for Iago and Roderigo, the request would become operative only for Desdemona. The problem is that, in (1), Othello is *not* addressing Iago and Roderigo. He cannot be said to be making a request of all three of them. The only addressee of his request is Desdemona. This is why we introduced the notion of participant in the first place. Categorizing all three hearers as addressees of the request is simply incorrect.

The same goes for other more complicated vocatives. In requests, the addressees are the requestees—the hearers who are to do what the speaker is requesting (Searle 1969; Bach and Harnish). In (32), that hearer isn't *both* Alistair *and* Fergus, as the conditional analysis in (49) would have it, but only the one who leaves last, precisely as specified in the vocative. If we change (32) to an apology—*The last one of you to leave, I apologize for not showing you out*—then the hearer to whom George is apologizing is still *either* Alistair *or* Fergus, but not both. Because the conditional analysis of vocatives systematically miscategorizes non-addressees as addressees, it must be incorrect.

For other vocatives, the conditional analysis gives the wrong result altogether. It would claim, for example, that (42) is equivalent to the following:

(52)   Adam, to Cain and Abel: *If you (yourself) are one of the two of you* [or: *If you are either Cain or Abel but not both*], *give me a hand.*

The conditional here would be true for both Cain and Abel separately, specifying they should both help Adam; but in (42), Adam wants only one of them to help him. For this reason, too, the conditional analysis of vocatives is unworkable.

Performatives

The informative analysis is a close cousin of what has been called the *constative analysis of performative utterances* (cf. Bach and Harnish). Consider this example of what Austin called "performative utterances":

(53)   Oscar, to Diana: *Diana, I request you to come.*

According to the constative analysis, this is both an assertion and a request, and the request is performed by the means of the assertion. Oscar is asserting to Diana that he is requesting her to go with him; and he is *thereby*, according to a convention of language use, requesting her to go with him. The arguments for such an analysis (see Bach and Harnish, 203–33), and against the major alternative (the "performative hypothesis"—see Gazdar, 15–35), are very strong indeed.[22]

The informative analysis is like the constative analysis in several ways. First, both Othello and Oscar make their requests by means of an assertion-like illocutionary act. In Othello's case, it is an informative; in Oscar's, an assertion. Second, the targets of Othello's informative and Oscar's assertion may include hearers other than the addressee of the request. In Othello's case, they include Iago and Roderigo; in Oscar's, they may also include others, e.g.,

(54)   Oscar, to Diana, Ian, and Robert: *I request the one of you who has my keys to come.*

Third, the connections between Othello's informative and request, and between Oscar's assertion and request, are both based on convention.

The informative analysis can be viewed as an extension of the constative analysis to include hearers other than addressees. First, note that there can be more than one performative verb per utterance, each with its own addressees:

---

[22]Linguists such as G. Lakoff 1975, Ross 1970, and Sadock 1974 have proposed handling performative utterances like (53) by treating their illocutionary force as part of the sentence meaning. In reviewing the evidence and arguments for this "performative hypothesis", Gazdar (15) argues convincingly that the hypothesis is seriously inadequate: "So inadequate, in fact, that it requires replacement rather than repair." As for other arguments for the constative analysis, see Åquist 1972, Bach 1975, Harder 1978, Heal 1974, Kempson 1977, Lewis 1970, Warnock 1973, and Wiggins 1971.

(55)   Professor, to students: *I announce to those of you who are interested that I hereby promise those of you who come early tomorrow that I will answer your questions about the last exam.*

The over-all assertion is directed at all the students; the announcement is directed at the interested students; and the promise is directed at the interested students who come early the next day. As (55) shows, there is nothing odd about using one illocutionary act as a means of performing another, each with different addressees. It is a simple thing to view the assertion itself as performed by means of yet another illocutionary act with its own more inclusive set of target hearers. Imagine adding, in (55), two teaching assistants who know what the professor is going to announce.

(56)   Professor, to students, in front of two teaching assistants: *I announce to those of you who are interested that I hereby promise those of you who come early tomorrow that I will answer your questions about the last exam.*

To handle the two extra side-participants, (56) requires an even higher illocutionary act—namely, the informative—which is directed at all the participants, i.e. the students plus teaching assistants. The informative, therefore, is like an extra higher performative that is added to inform the participants of what is being performed.

The Informative Analysis

What precisely is the connection between informatives and their associated addressee–directed illocutionary acts? What do we mean by saying that Othello performs his informative A as a means for performing his request B—i.e., that his informative "comes first"? Austin, in his original discussion of locutionary, illocutionary, and perlocutionary acts, drew parallels with the component acts of shooting a gun. We will appeal to a general analysis of such intentional human acts by Goldman.

The connection between Othello's A and B appears to be the same as that between pairs of what Goldman has called "level-generational" acts. Consider John's pulling the trigger of a gun (act X) and John's shooting the gun (act Y). Just as act Y is performed by means of act X, so Othello's act B is performed by means of act A. That is, the relation between A and B, as between X and Y, is asymmetric, irreflexive, and transitive. Nevertheless A and B, like X and Y, are performed simultaneously, and over the same time interval—neither one being a temporal part of the other. These are properties of level-generational acts.

One sub-type of level-generational acts is generated by convention, e.g., John's extending his arm out the car window and his signaling for a turn. Likewise, there is a convention according to which Othello's performance of the informative A justifies the further ascription to Othello of his making the request B. The informative is first, therefore, only in the sense that it is the means by which the addressee-directed illocutionary act is performed.

5 Indirectness

In "talking" to side-participants, speakers often do more than merely inform. They ask questions, criticize, offer congratulations, make requests, and do many other things. How do they do this? We have argued that they can perform these indirect acts only by means of informatives; now we consider how this might be done. Somewhat surprisingly, we are forced to argue that the standard analysis of indirect speech acts is not just incomplete, but in certain respects incorrect.

Lateral Indirect Speech Acts

Let us return to the indirect requests in Section 1, repeated here for convenience:

(5)   Ann, to Barbara, in front of Charles, *Barbara, I insist that you tell Charles who we met at the museum today.*

(6)   Ann, to Charles, in front of Barbara: *Charles, I insist that Barbara tell you who we met at the museum today.*

In (5), the indirect request has the same addressee, Barbara, as the direct assertion; so it is a *linear* indirect request. In the standard theories (see Bach and Harnish 1979, Clark 1979, Grice 1975, Morgan 1978, and Searle 1975), Ann makes the assertion as a means of making the request—a relation that might be diagrammed like this:

(57)   Assert(A, B, 'B must tell C who A & B met')
        $\downarrow$
        Request(A, B, 'B tell C who A & B met')

The single arrow represents a "by-means-of" relation that we will keep distinct from the relation represented by the double arrow, which is subject to different conventions.

Because of the informative analysis, however, we must add two informatives to this diagram. First, Ann is informing both Barbara and Charles of her assertion to Barbara, and is thereby making that assertion:

(58)   Inform(A, B & C, I_1)

   ↘

   I_1 = Assert(A, B, 'B must tell C who A & B met')

Also, Ann is informing both Barbara and Charles of the indirect request she is making of Barbara. By the informative analysis, this part is diagrammed as follows:

(59)   Inform(A, B & C, I_2)

   ↘

   I_2 = Request(A, B, 'B tell C who A & B met')

That is, in the circumstances we are assuming, both Barbara and Charles are m-intended to recognize the request Ann is making of Barbara. But for *Charles* to recognize the indirect request, the "by-means-of" arrow cannot connect "Assert" and "Request" themselves, as in (57). This is impossible by the Principle of Inclusion, Charles isn't a target of either of those two illocutionary acts. Instead, the arrow must connect the "Inform" for the "Assert" and the "Inform" for the "Request", as follows:

(60)   Inform(A, B & C, I_1) ⟹ I_1 = Assert(A, B,
    ↓   'B must tell C who A & B met')
  Inform(A, B & C, I_2) ⟹ I_2 = Request(A, B,
             'B tell C who A & B met')

Note that, if Charles weren't present, all that would change would be the informatives—which would be directed at Barbara alone. This is as it should be, since the only difference with and without Charles present is in who is being informed of the assertion and the request.

The diagram in (60) represents all we want to say, at this level of detail, about Ann's indirect request in (5). Ann is informing Barbara and Charles both about her direct assertion and about her indirect request. She is making her request indirectly. And, conforming to the informative analysis, she is making both her assertion and her request by means of informatives. What (60) spells out (but (57) doesn't) are Ann's intentions toward Charles. If Charles could make his reasoning explicit, it would go roughly as follows: *Ann is informing me that she is insisting to Barbara that Barbara tell me about someone they met. Why would she be informing Barbara and me of that assertion? If she is being cooperative in these circumstances, she must be indirectly informing both of us that she is also requesting Barbara to tell me about that person. In so doing, of course, she is also requesting Barbara to tell that to me.*

Let us turn to (6), in which Ann is making the same request of Barbara as in (5)—though her assertion is addressed not to Barbara, but to Charles. In the traditional analysis, the diagram parallel to (57) would be as follows:

(61) Assert(A, C, 'B must tell C who A & B met')
      $\downarrow$
      Request(A, B, 'B tell C who A & B met')

This, of course, is impossible by the Principle of Inclusion, since the target of the "Assert", Charles, doesn't include the target of the "Request", Barbara. Further, example (61) doesn't spell out the needed informatives. For all the reasons we brought up for (5), the needed representation is the following.

(62) Inform(A, B & C, I_3) $\implies$ I_3 = Assert(A, C,
      $\downarrow$ 'B must tell C who A & B met')
      Inform(A, B & C, I_2) $\implies$ I_2 = Request(A, B,
                                                'B tell C who A & B met')

With the informative analysis, therefore, (5) and (6) are given a uniform treatment, yielding the parallel representations in (60) and (62). The only difference between (60) and (62) is in the addressees of the direct assertion: in (5), it is Barbara, and in (6), it is Charles. So this analysis provides a natural extension from linear indirect speech acts (like (5)) to lateral indirect speech acts (like (6)). The standard theories, as we noted, say nothing about examples like (6); and it is hard to see how they could be extended to cover them. All this is further evidence for the validity of the informative analysis.

Complex Indirect Speech Acts

With ordinary linear indirectness, utterances can become very complicated; but with lateral indirectness, the possibilities almost defy imagination. For a relatively simple example, consider this:

(63) Ann, to Barbara, in front of Charles, David, and Ewan: *Barbara, I insist that Charles tell you the joke about the two Irishmen.*

At one level, Ann is informing everyone that she is asserting to Barbara that she insists Charles tell her a joke; she is thereby making that assertion to Barbara. At a second level, dependent on the first, she is also informing everyone that she is asking Charles to tell Barbara that joke, and she is thereby asking Charles to tell it. Suppose, however, that it is common-knowledge among Ann, David, and Ewan—but not Barbara and Charles—that David can't stand Charles' jokes, which he has heard many times before. By informing David and Ewan of her request to Charles, then, Ann is also informing the two of them that she is warning David to leave, and she is thereby warning David to leave. The situation can be diagrammed as follows:

(64) Inform(A, B & C & D & E, I_1) $\Rightarrow$ I_1 = Assert(A, B,
　　↓　　　　　　　　　　　　　　　　　　　　'A insist C tell joke')
　　Inform(A, B & C & D & E, I_2) $\Rightarrow$ I_2 = Request(A, C,
　　↓　　　　　　　　　　　　　　　　　　　　'C tell joke to B')
　　Inform(A, D & E, I_3) $\Rightarrow$ I_3 = Warn(A, D, 'D should leave')

A number of points should be noted here. First, there are distinct addressees at the three different levels of this diagram: Barbara, Charles, and David. In principle, there is no limit to the number of levels or distinct indirect addressees associated with these levels. Second, the participants change from one informative to the next: the participants for the first two informatives are Barbara, Charles, David, and Ewan, whereas those for the third are only David and Ewan. As specified by the Principle of Inclusion, the only requirement is that the participants in each indirect informative be included in those of the informative by which it is performed. Third, there is no obvious way of describing this situation in the standard theories.

Analyses like this make it possible to explicate utterances that turn on rather subtle effects:

(65) Mother, whispering to son, out of earshot of father: *Eat your peas.*

(66) Mother, aloud to son, in front of father: *Eat your peas.*

Suppose it is common-knowledge to the mother, father, and son that the father metes out punishment at the behest of the mother, and that she could well ask him to punish the son if he doesn't eat his peas. In (65), the only participant is the son, and so there is no immediately implied threat. In (66). since the father is also a participant, there *is* an immediately implied threat. The utterance in (65) might be diagrammed this way:

(67) Inform(M, S, I_1) $\Rightarrow$ I_1 = Request(M, S, 'eat peas')

What introduces the threat in (66) is the fact that the son realizes that the mother is not only informing the father of the request, but also indirectly requesting him to punish the son if he doesn't eat his peas. The utterance might be diagrammed like this:

(68) Inform(M, F & S, I_1) $\Rightarrow$ I_1 = Request(M, S, 'eat peas')
　　↓
　　Inform(M, F & S, I_2) $\Rightarrow$ I_2 = Request(M, F, 'punish if needed')
　　↓
　　Inform(M, F & S, I_3) $\Rightarrow$ I_3 = Warn(M, S, 'eat or else')

In (66), the mother's meaning *Eat your peas or else* is three-removes indirect.

In a traditional analysis of (66), one might be tempted to say that the mother is asking the son to eat his peas—and, because he knows the father might punish him if he doesn't, she is thereby also making a threat. This analysis, however, misses an essential element: the mother can make her threat only because the son recognizes that she is also indirectly asking the father to punish him if he doesn't eat his peas. The threat depends on the son's being informed of her conditional request to the father. The perspicuous characterization of (66) therefore requires all the apparatus in (68).

6 Conclusion

With the informative analysis, we are proposing a fundamental addition to the standard theories of speech acts. In our proposal, each traditional illocutionary act, which is directed at addressees, is performed by means of an informative—a logically-prior illocutionary act that is directed at participants. When only one hearer is present, there is little change from the standard analyses of illocutionary acts; this may be why informatives were not noted before. But when more than one hearer is present, informatives take on major importance. They are required, we have argued, to account for the cumulative nature of conversations, lateral indirect illocutionary acts, official and public side-participants, and the many ways in which addressees can be designated: collectively, distributively, attributively, indefinitely, and even singly by name.

With the introduction of informatives, the theory of speech acts gains enormously in power and breadth of application. It is no longer limited to illocutionary acts directed solely at one person: now it applies to genuine conversations in which three or more people address each other in a variety of ways, while adhering to their responsibility to keep everyone informed. It now recognizes an important reality of ordinary talk. Speakers make distinctions among addressees, participants, and overhearers—and in what they communicate to each.

8

Dealing with Overhearers

WITH EDWARD F. SCHAEFER

When we talk, we design our utterances for all the people we believe may be listening. But we don't treat listeners equally. We implicitly relegate them to a caste system depending on our responsibilities and intentions toward them. Our first responsibility is to our addressees—the people we are addressing directly. We also have responsibilities for any other participants there are in the current conversation. We even feel responsibilities toward anyone who may be overhearing us, although these responsibilities are quite different. When we go to formulate our utterances, we try to satisfy all these responsibilities at once. Doing that can be a genuine feat of engineering, because these responsibilities influence our formulations in a myriad of ways. This is a property of utterances called *audience design*, and it must be accounted for in any adequate theory of language use.

Why study audience design? For us there are two main reasons. One is that most theories of language use treat "one speaker, one listener" as if it were a constitutional guarantee. It isn't, of course. Any speaker can have a multitude of listeners in a multitude of roles. "But," you ask, "does that really change anything? All it may do is add new wrinkles to the old theories." We will suggest that it does much more than that. What is remarkable is how many essential aspects of language use it affects and, therefore, how many theories are incomplete, or wrong, without it.

The second reason for studying audience design is to investigate the role of common ground in language use. Common ground is the information shared by two or more people. Technically, it is the sum of their mutual knowledge, mutual beliefs, and mutual assumptions. The notion has played an essential part in theories that we and our colleagues have proposed about reference (Chapters 1, 3, 4, this volume), word meaning (Clark 1982; Clark and Clark 1979; Chapter 11, this volume), contributing to discourse (Clark and Brennan 1991; Chapters 9 and 5, this volume), and dialogues between experts and novices (Isaacs and Clark 1987). It has also been essential to theories of convention (Lewis 1969), speaker's meaning (Schiffer 1972), and illocutionary acts (Cohen and Levesque 1990; Stalnaker 1978). Despite this, there is skepticism in some quarters about whether it is really needed. We will argue that it is. Audience design revolves around the notion of common ground and cannot be accounted for without it.

The argument is that speakers design their utterances taking all potential listeners into account. Now there is wide recognition among linguists, psychologists, and philosophers that speakers take addressees and even other participants in the current conversation into account. But there is almost never any mention of overhearers. As it happens, it is complicated to deal with overhearers, because speakers can take a variety of attitudes toward them. Designing utterances for overhearers, then, offers us a new perspective on audience design and on language use in general.

This chapter is about how speakers deal with overhearers. But we can't look at that without looking at how speakers deal with addressees and participants too. We first try to characterize the responsibilities speakers have toward addressees, participants, and overhearers and, therefore, the attitudes they can take toward each of them. We then take up the logic of designing utterances for all three types of listeners. From there we turn to the techniques speakers have available for dealing with overhearers. And finally, we describe how speakers do things by the way they deal with overhearers.

1 Responsibilities toward Listeners

In conversation, we treat listeners both as individuals and as agents in certain roles. If we think Veronica is listening, we take note of her as an *individual*. We look at the common ground we share with her and design our utterances accordingly. But we also take note of her *role* in the current discourse, which shapes our utterances in other ways. Audience design is subject to judgments about listeners both as individuals and as holders of listener roles. To see how, we must first see the roles listeners can take.

Listener Roles

Speakers distinguish sharply among listeners. In Goffman's (1975) proposal, listeners have three main roles. There are *overhearers*, "whether or not their unratified participation is inadvertent and whether or not it has been encouraged" (260). There are the ratified participants in the current conversation, whom we will call simply *participants*, whether or not they are being addressed at the moment. And there are the *addressees*, "those ratified participants who are addressed, that is, oriented to by the speaker in a manner to suggest that his words are particularly for them, and that some answer is therefore anticipated from them, more so than from the other ratified participants" (260).

The scheme we propose is simply an elaboration of Goffman's. It assumes four basic contrasts among listeners. The first is self versus other listeners. Speakers, of course, listen to themselves in order to monitor what they say, so we will call them self-monitors or, more simply, *monitors*. The second contrast is between participants and nonparticipants, or overhearers. The third is between the two types of participants, the addressees and the rest. We will call the other participants *side participants*. The final contrast is between two types of overhearers. *Bystanders* are those listeners who have access to what the speakers are saying and whose presence is fully recognized. *Eavesdroppers* are those listeners who have access to what the speakers are saying, but whose presence is *not* fully recognized. To be more precise, speakers believe that they and the bystanders mutually believe that they, the bystanders, have access to what is going on. But speakers believe that they and the eavesdroppers, if there are any, don't have this mutual belief. At one point in Shakespeare's *Hamlet*, Hamlet realizes that King Claudius and Polonius are hiding behind a curtain listening to him talk to Ophelia, but he believes they don't know that he knows. In our terminology that makes Claudius and Polonius eavesdroppers.

Speakers assign listeners to the roles of addressee, side participant, and overhearer by the way they engineer their utterances in the current situation. Not, of course, that just anything is possible. Speakers must get listeners to recognize their assigned roles. In a conversation among Alan, Barbara, and Carl, it is easy for Alan to continue to treat Barbara and Carl both as participants. As participants in the previous turns, they will each assume they are still in the conversation unless Alan marks their exclusion. It should be hard for Alan suddenly to make Carl a bystander.

Speakers assign these roles for only limited periods of time. Alan might address Barbara with Carl as a side participant for one utterance and switch their roles in the next. Speakers can even switch addressees midutterance—and more than once per utterance. Take this utterance by Elsie to three others in conversation, as recorded by Goodwin (1981), where 0.2 marks a pause of 0.2 seconds:

See first we were gonna have [*turning to Ann*] Teema, Carrie and Clara, (0.2) a::nd myself. [*turning to Bessie*] The four of us. The four [*turning to Connie*] children. But then—uh:: I said how is that gonna look.

As Elsie gazes successively at Ann, Bessie, and Clara, she repeats and expands on *Teema, Carrie, and Clara, the four of us, the four children*, engaging each addressee singly, before going on. She designs each section of her utterance specifically for the woman she is addressing.

What, then, are these listener roles roles of? They cannot be roles with respect to utterances. For one thing, roles can change midutterance. For another, speakers can perform more than one illocutionary act—question, request, promise, or the like—with a single utterance, and these illocutionary acts may be addressed to different listeners. In an example invented by Searle (1969), "Suppose at a party a wife says, *It's really quite late.*" With the single utterance, she may (1) object to the host that it is late and, at the same time, (2) ask her husband to take her home. Her husband is the side participant for the objection, and the host is the side participant to the request. The three listener roles appear to be assigned, then, not for each utterance, but for each illocutionary act. Still, when there is no confusion, we will speak of these roles with respect to utterances.

Conversational Responsibilities

What distinguishes participants from overhearers is that the participants are taking part in what the speaker is currently doing, and the overhearers are not. What does it mean to take part in what the speaker is doing? The answer lies, we suggest, in the way conversations work. In the right circumstances, certain individuals, Alan, Barbara, and Carl say, consider themselves to be an ensemble of people who are "in a conversation." To be in a conversation is really to hold certain responsibilities toward each other:

Principle of responsibility. In a conversation, the parties to it are each responsible for keeping track of what is said, and for enabling the other parties to keep track of what is said.

The idea is that each party individually—Alan, Barbara, and Carl—keeps track of an accumulating body of information called the discourse record. This is a record of all the public actions the parties have taken, where by a public action we mean an action openly intended for all the parties. The discourse record is part of Alan's, Barbara's, and Carl's common ground. When Alan says *He's there* to Barbara in a conversation with both Barbara and Carl, he intends both Barbara *and* Carl to understand what he meant—for example, who *he* is, where *there* is, and that he is warning Barbara not to go *there* (see Chapter 7, this volume). That is the only way the three of them can guarantee the orderly accumulation of the discourse record. Let us call these their *conversational responsibilities*.

Listeners are overhearers to an utterance whenever they aren't taken as members of the ensemble "in the conversation" at the moment and therefore don't share in or benefit from their conversational responsibilities. If Alan, Barbara, and Carl consider Oscar a bystander, they needn't feel any responsible for making sure he understands. Conversely, if they don't feel responsible for making sure he understands, they are treating him as an overhearer. And if Oscar is a bystander, it would be rude of him to stop Alan to ask him what he was saying. That would be to intrude, to insinuate himself on Alan, Barbara, and Carl's conversation as if he were a party to it, and that is a social offense.

Collaborative Responsibilities

Speakers bear certain responsibilities toward addressees that they don't bear toward side participants. Or so it appears. For the participants in a conversation to fulfill their conversational responsibilities, they must try to reach what we have called the grounding criterion:

Grounding criterion. The participants in a conversation mutually believe that the current listeners have understood what the speaker meant to a degree sufficient for current purposes.

How do they reach this criterion? For two people talking, the answer is clear: They collaborate moment by moment in trying to *ground* larger or smaller stretches of what has been said (Clark and Brennan 1991; Chapters 9, 5, and 4 this volume). If Alan is talking to Barbara, he may ask her to confirm that she has understood what he meant, and she will spontaneously give evidence of her understanding or ask for repairs for anything she hasn't understood.

Most collaborative devices—at least the commonest and most direct ones—are possible only between two people. When there are three or more people in a conversation, collaboration has to be modified. Just how is not yet clear. It appears to us, but only from informal observation, that when the current speaker, say Alan, has singled out Barbara as the addressee, he is granting her a special status. If he wants to know what she did on her recent trip to Italy, he will orient toward her and pay her special attention. He will collaborate with her directly, much as if he would in a two person conversation with her. Not that he and Barbara forget their responsibilities toward Carl, the side participant. It is just that Carl isn't given the opportunity to collaborate directly. He has to be satisfied with clearing up misunderstandings in natural breaks in their talk, or when Alan and Barbara address him specially with information they think he needs. Let us call the Alan and Barbara's collaborative techniques *direct*, and Alan, Barbara, and Carl's *indirect*. Our conjecture is this:

Principle of collaboration. Speakers collaborate directly with addressees and only indirectly with side participants.

We will call these two responsibilities both *collaborative responsibilities*.

Politeness Responsibilities

People are responsible for being polite to each other no matter where they are. Politeness has to do with people's face, or image of themselves. According to Brown and Levinson (1987) and Goffman (1965), people have two face wants, one positive and one negative. The positive desire is to feel appreciated or esteemed—what we will call *self-esteem*. The negative desire is to be personally unhindered—to have what we will call *freedom of action*. For Alan to be polite to Barbara is to try to satisfy both of these desires. It is to maintain or enhance her self-esteem and not to infringe on her freedom of action. We will call these responsibilities toward others' face *politeness responsibilities*.

Now there are many ways of threatening another person's face by saying things. Alan can threaten Barbara's self-esteem by, for example: (1) asserting or implying bad things about her; (2) using language that is offensive to her; (3) making information public that is embarrassing to her; or (4) burdening her with sensitive information. And he can threaten her freedom of action by, for example: (1) obligating her to do things; (2) threatening her; (3) interrupting her while she is talking; or (4) interfering with her legitimate activities, e.g., by yelling. These are all *face-threatening* acts, as Brown and Levinson (1987) have called them, and they come in a great variety. There are also *face-enhancing* acts with the opposite effects. Alan can use them to raise Barbara's self-esteem or increase her freedom of action.

All of these actions, both face-threatening and face-enhancing, can be taken toward the other parties to a conversation. You can threaten, embarrass, obligate, or burden a fellow participant, for example, just by telling them things. Only some of these actions can be taken toward overhearers, and these include interrupting or embarrassing them, burdening them with sensitive information, and interfering with their activities. So Alan should feel a responsibility to be polite to Oscar even though he is only a bystander. He may, for example, avoid using profanity, gossiping about Oscar's best friend, or talking so loud Oscar can't continue reading. Libraries are places where bystanders conventionally have the right to silence. So speakers also have a responsibility that goes something like this:

Politeness responsibilities. Speakers try not to threaten other people's face without reason.

If speakers hold to this principle, they will be polite toward participants and overhearers alike.

Personal Acquaintance

The responsibilities people bear toward each other depend vitally on personal acquaintance. Suppose Alan and Oscar are close friends. They may have long standing obligations to keep each other informed about some topics and to avoid others. They will also know a great deal about what topics, language, and actions will please or offend the other. The story is quite different when they are strangers. They expect each other to know in general what they should and shouldn't be informed about and what topics, language, and actions will please and offend, but they cannot expect anything more specific. And there are many degrees of acquaintance between close friends and total strangers.

Personal acquaintance is generally critical in determining listener roles in the first place. Strangers are more likely to be bystanders than friends are. When you join Jane and Ken in order to speak to Jane, you may find it possible to treat Ken as a bystander if you don't know him, but impossible if you do, especially if you know him better than Jane. The prototypical bystander may be a stranger, but he needn't be.

It is politeness that is most clearly regulated by personal acquaintance. If Alan and Oscar are friends, then Alan will know precisely what will and won't threaten Oscar's self-esteem and restrict his freedom of action. To be polite, Alan must attend to these threats and restrictions. Alan's responsibilities are regulated in part by Oscar's current role. He is clearly responsible for being polite when Oscar is a participant. He is even responsible when Oscar is a bystander. He realizes that he and Oscar mutually know that Oscar may be listening in, so if he says something to threaten Oscar's self-esteem, and if Oscar thinks he could have avoided it, Oscar will conclude that Alan threatened his face on purpose, and that is a clear social offense. But when Oscar is an eavesdropper, and the two of them do not mutually know he is listening, he can't hold Alan responsible for deliberately offending him. Although he may think Alan is crass, he can't accuse him of a deliberate slight.

In summary, speakers hold several major responsibilities toward their listeners—conversational, collaborative, and politeness. How these apply depends on whether the listeners are addressees, side participants, bystanders, or eavesdroppers.

2   Attitudes toward Listeners

Speakers may hold a range of attitudes toward their listeners regardless of the responsibilities they feel toward them, and these attitudes affect the design of their utterances in radically different ways. Some of the attitudes we will call legitimate: they are fully compatible with a speaker's responsibilities. Others are illegitimate: In one way or another, they are *not* compatible with a speaker's responsibilities. To understand the attitudes speakers can take toward overhearers, we must first recognize the attitudes they can take toward participants.

Attitudes toward Participants

There is really only one legitimate attitude speakers can take toward other parties in the conversation, and that is to be openly informative. They must be sincere in what they tell, ask, promise, and offer their addressees and in letting the side participants know what they are doing. Not that everything they do is serious. They may be ironic, sarcastic, or facetious. They may overstate or understate. They may tell tall stories or jokes. They may overdramatize for effect. But all these devices are intended to be recognized for what they are: nonserious uses of language. Like all serious uses of language, these are intended to be *mutually* recognized by all parties of the conversation. They would be illegitimate uses if they weren't.

Speakers, of course, can choose to violate one or more of their responsibilities. They can fail to keep track of what has been said. They may repeat things others say, fail to presuppose what they all take to be common ground, or otherwise ignore what their partners know from the conversation so far. They can decide to be obtuse or obscure, saying things they know cannot be understood. They can fail to give their partners a chance to repair uncertain interpretations or failures in understanding. Or they can offend their partners directly or indirectly by using offensive language or bringing up threatening topics. There are many ways speakers can deal with the other participants in violation of their principles of responsibility and collaboration.

Attitudes toward Overhearers

In dealing with overhearers, in contrast, speakers can legitimately choose among a range of attitudes. Since they aren't responsible for making sure overhearers understand what is said, they are free to choose among four attitudes:

1. **Indifference.** For any part of what they mean, speakers can be indifferent about whether or not the overhearers can grasp it.

2. **Disclosure.** For any part of what they mean, speakers can design their utterances so that the overhearers can grasp it fully.

3. **Concealment.** For any part of what they mean, speakers can design their utterances so that the overhearers cannot grasp it and will recognize that they cannot do so.

4. **Disguisement.** For any part of what they mean, speakers can design their utterances so that the overhearers will be deceived into thinking it is something that it is not.

We will reserve the term *concealment* for overt attempts to conceal and *disguisement* for covert attempts.

Are these four attitudes always legitimate? Not at all. It depends on the circumstances. Overhearers may have no rights to the information being exchanged, but they do retain the right to self-esteem and freedom of action. It would be illegitimate, in our sense, for a speaker to disclose information that would threaten their self-esteem or freedom of action. Indeed, it might be illegitimate *not* to conceal, or even disguise, that sort of information. The right to save face limits when and where speakers can take these four attitudes.

Here there is a question of ethics. We don't ordinarily worry about *all* the eavesdroppers who could conceivably be listening in on us. It is always possible that the CIA or your boss or a blackmailer has bugged the room and is recording every word we say. Many paranoids live in just this fear. Should we moderate our talk just because of this remote possibility? Most of us would say no, so here is a good case for the attitude of indifference. To worry about eavesdroppers everywhere is to become a certified paranoid. But in circumstances in which there *is* a chance someone is overhearing us, we may feel morally obligated to worry about that person's face. That may be why some people who use profanity in the locker room or by themselves would never use it anywhere else. They don't want to run the risk of any offense that might incur.

So speakers can take many attitudes toward their listeners and still live up to their conversational, collaborative, and politeness responsibilities. With addressees and side participants, they have little choice but to be informative and polite. But with overhearers, they can choose among indifference, disclosure, concealment, and disguisement. The question is how they achieve these ends.

3   Designing Utterances

Speakers are primarily responsible, as we have argued, to other participants in the conversation, with special responsibilities to addressees.
Unless they fulfill these responsibilities—keeping everyone informed
about everything said—the conversation is open to failures, errors, misunderstandings. Indeed, when most theorists speak about the design
of utterances, they have only addressees in mind—and usually only one
addressee at that. So let us begin with the logic behind how speakers
tailor utterances for particular addressees. Our proposal is that the
form these utterances take depends fundamentally on what speakers
take to be their common ground with the addressees. As background,
let us briefly recount what is in two people's common ground (see
Chapter 1, this volume).

Common Ground

The common ground between two people—here, Alan and Barbara—
can be divided conceptually into two main parts. Their *communal
common ground* represents all the knowledge, beliefs, and assumptions
they take to be universally held in the communities to which they
mutually believe they both belong. Their *personal common ground*
represents all the mutual knowledge, beliefs, and assumptions they
have inferred from personal experience with each other.

Alan and Barbara belong to many of the same cultural communities. These communities are defined by such characteristics as these:

1. *Language*: American English, Dutch, Japanese
2. *Nationality*: American, German, Australian
3. *Education*: University, high school, grade school
4. *Place of residence*: San Francisco, Edinburgh, Amsterdam
5. *Occupation*: Physician, plumber, lawyer, psychologist
6. *Religion*: Baptist, Buddhist, Muslim
7. *Hobbies*: Classical piano, baseball, philately
8. *Subcultures*: Rock music, drugs, teenage gangs

Within each community, there are facts, beliefs, and assumptions that
every member believes that almost everyone in that community takes
for granted. So if Alan and Barbara mutually believe they both belong
to these communities, this is information they can take to be communal
common ground.

What sort of information is this? As English speakers, Alan and
Barbara take for granted a vast amount of knowledge about syntax,
semantics, phonology, word meanings, idioms, and politeness formu-

las. As educated American adults, they take for granted a certain acquaintance with American and English literature, world history and geography, and recent news events—disasters, election results, military coups, films. They also take for granted such broad concepts as the nature of causality, religious beliefs, and expected behavior in standing in lines, paying for food at supermarkets, and making telephone calls. As physicians, they take for granted facts about basic human anatomy, the major diseases and their cures, and the technical nomenclature taught in medical school.

Regardless of the information Alan and Barbara share as English speakers, San Franciscans, and physicians, it isn't part of their common ground until they have established the mutual belief that they both belong to these communities. They can establish this in many ways— by assertion (*I'm a pediatrician*; *Ah, so am I*), by showing (they both recognize each other speaking American English), and by other means (Isaacs and Clark 1986; Krauss and Glucksberg 1977; Schegloff 1972). The more communities they establish joint membership in, the broader and richer is their communal common ground.

Once Alan and Barbara meet, they begin openly to share experiences, and these form the basis for their personal common ground. Most joint experiences originate in one of two sources—*joint conversational experiences* or *joint perceptual experiences*. Whenever Alan and Barbara participate in the same conversation, as we have noted, they are responsible for ensuring that everyone understands what has been said, and everything they succeed on they assume to be part of their common ground. For example, if Alan asserts, *I'm leaving for Edinburgh in the morning*, and he and Barbara establish to their mutual satisfaction that she has understood him as intended, that becomes part of their personal common ground. Likewise, whenever Alan and Barbara attend to the same perceptual events, such as a shot in a basketball game, and realize they are both doing so, they can ordinarily assume that everything they are jointly attending to is also common ground (Schiffer 1972; Chapter 1, this volume). Even if at first they didn't know they were at the same basketball game, once that becomes mutually known, they can assume that its salient public parts are common ground.

People must keep track of communal and personal common ground in different ways. For communal common ground, they need encyclopedias for each of the communities they belong to. Once Alan and Barbara establish the mutual belief that they are both physicians, they can immediately add their physician encyclopedias to their common ground. For personal common ground, they need to keep diaries of their personal experiences. But not personal experiences alone. Alan's diary, to be useful, must record for each personal experience who else was involved in it—who else was openly copresent with him. Alan can count as personal common ground with Barbara only those diary entries for which the two of them were openly copresent. The more entries there are, the larger and richer their personal common ground.

Interpreting Utterances

The parties to any conversation, as we noted earlier, accumulate common ground in a regular way. Alan and Barbara begin a conversation with a certain initial communal and personal common ground. When Alan issues his first utterance, they add its content to their initial common ground, and with each further utterance, they add to the common ground that has accumulated so far—the current common ground. At least, this is the view assumed in most theories of discourse (Gazdar 1979; Heim 1983; Kamp 1981; Lewis 1979; Stalnaker 1978). This process can only work if Alan and Barbara ground what they say as they go along (Chapter 5, this volume). They must establish the mutual belief that what is said has been understood well enough for current purposes, and only then does it become part of the discourse record.

Alan tries to design each of his utterances to be interpreted against his and Barbara's current common ground. Suppose Alan utters one of these three sentences:

1. Where is Jack?
2. I just did three houses.
3. Do you have ten dollars?

For each utterance, Alan must ordinarily assume mutual knowledge of English. For 1, he must also believe that Jack is mutually identifiable to Barbara and him. The two of them may know many Jacks, but this Jack must be uniquely identifiable from their current common ground. For 2, he must assume that what he did to the three houses—whether it was to carpet, torch, or ransack them—is also mutually identifiable from their common ground. For 3, he must assume that what he is saying indirectly—he is reminding Barbara to buy a ticket to an orchestra concert that night—is also uniquely identifiable from their common ground. Each example requires both communal common ground (e.g., mutual knowledge of English) and personal common ground (e.g., mutual beliefs about Jack, Alan's business, and orchestra concerts). And Barbara can be confident, ordinarily, that Alan has tried to provide her with conclusive evidence of what he meant.

If Oscar is only an overhearer to 1, 2, and 3, he begins at a distinct disadvantage. He realizes that Alan doesn't bear any responsibility toward making sure he understands what Alan said. Worse than that, Alan doesn't even have to reveal whether his attitude is indifference, disclosure, concealment, or disguisement. For all Oscar knows, Alan and Barbara may have devised a secret code in which *Jack* is the name of a battleship, and *ten dollars* means "George's telephone number." Even if he assumes that Alan has taken the attitude of indifference, he still can't know what Alan means without knowing what is in Alan's and Barbara's common ground. That forces him to make assumptions about their common ground, about what Jacks they mutually know, what Alan does to houses, what social relations they have with each other. These are things he can only guess at. Unlike Barbara, Oscar can never be sure he has conclusive evidence of what Alan meant.

There is, then, a fundamental difference between the inferences that participants and nonparticipants make in trying to understand what is said. We will call this a difference between *recognition* and *conjecture*:

Recognizing speaker's meaning. Addressees and side participants are intended to *recognize* what speakers mean—that is, infer it from conclusive evidence.

Conjecturing about speaker's meaning. Overhearers can only *conjecture* about what speakers mean—that is, draw inferences about it from *in*conclusive evidence.

Barbara tries to recognize what Alan meant by 1, 2, and 3, but Oscar can only conjecture about it.

How does conjecturing differ from recognizing? Suppose Oscar isn't acquainted with Alan and Barbara—he is overhearing them sitting on a bus in San Francisco. When he hears Alan utter 1, *Where is Jack?* all he has to go on are general assumptions about middle class San Franciscans and how they talk. If he assumed that Alan took for granted Alan's and Barbara's mutual knowledge of American English, he might conjecture: *The man could be asking the woman about the location of a man named Jack—though, come to think of it, Jack could be a dog, a cat, or even a car. The man must also believe that Jack is mutually identifiable to him and woman.* Of course, the more Oscar knows about Alan and Barbara, the better his conjectures may be. Yet as long as he is an overhearer, he should realize that his conjectures can never be any more than just that—conjectures.

Overhearers like Oscar are forced to work backward. Let us denote Alan and Barbara's current common ground as CG(a,b), his utterance to her as U(a,b), and his meaning for her with the utterance by SM(a,b,U), where SM stands for "speaker's meaning." Barbara, as addressee, should go about recognizing SM(a,b,U) by the first schema, and Oscar, as overhearer, should go about conjecturing about SM(a,b,U) by the second:

Participant's recognition schema:
1. Assume CG(a,b).
2. Identify U(a,b).
3. Given U(a,b) in relation to CG(a,b), infer SM(a,b,U).

Overhearer's conjecture schema:
1. Identify U(a,b).
2. Conjecture CG(a,b) and SM(a,b,U) such that:
   1'. Assume CG(a,b).
   2'. Assume U(a,b).
   3'. Given U(a,b) in relation to CG(a,b), infer SM(a,b,U).

So Barbara's and Oscar's routes begin in different places. Barbara starts with her current common ground with Alan and asks, *How does Alan intend his utterance to increment our common ground?* Oscar starts instead with Alan's utterance and asks, *What common ground is the man presupposing such that he can use his utterance to add to it and mean something reasonable?* The two routes also differ in the evidence they assume is available. Barbara's assumes her evidence is conclusive. Oscar realizes his is inconclusive.

What complicates the picture, as we noted earlier, is that Alan and Barbara also ground what he says. If Barbara doesn't understand—if she believes the evidence she has registered isn't conclusive enough— she can ask for confirmation of an interpretation (for 1, *Jack Sears?*), for clarification (*Jack who?*), or even for a repeat of the utterance (*What did you say?*). Still, the grounding process itself works by the same recognition schema. When Barbara asks *Jack Sears?* she assumes a certain common ground between Alan and her—adjusted slightly from what Alan had just assumed—and intends him to recognize what she means against it. Grounding adjusts to slight differences in judgments about the conclusiveness of the evidence. If Alan misjudges the clarity of his utterance, or what Barbara assumes to be common ground, that will get sorted out in the process of grounding.

Alan's job in designing each utterance, therefore, is to play to these schemas. He must think primarily about Barbara—and any side participants such as Carl. For them he needs to assess their current common ground and formulate an utterance so they will recognize what he means. But in considering Oscar, he needs to do a great deal more. What he does depends on whether his attitude is indifference, disclosure, concealment, or disguisement.

4 Designing Utterances for Overhearers

For speakers to deal with overhearers, they must estimate how much the overhearers can conjecture, and design their utterances accordingly. When Alan is talking to Barbara, and Oscar is an overhearer, he needs to estimate one main piece of information: Oscar's assumptions about $CG(a,b)$, Alan and Barbara' s common ground. With this, he can judge whether Oscar will be able to apply the overhearer conjecture schema successfully or not. Only then can he decide how to disclose, conceal, or disguise what he is saying to Barbara. Let us look at the logic of designing utterances for overhearers.

Open and Closed Information

Both the recognition and the conjecture schemas are built on the common ground between Alan and Barbara, $CG(a,b)$. Now although $CG(a,b)$ is something Alan and Barbara themselves can take for granted, it is something Oscar can only conjecture about. If he makes the right conjectures, he can also conjecture correctly about what Alan meant, and if not, he can't. What Alan needs to estimate, then, are these two parts of $CG(a,b)$:

Open information. Information that O believes, or could readily guess, to be in $CG(a,b)$.

Closed information. Information that O doesn't believe, and could not readily guess, to be in $CG(a,b)$.

But what is open and closed to Oscar may not be open and closed to another overhearer, so dividing $CG(a,b)$ into these two parts depends on Alan's analysis of Oscar as an individual, if he happens to know him, or as a type, if he does not.

What information *is* closed to Oscar? Alan might first consider communal common ground. For that he needs to find cultural communities that he and Barbara belong to but that Oscar has no knowledge about. He might come to one of these judgments:

1. *Language*: Alan and Barbara know Japanese, and Oscar doesn't.
2. *Nationality*: Alan and Barbara are American, and Oscar is German.

3. *Education*: Alan and Barbara are adults, and Oscar is eight years old.
4. *Place of residence*: Alan and Barbara are San Franciscans, and Oscar is a New Yorker.
5. *Occupation*: Alan and Barbara are physicians, and Oscar is a lawyer.
6. *Religion*: Alan and Barbara are Episcopalians, and Oscar is a Buddhist.
7. *Hobbies*: Alan and Barbara are both birders and mountain climbers, and Oscar is neither.
8. *Subcultures*: Alan and Barbara are both part time rock musicians, and Oscar is known to abhor rock music.

It is discrepancies like these that Alan must exploit if he is to conceal or disguise his meanings from Oscar, or that he must avoid if he is to disclose them to Oscar.

For information closed to Oscar, Alan might also consider his and Barbara's personal common ground. First he must find conversations that he and Barbara were both participants in, or perceptual experiences that they were copresent at, and that Oscar couldn't know about. But it isn't enough to pick just any information from these sources. Alan must assure himself that Oscar couldn't even guess the information to be common ground. Even though Oscar didn't see *Night at the Opera* with Alan and Barbara, he could have seen it on his own and guess what Alan is talking about when he speaks of "the stateroom scene." For closed information, Alan must set his criterion very high. He must be sure Oscar is not only ignorant of that area of CG(a,b), but not even able to guess it is an area of CG(a,b).

The notions of open and closed information, properly formulated, are just what we need to account for the four main attitudes speakers can take toward overhearers.

Indifference

The simplest attitude Alan can take toward Oscar is indifference: He doesn't care whether Oscar understands what he is saying or not. Once he takes that attitude, he can design his utterances as if Oscar weren't there. But he cannot always take this attitude. By *indifference*, we mean "conversational indifference" and not "personal disregard." Alan is still responsible for not threatening Oscar's self-esteem and freedom of action. He must still try to be polite. He may be forced to conceal or disguise all or part of what he is saying from Oscar. Or he may have to soften his use of profanity.

Disclosure

With disclosure, Alan tries to provide Oscar with enough evidence so that he, Oscar, can come to the right conjectures about Alan's meaning. To do this, Alan must design his utterances to be interpretable against those parts of CG(a,b) that are open to Oscar. For example, he shouldn't use Japanese or medicalese unless he thinks Oscar speaks Japanese or medicalese. Nor should he design his utterances around personal common ground that is closed to Oscar.

To illustrate, let us set up a scenario, a web of information against which Alan must design utterances like 1, 2, and 3:

Scenario A. Barbara's father is named Jack McCall; Alan is a professional arsonist; Barbara needs ten dollars for a Beethoven concert she and Alan intend to go to. Alan takes these three facts to be salient parts of Alan and Barbara's common ground, CG(a,b), but believes they are closed to Oscar.

Under Scenario A, Alan couldn't use utterances 1, 2, or 3 (repeated here) and be sure of complete disclosure:

1. Where is Jack?
2. I just did three houses.
3. Do you have ten dollars?

He couldn't be at all confident that Oscar could infer that Jack was Barbara's father, that to *do a house* would be to torch it, or that Alan was reminding Barbara of the concert. To ensure disclosure, he might instead say something like 1', 2', and 3':

1'. Where is your father?
2'. I just torched three houses.
3'. Have you bought your ticket for the Beethoven concert tonight yet?

With these, not only should Barbara be able to understand, but so should Oscar by making the obvious assumptions.

Disclosure should be easy when Oscar is a close friend of Alan's, and hard, maybe even impossible, when Oscar is a stranger. When Oscar is a friend, Alan can be sure of finding open areas of CG(a,b) to work with. When Oscar is a stranger, Alan can never be sure of doing that. What if Oscar speaks only French, or Tagalog, or Finnish? What if he speaks English but doesn't know the slang interpretation of *torched*— he thought it meant "shine a light, a torch, on"? What if he doesn't know of the Beethoven concert? All Alan can do is make broad guesses at the type of person Oscar is—say, middle class educated American,

English speaking—work with open parts of communal common ground, and hope for the best.

Disclosing to an overhearer may look at first just like informing a side participant, but it isn't. When Alan treats a listener as a side participant, he intends the listener to infer what he means by recognizing that very intention (Grice 1957 1968). When he treats the listener as an overhearer, he no longer has that full intention. The difference lies in what he leads the overhearer to believe. If he leads Zoë, a listener, to think she is guaranteed to have everything she needs to understand him, he is treating her as a side participant. If he gives her any reason to doubt this guarantee, he is treating her as an overhearer. In practice, the opportunity for collaboration makes a big difference. If Zoë feels she can check on what Alan meant through delayed or indirect collaboration, she can consider herself a side participant. If not, she can't be guaranteed of success, and she must consider herself an outsider. If she is an eavesdropper, that is, if she doesn't think Alan knows she is listening, she can't be sure he is making himself comprehensible to her. So, like it or not, Zoë is once again stuck with the conjecture schema.

Concealment

With concealment, Alan tries to deprive Oscar of enough evidence to conjecture correctly about what Alan means—at least about the *targeted parts* of what he means. For this, Alan must design his utterance so that Barbara understands, as usual, on the basis of CG(a,b), but on parts of CG(a,b) that are closed to Oscar. For Scenario A, he couldn't use 1', 2', or 3', for these are designed around open parts of CG(a,b). He might well use 1, 2, and 3. But if he did, he would be concealing only selected parts of what he was saying—in 1 who he was referring to with *Jack*, in 2 what he meant by *doing a house*, and in 3 what he was reminding Barbara of. He would be making no attempt to hide the fact in 1 that he was asking Barbara where someone or something was, or in 2 that he was doing something to three houses, or in 3 that he was ostensibly asking Barbara if she had ten dollars.

To conceal every last scrap of what he means, Alan would have to go to a lot more trouble. One way would be to use closed parts of communal common ground. If he and Barbara knew Japanese and he thought Oscar didn't, he could switch to Japanese. If he and Barbara were adults and he thought five-year-old Oscar didn't know how to spell, he could switch to spelling. If he and Barbara had the foresight, they could set up a special code ahead of time that would be part of CG(a,b) but impervious to Oscar's conjectures. Whether the talk is in Japanese, spelling, or spy codes, Oscar is still likely to identify pieces of what Alan means, even if the pieces are of little importance. For example, any utterance that Alan openly addresses to Barbara would suggest that he is trying to communicate with her. With skill, Alan and Barbara may be able to forestall even this conjecture.

Just how easily Alan can conceal his meaning from Oscar depends on his knowledge of Barbara and Oscar. If both are strangers, and there are no obvious communities Alan and Barbara but not Oscar belongs to, concealment may be all but impossible. Where could Alan find parts of CG(a,b) that are closed to Oscar? It should also be difficult if Oscar is a friend and Barbara a stranger. Imagine asking directions from a stranger in an airport while trying to conceal what you are doing from your bystanding spouse. It won't be easy to find a piece of common ground with the stranger that is closed to your spouse. Concealment should also be tricky when Alan, Barbara, are Oscar are all intimate friends. They belong to most of the same cultural communities, have shared many of the same experiences, have talked about many more, and will be able to guess many of the rest. It should be hard to find a corner of CG(a,b) that is closed to Oscar. Concealment is probably easiest when Barbara is a friend and Oscar a stranger of an obvious type. In this case Alan and Barbara have vast areas of personal and communal common ground to work with.

Even in optimal circumstances, concealment isn't easy. In an experimental setting (Chapter 9, this volume), we gave pairs of Stanford University students each eight photographs of the Stanford campus and asked one of them, the director, to get the other, the matcher, to arrange them in a particular order. They were to do this all while not allowing an overhearer, also a Stanford student, to arrange his or her photographs in the right order. So the director and matcher had to conceal their references. The director and matcher were always friends, and the overhearer a stranger. Even so, they managed to conceal their references only 45% of the time. Why?

Try as they might, the director and matcher found it difficult to identify information that was *completely* closed to the overhearer. They were almost perfect at finding pieces of common ground that weren't known to the overhearer. Only once did the bystander happen to identify a person the director and matcher assumed he couldn't identify. What they misjudged was how deft the overhearer was at using other information to infer the references. Once when a director told a matcher *This is where someone wanted to put my teddy bear*, the overhearer was successful because there was only one picture of a thing where one might put a teddy bear.

Speakers can also conceal through the collaborative techniques they normally use in conversation. In our study, the director and matcher's main strategy, as expected, was to seek, find, and then exploit closed parts of their common ground. They used collaborative tactics on top of this. Directors often began with queries like *Okay, remember in Hiltonhead* to establish areas of common ground before they keyed on them in their references. They also tried out exotic areas of their common ground, confident that their partners would ask for repairs if the areas were too obscure. They sometimes talked faster to make it hard for the overhearer; again, they relied on matchers asking for repairs if necessary. And, finally, once matchers believed they understood a reference, they would often cut directors off midsentence to keep them from revealing any more than they already had. All of these techniques were possible only through moment by moment collaboration.

Disguisement

With concealment, overhearers normally see they are being kept in the dark. When Alan tells Barbara *You-know-who finally did you-know-what*, Oscar realizes that they don't want him to know who did what to whom. That may be a problem. Oscar may be offended that they think there are things he shouldn't know, even if he is an overhearer. Or they may not want Oscar to know they are gossiping. If so, they may want not merely to conceal what they are saying, but to disguise it as something else.

Disguisement is the most complicated attitude of all. In designing an utterance for Barbara, Alan must, as usual, depend on his common ground with her, CG(a,b). Then, to conceal his meaning from Oscar, he must key on closed parts of that common ground. But, also, to mislead him, he must key on open parts of that common ground. Disguisement is really the disclosure of a misrepresentation, and that takes careful engineering.

For an example, let us return to utterances 1, 2, and 3. To use them without change would merely conceal what Alan meant. To disclose a misrepresentation, Alan needs other information:

Scenario B. Everything in Scenario A is true. In addition, Jack McCall's nickname is Mac; Alan has been looking for Jack; and Alan and Barbara jokingly call Ludwig Beethoven Louis. Alan takes all this to be common ground to Barbara and him but *closed* to Oscar. Further, Mac is also the name of John Macleod, a good friend of Alan and Barbara's; and Louis Levesque is lecturing that night at the University. Alan takes this to be common ground to Barbara and him and *open* to Oscar.

Alan could now say to Barbara, perhaps with a private wink:

1″. Where is Mac?

2″. I just installed heating systems in three houses.

3″. Do you have ten dollars for your Louis ticket?

Barbara should interpret these utterances correctly (the same as 1, 2, and 3, or 1′, 2′, and 3′), but Oscar should interpret them incorrectly. He should take them to mean *Where is John Macleod?*, *Alan just installed three furnaces*, and *Do you have ten dollars for Louis Levesque's lecture?* Further, he should have no reason to suspect Alan meant anything else. If Alan is successful, he will have deceived Oscar without Oscar realizing it.

What makes disguisement so difficult is that the circumstances have to be just right for Alan simultaneously (a) to get Barbara to recognize what he means, (b) to conceal this from Oscar, and (c) to get Oscar to think he means something else. With Scenaro B, we had to create a very special situation. It is hard to imagine how Alan could achieve these conditions if he, Barbara, and Oscar were all strangers, or if Barbara was a stranger and Oscar a friend. Like concealment, disguisement should be easiest when Alan and Barbara are friends and Oscar is a stranger of an identifiable type. Also, it is hard enough to disguise parts of what is meant—such as references to people, places, or objects—and to disguise hints and other indirect speech acts. It is much harder to create larger disguises and sustain them.

In dealing with overhearers, then, Alan must make delicate judgments not only about his common ground with Barbara, but about his common ground with Oscar. Here are the areas we have identified for A, B, and O (speaker, addressee, and overhearer):

1. *A and B's common ground*: A's saying anything to B.
2. *Open parts of 1*: A's disclosure to O; A's disguisement from O.
3. *Closed parts of 1*: A's concealment and disguisement from O.
4. *A and O's common ground*: A's decision of whether or not to be indifferent to O.

Mutual beliefs, and conjectures about mutual beliefs, are crucial at every step in the process. It is hard to see how to deal with addressees and overhearers without them.

5 Uses of Audience Design

Speakers, as we have noted, have many goals in designing utterances. Their primary ones deal with addressees and side participants. Publicly, they may want to tell their addressees things, ask them questions, offer them things, order them to do things. At the same time, they will inform the participants of what they are doing with their addressees. Privately, they may want to impress the participants, confuse them, get them to stop talking, or induce them to change topics, all without their goals becoming public. All these goals are generally recognized as influencing the design of utterances.

What is less well recognized are speakers' goals toward *non*participants. These are what lead them to disclose, conceal, disguise, or be indifferent. When speakers conceal what they mean, their aim isn't merely to conceal what they mean. It is to do something by means of the concealment. What speakers can do with these four attitudes is in principle without limit, but it is instructive to look at examples. These examples highlight the possible uses of audience design and point up the deficiencies in theories that deal only with participants.

Indifference

Theories of language use that ignore overhearing—and almost all do—tacitly assume that the default attitude toward overhearers is indifference. They take for granted that speakers don't take overhearers into account unless they have to. Let us call this the *default attitude hypothesis*. At first blush, the hypothesis is plausible enough. Still, we suggest that it is incorrect.

The problem is that speakers cannot know whether to take overhearers into account without taking stock of the situation. As they plan an utterance, they must ask themselves, *Are there any overhearers around? If so, what effect will the utterance I am planning have on them? Will it offend, divulge a secret, or have any other untoward effects?* Or they might ask, *Could the utterance I am planning have untoward effects on anyone other than the participants? If so, are there any overhearers around who fit that description?* If either series of questions ends in *yes*, speakers must choose an attitude other than indifference. Speakers cannot be indifferent without choosing *not* to disclose, conceal, or disguise.

Indifference has its uses precisely because it contrasts with the other three attitudes. With it, speakers might show bystanders they have nothing to hide or disclose. In the right circumstances, they can confer status by reassuring bystanders that their presence isn't a problem—that they can be trusted with what is being said. In other circumstances, they can show bystanders that they are so unimportant that it doesn't matter whether or not they hear. In British novels, when a household gossips in front of the servants, they sometimes imply trust and sometimes imply insignificance. So overhearers can assume speakers have taken them into account and draw their inferences accordingly.

Disclosure

What can speakers do by disclosing what they are saying? That depends on whether the overhearers are bystanders or eavesdroppers. Let us consider disclosure to bystanders first.

In a California restaurant, a man and a woman found themselves being served by an inept waitress. At one point, the waitress dropped the man's forks on the floor and took them away to replace them. When she returned with food, she didn't bring any new forks and gave no hint that she realized she had forgotten them. Just as she turned away and was still within earshot, the man said politely to his companion, *Could I use one of your forks?* When one of us questioned him after the waitress had left, he said he was just trying to be polite. He intended the waitress to hear him without recognizing that he had intended her to hear him. This way he could get her to bring a fork without having to confront her about her lapse in conduct.

In a California post office, a woman and her son were speaking German as they waited in line to be served by a postal clerk. When her turn came—one of us was behind her—she started rummaging through her purse and, while the clerk waited, turned to her son and asked, now in English, *What did I do with my wallet?* Apparently, she disclosed her question to the clerk to account for her delay in stepping up to the counter. She switched to English so he could understand and draw that inference.

When people have partners to talk to, as in the last two examples, it is easy to create utterances to be overheard. What if they are alone? They can always speak to themselves in what Goffman (1978) called *self-talk.* Suppose you are sitting at the counter of a cafe when you accidentally knock over a glass of water. You exclaim to yourself *Damn* just loud enough for the strangers on both sides to hear. But why talk to yourself here when it is considered impolite, even slightly deranged, to talk to oneself in public? According to Goffman, you do so to account for yourself to the bystanders. In uttering *Damn,* you show them you recognize your blunder and are still fully in control. You use disclosure to get the bystanders to draw just the right inferences. Self-talk of this type Goffman called *response cries.*

Response cries are an essential part of most spectator sports. In American football, when a quarterback muffs a handoff, or a receiver drops a pass, and they are clearly to blame, they are obliged to do a little theater. They put on a hangdog look, stare at the ground or into the sky, beat one fist into the other palm, and, under their breath but clearly enough for the television audience to identify, utter a juicy expletive. Their aim isn't just to exclaim to themselves—if it is that at all. It is to disclose their disappointment to the spectators—to show them they recognize their blunder. Television audiences must enjoy these theatrics, for television cameras invariably focus on the quarterback and receiver for their reactions. What would football be without it?

Disclosure can be used for quite a different purpose with eavesdroppers. If you think your superior, say Verona, might overhear you, it may serve your purpose to disclose information that is flattering or critical. Your disclosure would be most effective if she were eavesdropper—if she thought you didn't know she was listening in. As a bystander, she could suspect you of calculated effects. As an eavesdropper, she would have more reason to take your statements as sincere. In a study by Walster and Festinger (1960), overhearers were more persuaded by what they heard if they were eavesdroppers than if they were bystanders.

Disclosure can also be used in teasing. In a technique described by Philips (1975), one boy A was telling a second boy B a number of things that were false. The real audience, however, wasn't B, but a third boy, O, a bystander, to whom A was disclosing all this information and who knew it to be false. With this technique, A and O could play a joke on B at his expense and without his knowledge.

Concealment

If Alan wants to tell Barbara something but keep it from Oscar, he has several options. He might postpone telling her, or whisper, or scribble a note to her. If these options are impractical—he is on the telephone and he has to tell her now—he may have to speak but conceal what he is saying.

The most extensive use of concealment is probably for transmitting diplomatic, military, and commercial information. There are many schemes for encrypting written messages between diplomats, between spies, between commanders, and between banks. There are audio scramblers for encrypting telephone signals between government officials, and video scramblers for encrypting television transmissions to paying customers. All of these devices are meant to keep overhearers from identifying the information being passed. And they don't conceal the fact that they are concealing.

In World War II, the American military discovered a simpler method of concealment with the use of Navaho (Kahn 1967). Although thousands of Navahos spoke the language, the military assumed only a handful of non-Navahos did, and they weren't likely to be in Europe, especially on the German side. So the military had Navaho soldiers transmit secret messages in Navaho, confident that the language was a closed part of these soldiers' common ground.

Virtually the same strategy is used by bilinguals in special settings. Many a second generation American child has complained of their parents speaking in Italian, Tagalog, or Polish to talk privately in front of them. Dutch tourists in Japan can speak privately in Dutch pretty much with impunity too. The more confined the language or the more foreign the setting, the more likely the strategy will work.

The same logic lies behind underworld argots and ingroup slang. In each new generation, according to many sources, British thieves have developed a special lexicon for speaking about victims, loot, fences, techniques, and other trade information. So, apparently, have drug traffickers, confidence men, smugglers, and other groups with information to conceal. As for teenage slang, its primary purpose may be to differentiate an ingroup from an outgroup, but it may also be used as a private language, closed to the prying ears of parents, teachers, and other outsiders.

Concealment may be harder without a private language, but it is still done. Without such a language, people are forced to rely on closed areas of personal rather than communal common ground—as with phrases like *you know who*, *the event we talked about yesterday*, and *the thingamabob* (Chapter 9, this volume). From our informal observations, people use these techniques for gossiping on crowded busses and at crowded parties, for speaking privately on the telephone near inquisitive coworkers, and for talking in front of children. Whether it is always effective is another matter.

Finally, there are private signals between partners of long standing. Many partners and families have private words for signalling that it is time to go home from a party, that a man's fly is unzipped, or that the family should hold back on the food.

Disguisement

When speakers conceal what they mean from overhearers, it is usually obvious to everyone that they are doing so, and that may not suit their purposes. Hide what you are saying, and overhearers will suspect you of having something to hide. Disguise what you are saying, and they may suspect nothing. The trouble is, disguisement is hard. If it were easy, it would probably be preferred to concealment. As it is, it is rare. We have only a few examples.

Just before Pearl Harbor in World War II, the chief of the American bureau of the Japanese Foreign Office talked with an associate of the Japanese Ambassador to the United States on the telephone. They suspected a wiretap and tried to disguise what they were saying with a pre-arranged code that made their talk sound personal and mundane. In referring to Japanese-American negotiations, for example, they spoke of a *matrimonial question*, so when the associate said *The matrimonial question seemed as if it would be settled*, he meant *It looked as though we could reach an agreement* (Kahn 1967). Unfortunately, their disguise wasn't very effective.

Argots may sometimes be attempts to disguise as much as to conceal. When the terms *tea, grass, weed*, and *Mary Jane* were coined for marijuana, one might suspect they were chosen to sound innocent to an overhearer. Still, they may merely have been euphemisms used to enable members of an ingroup to identify one another (Nunberg 1979).

Disguisement is easier when overhearers have access to only one side of the conversation. One of us, Clark, was once telephoned by an acquaintance who wanted confidential information about a student he was thinking of hiring. Trouble was, the student was sitting in Clark's office at that moment. Clark disguised what he was doing from her by responding to the caller with such nonsequiturs as *Yes, I see* and *I'll do that* until the caller caught on, saying, *Ah, she's in your office now. Let me call back later.* The talk the student heard sounded innocent, and the disguise seemed to work. So although the disguise was spontaneous, it was possible because the acquaintance did all the work out of the overhearer's earshot.

Attitudes toward overhearers, then, have their uses. Speakers can accomplish a range of goals by disclosing, concealing, disguising, and being indifferent. Some of these goals can only be achieved by exploiting one of the four attitudes. Indeed, for Goffman's response cries, the speaker's goal isn't to affect the addressee, but to deal with the overhearer.

6 Conclusion

In designing utterances, speakers have to worry simultaneously about *all* their listeners—addressees, side participants, bystanders, and possible eavesdroppers. When Alan addresses Barbara, and Carl is a side participant, he must try to get both of them to understand what he means. But he must also attend to Oscar, an overhearer. Although his only responsibility toward Oscar is to be polite, he can choose to disclose, conceal, disguise, or be indifferent, depending on his purposes.

We have looked at the logic of dealing with overhearers. When Alan designs an utterance for Barbara alone, he has to take their common ground into account. She is to recognize what he means by considering his utterance against their current common ground. To deal with Oscar at the same time, Alan has to work with areas of his and Barbara's common ground that are open or closed to Oscar. For disclosure and disguisement, he needs to exploit the open parts, and for concealment and disguisement, the closed parts. Without working from their common ground, Alan cannot guarantee that Barbara will recognize what he means while at the same time disclosing, concealing, or disguising it for Oscar.

How does Alan carry out these complex plans? About this, almost nothing is known. Dealing with Barbara and Carl alone is complicated enough. Adding Oscar should make the process more elaborate. One thing is certain. Theories about everything from utterance formulation to Gricean implicatures will change once they accept that speakers deal with overhearers and side participants as well as addressees.

9

Concealing One's Meaning from Overhearers

WITH EDWARD F. SCHAEFER

Two people talking, as at a crowded party, may try to conceal all or part of what they mean from overhearers. To do this, it is proposed, they need to build what they wish to conceal on a *private key*, a piece of information, such as an event mentioned in an earlier conversation, that is common ground for the two of them and yet not inferable by the overhearers. What they say must be designed so that it cannot be understood without knowledge of that key. As evidence for the proposal, pairs of friends were required, as part of an arrangement task, to refer to familiar landmarks while concealing these references from overhearers. As predicted, the two of them used private keys, which they often concealed even further by using certain collaborative techniques. Still, the two partners weren't always successful.

In standard theories of language use, the speaker (call her Ann) has one main purpose in issuing each utterance, and that is to get her addressee (say Ben) to recognize certain of her intentions. She may want to tell Ben something, ask him a question, or offer him something, and she issues an utterance to do this. The primary question for these theories is how Ann designs her utterances to achieve these goals.

But this picture leaves out overhearers. At a crowded party, Ann may want to conceal parts of what she tells Ben from obvious bystanders or unnoticed eavesdroppers. If so, she has several courses of action open to her. She can whisper, or postpone talking about the parts she wants to keep private. Or she can switch into a mode of speaking we will call *concealment*. Example: *You-know-who finally did what she told us she'd do to our fashionable friend.* With concealment, Ann tells Ben what she wants to tell him but, at the same time, overtly conceals from overhearers particular parts of what she means—here, who the two people are and what the first did to the second.

Concealment is an instance of a general property of language use called *audience design.* Speakers design what they say for the particular people they believe are or might be listening (Bell 1954; Chapter 7, this volume; Clark and Murphy 1983; Garfinkel 1967; Sacks, Schegloff, and Jefferson 1974). They plan their utterances to be understood not by just anybody, but by the addressees and other participants in the conversation at the moment. Yet they can also take one of several attitudes towards overhearers. They can disclose all or part of what they mean to the overhearers; they can conceal all or part of it from them; they can even disguise all or part of it from them. They can show overhearers various forms of respect or disrespect— for example, by using polite language versus profanity, or by choosing pleasant versus disgusting things to talk about. Rarely are people entirely indifferent to bystanders. The attitude we focus on here is concealment.

Concealment, like the other attitudes toward overhearers, raises two issues for theories of language use—one about logic and the other about process. First, by what logic can speakers get their addressees to recognize certain of their intentions and yet conceal the same intentions from overhearers? The standard theories of speech acts (e.g., Austin 1962; Bach and Harnish 1979; Grice 1968; Searle 1969, 1975), discourse (e.g., Heim 1983; Kamp 1981; Stalnaker 1978), and reference (Donnellan 1978; Kripke 1977; Russell 1905; Strawson 1950) have nothing to say about the issue, even though concealment is a potential factor in the design of any utterance. Second, how in practice do speakers accomplish these two goals—getting addressees to understand while concealing from overhearers? What techniques do speakers try, and how successful are they? Theories of production have no answers to these questions, even though, in some circumstances, concealment plays a critical role in the formulation and execution of utterances.

In this paper we take up both issues. We first sketch a logical scheme by which people can speak to addressees while concealing information from overhearers. We then report an experiment in which pairs of people were asked to talk about familiar places while concealing from an overhearer which places they were referring to. We use the findings to characterize some techniques that speakers exploit for concealment and how successful they are in using them.

1 An Analysis of Concealment

In concealment, the problem a speaker like Ann faces is how to get Ben, her addressee, to understand her while keeping Oscar, an overhearer, from doing so. To see how she might do this, let us turn the problem around and ask how Ben and Oscar should go about understanding her (see Chapters 7 and 2, this volume).

Ben, as Ann's addressee, is confident she is trying to provide him with sufficient evidence of what she means. All he needs to do is consider her utterance against their current common ground—their mutual knowledge, beliefs, and suppositions—and infer what she means. The process of inferring from sufficient evidence we will call *recognizing*.

Oscar should realize all this too—that Ann is providing Ben with sufficient evidence of what she means. But, as an overhearer, Oscar should also realize she need not provide him, Oscar, with sufficient evidence. He isn't part of the conversation, so she isn't obligated to let him know what she is saying. All Oscar can do is consider her utterance against what he believes *might* be Ann and Ben's current common ground, and about that he can never be certain. The process of inferring from *in*sufficient evidence like this we will call *conjecturing*. So what Ann must try to do is (1) give Ben evidence he needs to recognize what she means and yet, at the same time, (2) deprive Oscar of evidence he would need to conjecture what she means.

Ann's concealment may be total or selective. If she wanted to conceal *all* of what she means, she might favor one class of techniques, such as switching into a language Ben knew but Oscar didn't. If she wanted to conceal only *selective* parts of her meaning—certain referents (people or things she is referring to), predications, direct or indirect illocutionary acts, or implicatures—she might favor other techniques. To make the issue tractable, we will focus on the selective concealment of referents.

The Concealment Scheme

How, then, should Ann proceed? Her primary goal, whether she conceals or not, is to get Ben to recognize her meaning. She must design her utterance so that he can do this given their current common ground. If she says, *Derek has just arrived*, Ben should be able to figure out Derek's identity by appealing to their shared knowledge of a man named Derek of whom she could predicate just arriving. Now suppose Ann wants to conceal Derek's identity from Oscar. She cannot use *Derek has just arrived* if she thinks Oscar knows Derek by name or could conjecture his identity from the name. But if she and Ben had talked about Derek the night before, and if she thought Oscar didn't know and couldn't guess that, she could use *The man we talked about last night has just arrived*. That should make her confident that Ben will be able to identify Derek and Oscar will not. But why?

Concealment from overhearers, we argue, depends on a special use of common ground. Let us describe all those parts of Ann and Ben's common ground that Oscar isn't privy to and cannot guess as *closed* to Oscar. A speaker like Ann, then, should proceed as follows:

The concealment scheme. If the speaker wishes to conceal from an overhearer some part of what she means, she must try to design her utterance so that the addressee cannot recognize that part of her meaning without a piece of common ground she believes is closed to the overhearer.

Let us call this crucial piece of Ann and Ben's common ground a *private key* to the concealment part of her meaning. For successful concealment, then, Ann must find a piece of common ground she thinks is closed to Oscar (e.g., Ann and Ben's having talked about Derek the night before) and make it a private key to what she means.

Private Keys

Where should Ann search for information she can use as a private key? Very broadly, the common ground between two people consists of two types of information—*communal* and *personal* common ground (Chapter 1, this volume). Both should be potential sources for private keys.

Ann and Ben's communal common ground is what they take to be known, believed, or assumed by everyone, or almost everyone, in the various communities to which the two of them mutually believe they both belong—e.g., English speakers, U.S. residents, Californians, San Franciscans, bridge players, university graduates, physicians, and classical music buffs. For example, once Ann and Ben establish they are both San Franciscans and classical music buffs, they could take as common ground that they know what goes on at the Herbst Theater, Davies Hall, and the Opera House and where they are.

Communal common ground is an important potential source for private keys. If Ann can identify communities in which she and Ben, but not Oscar, are members, she can use information restricted to these communities. This tack leads to a family of methods as illustrated here:

1. **Use a foreign language.** Suppose Ann and Ben mutually know they are both speakers of Vietnamese. If Ann thinks it is unlikely that Oscar is too, she can switch to Vietnamese for anything she wishes to conceal from him.
2. **Use spelling.** Talking in front of a pre-literate child, Ann and Ben, as literate people, could conceal by spelling, as in *What about a T-R-I-K-E for X-M-A-S?*
3. **Use ingroup jargon.** If Ann and Ben are both physicians and mutually know it, they can conceal diagnoses from overhearing patients by using technical jargon.
4. **Use cryptography.** As spies, Ann and Ben may belong to an intelligence community with special codes designed for concealing what is said from anyone outside that community.

Ann and Ben's personal common ground, on the other hand, is what they take to be mutually known, believed, or assumed based on personal experiences the two of them have shared. One part consists of what was said in previous conversations in which both were participants—and that includes the current conversation so far. Another part consists of what the two of them have jointly seen, heard, or otherwise experienced openly in each other's presence, for example, at a symphony concert.

This personal common ground is a second potential source for private keys. Ann can search for conversational or perceptual experiences she has shared with Ben and not with Oscar and use these as private keys, as in our example, *The man we talked about last night has just arrived.* Most methods based on communal common ground—foreign language, spelling, jargon, cryptography—come prefabricated, ready for any occasion that requires them. But those based on personal common ground tend to be impromptu. A speaker like Ann must choose or devise them spontaneously, on the fly, taking account of overhearers in the very process of formulating her utterance. That makes them important to study as a component of formulating utterances.

Indirect Reference

Ann can hide private keys even further by the use of *indirect reference* (Clark 1978; Nunberg 1979). Compare Ann's *My car is parked down the street* with *I am parked down the street.* Or compare *The voters who live on Lincoln Avenue voted Republican last election* with *Lincoln Avenue voted Republican last election.* With *my car* and *the voters who live on Lincoln Avenue*, Ann refers directly to her car and the voters, but with *I* and *Lincoln Avenue*, she does so indirectly. With *I* she refers to herself and, via a *reference function* that maps cars onto people, thereby refers to her car. Ben, to make the link from her to her car, has to compute this reference function based on their common ground. The same holds for *Lincoln Avenue*.

Indirect references are ideal for concealment. They cannot be interpreted without knowledge of their reference functions, and Ann, if she is clever, can base these functions on private keys. Suppose Ann and Ben had talked about Derek's house in Guernsey. Ann could conceal Derek's identity by referring to him directly, as in *The man who has a house in Guernsey has just arrived*. She could be even more cryptic by doing so indirectly as in *Guernsey has just arrived*. It should be hard enough for Ben to work out the mapping from Guernsey to Derek. It should be impossible for Oscar.

Collaboration in Concealment

In everyday conversation, speaking is a collaborative process (Goodwin 1981; Sacks et al. 1974,; Schegloff 1982), and that is especially true of reference (Clark and Schaefer 1987; Chapter 4, this volume; Cohen 1984; Isaacs and Clark 1987). According to the collaborative model of referring (Chapter 4, this volume), the current speaker and her addressee try to reach the mutual belief, for each reference, that the addressee has identified the intended referent correctly. In the simplest cases, the speaker presents a noun phrase (e.g., *the man who went to Guernsey,*) and the addressee accepts it by allowing the conversation to proceed. In more difficult cases, the speaker may present a noun phrase that she and her addressee then repair, expand, or replace in an iterative process taking several turns to complete. The process ends when the two of them mutually accept that the description finally arrived at is adequate for identifying the intended referent.

The collaborative process has many features that could be exploited for concealment. One is that it works over time, over more than one conversational turn, allowing private keys to be introduced bit by bit. Suppose Ben stops Ann in downtown San Francisco to ask for directions, and she needs to refer to the arch at Grant and Bush. Here is a hypothetical conversation:

Ann: Are you from San Francisco? [preface]
Ben: Yeah. [confirmation]
Ann: Well, then, go to *the arch at Grant and Bush?*
      [presentation of a trial noun phrase]
Ben: Right, the entrance to Chinatown. [confirmation + expansion]
Ann: Yes. And then ... [confirmation + continuation]

Aspects of Ann's reference to the arch are distributed over five turns. She uses her preface to establish how much common ground she has with Ben and selects the definite description *the arch at Grant and Bush* accordingly (Krauss and Glucksberg 1977; Schegloff 1972). To that noun phrase she adds a question intonation, a *try marker* (Sacks and Schegloff 1979), to show she isn't quite sure Ben will identify the arch and to ask him for confirmation. He says *right* to assert he has identified it and adds *the entrance to Chinatown* to display his identification further. She says *yes* to confirm his expansion, accepting that he has understood her reference, and continues on.

Each of these features could be used in concealment. If Ann wants to try out an esoteric key, she could use a preface to check on its viability and abort the process if the check fails. Or she might present her description with a try marker to check whether the key has been grasped; Ben, for his part, might offer an expansion of his own to check whether he has understood her key.

So far we have described techniques that people *might* use for requiring the concentrated use of whatever techniques they had at hand. So the task was able to reveal a wide range of their techniques precisely because it was so demanding.

2 Methods

Pairs of Stanford University students, separated by a screen, were given identical sets of pictures of eight well-known Stanford landmarks or scenes. For the student designated the *director*, the pictures were in a set order, and for the student designated the *matcher*, they were in no particular order. (For convenience in *our* references, we will consider the generic director to be female and the generic matcher male, even though both sexes assumed both roles in different pairs.) The goal was for the matcher to arrange his pictures in the same order as the director's. Although the director and matcher couldn't see each other, they could talk as much as they liked. The director's pictures were then reshuffled and the procedure repeated five more times for a total of six trials.

The catch was that there in the same room, behind another screen, was an overhearer obviously able to hear everything they said. (The generic overhearer will be considered male.) There were two conditions. In the *concealment* condition, the two partners knew that the overhearer was another Stanford student with the same eight pictures, and their job was to prevent him from arranging his pictures in the right order. In the *indifference* condition, as a control, no mention was made of the overhearer or of concealment: the two partners were indifferent to whether the overhearer understood or not.

Impromptu methods of concealment, according to our analysis, should generally be impossible for two unacquainted people from the same communities as the overhearer. So we chose as director and matcher pairs of friends. They had known each other a median of 1.6 years (ranging from one to nineteen years) and rated that they knew each other an average of 6.4 on a scale of 1 (not at all) to 7 (very well). There were sixteen pairs of directors and matchers in all, eight in the concealment condition and eight in the indifference condition. The overhearer was always unacquainted with the director and matcher before the experiment. All students were native English speakers enrolled in an introductory psychology course and received either course credit or payment for participating.

In the concealment condition, the three students were led together into a small room and seated at three desks separated by screens. One of the two friends at random was designated the director, and the other, the matcher, and then all three listened to all the instructions. They were told they all had identical sets of eight pictures, and the director and matcher were to try to arrange theirs in the same order without letting the overhearer do so. They were each supplied with a matrix of two rows of four spaces into which to place the pictures; the positions were numbered one through eight to help them keep track. The director's pictures were then shuffled and placed in the eight places of the matrix in front of her; the matcher's and overhearer's pictures were scattered around the perimeters of their desks. The director and matcher were instructed to go through the pictures in numerical order, though they could backtrack to fix mistakes, and they were not allowed to use a foreign language. They were told they would be timed, and they should try to be accurate. The overhearer was asked not to talk during the session. The director's pictures were reshuffled before each new trial, and the procedure was repeated. No one was told of any errors until the experiment was over.

Via questionnaires, all three students were each asked after each trial to estimate which of the pictures the matcher had got right and which the overhearer had got right. After the last trial, the director and matcher were asked how each description used on that trial was related to its corresponding picture, and the overhearer was asked to say, for each picture, what if anything the director and matcher had said revealed its identity. The concealment sessions took about sixty minutes.

In the indifference condition, the two friends were led through the same procedure as in the concealment condition, but without mention of overhearers or concealment. The overhearer was the experimenter himself. We considered having a third student at the third desk, but judged that the two partners would be suspicious of what we were up to and wouldn't simulate ordinary cases of indifference. The experimenter had a legitimate reason for being there and wouldn't raise such suspicions. The two students were each asked via questionnaires after each trial to judge which pictures the matcher got right. The indifference sessions took about twenty minutes.

The eight pictures were black and white photographs from a book about Stanford that depicted: Hoover Tower, the front of Memorial Church, an arcade at Stanford Medical Center filled with bicycles, an academic procession at commencement with robed faculty and flag bearers, a fountain commonly known as "The Claw" in front of the Stanford Bookstore, an aerial view of Stanford Stadium with much of the campus visible behind it, three palm trees in the central quadrangle, and a view down a long columned passageway in front of Memorial Church showing tiles with graduation years on them. The landmarks and scenes seemed familiar to everyone. The photographs were mounted on stiff cards measuring fifteen by twenty centimeters.

Microphones were attached to the director's and matcher's lapels, and each session was tape recorded and later transcribed. The transcripts marked all speaker changes, interruptions, starts and ends of overlapping speech, unusual pauses and intonation, and nonspeech vocalizations such as laughter and coughing.

3 Results

The results will be divided into three parts—difficulty in concealing, methods of concealing, and failures in concealing.

Difficulties in Concealing

The referential process in our task is well described by the collaborative model of reference. In the indifference condition, the director (D) typically would indicate a position and then describe or refer to the picture that belonged there, as here:

D. Picture number 2 is the Claw.
M. Okay.

(All cited and italicized examples come from our transcripts verbatim but with names changed for anonymity.) In easy cases like this, the matcher (M) would then say *okay*, and the director would go on to the next picture. In more difficult cases, the matcher would expand on the director's initial description, or ask for an expansion or correction, and the director would go on only when both were satisfied the matcher had understood, as here:

D.   The long view of the quad uh walkway
M.   those
M.   ⌈ numbers right?
D.   ⌊ is number 5
M.   Mkay
D.   Yeah with the numbers on the bottom.

These patterns are typical of tasks of this sort (Chapter 4, this volume; Isaacs and Clark 1987).

Time and Effort

The referential process should take more time and effort when the director is trying to do two things at once—refer for the matcher *and* conceal from the overhearer. With indifference, the director can offer the most obvious description that distinguishes the target picture from its neighbors, like *Memorial Church* or *commencement*, and it should usually be accepted immediately. With concealment, the director must avoid the obvious description and cast about for a private key, as in *where you worked one time? when I didn't?* Since these keys are often esoteric, she may need to try more than one or clarify them further before they are accepted. So two partners should take much longer for concealment than for indifference.

Figure 1 plots the average time each pair spent per picture in the concealment and indifference conditions. For the concealment condition, we have plotted two subgroups separately. The four pairs in Group 1 used the same private keys from Trial 1 on, whereas the four pairs in Group 2 changed one or more of their keys on each new trial. Since these subgroups were identified post hoc, we cannot apply statistical tests for differences between them. Yet, interpreted with caution, the differences suggest that their contrasting strategies had an important influence.

As expected, concealment took a great deal longer than indifference. As Figure 1 shows, two partners took an average of 25.6 seconds per picture in the concealment condition, but only 3.0 seconds per picture in the indifference condition, a ratio of more than eight to one ($F(1,14) = 33.44$, $p < .001$). On Trial 1, these two times were 65.4 and 4.7 seconds ($F(1,14) = 50.38$, $p < .001$), and on Trial 6 they were 18.8 and 2.2 seconds ($F(1,14) = 6.05$, $p < .027$). So the time difference remained through Trial 6. The same pattern was reflected in the number of words used by the two partners together on each picture. As shown in

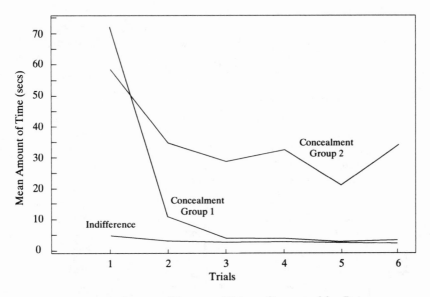

FIGURE 1 Average Time per Picture Consumed by Pairs
in Groups 1 and 2 of the Concealment Condition and
by Pairs in the Indifference Condition

Table 1, the concealment pairs averaged 49.0 words per picture, and
the indifferent pairs, only 6.6 words per picture ($F(1,14) = 21.35$, p
$< .001$). This difference also remained through Trial 6. This pattern
isn't surprising, since the more time a pair took, the more words they
uttered.

Concealment should also require more turns per picture than indifference. In all but the simplest conversations, however, what counts as
a turn depends strongly on the theory of turn taking one adopts. The
conversations in the concealment condition were very complex indeed,
and included a host of speech overlaps, interruptions, partial utterances, back channel responses and repairs. What we could count was
the alternations of speakers on each trial. As summarized in Table
1, concealment averaged 7.8 alterations per picture, and indifference,
only 1.3 per picture ($F(1,14)=25.58$, $p < .001$).

By the collaborative model, two partners should use briefer descriptions and need less refashioning as they refer more than once to the
same picture (Chapter 4, this volume). On each new trial they can
use the description mutually accepted on the previous trial and yet
make it briefer and this is what is generally observed (see Carroll 1985;
Chapter 4, this volume; Isaacs and Clark 1987; Krauss and Glucksberg

286 / Audience Design in Language Use

Average Time, Number of Words, Speaker Alternations, and Accuracy
by Participants in the Concealment and Indifference Conditions

MEASURE	CONCEALMENT			INDIFFERENCE
	GROUP 1	GROUP 2	ALL	
AVERAGE TIME PER PICTURE (S)				
Trial 1	72.2	58.6	65.4	4.7
Trial 6	3.3	34.3	18.8	2.2
All trials	16.2	35.0	25.6	3.0
AVERAGE NUMBER OF WORDS PER PICTURE				
All trials	32.7	65.2	49.0	6.6
AVERAGE NUMBER OF ALTERNATIONS PER PICTURE				
Trial 1	24.8	16.5	20.7	1.9
Trial 6	1.0	9.0	5.0	1.1
All trials	5.8	9.7	7.8	1.3
MATCHER ACCURACY (PERCENTAGE CORRECT)				
Trial 1	93.8	68.8	81.3	100.0
Trial 6	100.0	93.8	96.9	100.0
All trials	97.4	86.5	91.9	99.2
OVERHEARER ACCURACY (PERCENTAGE CORRECT)				
Trial 1	53.1	37.5	45.4	—
Trial 6	65.6	31.3	48.5	—
All trials	64.1	29.7	46.9	—

1977; Krauss and Weinheimer 1964). One director in the indifference
condition made these references to one picture over the six trials: *the
medical school with a bunch of bicycles, bicycles at the med school, the
bicycles at the med center, the bikes, the bikes,* and *the bikes.*

The result, as Figure 1 shows, is that time per picture tended to
decrease over the six trials. The indifference group took 4.7 seconds
per picture on Trial 1 and decreased to 2.2 seconds per picture by Trial
6. The linear decrease, as tested in a linear trend analysis, was reliable
($F(1,35) = 27.16$, $p < .001$). In the concealment condition, Group 1
can take advantage of their repeated use of the same keys and become
much faster over trials. Group 2, who tended to change keys from trial
to trial, can too, but less often. The times decreased over the six trials
from 72.2 to 3.2 seconds per picture for Group 1, and from 58.6 to only
34.3 seconds per picture for Group 2. The decrease for Groups 1 and 2
together was highly reliable (linear trend, $F(1,35) = 38.54$, $p < .001$).

With concealment, the two partners should find it more difficult to
formulate how to talk about a picture. Time, number of words, and
number of speaker alternations all attest to this, but there is qualitative
evidence as well. The indifference pairs always used equative sentences
with definite descriptions, like *The second picture is the medical center*

or, on later trials, noun phrases or nominals alone, like *medical center*. These are the forms one would use under optimal conditions. The concealing pairs, however, used many other forms as well. On the first mention of a picture on Trial 1, they used mostly descriptions, as in *Um, number four involves my summer job?*; *It looks like what we tell our, w– what we tell people to do when we work*; or *Okay, um, let's see, the sixth one is, let's see, I usually go tearing down here?* They also used many forms that would be judged ungrammatical by standard theories, such as *Uh first one is Maria works in front of it?* The point is, they exploited a variety of complex expressions never used by the indifferent partners.

Errors

Concealment also led to more errors than indifference, as shown in Table 1. The matchers, who were meant to get everything right, were correct 99% of the time in the indifference condition, but only 92% of the time in the concealment condition, a reliable drop in accuracy ($F(1,14) = 4.94$, $p < .05$). The overhearers in the concealment condition, who were not meant to get anything right, were correct fully 47% of the time. This is reliably greater than chance at 12.5% ($F(1,7) = 18.28$, $p < .004$), but reliably less than the 92% for matchers ($F(1,14) = 44.70$, $p < .001$). The matchers in the concealment condition improved over trials, from 81% on Trial 1 to 97% on Trial 6 (linear trend, $F(1,35) = 10.87$, $p < .01$), but the overhearers did not. So in trying to conceal, directors didn't do as well as they could have with their matchers, nor were they always successful in keeping their overhearers in the dark.

Techniques for Concealment

What techniques did the two partners use for concealment? If our proposals are right, their primary resource should be the use of private keys. The director should have described some relation to the picture (e.g., *I usually go tearing down here* or *where you worked one time? when I didn't?*) that she believes is part of her common ground with the matcher but is closed to the overhearer. Their secondary resource is the collaborative process itself. The two partners should help hide their keys via some of the same techniques they would ordinarily use in collaborating on references.

Private Keys

Two concealing partners should try to build their references on private keys. To see how they did this, we identified the keys each pair attempted to use for each picture on each trial. We defined a key as a bundle of information around a coherent theme that could have been expressed as a definite description for that picture.

The two partners were not as efficient in concealing referents as they could have been. If they had found the perfect keys right away, they would have used one key per picture for all six trials. In fact, they tried an average of 4.4 different keys per picture over the six trials. For Group 1, who used the same keys from Trial 1 on, the average was 2.7, whereas for Group 2, who changed many of their keys on each new trial, it was 6.2. Not surprisingly, most of the keys were introduced by the director, but 15% were introduced by the matcher.

The attempted keys should be based mainly on personal and not communal common ground, and they were. Almost all (97%) were built around people, events, situations, appearances, or conversations the two partners knew from joint personal experience. Exclusively communal common ground was used in only 3% of the attempted keys, and even some of these are debatable. One pair of friends from Atlanta alluded to a well-known tower there to refer to Hoover Tower. Another pair discovered by chance on entering the room that the overhearer hadn't been at Stanford the year before; later, they alluded to a time capsule buried the year before that he presumably couldn't have known about.

The relations chosen from personal experience were of many kinds. They included events (e.g., *the place where he served me coffee*), habitual activities (*where Jim works*), similarity (*it looks like the infield*), locations (*this picture is the closest place to where I live right now*), and many other types of experiences. They involved the central object depicted (e.g., Hoover Tower or Memorial Church), incidental objects (e.g., the flags at commencement, or the bicycles at the Medical Center), and even perspective (e.g., that the picture of Stanford Stadium was an aerial view).

Almost every key bore a relation to all or part of the landmark in the picture. These relations took two main forms. About half (49%) described a connection with the *particular* place or object depicted, as in: *Is it where I had trouble with Paul?* (Memorial Church); *Do you know where I go for my Bach Orchestra?* (Memorial Church); and *Scott works there?* (Hoover Tower). Most of the rest (44%) described something in relation to the *type* of place or objects depicted, as in: *The century* (a bicycle race, which alluded to bikes at the medical school); and *For the one, think of what Mariel makes fun of* (the Catholic church, an allusion to Memorial Church). This second type of relation never occurred in the indifference condition. Another 5% of the keys were built on incidents in the experiment itself (e.g., *the one we had so much trouble with last time*). The remaining 2% were uncodable.

The keys were constructed on a system of levels. Take the picture of the Claw fountain. At Level 1, it could be described as itself, e.g. as *the Claw*. At Level 2, it could be described in relation to another object, event, or process, e.g., as *where someone wanted to put my teddy bear*. At Level 3, it could be described in relation to the object mentioned at Level 2, e.g., *Chico's present to me* (the teddy bear). And so on. In the indifference condition, all descriptions should be at Level 1, and they were, as partners invariably described each landmark directly. In the concealment condition, all descriptions should be at Level 2 or above, and they were, with one exception. In that case, the director said, *Med school, oh, shit, [laugh], um*, recognizing it as a mistake.

The keys used for concealment ranged from 2 to 7 levels deep, constituting 43, 47, 8, 1, 0, and 1% of the attempted keys, respectively. (This excludes seven keys we couldn't classify.) In Group 2, many keys were built on keys from previous trials in a form of chaining. A new key (e.g., *Chico's present to me*) was created at a higher level on the basis of a previous key (e.g., *where someone wanted to put my teddy bear*), which is what accounts for most of the keys above two levels. In the one key seven deep, the director referred to the name of a woman who had a friend whose home town was near a city that had the same name as a dormitory where a friend of theirs lived with the same last name as someone they thought was in the commencement picture. Overhearers should have a difficult time penetrating baroque descriptions like this. Indeed, they identified the referents only 30% of the time for the pairs who chained after Trial 1 (Group 2) compared to 64% of the time for the pairs who didn't (Group 1) ($F(1,6) = 11.29$, $p < .02$). The matchers also had more difficulty with chained descriptions. They made 14% errors in Group 2 compared to only 3% in Group 1.

Many of these keys were used, as expected, in indirect references. In the indifference condition, directors almost always referred directly to something depicted, as with *Memorial Church, the Claw, Hoover Tower*, and *the stadium*. They continued to do so through Trial 6. In the concealment condition, directors regularly referred to what was depicted indirectly. On Trial 1, they tended to describe things in the pictures, as noted earlier. But by Trial 6, almost every reference was indirect. Examples from Trial 6: *Tsk um Arne and me* ["the place that looks like the desert island where Arne and I want to live"]; *Okay, 2 gummi bears* ["the place where you and I ate gummi bears (a type of candy)"]; and *four, silk dress* ["the place where a friend put her silk dress"]. In the last example, the director referred directly to a silk dress and, via an unexpressed reference function from silk dresses to places, thereby referred to the fountain. She was confident that the matcher could work out the function, and that the overhearer couldn't.

So, in concealing, the two partners created private keys from events, processes, people, and objects in their personal common ground. They seemed willing to try any relation so long as their partners would get it and their overhearers couldn't. Sometimes, they tried to hide them further by chaining new keys to previous ones, and by leaving the relations unexpressed in indirect references.

Collaborative Techniques

Two partners also collaborated in concealing in their use of prefaces, special modes of presentation, special interruptions, and speed.

1. *Prefaces.* In the concealment condition, the two partners should have tried hard to find areas of common ground that were closed to the overhearer and yet accessible to the two of them. So if the director wanted to use an esoteric key, she should try to establish that it, or its general area, is mutually recognizable before going any further. Prefaces are an ideal way of doing this. In fact, they were legion in our transcripts, as in these three examples:

(1) Okay, remember in Hiltonhead? [M. Uhhuh?]

(2) The first picture, we're gonna take, um, you know where we, you know uh, you know where the dorm was last year right [M. Yeah?]

(3) Okay, Ben, do you remember the place that- [M: Yes?] um, John came and sang. John and Dick and Bill sang happy birthday to me? couple days ago? [M: no]

Most prefaces asked the matcher to recall some event, though a few simply oriented the matcher to some area of common ground. Many prefaces were successful in bringing an area of common ground into joint focus, but many, like the last example, were not. Prefaces were used an average of 1.9 times per pair on Trial 1, but only 0.2 times per pair on each trial after that. They were never used in the indifference condition.

2. *Try markers.* Another common technique was to pronounce a noun phrase with a try marker, a rising intonation, as in *the fourth one is um my bestfriend on the ski team?* The try marker here is interpreted, not as *Is the fourth one my best friend on the ski team?* as if it were an ordinary question, but as *Do you understand what I am referring to with* my bestfriend on the ski team? With it, the director solicits confirmation of a description she was unsure the matcher would

grasp. In the indifference condition, try markers were used an average of 2.0 times per pair on Trial 1 and never on Trials 2 through 6. In the concealment condition, they were used 7.9 times per pair on Trial 1 and 2.2 times on each trial after that. The mean frequency over trials was reliably greater in concealment than in indifference ($F(1,14) = 11.54$, $p < .004$). The concealing director's goal was apparently to try out a key and expand on it only if asked.

Try markers were useful in a strategy of *gradual revelation*. The idea was for the director to present one key bit by bit, or several keys one at a time, until the matcher had identified the referent. For Memorial Church, one director named a series of religious acquaintances, asking after each whether the matcher had identified the picture yet. For the passageway with graduation tiles, another director listed objects in the time capsule under the tile laid the previous year, again asking about recognition after each object. With this technique the two partners don't reveal any more information than necessary, since they stop immediately when the matcher has understood. It is like unveiling a sculpture inch by inch until the observer can identify what it is. Someone less familiar with the sculpture than the observer should still not be able to identify it.

3. *Truncation*. Another technique for closing off a gradual revelation is truncation. In conversations without overhearers, a speaker can try out one definite description, and if that doesn't work, try out another, and then another, until the addressee cuts her off, as in this example (from Sacks, quoted by Jefferson, 1973, 59):

A. I heard you were at the beach yesterday. What's her name, oh you know, the tall redhead that lives across the street from Larry? The one who drove him to work the day his car

A. ⌈was -
B. ⌊Oh Gina!

A. Yeah Gina. She said she saw you at the beach yesterday.

A in effect invites B to cut her off the moment he has identified the woman she is referring to, and eventually he does, with *Oh Gina*. B's utterance here we will call a *truncator*.

Most partners used some truncation, as in this example from the concealment condition:

D. My class at the beginning of this quarter

D. ⌈was there
M. ⌊yeah yeah yeah yeah yeah yeah

The truncators included *yeah yeah, right right*, and *okay okay*. In the concealment condition, they were used on 61% of the pictures in Trial 1 and 6% in later trials; in the indifference condition, the two percentages were only 9 and 2%. The overall percentage was reliably higher for concealment than for indifference ($F(1,14) = 6.09$, $p < .027$). To our ears, the truncators seemed to be used in concealment to keep the directors from revealing too much, but in indifference to speed up the task.

4. *Speed*. The four pairs in Group 1 of the concealment condition all sped up their talk after Trial 1. On being questioned afterwards, three of the four pairs said they did so to make understanding harder for the overhearer. Their rationale was that the overhearers, with enough time, might be able to figure out some of the keys. The way to prevent that was to give them too little time.

The two partners, then, used a variety of collaborative techniques in conjunction with private keys. They used prefaces to try out esoteric pieces of common ground, presented tentative descriptions to be expanded on if needed, invited truncators to cut off too much revelation, and sped up. Their main aim, it appeared, was to reveal their keys in stages to avoid revealing any more information than necessary.

Failures of Concealment

The two partners, despite their effort, often failed to conceal the identities of the pictures from their overhearers. Why did they fail? What clues did they let slip through their fingers? And did they realize how badly they were doing? We first consider the judgments of the participants as to how well everyone did and then look at some reasons for the partners' failures.

Judgments of Success

Each participant in our experiment was asked after each trial to estimate which pictures the matcher got right, and which the overhearer got right. Table 2 shows the percentages of pictures, but only in the concealment condition, that each participant estimated had been correctly identified by the matcher and by the overhearer. Everyone thought the matchers had done splendidly—that they had been right 99% of the time—when they were actually right 92% of the time. More surprisingly, everyone thought the overhearers had been right in the neighborhood of 43% of the time, not 12.5% of the time, which was chance. In fact, overhearers were right 47% of the time. So everyone was pretty accurate at judging how *many* pictures the matcher and overhearer would get right.

The three participants, however, varied greatly in how accurately they predicted which *particular* pictures the overhearer got right. Suppose a director predicted that her overhearer got pictures 1, 2, and 8

TABLE 2

Percentages of Pictures That the Director, Matcher, and
Overhearer Estimated Had Been Correctly Identified by the
Matcher and Overhearer in the Concealment Condition

IDENTIFIER	SOURCE OF ESTIMATE	PERCENTAGE
Matcher	Director	99.5
	Matcher	98.5
	Overhearer	99.0
	Observed	91.9
Overhearer	Director	50.0
	Matcher	35.4
	Overhearer	44.8
	Observed	46.9

right and 3–7 wrong, when the overhearer actually got 1 and 3 right
and 2 and 4–8 wrong. The director was accurate in five of the eight
predictions, or 62% of the time. But given that she predicted he got
three right and five wrong, and given that he actually got two right
and six wrong, she would have been correct an average of 56% of the
time even if she had assigned her three rights and five wrongs at random. Her actual predictions were 6% better than this chance figure.
By averaging over individual cases like this, we calculated the three
percentages (corresponding to 62, 56, and 6%), for each type of judge,
for the matcher's accuracy and for the overhearer's accuracy. Those
percentages are listed in Table 3.

The overhearers were more accurate than the directors or matchers
at predicting which pictures they, the overhearers, got right. Overhearers made correct predictions 72% of the time, and the directors
and matchers, only 59 and 57% of the time. Only the first percentage
is above chance ($F(1,7) = 19.40$, $p < .003$), and it is reliably larger
than the second and third, whether they are corrected for chance or
not (when corrected for chance, $F(1,7) = 6.60$ and 6.88, $p < .05$). The
three percentages for the matcher's identifications are too near ceiling
to tell us anything.

So two partners suspected the overhearer of having identified three
to four pictures each trial, but couldn't tell which ones they were. The
overhearer was better at judging which ones he got right, but he still
wasn't perfect.

Sources of Failure

The postexperiment questionnaires revealed two major sources of failure—revealing too much adjunct information and using risky keys.

TABLE 3

Percentages of Pictures that the Director, Matcher, and
Overhearer Correctly Predicted Had and Had Not Been Identified
by the Matcher and Overhearer in the Concealment Condition

IDENTIFIER	JUDGE	CORRECT PREDICTIONS	CHANCE PREDICTIONS	DIFFERENCE
Matcher	Director	91.9	91.7	+0.2
	Matcher	91.4	91.0	+0.4
	Overhearer	91.4	91.4	0
Overhearer	Director	58.6	55.7	+2.9
	Matcher	56.5	53.3	+3.2
	Overhearer	71.9	57.7	+14.2

Adjunct information. For every reference used for concealment, one can divide the information the two partners made public into two parts—the private key proper and adjunct information. Consider one director's presentation, *this is where someone wanted to put my teddy bear.* Now the private key is the event, mutually known by the director and matcher in which a friend of the director's wanted to put her teddy bear into the Claw fountain. That event itself was closed to the overhearer. But in talking about it, the director displayed or presupposed adjunct information she surely believed was *not* closed to the overhearer: that the director had a teddy bear; what teddies are; what putting is; what sorts of things a teddy is likely to be put into; etc. For a successful concealment, the referent must *not* be conjecturable from the adjunct information alone.

Directors often misjudged how much could be conjectured from the adjunct information alone. The overhearer to *where someone wanted to put my teddy bear* looked through the pictures for something one could sensibly put a teddy into and chose the Claw fountain. He was right. Other overhearers were correct in choosing Hoover Tower for *I might hang a picture of Glenn off of this for his birthday* and for *where I was paid and getting dizzy,* the commencement picture for *we want to someday do this,* and Stanford Stadium, where the Olympic soccer matches had been held, for *Number 3 you heard a lot of noise from, this summer.* Many failures seemed to be of this sort, perhaps a majority. So although the directors used private keys, they often provided so much adjunct information that the keys weren't absolutely necessary.

Risky keys. The keys people used ranged in the risk they ran of being discovered. Most keys were safe, built on private experiences the two friends could be fairly certain the overhearer, a stranger, had no knowledge of. Examples: *we were talking about the aesthetic value of this on the way over; Sam and Joey; where Jim works,* and *this is that class that Andy and Eric were in.* Although one key backfired when the overhearer happened to know the person named, the risk was generally minimal.

Other keys were riskier, often much riskier. They were built on information a director, on reflection, should have expected to be common ground in communities the overhearer might well belong to. Examples: events from the movies *Repo Man* and *Young Frankenstein;* the golden arches for McDonald's Restaurants as a clue for the arches in front of Memorial Church; *something that's going to happen in June* for the commencement picture; and *cluelessness* and *black holes* for the long hallway. Directors tended to use such keys when only two or three pictures remained and they could assume the matchers but not the overhearers knew which. They were sometimes wrong in these judgments.

For a few keys, it was the adjunct information that was critical anyway. One director said, *Patricia always says I want a baby?*, referring to the Medical Center with the bicycles, since one bicycle had an infant seat on the back. What is critical to identifying this picture was not the private information about Patricia, but the adjunct information about babies. What the director should have said is, for example, *Remember what Patricia always says I want?* Another pair exchanged *Are there going to be a few people at our wedding* and *mm yeah just a few* to identify a picture with just a few people in it.

So two partners often gave the overhearer too much information by using risky or irrelevant keys. They seemed to underestimate how much overhearers knew about the risky keys and how far overhearers had already narrowed the options.

4 Conclusion

We have argued that audience design is an essential feature of language use: Speakers design what they say for the particular people they believe are or might be listening. Theories of language use have acknowledged this only gradually. At first they tended to treat all listeners alike; speakers designed utterances mainly to be true or false. The next generation of theories (e.g., Austin 1962; Grice 1968; Searle 1969) dealt with how utterances are designed for addressees, but they focused exclusively on speaking to single addressees. These theories had to undergo basic revisions to account for speakers talking to more than one conversational participant at a time (Chapter 7, this volume). They need still further revisions to say how speakers deal with overhearers (see Clark 1987). The research reported here is intended to help specify those revisions.

Audience design is especially obvious in definite reference. In the main theories, when Ann is addressing Ben and wants to refer to Derek, she must try to design a definite description—e.g., *Derek* or *that tall guy*—so that Ben can identify Derek based on that description plus their current common ground (see Chapters 1 and 3, this volume). But, as before, Ann's design has to change when she and Ben are joined by other participants. It changes even more radically when she and Ben can interact directly, as in a conversation. There, according to a good deal of evidence, she and Ben collaborate on the making of each reference (Clark and Schaefer 1987; Chapter 4, this volume; Cohen 1984; Isaacs and Clark 1987). Their goal is to establish the mutual belief that Ben has understood Ann's reference, and it may take them several exchanges to reach that goal.

Dealing with overhearers, we have argued, alters the process still further, depending on the speaker's attitude toward the overhearers. If Ann is indifferent to whether or not her overhearer Oscar understands, she can refer to Derek as she normally would with Ben—say, as *Derek*. But if she wants to make certain that Oscar too can identify Derek, she may need to expand on or change that reference—say, to *Derek Aitken from Denver*. If she wants to conceal his identity, as we have seen, she might use instead *the man we talked about last night*. She may even want to disguise Derek's identity so that Oscar thinks she is referring to someone else, and that would require other considerations. These four attitudes—indifference, disclosure, concealment, and deception—each follow a different logic. Each requires Ann to design her reference for two different purposes at the same time.

In this paper we have brought out two main points about concealment. The first concerns its logic. Ann's goal is to design her reference (a) to enable Ben to identify the referent and, simultaneously, (b) to prevent Oscar from doing so. To achieve this, according to our proposal, Ann must build her reference on a private key. That key is a piece of Ben's and her common ground (satisfying requirement a), but one she believes is closed to Oscar (satisfying requirement b). The students in our task tried to do just that. Almost all their keys were built around events, processes, states, and objects from joint personal experiences that excluded the overhearer and yet bore some relation to the landmarks whose identities were to be concealed. And each pair of partners worked hard at finding these areas. Two partners took much more time when they were trying to conceal than when they were indifferent.

The second point is about the process of concealment. Finding and using private keys that fit this logic can be difficult, especially on the fly. This poses two main problems. Ann and Ben need procedures for discovering and focusing on the right private information in the first place. They also need techniques for expressing the keys in such a way that adjunct information doesn't give them away. In our task the students solved these two problems in an ingenious way. They used a variety of collaborative techniques that they had available anyway for other purposes.

Their main strategy was to reveal their keys gradually turn by turn. The director would search for closed areas of personal common ground by the use of prefaces (e.g., *Okay, remember in Hiltonhead?*) and check on the understanding of a key with a try marker (e.g., *my bestfriend on the ski team?*). If these failed, she would try another private area or key. She would often try one key after another until the matcher caught on and cut her off with a truncator (e.g., *right right*). When the director did refer to a landmark or scene, she tended to do it indirectly, as in *Position eight is gummi bears* instead of *Position one is the place where you and I ate gummi bears*. These techniques enabled the two partners to focus on private, shared experiences without divulging too much information to their overhearers.

Our task made concealment particularly hard because it was so demanding. The two partners were no more familiar with the pictured landmarks than the overhearers were, so they had to worry about divulging too much. Also, with only eight pictures, the overhearers could narrow down the alternatives with relatively little information. And the partners had no choice but to conceal each reference; they couldn't postpone talking about a landmark just because it was hard to conceal. So the time and errors we found may not reflect most everyday attempts at concealment.

Still, the failures in our task reveal difficulties people can have in finding and using private keys. Two partners sometimes chose a proper key but, in making their reference, divulged adjunct information that gave it away. The idea was right, but the execution was faulty. Other times they overestimated the opacity of their keys. It was too easy for the overhearers to conjecture which pictures the keys were about. Yet the two partners seemed to know how often they let revealing information slip through their fingers.

In general, then, speakers take account of overhearers as well as addressees and other participants as they formulate and execute utterances. Any theory of these processes, to be adequate, must do so too.

Part IV

Coordination of Meaning

Introduction to Part IV

When you and I talk, we have to coordinate on what each word we use means. When I use *hot* to mean "lucky," I must be confident you will see that it means "lucky" and not "spicy" or "extremely warm" or "radioactive" or "angry" or "lascivious" or "stolen." The standard view is that coordination of word meaning is easy. You and I have a short list of conventional meanings for *hot* stored in our mental lexicons, and when I use *hot*, you search the list and, given the circumstances, pick the most reasonable meaning.

I became interested in the coordination of meaning when I realized that the standard view simply couldn't be correct. About 1975 I started looking into what I called *shorthand expressions*. Here are three examples, with the shorthand expressions in italics:

1. Service for eight includes dinner plates, *salads*, cups, saucers, *soup/cereals* plus oval platter, oval *vegetable*, *sugar* with lid, creamer (newspaper advertisement for china)
2. *Gold* falls to new *lows* (newspaper headline)
3. I bought two *William Blakes*.

When you look up *salad* in your mental lexicon, you surely won't find "small plate on which a salad is served." That is an interpretation you create on the spot based on your common ground with the author. The same goes for *soup/cereals*, *vegetable*, *sugar*, *gold*, and *lows*. As for the two William Blakes, are they paintings, poems, or autographs by Blake, books about Blake, people with that name, or what? Without evidence of what the speaker intended, there is an infinity of possible interpretations. So to understand these expressions, you must create interpretations in coordination with the speaker or author.[1]

---

[1] I presented this analysis in a paper called "Inferring what is meant" at the 1975 International Congress of Psychology in Paris; it was published in 1978 in *Studies in*

About the same time Eve Clark and I also became interested in how people create and interpret novel word coinages. We focused on verbs derived from nouns, as in these examples:

4. A hawk *landed* in the very top of that tree.
5. Did the paperboy *porch* the newspaper this morning?
6. My sister managed to *Houdini* her way out of the closet.

From 1975 on, we amassed a collection of over 1000 denominal verbs. Many of these verbs, like *land*, were already "lexicalized" or well established in the lexicon, but many others, like *porch* and *Houdini*, were innovations. Like shorthand expressions, innovative denominal verbs have in principle an infinity of possible interpretations. The issue, then, is how speakers and their addressees coordinate each time on precisely what interpretation is intended. This was the issue that Eve Clark and I addressed in our paper "When nouns surface as verbs," which appeared in *Language* in 1979.

Chapter 10, "Making sense of nonce sense," grew out of these two projects. Both shorthand expressions and denominal verbs suggest that many standard assumptions about parsing and interpreting utterances are simply untenable. Nonce sense is the sense that the speaker intends an expression to have for the nonce. It is an entirely accepted part of everyday language and yet isn't accounted for by any of the standard models of understanding. What is needed is a model of the processes by which speakers and addressees coordinate on nonce sense, and these processes will be founded on very different principles. I presented this argument at the 1981 International Congress of Psychology in Leipzig, and it was published in 1983 in *The Process of Language Understanding*, edited by Giovanni B. Flores d'Arcais and Robert Jarvella.

As Eve Clark and I realized, eponymous expressions offer a special challenge to standard theories of word meaning. A proper name like *Houdini* doesn't have a meaning in the usual sense. Unlike common nouns such as *land* and *porch*, it refers directly to a historical individual. So to understand "My sister managed to Houdini her way out of a closet," we must appeal not to the meaning of the noun *Houdini*, but to historical facts or legends in our common ground about the referent of *Houdini*, namely Harry Houdini himself. How do we search this historical information and create the intended meaning? Richard Gerrig and I examined the process empirically for eponymous verb phrases, as in "The Allies hoped that Hitler would *do a Napoleon* when he attacked

---

the Perception of Language, edited by Willem J. M. Levelt and Giovanni B. Flores d'Arcais.

Russia, and he did." Unlike other eponymous expressions, these never lexicalize, and that makes them a pure case of sense creation as opposed to sense selection. We reported our experiments in "Understanding old words with new meanings" in 1983 in the *Journal of Verbal Learning and Verbal Behavior*. The paper appears here as Chapter 11.

Creating a sense for the nonce isn't confined to eponymous expressions, novel denominal verbs, or shorthand expressions. It is a ubiquitous feature of everyday word use. What makes it ubiquitous is a basic principle of language use, in the spirit of Grice, that I have called the *choice principle*: Speakers choose each expression they use from a set of possible expressions for a purpose that they reflexively intend their addressees to recognize. When I describe a thing as a *hound*, I chose *hound* over *dog*, *animal*, *beagle*, *mongrel*, and other possibilities for a reason, and I intend you to recognize that reason as part of what I mean. Eve Clark and I applied this principle, in effect, in accounting for the phenomenon of pre-emption, why we can say *to hospitalize* but not *to hospital* with the same meaning.

How does this principle apply more generally? In 1989 I took up the issue at a conference celebrating a former professor of mine, Wendell R. Garner of Yale University. Garner had been the source of a principle I had carried with me since graduate school. I have called it the *principle of possibilities*: We understand *what an entity is* with reference to *what it could have been*—the set of possibilities we infer it came from. This was a principle Garner applied to the representation of what we see, but it seemed to me to apply just as readily in language use. There it becomes, in effect, the choice principle. The choice principle, in turn, is needed in accounting for the everyday uses of such ordinary terms as *red*, *several*, *New Yorker*, and *row*. The full argument appears in Chapter 12, "Words, the world, and their possibilities," which was published in 1991 in *The Perception of Structure*, edited by Gregory Lockhead and James Pomerantz.

10

Making Sense of Nonce Sense

A 'parser' is a device, either human or mechanical, that is designed to analyse a person's utterances as a part of deciding what that person meant. Most mechanical parsers do this by breaking down, or 'parsing', each utterance into parts, selecting senses for each part, and combining these senses into a meaning for the whole utterance. How human parsers do this is a question in which researchers have invested much time and energy, and for good reason. It is hard to imagine a model of language understanding without a parser of one sort or another.

One of the main stumbling blocks for parsers is ambiguity. When a parser encounters the word *post*, it must decide whether it means 'pole', 'mail', or something else. When it meets the phrase *good king*, it must decide whether it means 'king who rules well', 'king who is a good person', or something else. When it meets the clause *that he knew* in *He whispered to the woman that he knew*, it must decide whether it modifies *the woman* or is a complement of *whisper*. Parsers so far have been outfitted with syntactic, semantic, and pragmatic strategies for resolving ambiguity. For each expression, they anticipate the right meaning, or a small set of meanings, and thereby avoid the expensive computation of unintended meanings. Or they select the right meanings after the fact, pragmatically.

At the heart of what I will call traditional parsers is the *sense-selection assumption*. The idea is this. Each parser is in possession of a lexicon, or dictionary, that lists the potential senses for each word (like *post*), each morpheme (like *pre-*), and each idiom (like *kick the bucket*). For *post*, let us say, the lexicon lists six distinct senses. When a parser encounters *post* in an utterance, it selects from among these six senses the one that the speaker must have intended on this occasion. When it encounters *good king*, it parses the phrase into *good* and *king*,

305

combines the possible senses of the two separate words by appropriate rules of combination, and arrives at, say, twelve possible senses for the phrase. From among these twelve it selects the sense the speaker must have intended. The skill to parsing is in making these selections deftly, with the minimum fuss and computation. Still, the assumption that is virtually always made in traditional parsers is this: each constituent of an utterance has a finite number of possible senses, and people *select* the intended sense from among them.

The sense–selection assumption seems so natural, so obviously true, that it isn't even open to dispute. Yet in the last few years, more and more evidence has been brought to the fore suggesting that it is in fact false. The problem is this. Not only can expressions be ambiguous, but they can also be *semantically indeterminate*. Many expressions, contrary to the assumption, do not possess a finite number of senses that can be listed in the parser's lexicon. Nor can they be assigned their possible senses by any rule. Each expression of this sort, instead, has only a *nonce sense*, a sense 'for the nonce', for the occasion on which it is used. It would be hard enough for traditional parsers if there were *any* such expressions, but, as I will argue, they are ubiquitous. No parser can avoid them, yet when traditional parsers meet them, they break down.

In this chapter I have two main aims. The first is to describe two fundamental problems that nonce sense poses for traditional parsers. In doing this, I will demonstrate how natural and ubiquitous nonce sense is in daily usage. The second aim is to argue for a new view of parsing altogether. In this view, the goal is to infer the speaker's intentions in using each word and constituent that he used. The idea is to meet nonce sense head-on, to treat nonce sense as an intrinsic part of language, which it is.

1 Two Parsing Problems

For examples that will stymie any traditional parser, we need look no further than the daily newspaper, which is replete with them. The passage I have selected is from a column in the *San Francisco Examiner* by satirist Erma Bombeck about her daughter's difficulties in finding a roommate. Bombeck is quoting her daughter:

> We thought we were onto a steam iron yesterday, but we were too late. Steam irons never have any trouble finding roommates. She could pick her own pad and not even have to share a bathroom. Stereos are a dime a dozen. Everyone's got their own systems. We've just had a streak of bad luck. First, our Mr. Coffee flunked

out of school and went back home. When we replaced her, our electric typewriter got married and split, and we got stuck with a girl who said she was getting a leather coat, but she just said that to get the room.

As newspaper prose, this paragraph is unremarkable. Yet of the eight sentences, six will fail on the traditional parser. Why? Not because the six sentences sound odd, or use a peculiar vocabulary, or are in a strange dialect. It is only because they each contain a noun phrase used in a nonce sense—*a steam iron, steam irons, stereos, our Mr. Coffee,* and *our electric typewriter.* For *steam iron,* the parser will search its lexicon for the sense Bombeck intended for it—'a person who has a steam iron'. Since this sense won't be in the lexicon, it will search in vain. It will fail to deal with *steam iron* just as it will fail on the other five instances of nonce sense. Clearly, Bombeck isn't at fault. The parsers are.

The difficulties that parsers run into in this passage are of two kinds—non-parsing and mis-parsing. Consider *Our electric typewriter got married.* A traditional parser would meet *electric typewriter* and then *got married* and would search among the listed or computed senses for the two expressions to find ones that fit together sensibly. Because it wouldn't find any—electric typewriters, not being humans, cannot marry—it would fail to come to any interpretation. It would mark the utterance as uninterpretable nonsense rather than as interpretable nonce sense. This is what I will call the *non-parsing problem.*

The problem posed by *Stereos are a dime a dozen* is superficially quite different. As a sentence, this one is quite unremarkable and, unlike *Our electric typewriter got married,* is not semantically anomalous on the face of it. The traditional parser would work its way through the sentence and arrive at roughly the interpretation, *Phonographs are very common.* The trouble is this isn't what Bombeck meant. She meant, *People who possess phonographs are very common.* Since the traditional parser would never list in its lexicon the nonce sense *person who possesses a phonograph* for *stereo,* it could never come up with Bombeck's intended sense. It would discover an interpretation it would be willing to accept, but it is the wrong interpretation. This is what I will call the *mis-parsing problem.*

The difficulties underlying these two examples, however, are identical: *Electric typewriter* and *stereo* are both being used with nonce senses. The lexicons of traditional parsers list only the conventional senses of words, morphemes, and idioms, and rightly so. They couldn't possibly list—or store in memory—all the possible nonce senses a word, morpheme, or idiom might, be used with. As I will argue, there is no end to the nonce senses for words like *electric typewriter* or *stereo*; furthermore, these nonce senses cannot be enumerated by rule. As a consequence, these parsers will invariably fail to parse utterances like *Our typewriter got married* and will invariably mis-parse ones like *Stereos are a dime a dozen*.

2 The Ubiquity of Nonce Sense

For nonce sense like Bombeck's to pose a significant threat to traditional parsers, it must be more than a marginal part of language. I will argue both that nonce sense is ubiquitous and, more importantly, that it is a regular part of the language. When we encounter it, we perceive it to be natural and proper. We don't hear it as only partially acceptable or grammatical. Any parser that is to handle ordinary language must therefore be able to interpret nonce sense in the natural course of processing.

Contextual Expressions

It is well known that while some expressions have a fixed reference, others have a shifting reference. Those with a fixed reference are proper names, like *George Washington*, *the Second World War*, and *France*, which rigidly designate certain individuals. Those with a shifting reference are indexical expressions, like *I*, *now*, and *the bachelor over there*, whose referents depend on the time, place, and circumstances in which they are uttered. It has been virtually unrecognized, however, that while some expressions have fixed senses, others have shifting senses. Those with fixed senses might be called 'purely intensional expressions', like *bachelor*, *blue*, and *colorful ball*, each of which has a small number of conventional senses known to almost everyone in a speech community. Those expressions with shifting senses—what I am concerned with here—are called *contextual expressions*. Their senses depend entirely on the time, place, and circumstances in which they are uttered (Clark and Clark 1979). Thus, we have the following two analogies:

sense : reference :: purely intensional expression : proper name
:: contextual expression : indexical expression

And:

fixed : shifting :: proper name : indexical expression
:: purely intensional expression : contextual expression

These two analogies lead to the four-way classification given in Table 1.

TABLE 1
Classification of Expressions

ASPECT OF MEANING	ALTERABILITY OF ASPECT OF MEANING	
	FIXED	SHIFTING
Sense	Purely intensional expression (e.g., *bachelor*)	Contextual expression (e.g., *to teapot*)
Reference	Proper name (e.g., *George Washington*)	Indexical expression (e.g., *he*)

For the main properties of contextual expressions, which have shifting *senses*, let us first look at indexical expressions, which have shifting *references*. One such indexical expression is *he*, which has two important characteristics. First, it has an indefinitely large number of potential referents, and these referents are not denumerable. *He* can be used to refer to any of an indefinitely large number of males, past, present, and future, real and imaginary. These males cannot be listed, even in theory, since someone can always imagine another male and refer to it with *he*. Let me call this property *non-denumerability*. Second, what *he* is actually used to refer to on a particular occasion depends on who uttered it, where, what he was pointing at, who had just been mentioned in the conversation, what his addressee knew and didn't know, and many other points of coordination between the speaker and addressee (see, e.g., Chapter 1, this volume). Let me call this dependence on moment-to-moment coordination *contextuality*. These two properties—non-denumerability and contextuality—are characteristic of indexical expressions but not of proper names.

Non-denumerability and contextuality should also be characteristic of contextual expressions but not of purely intensional expressions. Imagine that Ed and I have a mutual friend named Max, who has the odd occasional urge to sneak up behind people and stroke the back of their legs with a teapot. One day Ed tells me, *Well, this time Max has gone too far. He tried to teapot a policeman.* Ed has used the noun *teapot* as a verb with a nonce sense, namely 'rub the back of the leg of with a teapot'. As for non-denumerability, note that the verb *teapot* could have been preceded by an indefinitely large number of introductory scenarios and could have possessed an indefinitely large number of different meanings. Neither the distinct scenarios nor the distinct senses it could possess are denumerable. As for contextuality, note that what *teapot* means depends crucially on the time, place, and circumstances in which Ed used it. He couldn't have meant just anything by it, and he could only have intended it to mean 'rub the back of the leg of with a teapot' for addressees who had just the right background knowledge. The verb *teapot*, then, is a contextual expression, and so are innovative denominal verbs in general (Clark and Clark 1979).

Some Types of Contextual Expressions

Most contextual expressions are word innovations that are formed from well established words or morphemes. The verb *teapot* is a novel construction built on the noun *teapot* plus a change in form class from noun to verb. This sort of word formation is often called zero-derivation, as if the noun *teapot* is provided with a zero suffix to form the verb *teapot-ϕ*. Not every innovation, however, is a contextual expression. Nouns formed from adjectives by adding *-ness*, as in *fakeness* and *chartreuseness*, aren't contextual expressions, as I will spell out later, whereas verbs formed from nouns by adding the zero suffix, as in *to teapot* and *to apple*, are. It is an important empirical question which constructions produce contextual expressions and which do not.

To give an idea of the range of contextual expressions, I will list some construction types that I believe contain contextual expressions. Some of these types contain well-documented cases of contextual expressions. Others contain cases I only conjecture to be contextual expressions. My conjectures are based on examples that work like the verb *teapot* in exhibiting the properties of non-denumerability and contextuality. Since it would be impossible to give the whole range of such construction types, I will restrict myself to expressions formed from concrete nouns. I will list the categories of contextual expressions by the form class of the derived word—by whether it is a noun, adjective, or verb. There are undoubtedly many types of contextual expressions other than those listed here.[1]

1. **Indirect Nouns.** The nouns in such expressions as *the horse*, *a car*, and *some water* appear to denote concrete things in an obvious way. Appearances, however, are deceiving. One way to ask for a glass of water in many contexts is to say *One water, please. Water*, of course, is a mass noun that denotes the substance water. To get it to denote a glass of water, one must take *one water* in the nonce sense *one glass of water*. In other contexts, the same phrase could be used to denote one tub of water, one type of water, one drop of water, one teaspoon of water, one person who ordered water, and

---

[1]Novel metaphors are one such type. They appear to pose the same problems for traditional parsers as do the contextual expressions I will discuss, and they appear to require the same new view of parsing that I will propose. In this chapter, however, I will stick to expressions that are ordinarily considered non-metaphorical.

so on indefinitely. Other examples of indirect nouns include: *Last night they played a Beethoven*; *I saw a Henry Moore today*; *That ten minutes was too long for a commercial*; *Stereos are a dime a dozen*; and *Our electric typewriter got married.* These expressions have been studied under various names—'beheaded noun phrases' (Borkin 1970), 'shorthand expressions' (Clark 1978), and 'deferred reference' (Nunberg 1979). It is important to notice that on the surface they are often impossible to distinguish from purely intensional expressions. *The water* could be used in the conventional sense *the substance called water*, or in some nonce sense *the glass, or pail, or drop, or the teaspoon, or ...*, *of water.* One can only tell from context.

2. **Compound Nouns.** In English, idiomatic compound nouns like *dog sled, tea garden*, and *apple pie* are common. Because they are idiomatic, their conventional senses are listed in the dictionary and, presumably, in most people's mental lexicons. Compound nouns with nonce senses, however, like *finger cup, apple-juice chair*, and *Ferrari woman*, are also common, and their meanings will not be found ready-made in the dictionary or in mental lexicons. Although Lees (1960), Levi (1978), and Li (1971) have all assumed that such compound nouns fall into a small number of paradigms, Downing (1977), Gleitman and Gleitman (1970), Jespersen (1942), Kay and Zimmer (1976), and Zimmer (1971, 1972) have argued that they do not. Both Downing, and Kay and Zimmer, have shown, in effect, that innovative compound nouns are contextual expressions since their possible meanings aren't denumerable and what they mean on any occasion depends on the close coordination of the speaker and addressee.

3. **Possessives.** We tend to think of the so-called possessive construction as denoting possession and a small range of other things. *John's dog* means *the dog John possesses.* Yet in the right contexts, *John's dog* could also mean *the dog John is standing in front of, the dog John saw yesterday, the dog John always wanted*, and any number of other things. The possibilities are in theory unlimited in number and cannot be enumerated, and what it is taken to mean on any occasion relies heavily on the coordination of the speaker and addressees. Possessives, in short, are contextual expressions.

4. **Denominal Nouns.** Nouns like *Nixonite, bicycler*, and *saxophonist* are formed from concrete nouns like *Nixon, bicycle*, and *saxophone* by derivation. There is a plethora of idiomatic cases of

this sort in English, but what innovative examples mean can vary enormously from one occasion to the next, depending on certain cooperative measures between the speaker and addressees. Each has an unlimited number of possible meanings, or so it appears. Denominal nouns, then, although they have stricter requirements than, say, possessives or compound nouns, are also contextual expressions.

5. **Denominal Verbs.** It is easy to turn nouns into verbs, as in *to graphite the locks*, *to farewell the guests*, and *to Houdini one's way out of a locked closet*. Some denominal verbs are already well established in the language, but many are being invented all the time. Eve V. Clark and I (Clark and Clark 1979) have argued in detail that innovative denominal verbs are contextual expressions. The denominal verb *teapot* has an unlimited set of potential senses, and what it means on each occasion depends on the coordination of speaker and addressees.

6. **Eponymous Verbs.** In *The photographer asked me to do a Napoleon for the camera*, the expression *do a Napoleon* is being used innovatively. I will call this expression an eponymous verb—because it is built on the name of its eponym Napoleon— even though it consists of a proverb *do* and an indirect noun as direct object. Eponymous verbs can only be understood if the speaker and addressees coordinate their knowledge of the eponym, here Napoleon, so that the addressees can identify the act of the eponym that the speaker is alluding to. Since there are, in principle, an unlimited number of acts one could know and allude to about an eponym, there are also an unlimited number of senses that could be assigned to the verb. Eponymous verbs are never idiomatic. Each one we meet we are forced to treat as a contextual expression.

7. **Pro-act Verbs.** In *Alice did the lawn*, *do* is what I will call a pro-act verb. It denotes an act like mowing, raking, fertilizing, or an unlistably large number of other things that one can do to lawns. Its senses are not denumerable, and what it is taken to mean depends critically on the time, place, and circumstances in which it is uttered. pro-act verbs appear to be genuine contextual expressions.

8. **Denominal Adjectives.** Adjectives derived from nouns, like *gamey*, *impish*, and *athletic*, from *game*, *imp*, and *athlete*, are common in English. Although most such adjectives are idiomatic and have conventional senses, many of them can be innovative, with

meanings dependent on the time, place, and circumstances of the utterance. *Churchillian*, for example, might mean *with a face like Churchill, smoking a cigar like Churchill, with a speaking style like Churchill*, or any number of other things. In principle, the list is unlimited; in practice, it is limited by what the speaker can assume the addressees know about Churchill and will be able to see that he is alluding to.

9. **Non-predicating Adjectives.** Closely related to the first noun in noun compounds are the so-called non-predicating adjectives, like *atomic, manual*, and *marine* (Levi 1978). These adjectives, formed from Latin and Greek roots, serve virtually the same purpose as the equivalent English nouns would serve in the same position. Just as there are *atomic bombs, manual labor*, and *marine life*, there are *atom bombs, hand labor*, and *sea life*. These adjectives are non-predicating in that one cannot say, with the same meaning as in *marine life*, that *life is marine*. For all these reasons, these adjectives share many properties with the first nouns of compound nouns and also with possessives (Levi 1978). Innovative uses of non-predicating adjectives appear to possess both of the critical properties of contextual expressions—non-denumerability and contextuality. *Atomic*, for example, may indicate any of an indefinitely large set of unlistable relations between atoms and the things denoted by the noun that *atomic* modifies.

10. **Eponymous Adjectives.** In examples like *She is very San Francisco* and *That is a very Picasso painting*, the adjectives are formed from the names of people or places—their eponyms—and allude to one of an indefinite number of unlistable properties of those eponyms, of San Francisco and Picasso. What the adjectives actually allude to depends on the time, place, and circumstances in which they are uttered. They too are contextual expressions.

The types of contextual expressions I have just laid out are summarized in Table 2.

Ubiquity and Naturalness

With so many different types available, contextual expressions ought to be ubiquitous, and they are. They occur everywhere and generally without our being aware that their senses are nonce senses. Absolute numbers are difficult to estimate. One reason is that the line between contextual expressions and purely intensional expressions is difficult to draw (Clark and Clark 1979). A sense may be conventional within

TABLE 2
Ten Types of Contextual Expressions

CATEGORY OF DERIVED WORD	TYPE OF EXPRESSION	EXAMPLES
Noun	Indirect nouns	*one water, a Henry Moore.*
	Compound nouns	*finger cup, apple-juice chair.*
	Possessives	*John's dog, my tree.*
	Denominal nouns	*a waller, a cupper.*
Verb	Denominal verbs	*to farewell, to Houdini.*
	Eponymous verbs	*to do a Napoleon, to do a Nixon.*
	Pro-act verbs	*to do the lawn, to do the porch.*
Adjective	Denominal adjectives	*Churchillian, Shavian.*
	Non-predicting adjectives	*atomic, manual.*
	Eponymous adjectives	*very San Francisco, very Picasso.*

one community, as among newspaper reporters or computer users, but it may be a nonce sense for the people being addressed. All I can do is give a feel for the numbers involved. As examples I will offer both deliberate uses by literary people trying for special effects and unpremeditated use by ordinary people trying to talk efficiently. Both types are common.

Many literary uses are designed for humour. When Bombeck has her daughter say, *We're looking for a size 10 with a steam iron,* meaning 'a person who wears dresses of size 10 and comes with a steam iron', she is making a point of her daughter's materialism. There is similar motivation behind the following examples (the obvious nonce uses in italics):

Subjected to the musical equivalent of 72 hours in a dentist's waiting room, Bradley was apparently in real danger of being the first tourist ever *Muzakked* to death.   (*SF Examiner*)

We've redone the entire living room in *Nelson Rockefeller* [alluding to Rockefeller's business of selling reproductions of art from his private collection].   (*New Yorker* cartoon)

I divide the world into two groups—the *'for me's* and the *'against me's.*   (Mal cartoon)

The fire department capped the plug and the police department *jugged* the guest. (Herb Caen, *SF Chronicle*)

J. W. Marriott Sr. and J. W. Jr. *Pan Am'd* out of here Sat. for Peking. (Herb Caen)

Tuesday is a good day for *noistalgics* who miss the daily noon siren sound from the Ferry Building. (Herb Caen)

Alexander Zinchuk, the USSR's consul General, inviting the local wretched *inkstains* to a reception May 3 in observance of—get set—'The Day of the Press'. (Herb Caen)

The bank's *buzzier guessips* tried to connect this odd coincidence with the Alvin Rice hoo-ha—Alvin being the former *No. 2* of B of A now being *grand-juried* for possible conflict in real estate loans—but at least two of the *Vanishing Bank of Americans* say coolly "We resigned." (Herb Caen)

Newspaper reporters and other writers rely on contextual expressions in everyday expository writing. This is illustrated in the following examples:

Gold plunges to new *lows* [the price of gold, new low levels]
(headline, *SF Chronicle*)

I stopped in Perry's for a *quick crab*. [dish of crab meat that could be consumed quickly] (Herb Caen)

The initiative is aimed at preventing the *New Yorking* of the San Francisco skyline. (TV news)

Twenty-two nations and five international agencies agreed here yesterday to send a delegation to Cuba to urge Fidel Castro to ease the plight of thousands of his countrymen seeking to leave the island, and to regularize their departure. [Representatives from 22 nations and five international agencies] (*LA Times*)

I had a *teletype* on the situation half a hour ago. [a message sent by the teletype machine] (novel)

The *telephone* managed to get a word in. [The person on the other end of the telephone line] (novel)

Service for 8 includes dinner plates, *salads*, cups, saucers, *soup/- cereals* plus oval platter, oval *vegetable*, *sugar* with lid, creamer.
(advertisement)

Only a few of these examples stand out as innovations—the telephone and New Yorking examples, perhaps. The rest strike us as mundane and quite unremarkable.

You don't have to be a professional writer to come up with contextual expressions, as illustrated in these attested spontaneous examples:

In this program I could either *and* it or *or* it. [Use the computer language connectives '*and*' and '*or*'] (computational linguist)

(Can you tell a person by his car?) I'm *a Dodge Power Wagon*. That's what I've got. (*SF Chronicle*, 'Question Man')

(What's good cheap entertainment?) Today I'm going *gallerying*. ('Question Man')

He's home today *jetlagging*. [Recovering from the effects of jet-lag] (a friend)

Having *porpoised* my way through the arguments, I gave them my conclusion. (a well known psychologist)

I know that it's across from a quarry. That's the only way I can *landmark* it. (Person talking about finding a beach)

Once again, there is nothing particularly remarkable about most of these contextual expressions. We may identify many of them as novel, but we take them as a legitimate part of English.

Contextual expressions have to be legitimate in order to account for how new words come into English, which happens at an often alarming rate. Consider this example. In the *San Francisco Chronicle*, the 'Question Man' one day asked 'What's good cheap entertainment?' One woman replied, *Bouldering is great*. For readers like me, *bouldering* was an expression with no conventional meaning. In context, we took it to mean 'climbing on boulders'. Yet it was clear from the rest of the woman's answer that she took *bouldering* to be a conventional term for that activity—perhaps within the community of rock climbers. We understood her even though that conventional sense hadn't yet spread to the larger community of readers. For her convention to spread to the larger community, the rest of us must be able to interpret her term readily and as a matter of course. We must be willing to accept its Janus–like character for a while—as a conventional term for some of us and as an innovation for others. A good deal of the conventional vocabulary appears to have entered the language by just this route—from contextual expressions solidifying and petrifying into purely intensional expressions (see Clark and Clark 1979).

3   Traditional Parsers

Which parsers in the literature run into trouble with contextual expressions? Most of them, I will argue, or so it appears. The caveat *or so it appears* is critical. For parsers in the psychological tradition, there have been few characterizations of the lexicon—of what lexical entries would look like and how they would be organized. Yet these parsers proceed as if they were making the sense-selection assumption and don't appear able to handle contextual expressions. In the artificial intelligence tradition, more attention has been paid to the lexicon, but only a few of the parsers have been spelled out in any detail (e.g., Winograd 1972). Yet these parsers also appear to follow the sense–selection assumption, and so they too will fall victim to the problems of nonce sense. To handle contextual expressions, both types of parsers will need to undergo major revisions. I will illustrate this point by considering several of the psychological parsers that have been proposed.

Heuristic Parsers

Psychological approaches to parsing have followed two main traditions. The first, which I will call the *heuristic tradition*, has its roots in Miller and Chomsky 1963 and Fodor and Garrett 1966. But it is most clearly identified with Bever (1970), who set out a series of processing strategies, or heuristics, to account for the difficulties of people trying to understand complex sentences. Later, Kimball (1973, 1975) put these strategies into a systematic framework, and his is still the best description of this tradition. He proposed seven 'principles of surface structure parsing' and showed how they accounted for the phenomena Bever had identified and more. Frazier and Fodor (1978) have since offered a version of Kimball's parser, called the "sausage machine", but it is like Kimball's parser in the ways that matter to the point I want to make.

For Kimball, parsing meant dividing an utterance into its constituents and labelling these constituents with the correct syntactic categories. His parser proceeded word by word through an utterance, deciding when to begin and end each constituent as it went. The main information it needed was the form class of each word from the lexicon, rules about the composition of surface constituents, and Kimball's seven heuristic principles. Take the utterance *George managed to read the newspaper yesterday*. When the parser reached the word *to*, it would look it up in the lexicon and find it to be either a preposition or an infinitive marker. So it would mark *to* as the beginning of a constituent—either a prepositional phrase or an infinitive complement. When it reached *read*, it would look up *read* in the lexicon, find it to be a verb, and then eliminate the prepositional phrase interpretation. And so on. The parser didn't deal directly with word or constituent meanings, although at critical times it made reference to these meanings in selecting between alternative parsings.

The first place where Kimball's parser would get into trouble is with words that aren't in the lexicon. Take *George managed to porch the newspaper yesterday. Porch*, though only a noun in the lexicon, is being used in this utterance as a verb. The parser would automatically classify *porch* as a noun and then not be able to parse the rest of the infinitive complement. The problem might be handled by outfitting the parser with lexical rules that change nouns into verbs, verbs into adjectives, verbs into nouns, and so on. This solution, however, won't work because of the mis-parsing problem. For *porch*, the parser, not being able to parse the noun *porch*, could be made to go to a lexical rule that changes nouns to verbs. Then it could identify *porch* as a verb and parse the other constituents correctly. But consider *George set out to Jesse Owens down the street* in circumstances in which *Jesse Owens* is intended to mean 'sprint', after Jesse Owens the Olympic sprinter. In parsing this sentence, there is nothing to force the parser to go to a lexical rule, since the sentence makes good sense with *Jesse Owens* as a noun. To get the analysis right the parser would have to consult the speaker's intentions in using *Jesse Owens*, which it might only be able to infer from non-linguistic context. Kimball's parser is not designed to do this.

Kimball's parser will run into other difficulties too. Imagine that Bombeck had written *The neighbor swore at our electric typewriter who got married.* Ordinarily, Kimball (1973, 25) argued, the parser would try to attach the relative clause *who got married* to the nearest noun phrase, here our *electric typewriter*. If the parser couldn't do this for semantic reasons, it would attach it instead to some earlier noun phrase, here *the neighbor*, so that the utterances would mean *the neighbor who got married swore at our electric typewriter.* Kimball's parser would be forced to take the second option. All it would have to go on would be the senses of *electric typewriter* listed in the lexicon. These wouldn't include *person who has an electric typewriter* or any of the indefinitely large number of other nonce senses it could have. The parser, then, would misidentify the surface structure of this utterance and of all other utterances in which a nonce sense had to be consulted in order to get the right parse.

Augmented Transition Networks

The second main tradition in psychological approaches to parsing is the *augmented transition networks*, or ATNs. This tradition had its start with Woods (1970) and Kaplan (1972) and has since evolved in papers by Woods (1973), Kaplan (1973a, 1973b, 1975), Wanner and Maratsos (1978), and Kaplan and Bresnan (1982). ATNs consist of a set of interconnected operations. An ATN parses each utterance word by word, applying its operations in a well defined order and identifying the intended constituents and their functions as it goes along.

An ATN can be viewed, whimsically but pretty accurately, as a medieval game played by a king on the country roads around his castle. The object of the game is for the king to get from his castle to his rival's castle along these roads (called 'arcs') using only the words in the sentence to guide him. He must leave his castle by the road signposted with the first word in his sentence. That will take him to a nearby village (called a 'state') where he will take the road signposted with the second word, and so on, until he reaches his rival's castle. Often, he can't leave a village directly, since there isn't a signpost with the next word on it. Instead, he must take detours signposted with the category of the word he is looking for (say, 'noun') or with the category of a constituent that contains the category of the word he is looking for (say, 'noun phrase'). The king discovers the category of each word in his pocket lexicon. He can pass along the route signposted 'noun' only if the word he is looking for is listed in his lexicon as a noun.

ATNs run into the same two problems that heuristic parsers run into. The king will be stopped by *porch* in *George managed to porch the newspaper*. He will look for a road signposted 'porch' or 'noun' or 'noun phrase' or 'sentence' and find none. He will be condemned to remain in that wretched village forever. If he adds to his lexicon a set of lexical rules that change nouns into verbs, verbs into nouns, and so on, he will have a different problem with *George set out to Jesse Owens down the street* when *Jesse Owens* is intended to mean 'sprint'. Since *Jesse Owens* is in the lexicon as a noun, and since there is a noun-detour available, he will take it and not even try the verb-detour. The noun-detour will lead him to the wrong destination, which he will never realize. If, instead, he tries the lexical rule first and takes the verb-detour first whenever he encounters a noun, he will take many wrong roads that he will have to retrace before trying another route. And he will now get the *Jesse Owens* sentence wrong when *Owens* is intended as a noun. So because of contextual expressions, the king will get stranded, or finish at the wrong castle, or wander around needlessly before arriving at the right castle.

ATNs also base certain parsing decisions on meaning. The king is often forced to select routes based on what the current word means. For decisions about word meaning, he still has only his pocket lexicon, and it doesn't contain nonce senses for Bombeck's *electric typewriter* or *stereos*, or for any other contextual expression. Adding lexical rules won't help. As I will show later, there would have to be an indefinitely large number of lexical rules to account for the possible senses of contextual expressions. So when the king needs to make choices based on meaning, once again he can become stranded (as with *Our electric typewriter got married*), or be led to the wrong castle altogether (as with *The neighbor swore at our electric typewriter who got married*). The king's lexicon could never be large enough to parse nonce sense.

Lexical Access

Aside from the heuristic and ATN traditions, there has been much experimental work on 'lexical access', the process by which people 'access' words in their mental lexicons in long-term memory. A significant problem for lexical access is ambiguity. Consider *The man was not surprised when he found several bugs in the corner of his room* (from Swinney 1979). When a listener hears *bugs*, he has to access *bug* in his mental lexicon. There, it has been assumed, he will find, say, two senses—'insect' and 'listening device'. He must decide which of these two senses was intended on this occasion. In a long series of experiments, it has been shown that resolving ambiguities takes time and effort (for reviews, see Clark and Clark 1977; Fodor, Bever, and Garrett 1974; Foss and Hakes 1978).

Lexical access of ambiguous words has almost invariably been characterized in accordance with the sense-selection assumption. Fodor, Bever, and Garrett (1974) talked about listeners "selecting among readings of ambiguities." Foss and Hakes (1978) argued that the findings by Foss and Jenkins (1973) demonstrated "that listeners always retrieve both interpretations of an ambiguous word from the mental lexicon and that the context then operates to help them decide among them." Clark and Clark (1977) characterized the same findings in similar language: "When listeners encounter an ambiguous construction, they compute multiple readings"; "using the context, listeners then attempt to select the most plausible reading."

These characterizations of lexical access ought to be inadequate for contextual expressions, and they are. Consider Swinney's (1979) 'post-decision model' of lexical access. As Swinney put it, his results "support the existence of a postaccess decision process which acts to select a single meaning from those originally and momentarily accessed for involvement in further processings." Listeners access all senses of *bug*, and only then do they use the context to select one from among them. Swinney argued against a 'prior decision model' in which listeners use the semantic context to guide lexical access—in which, for example, listeners use the prior context to access or activate only one sense of *bug*, the one appropriate to context.

Taken literally, the post-decision model has to fail on contextual expressions. When it encounters *porch* in *George managed to porch the newspaper yesterday*, it will have no lexical entries to access for the verb *porch* and hence no senses to select from. The model predicts that the verb *porch* cannot be understood. If lexical rules are added to derive the possible senses of the verb *porch* from the noun *porch*, the model has the opposite problem. The lexical rules, as I will show later, generate an indefinitely large number of possible senses for the verb *porch*. No model with a finite memory could access all of these senses, as the post-decision model requires, nor could any model select from among the possible senses in a finite amount of time.

With certain revisions, however, the post-decision model might be made to work. It would proceed roughly as follows. When it encountered the verb *porch*, it would access the senses for *porch* in the lexicon. These would consist entirely of *conventional* senses, such as the noun senses *covered entrance to a house* and *verandah*. The model would then select from among these senses the one on which it could create the intended verb sense. After all, the meanings of the verb *porch* are based on the meanings of the noun *porch*. How the model would decide which noun sense is the right one, and how it would create the intended verb sense from it, however, are matters that go beyond the assumptions of the post-decision model. They will be considered later. Yet with these emendations, the model could retain its most important property, the selection process that correctly predicts that ambiguous words should be difficult to understand.

Since virtually all current models of lexical access make the sense-selection assumption either explicitly or implicitly, they are open to the same criticisms as the post-decision model. These include the models of Cairns and Kamerman (1975), Forster (1976), Garrett (1978), MacKay (1970), Marslen-Wilson and Welsh (1978), Morton (1969, 1970), and

Tanenhaus, Leiman, and Seidenberg (1979), to name just a few. Like the post-decision model, many of these models could perhaps be revised to handle contextual expressions. But these revisions would require a view of parsing that is rather different from the one on which all these models are based.

Sentence Meanings

Most traditional parsers and models of lexical access are based on what I will call the *traditional view of sentences*, a view that has been held, explicitly or implicitly, by most investigators in these areas. According to this view, the grammar of English, including its lexicon of conventional senses for words, morphemes, and idioms, assigns readings to each string of words. If a string of words is assigned one or more senses that aren't semantically anomalous, as *Stereos are a dime a dozen* would be, it is adjudged to be a sentence of English. The readings assigned to it are called its *sentence meanings*. If a string of words can *not* be assigned any such readings, and *Our electric typewriter got married* could not be, it is adjudged *not* to be a sentence of English. In one terminology (e.g., Chomsky 1965; Katz 1964), it would be marked as 'ungrammatical'. In another terminology (e.g., Katz 1972, 1977), it would be marked 'sematically anomalous'. For convenience, I will adopt the first terminology.

The traditional view of sentences, then, is this. What the speaker meant in uttering a string of words is identical to, or derivable from, one of its sentence meanings—one of the readings assigned to it by the grammar. What a speaker could mean by *Stereos are a dime a dozen* is derivable from its only sentence meaning *Phonographs are very common*. And what a speaker could mean by *Our electric typewriter got married* is nothing, since this string of words yields no sentence meanings—since it isn't assigned any sensible readings by the grammar. (It might be treated as a 'semi-sentence', à la Katz (1964); I will discuss this possibility later.) This view of sentences fails to do justice to six of Bombeck's eight utterances. For those that are grammatical, what Bombeck meant is *not* derivable from any of the sentence meanings. For those that are not grammatical, Bombeck meant something that has no chance of being derived from a sentence meaning, since these strings don't *have* any sentence meanings.

Put in its strongest form, what a speaker means bears no direct relation to the sentence meanings assigned to it in the traditional view of sentences. Grammaticality as defined in this view bears no direct relation to ordinary language use. Consider these four types of utterances:

(1) A grammatical sentence used in one of its sentence meanings (like Bombeck's *We've just had a streak of bad luck*).

(2) A grammatical sentence used in something other than one of its sentence meanings (like her *Stereos are a dime a dozen*).

(3) An ungrammatical string used in one of the semantically anomalous readings assigned to it by the grammar (like *The rock cried*, meaning 'the stone wept', a made-up example).

(4) An ungrammatical string used in something other than one of the semantically anomalous readings assigned to it by the grammar (like Bombeck's *Our electric typewriter got married*).

According to the traditional view of sentences, speakers should only use sentences of type (1). These alone have sentence meanings from which one can derive the speaker's meaning. If a speaker used sentences of types (2), (3), or (4), they would be judged as mistakes. But as I argued earlier, cases (2) and (4) are ubiquitous. Furthermore, they sound perfectly natural. They are as much a part of ordinary English as case (1) is.

So long as parsers and models of lexical access are based on the traditional view of sentences, they will be inadequate. They will miss every utterance that falls into cases (2) and (4), misparsing the first and failing to parse the second. They will fail to handle a significant portion of what ordinary people consider to be ordinary English.

4 Two False Solutions

Two mechanisms that have been proposed and at first appear able to handle contextual expressions are the lexical rule and the semi-sentence. Yet neither of these mechanisms offers any real solution. It is important to see why.

Lexical Rules

The way a traditional parser would handle innovations is via *lexical rules* or via Miller's (1978) *construal rules* (which for present purposes are indistinguishable from lexical rules). Imagine that such a parser is confronted with the word *chartreuseness*, which is not in its lexicon. Nevertheless, the parser has in its lexicon the adjective *chartreuse*, the suffix *-ness*, and the following lexical rule:

$X_{\text{Adj}} + \textit{-ness}_{\text{N}}$ has these and only these possible senses:

(a) state of being X

(b) quality of being X

(c) condition of being X

(d) instance of the state of being X

(e) instance of the quality of being X

(f) instance of the condition of being X

With this rule, the parser will generate six senses for *chartreuseness* and then select from among the readings just as it would for a word already in its lexicon. The difference between the listed senses and the senses generated by such a rule is that whereas the first are actual, the second are virtual. Otherwise, the two types of senses function in the same way.

For lexical rules to be sufficient, they must be capable of generating every sense of every innovation. For words like *chartreuseness*, which are assigned a fixed number of senses, lexical rules do a good job. But similar rules have been offered for other types of expressions. For denominal verbs, McCawley (1971) suggested a rule that would go like this (where ϕ_V is the null verb-forming suffix of what is technically called 'zero-derivation'):

$X_N + \phi_V$ has this (and other) possible senses:

(a) causes an X to hold onto

With this rule, *John nailed the note to the door* is interpreted as 'John caused a nail to hold the note onto the door.' The rule would also capture the sense of *to tack*, *to scotchtape*, *to glue*, and many other like verbs. Green (1974) suggested another lexical rule for denominal verbs to handle cases like to *hammer*:

(b) as by using X(on) in the usual manner, for the purpose for which it was designed

For denominal verbs like to *porch*, as in *George managed to porch the newspaper yesterday*, there would also be this rule:

(c) cause to be on an X

Rule (c) would also generate the right senses for *to bench a player*, *to beach the boat*, and *to shelve the books*.

The problem is that for contextual expressions, there would have to be an indefinitely large number of such rules (Clark and Clark 1979). Take Ed's remark to me about Max, the man with the teapot compulsion: *He teapotted a policeman*. As a denominal verb, *teapot* would add still one more lexical rule to the list for $X_N + \phi_V$, namely:

(d) rub the back of the leg of with an X

But since there are an unlimited number of other nonce senses that *teapot* (or any other novel denominal verb) could have had, there must also be an unlimited number of such rules for generating them. There would have to be rules like these:

(e) strike on the back of the leg of with an X

(f) rub on the back of the ankle of with an X

(g) scratch on the back of the neck of with an X

(h) turn into an X

And so on indefinitely. That is, since *teapot* can have a different nonce sense in each different situation, it would have to have associated with it a different lexical rule for each situation. This undermines the reason for having lexical rules in the first place.[2]

The same problem arises for all other contextual expressions. In the domain of compound nouns, Levi (1978) has proposed lexical rules too. She has argued that all the possible interpretations of novel noun-noun compounds like *horse chair* are captured in the twelve rules in Table 3. An important feature of these rules is that they rely on only nine different predicates—*cause, have, make, use, be, in, for, from*, and *about*—which appear to capture the major relations that hold in English compound nouns.

It is easy to see that these rules don't capture the *full* meanings of innovative compound nouns. Consider Downing's (1977) example of a friend being asked to sit at the *apple-juice seat*, meaning 'the seat in front of which a glass of apple juice had been placed'. Levi would probably generate the meaning of this compound by Rule (i), giving it the analysis *seat that is located with respect to apple juice*. This paraphrase, however, hardly does justice to the meaning that was intended. It may offer a broad category into which the nonce sense fits, but it doesn't explicate the nonce sense itself. The intended sense would require a lexical rule something like this:

(i') Y in front of which there had been X.

This rule would be a subrule of Levi's rule (i), and there would be other subrules as well. If Downing, and Kay and Zimmer (1976),

---

[2]Lexical rules (a) through (c) may appear to be more general than rules (d) through (h), but this isn't really so. Rules (a) through (c) are incomplete. To *glue a stamp to an envelope* ordinarily means something more specific than rule (a)'s 'cause glue to hold a stamp to an envelope'. There are many extraordinary ways of causing glue to do this that wouldn't be called "gluing." Rule (a) is really a collapsing over a large set of related rules. This point is made later for the compound *apple-juice chair*. The broad types that do emerge in denominal verbs, and in other constructions, do so not because they reflect lexical rules, but because they reflect general categories of experience, of encyclopedic knowledge (see Clark and Clark 1979, 787–92).

TABLE 3
Possible Interpretations of Noun-Noun Compounds

$X_N + Y_N$ HAS THESE AND ONLY THESE POSSIBLE SENSES:	
SENSE	AS IN:
(a) Y that causes X	*tear gas*, 'gas that causes tears'
(b) Y that is caused by X	*birth pains*, 'pains caused by a birth'
(c) Y that has X	*apple cake*, 'cake that has apples'
(d) Y that X has	*lemon peel*, 'peel that lemons have'
(e) Y that makes X	*honeybee*, 'bee that makes honey'
(f) Y that X makes	*daisy chains*, 'chains that daisies make'
(g) Y that uses X	*voice vote*, 'vote that uses voices'
(h) Y that is X	*soldier ant*, 'ant that is a soldier'
(i) Y that is in X	*field mouse*, 'mouse that is in a field'
(j) Y that is from X	*olive oil*, 'oil from olives'
(k) Y that is for X	*wine glass*, 'glass for wine'
(l) Y that is about X	*tax law*, 'law about taxes'

are correct, novel compound nouns like this have an indefinitely large number of possible senses, and so there would be an indefinitely large number of such subrules. The problem with Levi's rules is that they are stated at an arbitrary level of abstraction; therefore, they capture an arbitrary amount of the sense of compound nouns like *apple-juice seat*. It is an illusion that there are only a small number of lexical rules. At the correct level, there would have to be an indefinitely large number of them (see also Carroll and Tanenhaus 1975).[3]

For other categories of contextual expressions, the problem is just as serious. With eponymous verbs like *do a Napoleon*, there are a few broad categories of senses one might identify:

Do a X_{PN} has these possible senses:

(a) do what X did (as in I *want you to do a Napoleon for the camera*)

(b) do what was done to X (as in *They did a Manhattan to downtown San Francisco*)

(c) do what happens in X (as in *The horse did a Pimlico*, or *a Derby, down the road*)

And so on. Yet the same problem arises as before. These categories are hardly fine enough to capture, for example, what a photographer meant in saying I *want you to do a Napoleon for the camera*. *Do a Napoleon*

---

[3]Jespersen (1942, 137) said this about noun compounds: "Compounds express a relation between two objects or notions, but say nothing of the way in which the relation is to be understood. That must be inferred from the context or otherwise. Theoretically, this leaves room for a large number of different interpretations of one and the same compound, but in practice ambiguity is as a rule avoided."

here doesn't mean 'do what Napoleon did' but 'pose with your hand inside the flap of your coat, as Napoleon did'. We would need a specific lexical rule to distinguish this meaning from other possible meanings of *do a Napoleon*, as in *The lawyer was asked to do a Napoleon for the legal system of Oahu, Hitler tried to avoid doing a Napoleon in attacking Russia in the winter*, and any number of other uses. Once again, the number of lexical rules is indefinitely large. No parser could manage that many.

Lexical rules, therefore, cannot solve the problems of nonce sense. Certain types of nonce sense, as in expressions like *chartreusness*, may be adequately captured with lexical rules, but other types are not. The types not captured are the contextual expressions. For them, there would have to be a new lexical rule for each new sense in which they were used. For them, lexical rules solve nothing at all.

Semi-sentences

Bombeck's utterance *Our electric typewriter got married* is an example par excellence of what in the traditional view of sentences would be called an ungrammatical string . Yet Katz (1964) has argued, and many others have followed suit, that a string of words doesn't have to be grammatical to be comprehensible. For this purpose, Katz has proposed a theory of *semi-sentences. Our electric typewriter got married* would be such a semi-sentence in that it is a string of words that isn't grammatical but can nevertheless be understood. Katz seems to have intended his theory to account for utterances like Bombeck's, for he offered as examples of semi-sentences *It happened a grief ago, I have over-confidence in you*, and *He expressed a green thought*, all of which contain innovations, although they don't all sound as natural as Bombeck's utterance.

The basic idea of the theory is this. When a listener is confronted with a semi-sentence, he associates with it a set of fully grammatical sentences called the *comprehension set*. The members of the comprehension set, in effect, enumerate all the possible meanings the semi-sentence could have. For *Man bit dog*, the comprehension set would be as follows:

Man bit dog is associated with this comprehension set:

(a) The man bit the dog
(b) The man bit a dog
(c) A man bit the dog
(d) A man bit a dog

Sentences (a) through (d) each represent a possible reading of the semi-sentence *Man bit dog*. They are created by what Katz called *transfer rules*, although he offered only the sketchiest examples of what these rules might look like (see also Ziff 1964). Katz's claim is that the listener's understanding of a semi-sentence is "nothing other than his understanding of the sentences in the set with which the semi-sentence is associated" (411), namely the comprehension set. The proposal is as ingenious as it is simple. It reduces the problem of understanding semi-sentences to the problem of understanding grammatical sentences, a problem that will presumably submit to the scientist's scalpel sooner or later.

For this scheme to work, the comprehension set associated with each semi-sentence must contain a finite number of sentences. As Katz put it (411), "the notion *sufficient structure to be understood* is analyzed as *structure that suffices to permit a semi-sentence to be associated with a finite number of sentences, each of which is a possible reading of the semi-sentence*" (all emphases are Katz's). This follows from Katz's general approach to semantics, which is to be able to enumerate for each sentence a finite number of readings. He wants to be able to do the same for each semi-sentence too. The requirement in this case has further value, according to Katz, since it distinguishes genuine semi-sentences like *Man bit dog*, which will have a finite comprehension set, from nonsense strings like *The saw cut his sincerity*, which will not.

Katz's theory of semi-sentences, however, cannot work for contextual expressions. The reason is simple. As I noted earlier, *Max teapotted a policeman* has an indefinitely large number of potential readings. It could mean *rub the back leg of with a teapot*, *rub the back of the shoulder of with a teapot*, *rub both ankles and knees of with a teapot*, and so on indefinitely. In the theory of semi-sentences, each of these readings would correspond to a grammatical sentence in the comprehension set associated with the ungrammatical string of words *Max teapotted a policeman*. Thus, the comprehension set for *Max teapotted a policeman* is not finite in size. But because the set isn't finite, the theory predicts that *Max teapotted a policeman* isn't comprehensible—that it doesn't have "sufficient structure to be understood." This prediction, of course, doesn't hold. For the same reasons, the theory also predicts as incomprehensible Bombeck's *Our electric typewriter got married*, Herb Caen's *I stopped in Perry's for a quick crab*, and *The photographer asked me to do a Napoleon for the camera*. These predictions obviously don't hold either.

The most glaring defect in this theory is that it requires each string of words to have a finite number of readings in order to be comprehensible. By definition, contextual expressions have an indefinitely large number of potential readings and, as we have seen, are taken to be a regular part of English. Conclusion: contextual expressions cannot be accounted for by the theory of semi-sentences.

A less obvious defect goes as follows. The basic assumption of the theory is that each meaning of a semi-sentence can be *precisely* and *completely* captured by at least one grammatical sentence of English. This assumption isn't really warranted. The raison d'etre for the use of many contextual expressions is to say things that could not be said any other way. Consider *Harry managed to Richard Nixon the tape of his conversation with the chief of police.* Here *Richard Nixon* cannot be paraphrased by *erase*, or *erase with malice and conniving*, or *erase as Richard Nixon would have done*, without losing something of the original. The point of the utterance is to compare Harry's actions and motives, in all their complexity, with those of Nixon, and no paraphrase can do that comparison justice. If this is so, a theory that requires each reading of every sentence with a contextual expression to correspond exactly to a sentence of English is doomed to failure.

An additional complication for the theory of semi-sentences is that it would require two distinct accounts of contextual expressions—one for those found in 'ungrammatical strings', the true semi-sentences, and another for those found in 'grammatical sentences'. Let us return to Bombeck's *Stereos are a dime a dozen*, in which *stereos* is being used innovatively to mean *people who have stereos*. The sentence itself is grammatical on Katz's criteria, but the meaning Bombeck intended is not one of those enumerated by Katz's rules of composition. *Stereos* is being used in something other than one of its conventional meanings. Since the theory of semi-sentences would not identify this utterance as a semi-sentence, it would need a new device to identify *stereo* as a contextual expression and to compute its possible meanings. It would interpret *electric typewriter* via the theory of semi-sentences and *stereos* via some other theory, when they ought to be handled by the same process. The underlying problem is that sentences that contain contextual expressions are sometimes grammatical and sometimes not. It was pure accident that *stereos* appeared in a grammatical sentence and *electric typewriter* didn't. As noted earlier, any theory that ties the interpretations of these expressions to grammaticality seems misdirected from the start.

In the end, the theory of semi-sentences fails for much the same reasons that lexical rules do. It is easy to see that Katz's transfer rules, which generate the comprehension sets for semi-sentences, have the same consequences as lexical rules. Both require the meanings of a sentence to be denumerable and to be definite in number. Both run afoul of contextual expressions, whose possible meanings are neither denumerable nor definite in number.

5 Indirect Uses of Language

Contextual expressions, one could say, are ordinary words that are used indirectly for momentary purposes. Another type of expression that might be described this way are indirect illocutionary acts. When I use *It's raining out* to remind my wife to take her umbrella, or to request her to close the window, or to offer to bring her a raincoat, I am using an ordinary sentence indirectly for some momentary purpose. This analogy gives a clue to the approach I will take to parsing utterances with contextual expressions. I will argue for a general procedure for computing indirect uses of language. To see how the process might work, I will first review some characteristics of indirect illocutionary acts.

Indirect Illocutionary Acts

By now there is a good deal known about indirect illocutionary acts (Gordon and Lakoff 1971; Sadock 1974; Searle 1975; Morgan 1978; Bach and Harnish 1979; Clark 1979; Cohen and Perrault 1979). There is even something known about how they are understood (Clark and Lucy 1975; Clark 1979; Clark and Schunk 1980; Munro 1977; Schweller 1978; Gibbs 1979). I will concentrate on five of their properties in order later to show a correspondence with contextual expressions. As my example, I will use the sentence *Do you know what time it is?*

1. **Simultaneous Meanings.** In the right situation, I could use *Do you know what time it is?* to ask someone to give me the time. In this instance, I would mean two distinct things at once. I would mean 'I ask you whether or not you know the time', a yes/no question, which I will call the *direct meaning*. I would also mean *I request you to tell me the time*, a request, which I will call the *indirect meaning*. Genuine cases of indirect illocutionary acts all involve more than one meaning—a direct meaning and one or more indirect meanings.

2. **Logical Priority.** In my use of *Do you know what time it is?*, the yes/no question is *logically* prior to the request. I perform the request by performing the question, and not vice versa. It is this that allows us to call the question the direct meaning and request the indirect meaning.

3. **Literalness of Direct Meaning.** The direct meaning of my utterance—the yes/no question—follows pretty directly, via conventions of language, from the literal meaning of the sentence *Do*

you know what time it is? This is one reason that the speaker's direct meaning is often called the literal meaning. In the traditional view of sentences at least, one needs to know little more, often nothing more, than the sentence's literal meaning to know the speaker's direct meaning.

4. **Non-denumerability of Indirect Meanings.** Given the sentence *Do you know what time it is?*, there is no way to enumerate the possible indirect meanings a speaker could have in uttering it. In the right circumstances, I could use it to mean *Please tell me the time, Don't forget your dentist appointment, You are late in getting home again, The party started an hour ago,* and so on indefinitely. Whereas the direct meaning is pretty well determined by the literal meaning, if any, of the sentence uttered, the indirect meaning could be any number of things.

5. **Contextuality of Indirect Meanings.** What I mean indirectly in saying *Do you know what time it is?* is critically dependent on the circumstances in which I utter it. In particular, if I directed this utterance at my wife, I would expect her to recognize that I was indirectly performing an illocutionary act that I had good reason to believe on this occasion she could readily compute uniquely on the basis of our mutual knowledge such that my direct meaning played some role. Thus, unlike my direct meaning, which is tied pretty closely to the literal meaning of the sentence I uttered, my indirect meaning is often completely dependent on my wife's recognition of my plans and goals in using that sentence on this occasion.

Indirect Uses in Contextual Expressions

The five characteristics of indirect illocutionary acts bear a close, though not exact, resemblance to five corresponding characteristics of contextual expressions. I will illustrate these for the denominal verb in my earlier example *Max teapotted a policeman.*

1. **Simultaneous Meanings.** In the circumstances I outlined earlier, Ed used the verb *teapot* to mean 'rub the back of the leg of with a teapot'. Without stretching things too much, we could say that Ed used the word *teapot* to do two things at the same time. He used it directly to denote teapots—those pots for brewing tea. He also used it indirectly to denote the act of rubbing someone's leg with a teapot. In other words, we can speak of a direct and an indirect meaning of the word *teapot*. These correspond, though are not exactly equivalent, to the direct and indirect meanings in my use of *Do you know what time it is?*

2. **Logical Priority.** In uttering *teapot*, Ed denoted the rubbing of someone's leg with a teapot by denoting teapots themselves. That is, he performed the act of denoting the leg rubbing by performing the act of denoting teapots, and not vice versa. The direct use is logically prior to the indirect use, and this too corresponds to what happens in indirect illocutionary acts.

3. **Literalness of Direct Use.** Ed's direct use of *teapot*—his denoting of teapots—follows directly from one of the conventional meanings of the noun *teapot*. This is analogous to my direct meaning in uttering *Do you know what time it is?* which follows fairly directly from the literal meaning of this sentence. In both instances, the direct use of the expression is tied to the conventional meaning of the expression in the language.

4. **Non-denumerability of Indirect Uses.** There is no way of enumerating the possible indirect uses a speaker could have in using the noun *teapot* as a verb. This is a defining characteristic of contextual expressions: for something to be a contextual expression, its possible senses must be *non-denumerable*. Once again, there is a parallel with indirect illocutionary acts.

5. **Contextuality of Indirect Uses.** What Ed meant indirectly in using the word *teapot* is critically dependent on the circumstances in which he uttered it. Indeed, Eve V. Clark and I (Clark and Clark 1979) have argued that there is a convention that governs how a speaker and addressee coordinate their use and understanding of innovative denominal verbs. The convention goes as follows:

The innovative denominal verb convention. In using an innovative denominal verb sincerely, the speaker means to denote:

(a) the kind of situation
(b) that he has good reason to believe
(c) that on this occasion the listener can readily compute
(d) uniquely
(e) on the basis of their mutual knowledge
(f) in such a way that the parent noun denotes one role in the situation, and the remaining surface arguments of the denominal verb denote other roles in the situation.

Here 'situation' is a cover term for states, events, and processes.

Once again, there is a striking parallel with indirect illocutionary acts, which also depend on a convention that refers to reasonableness in context, ready computability, uniqueness, and mutual knowledge of the speaker and addressee. The point at which indirect speech acts differ from denominal verbs is in condition (f). With denominal verbs, condition (f) makes reference to the conventional meaning of the parent noun (e.g., *teapot*) and the meanings of its surface arguments (e.g., *Max, a policeman*). With indirect illocutionary acts, condition (f) would make reference to the speaker's direct meaning, so that it perhaps would read 'in such a way that the speaker's direct meaning establishes a necessary condition for the speaker's indirect meanings'. In both cases, condition (f) makes reference to the direct use of the expression uttered, whether it is the whole sentence *Do you know what time it is?* or just the single noun *teapot*.

The parallels between indirect illocutionary acts and contextual expressions suggest that it ought to be possible to extrapolate from models of the understanding of indirect illocutionary acts to models of the understanding of contextual expressions. But how are indirect illocutionary acts understood? For an answer, we must consider the notion of *goal hierarchy*.

Goal Hierarchies

In interpreting complete utterances, listeners ordinarily infer a hierarchy of goals they believe the speaker is trying to attain, and they interpret the speaker's current utterance as a step in the plan for attaining one or more of those goals. This is the conclusion of a number of studies of indirect illocutionary acts—studies of their formal properties (Gordon and Lakoff 1971; Searle 1975), studies of their understanding in natural settings (Clark 1979; Merritt 1976; Goffman 1976), and studies of simulations in computer models (Cohen 1978; Cohen and Perrault 1979).

Consider an example from a study of my own on indirect requests for information (Clark 1979, Experiment 5). I had an assistant call up restaurants in the Palo Alto, California, area and ask whether they accepted credit cards. Two of the questions she asked were these:

> Do you accept American Express cards?
> Do you accept credit cards?

(I will abbreviate these as *American Express cards?* and *Credit cards?*) My assistant would call up a restaurant and ask either *American Express cards?* or *Credit cards?*, listen to the restaurateur's reply, say *thank you*, and hang up. The interest was in the replies and what they implied about the restaurateur's interpretation of what my assistant had asked.

The restaurateurs apparently imputed my assistant with a different hierarchy of goals depending on which question she asked. For *American Express cards?*, the hierarchy was something like this:

(1) She wants to decide whether or not to patronize this restaurant.
(2) She wants to know how to pay for her meal.
(3) She wants to know if she can pay with the credit cards she owns, which consists (almost certainly) of just the one card, the American Express card.
(4) She wants to know if the restaurant accepts American Express cards.

The question *Do you accept American Express cards?* directly reflects the lowest subgoal, number (4), but an answer to it would also fulfill the next higher subgoal, (3). Hence the only thing the restaurateurs needed to do, if they did accept American Express cards, was say *Yes* or *Yes, we do*. Indeed, 100 per cent of the restaurateurs who were asked this question and were able to say *yes* gave this response. They interpreted the utterance as a direct question and nothing more.

For *Credit cards?*, the restaurateurs inferred a very different hierarchy of goals. It was something like this:

(1) She wants to decide whether or not to patronize this restaurant.
(2) She wants to know how to pay for her meal.
(3) She wants to know if she can pay with one of her credit cards, which (probably) include most or all of the major credit cards.
(4) She wants to know if any of the credit cards acceptable to the restaurant are among the cards she owns.
(5) She wants to know if the restaurant accepts credit cards.

The question *Do you accept credit cards?* directly reflects the lowest subgoal, number (5), and hence the restaurateurs should ordinarily answer that question. In fact, 84 per cent of those who could have answered in the affirmative did. However, the caller's reason for asking the question couldn't have been just to attain subgoal (5), since that isn't sufficient information for subgoal (4), the next goal up in her hierarchy. She must be indirectly requesting the restaurant's list of acceptable credit cards. In fact, 46 per cent of the restaurateurs inferred the next higher subgoal and gave the caller a list of the credit cards they accepted. They took *Credit cards?* to be both a direct question and an indirect request for the list of credit cards they accepted.

The contrast between *American Express cards?* and *Credit cards?* is striking, for the two questions are identical except for the object of the verbs. It was the content of those noun phrases that forced the restaurateurs to infer very different goals and to construe *American*

Express cards? as merely a direct question while construing *Credit cards?* as both a direct question and an indirect request for a list of acceptable credit cards. Conclusion: it is the hierarchy of imputed goals that enables listeners to decide whether or not the speaker is performing an indirect speech act, and if so, what it is.

There are two main sources of evidence that listeners are intended to use in inferring the speaker's hierarchy of goals. The first is the utterance itself. It is pertinent whether or not a request is made via a conventional form like *Can you tell me the time?* or via a non-conventional form like *Do you happen to have a watch on you?*, whether or not a request is accompanied by *please*, and whether or not other 'linguistic' factors are present (Clark 1979). The second source of information is the remainder of the knowledge, beliefs, and suppositions that the speaker and listener share—called their *common ground* (Chapter 2, this volume). It was pertinent in the experiment reported earlier that my assistant was telephoning the restaurateur at his restaurant and not at his home, that the restaurant's telephone number was public and intended to be used for enquiries about the restaurant's services, and that other such 'non-linguistic' factors were present (Cohen and Perrault 1979). Listeners generally cannot, nor are they expected to, infer the speaker's hierarchy of goals accurately without consulting both the utterance and their common ground.

6 Intentional Parsers

Parsing an utterance can itself be viewed as reconstructing a hierarchy of goals. When a friend tells me *Julia is a virologist*, I realize that he has specific goals. In making an assertion, he wants me to believe, and to recognize that he believes, some state of affairs. One of his subgoals is to specify that belief. However, he can't do this in one step. First, he designates the thing the belief is about, which he does via the word *Julia*. Next, he predicates what it is that he believes about that object, which he does with the words *is a virologist*. He makes this predication in two parts. He specifies that the predication is equative and that it holds at the time of utterance by using the word *is*. He specifies the predication proper with the words *a virologist*. This, too, is accomplished in two steps. He specifies the category of interest with the word *virologist*, and he indicates that he is predicating membership in that category with the word *a*.

Described this way, my friend is performing a series of acts, each of which accomplishes a subgoal along the path to getting me to believe that Julia is a virologist. Furthermore, he performs each of these acts by means of a constituent in the utterance. With the noun phrase *Julia*, he is performing the act of referring to Julia. With the verb phrase *is a virologist*, he is performing the act of predicating something about her. With the verb *is*, he is performing the act of designating the predication as one of equation and the time it holds as the present. With the noun phrase *a virologist*, he is designating the predication as membership of the category of virologists. With the noun *virologist*, he is designating the concept of virologist as the category being predicated. And with the article *a*, he is specifying that the predication is membership in the so-designated category. All I have done here is expand on Strawson's (1959) and Searle's (1969) notions of reference and predication as speech acts.

These acts, with their goals, form a hierarchy that corresponds to the hierarchy of constituents in the sentence. In uttering *a* and in uttering *virologist*, my friend has two separate goals. But these are subgoals in his uttering the construction that contains those two constituents, the noun phrase *a virologist*. Likewise, his goal in uttering *is* and his goal in uttering *a virologist* are both subgoals in his act of predicating with the construction of *is a virologist*. And finally, his goal in referring with *Julia* and his goal in predicating with *is a virologist* are subgoals of the 'propositional act' that he performs with the whole utterance (see Searle 1969), the act in which he specifies the proposition to be believed, that Julia is a virologist. In general, the speaker's hierarchy of goals in uttering a sentence appears to have a many-to-one mapping onto the constituents of that sentence.

Parsing, therefore, can be viewed not simply as dividing a sentence into its parts—the traditional view—but as identifying the goals and subgoals the speaker had in uttering each part of the sentence, what I will call the *intentional view of parsing*. These two views might at first appear to be simple variants of one another—"notational variants" to use the jargon of the field—but they are not. In the traditional view, the aim of the parser is to yield one of the (traditional) sentence meanings, presumably the one the speaker intended. In the intentional view, the aim is to yield the speaker's intentions in uttering what he did. And for utterances such as Bombeck's *Our electric typewriter got married* and *Stereos are a dime a dozen*, the speaker's intentions are not derivable from any of the (traditional) sentence meanings.

These two views lead to different parsing implementations. Traditional parsers have been designed to rely totally, or almost totally, on the linguistic properties of the utterance. But recall that in order to understand indirect requests, listeners use *two* main sources of information. The first is the utterance itself, as in traditional parsers.

The second is the speaker's and addressee's common ground. The speaker's intentions can be inferred only through the *joint* use of these two sources. What is missing in traditional parsers is any systematic reference to the common ground.

Even though common ground has not been welcomed at the front door of traditional parsers, it has sometimes been sneaked in through the servants' entrance. Many parsers have been designed to parse discourse and therefore to resolve anaphoric reference (see Charniak 1972; Lockman and Klappholz 1980). In the sequence *Ned went home for dinner, he got lost on the way*, such a parser would identify Ned as the referent of *he*, and the route Ned was taking home as the referent of *the way*. These two referents are resolved in the second utterance mostly by referring to that part of the reader's and writer's common ground that was established in the first utterance. Indeed, some utterances could not be parsed correctly without knowledge of such referents. In the sequence *Ned was introduced to a woman at the party, he whispered to the woman that he knew*, the phrase *that he knew* would be identified as the complement of *whispered*, since *the woman* presumably refers to the woman Ned just met, who couldn't possibly be 'a woman that he knew'. Here again, the first utterance establishes certain common ground that is used in parsing the second.

Yet in resolving reference, as in these two examples, traditional parsers exploit common ground only to a limited extent. A genuine intentional parser would need to consult the common ground systematically. Nowhere is this easier to demonstrate than in the parsing of contextual expressions.

Contextual Expressions

With contextual expressions, reference to the speaker's and addressee's common ground is mandatory. When Bombeck wrote *Our electric typewriter got married*, she intended us readers to make use of the fact that she had just written about roommates and their possessions. She intended us to use this common ground in conjunction with the fact that she was uttering the phrase *our electric typewriter* and was predicating of its referent, that it got married. She intended us to use both sources of information in inferring her hierarchy of goals.

As an illustration of such a goal hierarchy, consider Ed's assertion to me *Max teapotted a policeman*. Ed's goal hierarchy in using *teapot* might be described as follows:

(1) Ed wants me to recognize that he is using *teapot* to denote *rub the back of the leg with a teapot*.

(2) Ed wants me to recognize that what he is asserting Max did to a policeman is the kind of action that he has good reason to believe that on this occasion I can readily compute uniquely on the basis of our common ground in such a way that teapots play one role in the action, Max is the agent, and the policeman is the patient.

(3) Ed wants me to recognize that he is using *teapot* to denote teapots.

I am to infer the lowest subgoal, (3), from the fact that Ed is using the noun *teapot*. I am to infer the next subgoal up, (2), from the fact that he is using it as a verb too. And I am to infer the highest subgoal, (1), from the computations required in (2).

The main addition to traditional parsers is subgoal (2). For contextual expressions, the speaker always intends the addressees to compute the novel meaning on the spot. As subgoal (2) makes clear, this requires the listener to consult the speaker's and addressee's common ground. But when does this addition need to be made? If *teapot* were actually in the lexicon as a verb with the sense *rub the back of the leg of with a teapot*, then I wouldn't have needed any goals but (1). I wouldn't have had to go beyond the conventional meaning listed in the lexicon. In Ed's utterance, it was partly because the verb *teapot* wasn't in my lexicon that I was forced to infer Ed's subgoals (2) and (3).

It need not work this way. Subgoals such as (2) and (3) need not be forced by a semantic anomaly. In Bombeck's *Stereos are a dime a dozen*, the noun *stereos* has a proper noun lexical entry meaning 'phonographs' that makes perfectly good sense in the sentence Bombeck uttered. Nothing in Bombeck's sentence per se forces us to look for a non-conventional interpretation. So subgoals such as (2) and (3) must always be present—or almost always. Virtually every word can be used with a nonce sense in at least some situations. It is just that in conventional cases, the computation required to capture these goals is trivial.

To see how this would work, imagine Arlene telling Bill *Stereos are a dime a dozen*, by which she means *Phonographs are very common*. The goal hierarchy for *stereos* would look like this:

(1) Arlene wants Bill to recognize that she is using *stereos* to denote phonographs.

(2) Arlene wants Bill to recognize that what she is asserting are a dime a dozen are the kind of thing that she has good reason to believe that on this occasion he can readily compute uniquely on the basis of their common ground such that this kind of thing has something to do with phonographs.

(3) Arlene wants Bill to recognize that she *is* using *stereos* to denote phonographs.

The use of *stereos* by Bombeck, in contrast, would have this goal hierarchy:

(1′) Bombeck wants us to recognize that she is using *stereos* to denote people who *possess* phonographs.

(2′) Bombeck wants us to recognize that what she is asserting are a dime a dozen are the kind of thing that she has good reason to believe that on this occasion we can readily compute uniquely on the basis of our common ground such that this kind of thing has something to do with phonographs.

(3′) Bombeck wants us to recognize that she is using *stereos* to denote phonographs.

The difference between Arlene's and Bombeck's uses of *stereos* lies entirely in goals (1) and (1′). For Arlene, the kind of object she intended to have something to do with phonographs are phonographs themselves. The relation to be computed in subgoal (2) is the identity relation. For Bombeck, the kind of object she intended to have something to do with phonographs are people who *possess* phonographs, a more complicated and indirect relation.

The point is that Bill, in parsing Arlene's utterance, can't ever be content with subgoal (1) alone. He can't ever know for certain, ahead of time, which words Arlene is using in their conventional senses, and which she is using in contextually innovative senses. How does he know she isn't using *stereos* to mean what Bombeck meant, or to mean something still different, as in *Nowadays monaural recordings are rare, but stereos are a dime a dozen?* Only by consulting his and her common ground can Bill recognize when *stereo* is to be construed as the identity relation and when as something else. Subgoals such as (2) and (3) are implicitly required wherever there is the possibility of a nonce sense.

Intentional parsers create senses and don't just select them from a predetermined list of senses. Subgoal (2) is an injunction to listeners to use the common ground, plus certain guidelines about rationality, to create the sense the speaker intended. The listeners need never have thought of the intended sense before, either as a sense of the word the speaker uttered or, for that matter, as a sense of any word they have ever heard before. When we first hear *The photographer asked me to do a Napoleon for the camera*, most of us have never before thought of *tuck one's hand into one's vest* as the sense for any word, let alone for *do a Napoleon*. We create this sense for this occasion alone. It is truly a nonce sense.

How intentional parsers can be made to work, and how they create the speaker's intended senses, are questions for future research. The argument is that parsers need to take account of the speaker's intentions in every step they take. Their goal must be to create the speaker's hierarchy of intentions in uttering the words he uttered on that occasion.

7   Conclusion

Nonce sense is a genuine puzzle for traditional parsers, for they don't even recognize its existence. It exists all right. In everyday speech, it is ubiquitous, sometimes taking shapes that are easily recognized as innovative expressions, but other times sounding no different from anything else in language. Parsers can no longer pretend that nonce sense doesn't exist. They must make sense of nonce sense or fail.

The failure of traditional parsers to handle nonce sense, I have argued, reveals a fundamental problem in their design. Traditional parsers generally do their job without regard to who uttered the sentence or to whom. Any concern that they show for the interlocutors is indirect and limited, as when they identify referents from the surrounding discourse. Yet understanding ultimately requires listeners to decide what the speaker meant—to reconstruct the speaker's intentions, or goals, in uttering what he did. The traditional assumption is that parsers need to take account of these intentions only after they have parsed the sentence uttered. The existence of nonce sense makes this assumption untenable. Parsers must worry about the speaker's intentions at every turn.

The current conception of parsing needs revision. It ought to be thought of not as the analysis of the sentence uttered, but as the analysis of the speaker's intentions in uttering the sentence. All that counts in the end is the speaker's meaning, even if it is only for the nonce.

11

Understanding Old Words with New Meanings

WITH RICHARD J. GERRIG

Most theories of comprehension assume that every word in an utterance is comprehended by selecting its intended sense from a short exhaustive list of potential senses in the mental lexicon. This assumption is challenged by novel words based on proper nouns, as in *After Joe listened to the tape of the interview, he did a Richard Nixon to a portion of it* [i.e., erased]. Experiment 1 demonstrated that people interpret verb phrases like *do a Nixon* against a hierarchy of information assumed to be shared by the speaker and his addressees: Nixon's identity; acts associated with Nixon; types of acts appropriate to the utterance; and the type of act specifically intended. Experiment 2 demonstrated that people expect the intended type of act to be coherent, and to be salient among the acts associated with Nixon. It is argued that creating senses, as with *do a Nixon*, works differently from selecting senses, and that many words require a mixture of both.

In most theories of moment-by-moment comprehension, listeners are assumed to have access to a mental dictionary, or lexicon, that contains all the words they know. When they hear a word in an utterance, they consult its conventional meanings in their lexicon and select the one that best fits the current utterance. According to some models (e.g., Blank and Foss 1978; Marslen-Wilson and Tyler 1980; Marslen-Wilson and Welsh 1978; Simpson 1981), listeners exploit the previous context to limit the number of meanings they access. According to other models (e.g., Forster 1976; Seidenberg, Tanenhaus, Leiman, and Bienkowski 1982; Swinney 1979; Tanenhaus, Leiman, and Seidenberg

1979), listeners ordinarily access *all* of the meanings for each word and use the context only afterwards to select out the right one. Both types of models make two strong assumptions. The first, or *enumerability*, assumption is that all of the possible meanings for each word are listed in or can be enumerated by mental lexicon. The second, or *selectivity*, assumption is that listeners *select* among these enumerable meanings in coming to the right one.

Both assumptions, however, appear to be incorrect, which challenges the completeness, even the correctness, of these models (Chapter 10, this volume). Consider a caller, as reported in the *San Francisco Chronicle* (November 24, 1980), who asked an operator at the telephone company's directory assistance about toll charges and was told *I don't know. You'll have to ask a zero.* The caller presumably had several conventional meanings for *zero* in her mental lexicon, including "naught," "freezing temperature," and "nonentity." If all she could do was access these meanings and select among them, she would have interpreted *zero* as "nonentity." But she did not. According to the report, she interpreted it as "person one can reach on a telephone by dialing zero." Surely, this meaning was not in her lexicon. She created it on the spot. To be sure, she started with "naught" from her lexicon, but she added elements from her knowledge about telephones, telephone operators, and public sources of information. Creating a word meaning based on world knowledge appears to be a very different process from merely selecting a well-established, or conventional, word meaning from a list. Our goal in this paper is to characterize some of the properties of sense creation.

The operator's *zero* is an instance of a large class of word constructions called *contextual expressions* for which word meanings must be created and not selected (Clark and Clark 1979; Chapter 10, this volume). The defining property of these expressions is that they can, in principle, take on infinitely many senses depending on the circumstances in which they are used. *Zero*, which is one common noun created from another, could have been used by a teacher in *All the zeros must redo their papers* to mean "person with a grade of zero on a paper," and by other speakers in other circumstances in principle to mean infinitely many other things. In the same fashion, novel verbs can be created from nouns, as in *The newsboy porched the newspaper yesterday* (Clark and Clark 1979); novel compound nouns can be created from two or more nouns, as in *apple–juice chair* (Downing 1977; Gleitman and Gleitman 1970; Kay and Zimmer 1976); novel count nouns can be created from mass nouns, as in *I'd like three waters please* (Clark 1978); novel adjectives can be created from nouns, as in

We had a parky vacation (Chapter 10, this volume), and so on (see also Nunberg 1979). All of these construction types yield contextual expressions.

Most contextual expressions are so prosaic that they escape notice. One dictionary lists the sense of *crab* that appears in *A crab scuttled along the beach*, but not the senses that appear in *I like crab* ["crab meat"], *There is crab on the menu* ["a dish with crab meat"], *How many crabs do you have there?* [said by a grocery clerk, "cans of crab meat"], and *I stopped in Perry's for a quick crab* ["meal of crab meat"] (from the *San Francisco Chronicle*). In *a quick crab* note that it is the meal, not the crab, that is quick. If we have no more entries in our mental lexicons than there are in the dictionary, then we created the last four senses and did so unwittingly. For a theory of comprehension to be adequate, it must say how we do this in the ordinary course of understanding.

To bring home how injudicious the enumerability and selection assumptions are, let us consider nouns, verbs, and adjectives freshly created from *proper* nouns. Suppose a friend, taking your photograph, asks you with a glint in her eye, *Please do a Napoleon for the camera.* Most people to whom we have offered this scenario report imagining, quickly and without reflection, posing with one hand tucked inside their jacket a la Napoleon. Arriving at this sense is a remarkable feat. The proper name *Napoleon*, though listed in the mental lexicon, does not have senses of the kind common nouns have (see, for example, Burge 1973; Donnellan 1970; Evans 1973; Kripke 1972; Searle 1958): according to the favored theories of proper names, all it contains are designations, or pointers, to individuals such as Napoleon Bonaparte and Napoleon III. In understanding the proper noun in *Napoleon died from arsenic poisoning*, listeners simply represent a designation to Napoleon Bonaparte. In understanding *do a Napoleon* too, you must represent a designation to M. Bonaparte, but you must also search his biography for a characteristic act fitting your friend's request in this context and create a sense around it. Your interpretation is built entirely around elements from your knowledge of Napoleon's life.

Sense creation without sense selection is characteristic of eponymous expressions—that is, expressions built around references to people, or eponyms, like Napoleon. Such expressions come in many forms. They may be verbs, as in *John managed to Houdini his way out of the locked closet;* adjectives, as in *Nixon took to giving crowds a Churchillian gesture;* or common nouns, as in the William Hamilton cartoon (June 23, 1977) of one businessman saying to another, *You misunderstand, Hayne—when I said what we need now is a Churchill,*

I was speaking of a cigar. Many eponymous expressions, like *to boycott, a cardigan,* and *a napoleon* (the pastry), have evolved into well-established words with conventional meanings (see Espy 1978, for an extensive list) and so are no longer contextual expressions. But eponymous verb phrases such as *do a Napoleon* rarely if ever enter the conventional lexicon, and so their meanings must always be created on the spot. This makes them an excellent choice for an investigation of pure sense creation.

In the study of understanding, one can distinguish the moment-by-moment process of creating meanings for utterances (call it *comprehension*) from the product of that process (call it *interpretation.*) The experiments we will describe are on interpretation, not comprehension. Yet models of interpretation constrain models of comprehension, and vice versa, so we will be able to draw certain general conclusions about comprehension too.

1 Eponymous Verb Phrases

When listeners interpret eponymous verb phrases, according to our proposal, they make two basic assumptions. They suppose there is a set of conventional constraints about the form these expressions can take, *formal constraints* they can exploit in interpreting what was meant. And they suppose speakers are cooperating by designing utterances their addressees can readily understand.

As for formal constraints, briefly, eponymous verb phrases consist of the main verb *do* plus an indefinite noun phrase, like *a Napoleon*, that designates a type of act. Theg are related to verb phrases like *do a job, do a handstand,* and *do a trick,* but the act is designated with a proper noun used indirectly as a common noun. Notice that when *Napoleon* is used as a proper noun, it cannot take an article or plural ending, but when used indirectly as a common noun, it can, as in *Please do a Napoleon for the camera* and *We all did Napoleons for the camera.* Proper nouns, however, can be used indirectly as common nouns to denote other things too, for example, objects (*He's a little Napoleon*) and events (*She met her Waterloo in Denver.*) So with eponymous verb phrases, listeners must realize that the noun phrases are being used to denote acts. They must also realize that the eponyms may be not only people, as in *do a Napoleon*, but also places, as in *The architects have done a Manhattan to downtown San Francisco* (compare *The initiative is aimed at preventing the New Yorking of the San Francisco skyline,* San Francisco television news, February 28, 1979), historical events, as in *A small boy and a girl came past close to me doing an Indianapolis on their tricycles*, a reference to the Indianapolis 500 auto race (from Dick Francis's *Blood Sport*), and other things.

These formal constraints are hardly enough. When your friend said *Please do a Napoleon for the camera*, you could have assumed these constraints and still interpreted the verb phrase as *smile* or *say 'fromage'* or *remove your glasses*. As we will argue, it was only because you assumed your friend thought you could figure out the meaning she had in mind that you chose "tuck your hand into your jacket."

We suggest that addressees assume they are intended to understand what was meant by using only what was said in relation to the rest of the common ground they share with the speaker (Chapter 2, 1, this volume). With eponymous verb phrases, their common ground includes the following hierarchy of beliefs:

1. **Identity of the Eponym.** The identity of the eponym is common ground. Your friend couldn't sincerely have said *Please do a Tallyrand for the camera* if she did not assume it was common ground to the two of you who Talleyrand was. It is not enough for her to know about Talleyrand. She must believe the knowledge is common ground.

2. **Acts by the Eponym.** Certain acts associated with the eponym are also common ground. Your friend knew about many acts associated with Napoleon—that he ruled France, crowned himself, laid siege to Moscow, was exiled to Elba, and so on—and she took at least one of these to be part of her and your common ground.

3. **Relevant Acts of the Eponym.** It is common ground that certain types of acts among those specified in (2) make sense in the sentence the speaker uttered. Your friend thought you could discover from among the types of acts associated with Napoleon in (2) at least one type that a person could do for a camera, such as frown, crown oneself, pose hand in jacket, and so on.

4. **The Type of Act Referred to.** It is common ground that the speaker assumed the addressee could readily and uniquely identify on this occasion the type of act the speaker intended from the types of acts in (3). Out of all the types of Napoleonic acts one could do for a camera, your friend believed that the hand in jacket pose was common ground to you both, and that you could readily infer that type to be the one she intended. This last constraint is a special case of a more general *reciprocity principle:* it is common ground between speakers and listeners that with sincere uses of language the speaker believes his addressees can readily infer what he means on each occasion.

We will demonstrate the importance of three properties of this hierarchy. In Experiment 1, we will show how listeners exploit the hierarchical nature of these constraints. In Experiment 2, we will demonstrate that listeners exploit the requirements that (a) eponymous verb phrases denote "types of acts," and (b) these types must be readily and uniquely identifiable on each occasion—in effect, "salient" in the speaker's and addressees' common ground.

2 Experiment 1: Knowledge of Eponyms

The people we confronted with our Napoleon scenario often reported that the right interpretation just popped out. Out of everything they knew about Napoleon, they immediately recognized that they were to pose with one hand inside the jacket. In models of pure sense selection, listeners are assumed to exploit two sources of information about a word's intended meaning—the word's senses in the lexicon, and the "context." In sense creation, we suppose listeners exploit the analogous two sources of information. In an *eponym-centered* process, they begin with beliefs they have about the eponym and build the intended meaning around them. And in a *context-centered* process, they begin with the context and narrow in on what the intended meaning could plausibly be. We assume it is these two processes working together that engender the feeling that the right interpretation just pops out. The eponym-centered process should be guided by the hierarchy of constraints we have presented. Listeners should begin at level 1 with the most general constraint and narrow down the possible interpretations by adding constraints at levels 2, 3, and 4. The further they can get, the more confident they should be that they have understood the utterance. Suppose your friend says:

(1) Please do a George Conklin for the camera.

(2) Please do a Homer for the camera.

(3) Please do a Franklin Delano Roosevelt for the camera.

(4) Please do a Napoleon for the camera.

Utterance (1) should seem the least interpretable since, presumably, you do not even know who George Conklin is. You cannot get past level 1 of the hierarchy. (2) should seem more interpretable, since you know who Homer is, but if you know any acts associated with him, none is one a person could do for a camera. You can't get past level 2. (3) should be still more interpretable, since you know who Roosevelt is, know acts associated with him, and may even know types of acts that fit this utterance. Still you cannot get past level 3 of the hierarchy. (4) should seem the most interpretable, since you can penetrate all four levels of the hierarchy. One goal of Experiment 1 was to test this prediction.

To be efficient, listeners also surely rely on a context-centered process. They probably do not develop each level of the hierarchy fully— deciding that they know the eponym, then registering acts associated with him, then registering acts that might fit the context, and finally deciding which act was intended. By exploiting the context, they can search immediately through the few types of acts that are at all consistent with the context for an act that is obviously associated with the eponym—for example, a pose obviously associated with Napoleon. This would be more efficient than considering all of the eponym's biography, which contains much information irrelevant to the current utterance.

Where should we see evidence of context-centered processes? Compare these two requests:

(1)   Please do a George Conklin for the camera.

(5)   Please do a George Conklin for me.

From the internal structure of (1) uttered by your friend in the circumstances, you could guess she was asking you to strike some sort of pose even if you didn't know who George Conklin was. For (5) in the same circumstances, you could not narrow down the possibilities this much. If you are working solely by an eponym-centered process, (1) and (5) should seem equally interpretable, since you cannot get past level 1 for either one. But with a context-centered process, you should find (1) more interpretable than (5). Another goal of Experiment 1 was to test for such a context-centered process.

Listeners often have a good idea why they cannot understand an utterance. For *Why can't you understand (1)?* you might reply, *Because I don't know who George Conklin is*. When asked about (2), you might reply *Because I don't know anything about Homer that would be appropriate to do for a camera*. These two reasons reflect levels 1 and 2 in the hierarchy of constraints and, therefore, give evidence of an eponym-centered process. Other reasons would reflect context-centered processes. So in Experiment 1, we gathered people's justifications for their successful and unsuccessful interpretations and analyzed them as evidence of eponym and context-centered processes.

Method

Students tried to interpret thirty-two utterances with eponymous verb phrases. They then rated their confidence in these interpretations and explained why they chose each interpretation or, if they found no interpretation, why they did not.

We composed sixty-four sentences in all. We chose thirty-two people, such as Richard Nixon and Elizabeth Taylor, as eponyms familiar to students and composed thirty-two sentences, one per name, on a variety of topics. We chose another thirty-two unfamiliar names at random from a telephone book (e.g., John Jacobs, Joan Sprague) and created a matched set of thirty-two sentences by replacing each known name in the first thirty-two sentences with an unknown name. By an entirely eponym-centered process, people should get stranded by the unknown eponyms at level 1 in the hierarchy, whatever the context; with the known eponyms, they should have more success. The known eponyms, however, varied considerably in familiarity. For those known only by name, most students should not get past level 2. For others, most students should have access to a range of possible acts, so they could get at least to level 3. With the range of known eponyms, we could elicit reasons reflecting levels 2 and 3 of the hierarchy too.

Each sentence had either a *restricting* or an *unrestricting* context. For 16 of the known eponyms, the interpretations were intended to be transparent, as in *After Joe listened to the tape of the interview, he did a Nixon to a portion of it* ("erased"). For the remaining 16, they were intended to be obscure, as in *I met a girl at the Coffee House who did an Elizabeth Taylor while I was talking to her.* With this contrast, we could test for the successful completion of level 4—the discovery of the precise type of act intended. The identical contexts were also used with the unknown eponyms in place of the known eponyms. By an entirely eponym-centered process, the verb phrases created around these unknown people should be equally obscure, since students can never get past level 1. But if the utterances with restrictive contexts are more interpretable than those with unrestrictive contexts, students must be exploiting a context-centered process.

Each student received one sentence for each of the thirty-two sentence frames; sixteen had known eponyms, and sixteen unknown ones, and of each of these sets, half contained restricting contexts and half unrestricting ones. In a counterbalanced design, one set of thirty-two sentences was given to half the students, and the complementary set of thirty-two was given to the other half. Each sentence was presented as follows:

> If, during a conversation with a friend, he were to say the following sentence: After Joe listened to the tape of the interview, he did a Nixon to a portion of it.

(1) What do you think he meant? (Answer only one of the four following choices)
   (a) He almost certainly meant:
   (b) He probably meant:
   (c) He might have meant:
   (d) I can't really tell.
(2) If (a) or (b), why do you think he meant that?
(3) If (c) or (d), what is it that you cannot understand and why?

Each sentence and its accompanying questions were printed on a single page, with plenty of room for answers, and the pages were placed in a random order individually for each student.

The questionnaires were completed by twenty-four Stanford University students participating either as a requirement for introductory psychology or for pay.

Results and Discussion

Interpretability

For the question *What do you think he meant?*, the answer *I can't really tell* was assigned an interpretability rating of 1, *He might have meant*, 2, *He probably meant*, 3, and *He almost certainly meant*, 4. These ratings were submitted to an analysis of variance in which both students and verb phrases were treated as random effects (Clark 1973). The mean ratings for the four types of sentences are shown in Table 1.

The ratings give clear evidence of an eponym-centered process. By such a process, a verb phrase should be more interpretable when the eponym is known, allowing the interpreter to penetrate to level 2, 3, or 4 of the hierarchy, than when it is unknown, barring the interpreter from getting past level 1, and it was, 2.77 to 1.65, min $F'(1, 49) = 49.17$, $p < .001$. Also, a verb phrase with a known eponym should be more interpretable when the context is restricting, enabling the interpreter to reach level 4, than when it is unrestricting, allowing him only to reach level 2 or 3, and it was, 3.44 to 2.10, min $F'(1, 49) = 53.40$, $p < .001$.

The ratings also give evidence of a context-centered process. Although the restricting contexts were designed for the known eponyms, they made verb phrases with unknown eponyms more interpretable too, 1.85 to 1.45, min $F'(1, 48) = 4.78$, $p < .025$.

Notice, however, that restricting the context aided interpretability by 1.34 units when the eponym was known, but by only 0.40 units when the eponym was unknown, min $F'(1, 47) = 16.60$, $p < .001$. What accounts for this asymmetry? When the eponym is known, the

TABLE 1
Mean Interpretability Ratings for Four Types of Sentences
(Experiment 1)

	CONTEXT		MEANS
	RESTRICTING	UNRESTRICTING	
Known eponym	3.44	2.10	2.77
Unknown eponym	1.85	1.45	1.65
Means	2.64	1.78	2.21

NOTE: 1 means *I can't really tell*, and 4 *He almost certainly meant.*

context could have cued students' recall of an event in the eponym's life that they might not otherwise have recalled. It would have then allowed them to move in levels from 2 to 3, from 2 to 4, or from 3 to 4, depending on what they could recall. But when the eponym is unknown, there can be no cuing of memory since there is nothing about the eponym in memory to cue. All the context can do is constrain the types of acts the verb phrase could denote, allowing a more educated guess at what the speaker might have meant. So ordinarily, the context-centered process does not simply narrow down the alternatives. It presumably helps cue the recall of relevant events in the eponym's life.

Reasons

Each answer to *Why do you think he meant that?* and *What is it that you can't understand and why?* was classified into one of eleven main types, later combined into the eight categories as shown in Tables 2 and 3. The eleven categories were decided on by Clark and an assistant; all answers were then coded by the assistant and checked by Clark. Of the 768 answers, fifty-one could not be put into these categories: forty-four were too vague, as in *I based it on Nixon's name* or *It was worded funny* or *I have heard athletic terms named after people*, and seven were blank. All the rest are included in Tables 2 and 3.

The reasons, the mean interpretability rating for each reason, and the number of students offering each reason are listed for the known eponyms in Table 2, and for the unknown eponyms in Table 3. For example, as shown in Table 2, 15 students offered reason (c), *I don't know how to limit the choices* for verb phrases with known eponyms, five times in restricting contexts and ten times in unrestricting contexts. The categories are ordered in each table from the most comprehensible to the least, according to the mean ratings for each reason. Because each mean rating was contributed to by different students interpreting different verbs, these means cannot be compared with clean statistical tests.

TABLE 2
Mean Interpretability Ratings for Reasons Given for
Interpretations of Eponymous Verb Phrases with Known
Eponyms (E) in Restricting and Unrestricting Contexts
(Experiment 1)

REASONS	CONTEXT RESTRICTING	CONTEXT UNRESTRICTING	MEAN
(a) E has these characteristics; or E has done these specific acts.	3.70 (151)	3.07 (77)	3.49
(b) Judging from the context; or this seemed obvious from the context; or that's what I would do.	3.00 (19)	2.89 (9)	2.96
(c) I don't know how to limit the choices.	1.80 (5)	1.70 (10)	1.73
(d) I know who E is, but I can't think why he'd fit into this sentence.	2.00 (5)	1.49 (50)	1.45
(e) I know who E is, but I'm not familiar with his characteristics.	2.00 (1)	1.33 (18)	1.37
(f) I'm not positive, but I think E is ...	3.00 (2)	1.00 (13)	1.27

NOTE: The number of instances for each mean is shown in parentheses.

The pattern of reasons and ratings in Table 2 is consistent with an eponym-centered process. As an illustration, suppose a student interpreted the verb phrase in *After Joe listened to the tape of the interview, he did a Nixon to a portion of it* as "erase", and gave as his reason, *Because Nixon erased a tape.* This reason was classified as reason (a), "E has done these specific acts." Although the student did not say so explicitly, he presupposed that he knew who Nixon was (level 1 in our hierarchy), knew acts associated with Nixon (level 2), knew acts that could fit this context (level 3), and believed that this type of act must be the one the speaker was referring to (level 4). Reason (a) presupposes levels 1, 2, 3, and 4. Similarly, reason (c), "I don't know how to limit the choices," presupposes levels 1, 2, and 3. Reason (d), "I know who E is, but I can't think of why he'd fit into this sentence," presupposes levels 1 and 2. Reason (e), "I know who E is, but I'm not familiar with his characteristics," presupposes level 1. Reason (f), "I'm not positive, but I think E is ...," doesn't even presuppose level 1. (Reason (b) is not directly related to the levels.)

TABLE 3

Mean Interpretability Ratings for Reasons Given for
Interpretations of Eponymous Verb Phrases with Unknown
Eponyms (E) in Restricting and Unrestricting Contexts
(Experiment 1)

REASONS	CONTEXT RESTRICTING	UNRESTRICTING	MEAN
(g) This seemed obvious from context; or that's what I would do.	2.88 (25)	3.00 (11)	2.92
(h) I don't know who E is, but judging from the context ...	2.78 (32)	2.71 (14)	2.76
(i) I don't know who E is.	1.35 (103)	1.10 (35)	1.21
(j) I don't know how to limit the choices.	1.27 (15)	1.14 (22)	1.19

NOTE: The number of instances for each mean is shown in parentheses.

In an eponym-centered hypothesis, reasons (a), (c), (d), (e), and (f) ought to be associated with less and less confident interpretations, and they were. The mean ratings declined as follows: 3.49, 1.73, 1.45, 1.37, and 1.27. This change from reason (a) to reason (c) marks the break between complete and incomplete understanding, so it is not surprising that it shows the largest drop in interpretability.

For other evidence of eponym-centered processes, compare the restricting and unrestricting contexts in Table 2. What the restricting context should do is allow the students to reach level 4 more easily. In agreement with this expectation, reason (a), which reflects the reaching of level 4, was offered 151 times for restricting contexts, but only 77 times for unrestricting contexts, min $F'(1, 46) = 21.00$, $p < .001$. Similarly, reasons (c), (d), (e), and (f) were each offered more often for unrestricting contexts than for restricting ones, 91 to 13. Put differently, we have confirmation here of why, with known eponyms, restricting contexts were rated as more interpretable than unrestricting contexts: With the restricting contexts, the students could more often justify their interpretations with "E has these characteristics, or E has done these specific acts," which reflect their arrival at level 4 in our hierarchy.

The best evidence for context-centered processes is found in the reasons offered when the eponym was unknown (see Table 3). Reasons (g) and (h), "This seemed obvious from context; or that's what I would do," and "I don't know who E is, but judging from the context ...," both directly reflect what it means to be "context-centered." They justify an interpretation not from knowledge of the eponym but from the context. If so, the mean ratings for reasons (g) and (h) should be higher than those for reasons (i) and (j), which reflect no such justification, and they were. Reasons (g) and (h) averaged 2.83, and reasons (i) and (j) only 1.21. Reasons (g) and (h) should also have been used more often when the context could truly be used, and they were. Reasons (g) and (h) were used 57 times with restricting contexts, but only 25 times with unrestricting contexts, min $F'(1, 48) = 7.02$, $p < .01$. In the complement of this finding, reasons (i) and (j), which arise from the inability to exploit the context, were offered 157 times for unrestricting contexts and only 118 times for restricting contexts, min $F'(1, 50) = 10.07$, $p < .003$. So even without knowledge of the eponym, students were willing to make a best guess based only on the context—at least, when they could.

The reasons demonstrate once again how the eponym- and context-centered processes work together. Consider reason (a) in Table 2, "E has these characteristics; or E has done these specific acts." Students offered this reason sometimes when the context was restricting (151 times) and sometimes when it was unrestricting (77 times). But even though they gave the same reason for both contexts, suggesting they had reached level 4 in both cases, they were more confident in their interpretation with restricting contexts than with unrestricting contexts. The difference was 3.70 to 3.07, min $F'(1, 43) = 22.37$, $p < .001$. Apparently the more converging evidence listeners have of the speaker's intention, the more confident they are.

3   Experiment 2: Salience and Coherence

One of the main findings of Experiment 1 remains quite mysterious. Compare two sentences we used in that experiment:

(6)   After Joe listened to the tape of the interview, he did a Nixon to a portion of it.

(7)   I met a girl at the Coffee House who did an Elizabeth Taylor while I was talking to her.

Sentences like (6), with "restricting" contexts, were judged to be more interpretable than sentences like (7), with "unrestricting" contexts? Why? For *do an Elizabeth Taylor*, we can think of perfectly acceptable acts associated with Elizabeth Taylor that fit the context—acts such as standing, flirting, behaving like a shrew, pouting, and looking Cleopatra–like. But as we will argue, there are two problems with these Taylor acts. First, as a collection they do not constitute a *coher-*

ent set: they don't define a "type of act," as required by the hierarchy presented earlier. And second, no one of these acts taken singly is any more appropriate than the others: no one of them is especially *salient*.

Salience is an obvious criterion for interpreting eponymous verb phrases. In the right contexts, *do a Napoleon* could be used to mean "pose with one's hand tucked in one's vest, as in *do a Napoleon for the camera*, "conquer by overrunning," as in *Hitler did a Napoleon to Poland in 1939*, or "go into exile" as in *The Shah of Iran did a Napoleon to an island off Panama in 1980*. Except in the most contrived contexts, it cannot be used to mean "eat" or "ask questions" or "sit down," which are also things Napoleon certainly did. A speaker couldn't say *I was in bed doing a Napoleon to a mystery story* and expect his addressee to understand him to mean simply "read." Why not? Intuitively, the type of act intended must be salient of Napoleon.

But salience is a relative notion—relative to the speaker, his addressees, and their particular common ground at the moment. Recently, a colleague heard a woman ask her husband as she was about to lift her baby into their car, *Couldn't you help me by doing a Chomsky?* Who would ever have thought *do a Chomsky* could have meant "Open the car door"? Yet, as it later came out, she and her husband had been out with Noam Chomsky the week before—her only visit with him—when he had courteously opened the car door as she struggled in with her baby. With *do a Chomsky*, she was alluding to an act associated with Chomsky that was especially salient in her and her husband's common ground—they had perhaps discussed Chomsky's courtesy in the meantime. It did not matter that the act was not part of the common ground she shared with anyone else. She was speaking to her husband, and so it had to be salient only in their common ground.

This example also suggests that for an act to be salient in two people's common ground, it must be readily accessible in memory—at least, believed to be so. Two months later, the same woman could not have expected her husband to understand *do a Chomsky* as intended unless they had discussed Chomsky's helpfulness in the interim. She had to suppose that the mention of Chomsky's name in the circumstances would give her husband access to the relevant act. Ready access also applies when the act is common ground to most people, as when reporters write about public acts. Informally, we noticed that while Alexander Haig was the American Secretary of State, *do an Alexander Haig* was sometimes used to mean "speak in Washington jargon and with mixed metaphors," as Haig was well known for doing. After his resignation, the expression quickly lost ground and disappeared, apparently because his characteristic speech was no longer readily accessible for most people. *Ready access* seems to be a necessary condition for the cooperative use of eponymous verb phrases.

For an act to be salient, it must also be distinctively associated with the eponym. Two complementary criteria of distinctiveness can be derived from Tversky's (1977) theory of similarity. First, the eponym must be more strongly associated with the intended act than with other contextually appropriate acts in common ground. And second, the act must be more strongly associated with the eponym than with other potential eponyms in common ground. For *Please do a Napoleon for the camera*, Napoleon is more strongly associated with posing hand in jacket than with any other act one could do for a camera. Also, this pose is more strongly associated with Napoleon than with any other readily accessible name in memory. What made *do a Chomsky* sound strange for us outsiders was that we could not imagine how these two criteria could have been met. Yet against the common ground of the woman and her husband, they were. *Distinctiveness* appears to be another necessary condition for the cooperative use of eponymous verb phrases.

The next issue is what constitutes a type of act. Compare the set of acts consisting of toasting, rissoleing, searing, parching, and flambeeing (set 1) with the set of acts consisting of sneezing, swimming, and arguing (set 2). Membership in set 1 has a clear rationale, whereas membership in set 2 seems arbitrary, without reason. The acts in set 1 have a common goal (the preparation of food for eating by browning without fat), a common location (the kitchen), and other common properties, whereas the acts in set 2 seem to have few common properties. Furthermore, the acts in set 1 contrast with all other types of food preparation—there are no other ways of preparing food whose special purpose is browning (Lehrer 1969)—whereas there seems no good reason why set 2 does not also include coughing, sailing, and talking. Set 1, in short, has a highly valued rationale for membership—a rationale based on human conceptual and perceptual principles (Clark and Clark 1979)—whereas set 2 doesn't. For now, we must be content with this informal characterization. We will call having such a rationale the property of *coherence.*

For *do a Napoleon*, what listeners seek is not a set or collection of acts associated with Napoleon, but a type or kind of act. In saying *Please do a Napoleon for the camera*, your friend does not want Napoleon to do something; she wants *you* to do something of a type Napoleon would do. Our proposal is that (a) listeners seek a type of act that is defined by a collection of acts they believe to be associated with Napoleon, and (b) the more highly valued its rationale, the more

TABLE 4

A Pair of Coherent Vignettes with Three Different Completions

ONE SALIENT ACT

Imagine your friend told you about his neighbor, Harry Wilson. Harry Wilson decided that it was time to rejuvenate his house and property. He started by using his electric shears to carve his hedges into animal shapes—an elephant, a camel with two humps, and a fat seal balancing a ball on its nose. Then he decided to paint the exterior of his house. He painted the clapboard walls with bright white and the trim with royal blue. For the final touch, Harry moved his furniture out to the porch, so that he could enjoy the evening breezes.

Later your friend told you, *This summer I plan to ...*

do a Harry Wilson. [unrestricting]
do a Harry Wilson to the hedges. [restricting]
do a Harry Wilson to a bar of soap. [extending]

THREE SALIENT ACTS

Imagine your friend told you about his neighbor, Harry Wilson. Harry Wilson decided that it was time to rejuvenate his house and property. He started by using his electric shears to carve his hedges into animal shapes—an elephant, a camel with two humps, and a fat seal balancing a ball on its nose. Then he decided to paint the exterior of his house. He painted the clapboard walls in the Bicentennial Spirit with red and white stars and the rim with bright blue stripes. For the final touch, Harry moved his summer furniture up to the roof, so that he could enjoy the evening breezes.

Later your friend told you, *This summer I plan to ...*

do a Harry Wilson. [unrestricting]
do a Harry Wilson to the hedges. [restricting]
do a Harry Wilson to a bar of soap. [extending]

acceptable a type of act it defines. So *do a Napoleon* cannot denote a type of act defined by the set "conquer by overrunning," "posing with one's hand tucked in one's jacket," and "going into exile," since these three acts do not constitute a coherent category. When listeners cannot come up with an acceptable type of act, they should find the verb phrase uninterpretable.

Method

Students read twelve vignettes, each ending with a sentence containing an eponymous verb phrase. For each vignette, they interpreted the verb phrase, rating their confidence in their interpretation.

Each vignette began with a sentence like *Imagine that a friend of yours told you about his neighbor, Harry Wilson* and continued with three or so sentences that described three of the neighbor's acts. The vignette ended with a "completion" sentence containing an eponymous verb phrase like *Later your friend told you, 'This summer I plan to do*

TABLE 5
A Pair of Incoherent Vignettes with Three Different Completions

---

ONE SALIENT ACT

Imagine that a friend of yours told you about his neighbor, Elvis Edmunds. Elvis loves to entertain his children in the evening with several card games he knows. He often plays canasta with them. During the day, Elvis is employed as an insurance salesman. He likes to work best on days when there is not a cloud in the sky. To supplement his income, Elvis carves fruit into exotic shapes for the delicatessen down the road.

Later your friend says, *I have often thought about ...*

    doing an Elvis Edmunds. [unrestricting]
    doing an Elvis Edmunds to some apples I bought. [restricting]
    doing an Elvis Edmunds to a piece of driftwood. [extending]

THREE SALIENT ACTS

Imagine that a friend of yours told you about his neighbor, Elvis Edmunds. Elvis loves to entertain his children in the evenings with several magic tricks that he knows. He often surprises them by pulling dollar bills out of his ear. During the day, Elvis is employed as a professional skywriter. He likes to work best on days when there is not a cloud in the sky. To supplement his income, Elvis carves fruit into exotic shapes for the delicatessen down the road.

Later your friend says, *I have often thought about ...*

    doing an Elvis Edmunds. [unrestricting]
    doing an Elvis Edmunds to some apples I bought. [restricting]
    doing an Elvis Edmunds to a piece of driftwood. [extending]

---

a Harry Wilson to the hedges.' We composed vignettes like this around twelve fictitious people.

To examine salience, we created two forms for each vignette, as illustrated in Table 4. In one form, two of the eponym's acts were mundane, and the other was highly unusual. In the upper example in Table 4, Harry Wilson painted his house ordinary colors and moved his furniture to the porch—both mundane acts—but also carved his hedges into animal shapes—a highly unusual act. In the second form of each vignette, all three acts were highly unusual so that, as much as possible, no one act was more salient than the others. In the lower example in Table 4, Harry Wilson painted his house in stars and stripes, moved his furniture to the roof, and carved his hedges into animal shapes—all three highly unusual acts. These two forms will be said to have one and three salient acts, respectively. Students should find it easy to interpret a bare eponymous verb phrase like *do a Harry Wilson* around the single salient act, but not around any one of the three equally salient acts. With three salient acts, the students should instead try to create the meaning around the three acts taken as a set.

TABLE 6
Mean Comprehensibility Ratings for Verb Phrases
with Different Completions
(Experiment 2)

TYPE OF VIGNETTE	SALIENT ACTS	TYPE OF COMPLETION		
		UNRESTRICTING	RESTRICTING	EXTENDING
Coherent	One	2.93	3.83	3.13
	Three	2.90	3.67	2.73
Incoherent	One	2.60	3.60	3.20
	Three	2.17	3.37	2.87
Means		2.65	3.62	2.98

NOTE: 1 means *I can't really tell*, and 4 *He almost certainly meant*.

To examine coherence, we created two types of vignettes, six with coherent sets of acts, and six with incoherent sets. Table 4 illustrates a vignette with a coherent set of acts. All three acts attributed to Harry Wilson are about improving his house, or getting his house ready for summer. Table 5 illustrates a vignette with an incoherent set of acts. For the three acts attributed to Elvis Edmunds, there is no obvious rationale for placing them in the same set. Students should find it easier to treat the coherent acts than the incoherent acts as defining a type of act. They should interpret *do a Harry Wilson* as "improve the house"; they should *not* interpret *do an Elvis Edmunds* as defined by the three acts in Table 5 taken as a collection.

For each vignette there were three completions, as illustrated in Tables 4 and 5. The *unrestricting* completions contained the bare eponymous verb phrase, as in *This summer I plan to do a Harry Wilson.* The *restricting* completions contained an additional qualifying phrase intended to narrow down the interpretation to the single salient act in each vignette with one salient act, or to the same act in its paired vignette with three salient acts. In Table 4, *This summer I plan to do a Harry Wilson to the hedges* was designed to select the interpretation "carving into animal shapes" for both forms of the vignette. The *extending* completion contained a qualifying phrase intended to pick out the same acts as in the restricting completion but to extend the meaning to another domain. In Table 4, *This summer I plan to do a Harry Wilson to a bar of soap* was designed to select the interpretation "carve into animal shapes," but to see this, students had to understand how carving shrubs could be extended to carving soap. In general, restricting completions should be the most interpretable of the three, since they pinpoint the most precisely which type of act the friend meant.

The thirty students in Experiment 2, from the same source as in Experiment 1, were divided equally into six groups. Each group was assigned one of the six versions of each vignette (one vs three salient acts, and three different completions) in a counterbalanced Latin square design. So each student read 12 vignettes, 1 for each of the 12 eponyms: half of the vignettes were coherent, half in coherent; half had one salient act, half had three; and there were equal numbers of unrestricting, restricting, and extending completions.

The students read each vignette on one sheet of paper and answered a questionnaire on a second sheet. The questionnaire had the following format:

Circle one alternative for question 1 and provide the right interpretation. Then answer question 2.

1. (a) Your friend almost certainly meant:
   (b) Your friend probably meant:
   (c) Your friend might have meant:
   (d) You can't tell what your friend meant.

2. (a) If you answered 1(a), why do you think your friend meant that?
      Why are you so certain?
   (b) If you answered 1(b), why do you think your friend meant that?
      Why are you only fairly certain?
   (c) If you answered 1(c), why do you think your friend might have meant that?
      Why are you so uncertain?
   (d) If you answered 1(d), why can't you understand what your friend meant?

Plenty of space was left for answers. The 12 vignettes were placed in an individually random order for each student.

Results and Discussion

Interpretability. The responses "Can't tell" through "Almost certainly meant" were assigned the interpretability ratings 1 through 4, as in Experiment 1, and were submitted to an analysis of variance. The mean ratings are shown in Table 6.

The three types of completions were not equally interpretable, min $F'(2, 38) = 9.44$, $p < .001$. The restricting completions were expected to be highly interpretable, since they pick out the target acts with such precision, and they were. Their ratings averaged 3.62 out of 4

TABLE 7

Percentages of Attempted Interpretations that were Narrow
for Verb Phrases with Different Completions

(Experiment 2)

Type of Vignette	Salient Acts	Type of Completion		
		Unrestricting	Restricting	Extending
Coherent	One	52 (25)	97 (30)	92 (26)
	Three	8 (24)	100 (29)	86 (22)
Incoherent	One	100 (22)	100 (28)	100 (25)
	Three	80 (20)	100 (27)	95 (21)
Means		58	99	94

NOTE: Numbers of students (out of 30) on which percentages are based are given
in parentheses; these exclude *can't tell* responses.

on the scale. The extending completions should be less interpretable
since they pick out the target acts only by analogy to a new domain,
and they were, with a mean rating of only 2.98. The unrestricting
completions should also be less interpretable since they very much
leave open which act was intended. Their mean rating was only 2.65.
The ratings of 2.98 and 2.65 are each significantly less than 3.62, min
$F'(1, 38) = 18.42$ and 8.02, respectively, $p < .01$. No other differences or interactions were reliable, most likely because there were so
few vignettes in each condition. To understand why the three types
of completions differed in interpretability, we must see how they were
interpreted.

Interpretations. Two basic strategies were adopted for interpreting
the verb phrases in these vignettes: The *narrow* strategy, in which
just one of the three acts served as the basis for interpretation; and
the *broad* strategy, in which the three acts were taken together as one
coherent act. For *do a Harry Wilson* in Table 4, a narrow strategy
would lead to a meaning like "carve into animal shapes," and a broad
strategy to "fix up the house." Table 7 lists for each of the 12 conditions the percentage of narrow interpretations and, in parentheses, the
number of instances on which each percentage is based. For example,
for coherent vignettes with one salient act and an unrestricting completion, twenty-five out of thirty students offered either a narrow or a
broad interpretation. Of these twenty-five, thirteen (or 52%) chose a
narrow interpretation, and the rest chose a broad one. The few remaining students (five of the thirty in the cell just cited) responded either
"can't tell" or, very occasionally, with an interpretation not classifiable
as either broad or narrow.

Each restricting completion was designed to be interpreted on the basis of what we will call a *target* act. For *do a Harry Wilson to the hedges*, the target was carving the hedges into animal shapes. The data in Table 7 fit these expectations. Of the 120 interpretations for restricting completions, 113, or 94%, were based on the target act. The sentential context was so specific that the target act became most salient no matter whether there was one or three salient acts, or whether the acts were coherent or incoherent. This helps explain why the verb phrases with restricting completions were judged to be the most interpretable.

The verb phrases with extending completions like *do a Harry Wilson to a bar of soap* were designed to be based narrowly on the same target acts as those with restricting completions, and for the most part, they were. Of the 120 interpretations, 87 (or 72%) were based narrowly on the target act; one more was based on a nontarget act. Only six interpretations (or 5%) were broad interpretations. So the students settled on the target act by looking for the most salient act analogous to what was required by the sentential context. We have no trouble interpreting *do a Napoleon for the camera*, even though Napoleon never posed for a camera, since his pose in paintings resembles the pose he would strike for a camera.

The unrestricting completions, like *do a Harry Wilson*, bring out salience and coherence most clearly. Without other context to constrain them, students have to search the content of a vignette for a highly valued type of act that is also the most salient in the vignette. If the three acts are coherent, students can adopt the broad strategy—as with "fix up the house" for *do a Harry Wilson*—and they often did. The broad strategy was used for 69% of the coherent vignettes, but for only 10% of the incoherent vignettes, min $F'(1, 21) = 16.43$, $p < .001$. In the few instances where the broad strategy *was* used for the incoherent vignettes, it yielded such special interpretations as "do unconventional things" or "be eccentric." Coherence, then, is an important criterion for the type of act chosen.

So too is salience, as we can also see in the unrestricting completions. When the vignettes were coherent, students could give either a broad or a narrow interpretation. They would be attracted to a narrow interpretation only if one and only one of the three acts was especially salient. Indeed, for the coherent vignettes, 52% of the interpretations were narrow when there was just one salient act; only 8% were narrow when there were three salient acts, min $F'(1, 17) = 5.64$, $p < .03$. All it takes is a single salient act associated with the eponym, as in *I have just done twenty John Hancocks*, for people to latch onto an interpretation they are happy with.

4 Sense Selection and Sense Creation

Listeners cannot comprehend words entirely by selecting senses from the mental lexicon, as many theories assume. They must also create senses from information they believe is common ground to the speaker and his addressees. Word comprehension, then, can be viewed as a mixture of sense selection and sense creation. What distinguishes the two processes? How are they interleaved? We first take up a pure case of sense creation—the interpretation of eponymous verb phrases.

Sense Creation

It is easy to see, informally, how speakers expect eponymous verb phrases to work. With *do a Napoleon*, the photographer wanted to denote a type of act—posing hand in jacket—which, let us suppose, reminded her of Napoleon. She believed you shared knowledge about Napoleon's pose, so if she simply alluded to Napoleon in this situation, you would see the type of act she was denoting. She realized she was not leading you along a conventional route from words to meanings. But by pointing you in the right direction, she was confident you could make the journey on your own.

To understand her, you had to suppose that she thought you knew about certain acts associated with Napoleon and that from her allusion you could fix on the type of act she was denoting. What this meant in practice was that you had to assume that the denoted act was definable from a *coherent* set of Napoleon's acts she believed was *salient* in your common ground—a set of acts distinctive of Napoleon in this situation and readily accessible in memory. In Experiment 2, the interpretations students created showed their appreciation for both salience and coherence. The information people have about the acts associated with eponyms, we have assumed, is hierarchical in form. In Experiment 1, there was evidence for both eponym and context-centered processes in the use of that hierarchy. In the eponym-centered process, they begin with the eponym's name—say, Nixon—and work within the following hierarchy of constraints: (1) Nixon's identity; (2) acts associated with Nixon; (3) types of acts associated with Nixon relevant to this context; and (4) the type of act from 3 that the speaker intended. The further down the hierarchy listeners can get, the more confident they are that they have created the right interpretation. In the context-centered process, listeners use the situation and sentential context as clues to what the speaker meant. The more constraints the context provides, the more confident they are that they are onto the speaker's meaning. These eponym and context-centered processes work together. It is un-

TABLE 8

Comparison of Selection Process with Creation Process

SELECTION PROCESS	CREATION PROCESS
1. Senses are conventional	1. Senses are not conventional
2. Senses are enumeratable by lexicon	2. Senses are not enumeratable by lexicon
3. Sense coherence is guaranteed	3. Sense coherence is created
4. Word has small number of senses	4. Word has many potential senses
5. Intended sense is selected	5. Intended sense is created
6. Word prompts access to intended sense	6. Word prompts recall of relevent information
7. All needed information is in lexicon	7. At least some needed information is world knowledge

likely that addressees consider all the acts they know associated with Nixon (level 2 in the hierarchy). The only ones they need to consider are those appropriate to the rest of the speaker's utterance and those the speaker could assume are readily accessible in memory. Experiment 1 yielded evidence consistent with this view.

Sense Selection

For comparison, let us consider a pure case of sense selection. Suppose you hear the word *radish* in *I have two radishes.* According to one dictionary, *radish* has two senses, "plant of the genus *Raphanus*" and "pungent root of such a plant." As summarized in Table 8, such senses are conventional: each is listed in the mental lexicon; each is guaranteed to be coherent—to become conventional a sense must be coherent; and there are only a small number of conventional senses. To understand *radish*, you consider the two senses in the mental lexicon, assuming the speaker is "pointing" to one of them, and select the one that fits best. With this utterance, you are led, say, to the first sense.

Sense creation in its pure form contrasts on all but one of these properties with sense selection. For *Napoleon* in *do a Napoleon*, the potential senses are *not* conventional, *not* listed in the lexicon, *not* guaranteed to be coherent, and *not* finite in number. To understand *Napoleon*, you must assume the speaker is prompting the recall of historical information as the basis for creating a sense. Whereas each conventional sense is a prepackaged bundle of information that is recognized as shared by most speakers—that is what it takes to be conventional—your beliefs about Napoleon are more loosely organized. Some of these beliefs are shared by other people, and others are not, and it is only on hearing *do a Napoleon* that you need to decide which ones are shared by your friend. Whereas you might, as some theories assume, automatically activate all the conventional senses of a word each time you hear it, it is unlikely that you activate all the acts you know associated with Napoleon—or Richard Nixon or Elizabeth Taylor. Nevertheless, the sense you do create is, like its selected counterpart, measured against the reciprocity principle.

Sense Selection Mixed with Sense Creation

Although sense creation is found in a pure form with novel eponymous expressions, it comes mixed with sense selection in most, perhaps all, other contextual expressions. In *You'll have to ask a zero*, the caller was intended both to select the conventional meaning "naught" and to create the novel meaning "person you can reach on a telephone by dialing [naught]." As the square brackets indicate, the created sense was built around the selected sense. This is always true in mixed cases. So there are constraints on how the two processes get interleaved: creating the intended sense cannot be truly complete until the right conventional sense has been selected.

For most words, however, listeners have no way of telling whether they should look for a conventional or a novel sense except by trying to understand what the speaker meant (Chapter 10, this volume). Words (and the sentences they are carried by) generally do not come inscribed "This has a conventional meaning" or "This has a novel meaning." When our caller heard *zero*, the sentence did not tell her whether the sense was conventional or novel. She discovered that only by trying to understand what the operator meant. A grocery clerk once asked one of us, Clark, *Do you have one or two radishes there?* For *radish*, Clark created the sense "bunch of [plants of the genus *Raphanus*]" instead of selecting the sense "plant of the genus *Raphanus*" only because it was obvious that he had many radishes and they came in bunches.

One possible model, the *strict serial model*, would assume that listeners (1) exhaustively try out all the conventional senses in the lexicon, evaluating each one for plausibility, and then (2) if none of these is plausible, try to create the intended sense around one of those conventional senses. Another model, the *parallel model*, would assume that listeners begin creating senses while they are accessing senses from the lexicon. They could use the situation to create a partial sense, such as "person one can somehow reach in the telephone company" for *zero* and "bunch of something" for *radish*, and then select a conventional sense to fill in the missing information—for "somehow" with *zero* and for "something" with *radish*. In Experiment 1, students often exploited a context-centered process, and that favors the parallel model. Still, the evidence we have examined is hardly definitive.

It isn't surprising that meaning creation should be required for understanding words, since it enters into almost every other type of understanding too. Analogous processes are needed for deferred reference, as in *My street* [i.e., the people on my street] *voted Democratic in the last election* (Clark 1978; Nunberg 1979), for demonstrative reference, as in *That woman* [pointing at an empty chair at a meeting] *is home sick with the flu* (Chapter 3, this volume; Nunberg 1979), and for nonconventional indirect speech acts, as in *Do you know how late it is?* used as a reminder of an appointment (Chapters 10 and 7, this volume; Gibbs 1979; Morgan 1978; Searle 1975). All these cases, like contextual expressions, have in principle infinitely many potential interpretations, exploit the common ground in their interpretations, and are not necessarily marked as deferred or indirect. Instantaneous meaning creation, as opposed to meaning selection, seems common in language from the word on up.

Listeners are sophisticated about handling word senses. They consider the information the addressees share with the speaker, evaluate the salience and coherence of potential interpretations against this common ground, and select or create interpretations as specific as this common ground allows—all with deceptive ease. They mix sense creation with sense selection even in the absence of sentential cues. For a theory of language comprehension to be correct, it must characterize how they manage this.

12

Words, the World, and Their Possibilities

By the principle of possibilities, we understand what an entity is with reference to what it could have been. The word *red*, for example, belongs to both a domain of lexical possibilities (all English words) and a domain of conceptual possibilities (all conceivable denotations). But on any occasion the word is intended to be understood against much narrower domains. Speakers and addressees restrict the domains on the basis of their momentary common ground—that information they believe they share and is readily accessible at the moment. For an utterance of *red potato*, the two domains might be the primary color words and the possible colors of potatoes. The color denoted by *red*, therefore, changes with the occasion of use; compare red cabbages and red hair, or a red face from sunburn, embarrassment, or clown makeup. Word meanings, it is argued, are not static dictionary entries, but products of a lexical process.

In communication we use words to signify things in the world around us. I might use *scholar* for a type of object, *eminent* for a type of state, *think* for a type of process, and *Garner* or *he* for a particular man. On the one side we have words—*scholar, eminent, think, Garner*—and on the other side, the world—its objects, states, events, and processes, both as types and as particulars. We use the words to talk about the world. But how? What is relation between the two? This is one of the fundamental questions of language use.

One of the basic insights into this issue was brought home to me by Wendell R. Garner in 1962 in his book *Uncertainty and Structure as Psychological Concepts*, and it has permeated my work every since.[1]

---

[1] I participated in a seminar with Garner on his book my very first semester in graduate school. (On the inside cover of my copy of the book is written "August

What he argued was this. We can never make sense of an entity—a word, object, process, state, event—on its own. Whatever meaning it has for us, whatever structure we see in it, comes from our understanding of the system it belongs to. If we "see a single stimulus as structured," Garner argued, it is only because we "generate an implied set of stimuli against which the particular stimulus can be contrasted, or within which the particular stimulus can be subsumed." Let me call this the *principle of possibilities:* We understand *what an entity is* with reference to *what it could have been*—the set of possibilities we infer it came from.

For Garner, this principle was crucial in understanding how two systems are linked. English words, he noted, bear relations to one another, and this he called internal structure. They also bear relations to French words; for example, *house* corresponds to *maison*. This he called external structure. The crucial point for Garner was that we cannot account for external structure without considering internal structure, the possibilities in each system separately. To translate from English to French, we need to know the inner workings of both English and French. Garner's arguments were drawn mostly from perception, but they are clearly more general than that. They apply to language use as well.

So how do words relate to the world? Most accounts have at their core a theory of word meaning based on the analogy of the dictionary. These *dictionary theories*, as I will call them, go like this: Every word has a lexical entry in memory that pairs a phonological shape, like /dog/, with a conventional meaning, like "canine animal." The conventional meaning is really a brief, partial description of some aspect of the world. All the words taken together form a list called the mental lexicon. When we need a word, we search this list for a word with the right conventional meaning. And when we hear the phonological sequence /dog/, we search the list for that shape and retrieve its conventional meaning. Although this may be somewhat of a caricature of the dictionary theories, it isn't far wrong.

Dictionary theories of word meaning, I will argue, are inadequate, and it is largely because they ignore the principle of possibilities. Let me call the domain of all possible words the *lexical domain*, and the domain of all possible objects, processes, states, and events in the world, as people conceive of them, the *conceptual domain*. Dictionary

---

1962.") So as a mere foundling in the field I was raised thinking that uncertainty and structure were important psychological concepts, and I continue to believe that. If that is a mistake, it is Garner who must be held responsible.

theories tend to disregard the internal structure of the two domains. They try to specify what words signify independently of the lexical and conceptual possibilities. The right account of signification, I will suggest, must assess both sets of possibilities. It will not be a static dictionary but a lexical process. One of my goals here is to suggest what that process might be like. As groundwork, I must begin by describing how words are used for coordinating in communication.

1 Words and Coordination

Communication is a collective activity, and collective activities take coordination. When Kate says to Jess, *Hand me that book*, the two of them have to coordinate. For one thing, they must synchronize his listening with her speaking. If he isn't listening and trying to understand precisely as she speaks, he is likely to miss what she says. They must also coordinate on content. Kate must be sure, among other things, that Jess knows English, that he sees she is the person speaking (to get *me* right), and that he notices what she is pointing at (to get *that book* right).

To coordinate, in turn, Kate and Jess must act on the basis of their current common ground—the knowledge, beliefs, and assumptions they believe they share at the moment. Their current common ground is itself based on three main sources of information (Chapter 1, this volume). The first source is their joint membership in various communities or cultural groups. If Kate and Jess know they are both English speakers, Californians, university graduates, clinical psychologists, and Giants' fans, they can take everything that is universally known, believed, or assumed within these communities to be part of their common ground. The second source is their prior conversation. All the information they have exchanged up to that moment, once they allow for memory loss, can also be assumed to be in common ground. The third source is their joint perceptual experiences. If they are both looking at a book on a table and see each other doing so, they can assume the book and its appearance are also in common ground. Two people's common ground is constantly changing. For Kate and Jess, it accumulates with every new bit of conversation and every new joint experience (Chapter 5, this volume; Lewis 1979; Stalnaker 1978).

Common ground is needed for coordinating on both the processes and the content of language use. Kate and Jess cannot synchronize her speaking with his listening without assessing who is doing what at each moment. For this they work from the joint perceptual evidence of eye gaze, gestures, facial expressions, and speech timing (Goodwin 1981;

Jefferson 1973; Schegloff 1984). Nor can they coordinate on content without appealing to common ground. Kate cannot use French with Jess unless she takes it as common ground that both know French. Nor can she mention rbi's, era's, or the infield fly rule without assuming baseball is common ground (Nunberg 1978).

What does all this have to do with signification? Signification, obviously, requires coordination too. When Kate uses a word, she must coordinate with Jess on what it signifies on that occasion. To do this, by the argument just presented, the two of them must rely on elements in their current common ground. But what elements?

The simplest assumption is that all they need is the mental lexicon. This is, in effect, what dictionary theories assume. For Kate to use *book*, she must assume that she and Jess have the same lexical entry for *book*. Most dictionary theories go no further. Indeed, they generally take for granted that everyone who speaks English has the same mental lexicon. That, of course, isn't true. Kate may know the whole field of baseball terms—*rbi, era, infield, shortstop, fly out*—while Jess doesn't. How can she discover what he knows? Here joint membership in a community or cultural group comes in handy. If it is common ground that they are both baseball fans, it is also probably common ground that they both know baseball jargon. Ultimately, every convention, such as a word meaning, is in common ground for a particular community or cultural group (Lewis 1969). *Maison* is conventional for French speakers, *rbi* for baseball aficionados, and *quark* for students of physics.

Yet, on the face of it, certain conceptual possibilities must be common ground as well. How can Kate really expect Jess to understand *rbi* if he doesn't know a lot about baseball, or *quark* if he doesn't know a lot about subatomic physics. Intuitively, it isn't enough for them to have *rbi* or *quark* in the lexical domain. They need to know the corresponding sets of possibilities in the conceptual domain as well. To see this, let us begin with a simple case and see what it requires for successful signification.

2 Conceptual Possibilities

Consider the word *red*. In dictionary theories, its lexical entry would pair the phonological shape /red/ with a conventional meaning something like this:[2]

---

[2]The *American Heritage Dictionary of the English Language* defines *red*: "Any of a group of colors that may vary in lightness and saturation, whose hue resembles that of blood; the hue of the long-wave end of the spectrum; one of the additive

red denotes the color of blood when predicated of most objects, except that *red* denotes

(1) tawny when predicated of a skin type;
(2) pinkish red when predicated of potatoes;
(3) orange when predicated of hair;
(4) purply red when predicated of wine;
(5) pinkish red when predicated of wood; and so on.

The precise color that *red* denotes depends on what it is predicated of, and the mental lexicon would have to list each of these exceptions. But there is something very wrong here. I submit that it comes from flouting the principle of possibilities and its role in coordination.

Suppose Kate is talking to Jess and uses the word *red*. In doing this, she takes as common ground two sets of possibilities. The first is the lexical field from which *red* is drawn. It might be represented this way:

primary brightness terms: ⟨black, white⟩
primary hue terms: ⟨red, yellow, green, blue⟩
secondary color terms: ⟨grey, pink, orange, brown, purple⟩
exotic color terms: ⟨maroon, ecru, chartreuse, etc.⟩
modifiers: ⟨light, dark, etc.⟩

Red belongs to the set of primary hue terms ⟨red, yellow, green, blue⟩, which contrast with the primary brightness terms on one side and with the secondary and the exotic color terms on the other. It also contrasts with *light red*, *dark red*, and other modified terms.

The second set of possibilities is the conceptual field she is talking about. Suppose that is skin color. What Kate and Jess know about that might include information like this: (1) Skin color in humans comes in a limited number of types. (2) Skin color is genetically determined. (3) Skin color is highly correlated with race. (4) Skin color can change with emotion and illness. (5) Skin color can change with exposure to the sun. (6) The skin colors determined by these factors have such and such appearances. Even if we never talked about skin colors, we would have tacit knowledge about their types, range, and origins.

But Kate and Jess also know that only part of the general color vocabulary gets applied to skin. The lexical field looks something like this:

---

or light primaries; one of the psychological primary hues, evoked in the normal observer by the long-wave end of the spectrum." I am concerned with the first part of this definition.

primary skin color terms: ⟨black, white, red, yellow, brown⟩
skin color from sun exposure: ⟨tan, brown, red⟩
skin color from emotions: ⟨red, white, pale, green, purple⟩
exotic skin color terms: ⟨sallow, ashen, livid, olive, etc.⟩

Ultimately, any color term could be applied to skin in the right circumstances.

When Kate speaks of *red skin*, just what color is she denoting? Well, it certainly isn't fire-engine red. If she is talking about the skin type, it is tawny. If she is talking about white skin with too much sun, it is the sort of dark pink that is caused by burning. If she is speaking of a red face from embarrassment, it is another sort of pink, the one caused by blood invading the capillaries. Let us focus first on the five common skin types. As English evolved, they got assigned color terms from the general vocabulary. Indeed, the commonest skin colors got covered by the commonest general color terms—*black, brown, red, yellow*, and *white*—even though they lay far from the focal colors denoted usually by these terms. (*Blue* and *green* didn't come up because there are no skin types in those regions.) The puzzle is why so–called white skin was called *white* instead of *pink*. The answer is that *white* is the commoner term, a basic brightness term, and so it is preferred over *pink*. That is, as English evolved, there was a preference for assigning the commonest possibilities in the lexical field to the commonest possibilities in the conceptual field, even when that led to distortions outside that field.

This example illustrates three broad constraints for taking the nomenclature for a general conceptual field (color in general) and applying it to a specialized conceptual field (skin color).

Similarity Constraint.   For each salient possibility in the specialized conceptual field, apply the term for the most similar possibility in the general conceptual field.

Preference Constraint.   For terms in the specialized lexical field, prefer common over uncommon terms from the general lexical field.

Exhaustiveness Constraint.   Partition the possibilities in the specialized conceptual field in such a way that, for most practical purposes, they are exhaustively covered by the chosen terms with the maximum amount of information value.[3]

These three constraints account not only for the color terms for skin types, but also for the color terms for sun exposure and emotions.

The same three constraints make sense of other conventional trans-

---

[3]This notion too was introduced to me in Garner's book *Uncertainty and Structure as Psychological Concepts*.

fers of the color vocabulary. In the local market, we find: red, brown, white, and russet potatoes; red and green cabbages; red, yellow, and green bell peppers; red, yellow, and white onions; red and white grapes; white and pink grapefruit; red, white, black, green, and yellow beans; and, of course, red, white, rosé, and green wine (green as in *green Hungarian*). Among hair colors, we find black, brown, red, blond (instead of yellow), gray, and white. None of these nomenclatures makes sense if we go strictly by the standard Munsell color chips. The reds in red hair, red potatoes, red cabbage, red bell peppers, red onions, red grapes, red beans, red wine, and red skin are very different from the blood red of the focal red Munsell chip. They are also very different from each other. They only make sense with the similarity, preference, and exhaustiveness constraints. And these constraints couldn't work if it weren't for the principle of possibilities.

To summarize so far, what we take someone to mean by a color term depends on two sets of possibilities in current common ground—those in the lexical field and those in the conceptual field. This example might tempt us into treating the mapping from one to the other as entirely conventional—as when *red* is applied to hair color—but we must not succumb to that temptation. To see why, we must look at other examples.

3   Situational Possibilities

What a word signifies depends not only on generic properties of the conceptual domain, but on the situation being described at the moment. Consider a study by Hörmann (1983) on the quantifiers *some, several,* and *a few*—or rather their German translations *einige, mehrere,* and *ein paar*.

In English there are many terms for quantifying number, and they form a rich lexical field with contrast sets such as these:

exact number: ⟨zero, one, two, three, four, ...⟩
existence: ⟨some, none⟩
universality: ⟨all, some⟩
contrastive number: ⟨many, a few⟩
estimates: ⟨a lot, numerous, several, a couple, ...⟩

When Kate says she has *six* or *some* or *a few paperclips*, Jess takes her as saying something about the number of paperclips she has. With *six* he may infer the number to be exactly six, but what about the other quantifiers? They are useful precisely because they suggest a range of numbers rather than an exact count. Still, that range is usually centered around a middle value. How do we compute that value?

Hörmann's study suggests an answer. He gave people expressions like *several crumbs* and asked them to judge how many objects were being denoted. For each judgment they were to provide a range of values. Indeed, their judgments varied with what was being described. The median estimate was 9.69 for *several crumbs*, 8.15 for *several paperclips*, 7.27 for *several pills*, but only 5.75 for *several children*, 5.50 for *several cars*, and 5.27 for *several mountains*. The numbers got smaller as people went from *several small cars* to *several cars* to *several large cars*. As Hörmann observed, the larger the object, generally the fewer objects inferred. But why?

The answer I will suggest depends crucially on the principle of possibilities. When we hear *several crumbs* or *several mountains*, we imagine a scene typical of crumbs or mountains. To decide how many crumbs or mountains we should put in that scene, we consider how many of them could possibly inhabit the scene. Let me call this the maximum number possible. That number should be larger for crumbs than for mountains because in a scene typical of crumbs or mountains, we will imagine more crumbs than mountains.

On the other side, within the lexical field, *several* contrasts with the other quantifiers. It cannot denote an exact number like one, two, three, or four because otherwise the speaker would have used *one, two, three,* or *four*. Also, it must contrast with *none* on the low side and with *all, many,* and *a lot* on the high side. That is, *several* will be more than *none*, different from *one, two*, etc., different from *a few*, and less than *many, numerous, a lot*, etc. So when the maximum number possible is large, as with crumbs, its median number should be high, and when the maximum number possible is small, as with mountains, the median number should be low. And this is what Hörmann found.

Other evidence Hörmann collected fits this view. Consider these sentences (translated from German) and people's median estimates for *a few*:

In front of the hut are standing a few people:	4.55
In front of the house are standing a few people:	5.33
In front of the city hall are standing a few people:	6.34
In front of the building are standing a few people:	6.69

The larger the space, the more possible people there can be, and the higher the median estimates. The same goes for these:

Out of the window one can see a few people:	5.86
Out of the window one can see a few cars:	5.45
Through the peephole one can see a few people:	4.76
Through the peephole one can see a few cars:	3.95

So people appear to assess the possibilities afforded by the physical situation and estimate the numbers accordingly.

People make surprisingly subtle judgments of the situation in assessing the possibilities, as shown in these three pairs:

In front of the city hall there are a few people standing:	6.34
In front of the city hall there are a few people working:	5.14
Out of the window one can see a few people:	5.86
Out of the window one can see a few people arguing:	3.60
In the morning he read a few poems:	4.59
In the morning he wrote a few poems:	3.44

In the scheme I am proposing, people can imagine more possible gawkers than workers, more possible silent people than arguing people, and more possible poems read than poems written in an average morning. That is the source of their differing judgments.

As Hörmann argued, it is impossible to provide a dictionary account for these findings. Suppose the entry for *a few* read as follows: "denotes from 2 to 20 with a median of about 10 when applied to crumbs, from 2 to 18 with a median of about 7 when applied to paperclips, etc." Already the definition is problematic, for it contains a long, perhaps infinite, list of items. But it has a more fundamental flaw. The number for *a few* isn't really fixed for each item on the list. For poems it changes with whether they are written or read. For people, it changes with whether they are in front of a hut or a city hall, standing or working, arguing or not arguing, or seen through a window or seen through a peephole.

Suppose, instead, the entry for *a few* read "denotes the 25th percentile (range: 10th to 40th percentile) on the distribution of items inferred possible in that situation." This comes close to the picture just presented. But, as I will argue, it still doesn't take account of the particular quantifiers that *a few* contrasts with in each situation, and these change with the situation. So a dictionary theory is problematic for quantifiers. What they signify is tightly constrained by the possibilities both in their lexical neighborhoods and in the situations being described (see also Morrow & Clark 1988).

4   Lexical Possibilities

But why should lexical neighborhoods matter? For an answer, let me start with the view of language use taken by the philosopher Paul Grice (1975). Conversations, he argued, "are characteristically, to some degree at least cooperative efforts; and each participant recognizes in them, to some extent, a common purpose or set of purposes, or at least a mutually accepted direction" (p. 45). So the participants expect each other to follow what he called the cooperative principle: "Make your conversational contribution such as is required, at the stage at which it occurs, by the accepted purpose or direction of the talk exchange in which you are engaged" (p. 45).

For people to contribute to the accepted purpose or direction of the talk exchange, they must get their addressees to recognize their own purposes. So at the core of Grice's program is a principle I will characterize this way:

Choice Principle. Speakers choose each expression they use from a set of possible expressions for a purpose that they m-intend their addressees to recognize.[4]

When Kate uses the word *dog*, as in *I have a dog*, she does so for a purpose that she expects Jess to recognize. "Of course, she does," you say. "She wants to denote a dog, and the way to do this in English is with the word *dog*." But she had options. She could have used *hound, German shepherd, animal, canine*, or many other terms. Why *dog*? Jess can assume she had a reason, and one she intended him to recognize. Once again, the principle of possibilities comes to the fore. Each expression is chosen from a set of possible expressions, and each choice means something.

The choice principle has many consequences, and one of the most fundamental is the so-called *principle of contrast* (E. Clark 1981, 1983, 1988): Every two forms differ in meaning. As linguists have long noted, there are no true synonyms in the conventional lexicon. Consider these three pairs: *try* and *attempt*; *often* and *frequently*; and *cop* and *policeman*. Although the two terms in each pair can be used to denote the same thing, the first term is of a lower register than the second. *Try, often,* and *cop* are appropriate for informal settings, and *attempt, frequently,* and *policeman* for more formal ones. What would Kate mean, then, by saying *I was approached by that cop* in a courtroom? In line with the choice principle, she would expect us to reason: *If Kate wanted to refer neutrally in a courtroom to a policeman, she would have chosen 'policeman', or even 'police officer'. Instead, she chose 'cop', a term from a less formal register. To do so is to express a less formal and, therefore, less respectful attitude toward the policeman than expected, and that becomes part of what she meant.* Reasoning by the choice principle, indeed, leads to meaning contrasts for all choices of words.

Effort counts as part of this reasoning. At any moment, some words

---

[4]For the notion of m-intention, which is essential here, see Grice 1957, 1968.

take less effort to retrieve, utter, or understand than others, and the choice of one over the other means something relative to that effort. (Let me assume that a word that is easy to retrieve and utter is also easy to understand, even though this assumption isn't always true.) Take *pink* and *light red* (McCawley 1978). Although they could conceivably denote the same color, the choice principle dictates otherwise. *Pink* is a common expression one word long, and *light red* a less common expression two words long. When Kate tells Jess *I just bought a light red dress*, he should reason: *If Kate's dress were true pink, she would have used the less effortful term 'pink'. But since she went to the extra effort of using 'light red', she must have a special purpose that she intends me to recognize. She is distinguishing light red from true pink—and from true red—so the dress is between true red and true pink.*

Reasoning about effort in word choice is everywhere in language use. It is needed for explaining the meaning differences we invariably find between a common word and its paraphrase. Compare *Jack killed the fly* with *Jack caused the fly to die* (McCawley 1978). With *kill*, the causation is taken to be the normal, standard, or prototypical type—direct causation—whereas with the more effortful *cause to die* it is ordinarily taken to be abnormal, nonstandard, or nonprototypical—indirect causation. Or compare *Jack is a New Yorker* with *Jack is a person who lives in New York*. With *New Yorker*, we take Jack to be a standard resident of New York, a native, but with the more effortful *person who lives in New York*, we take him to be nonstandard in some respect—perhaps he is there only temporarily. So it goes with paraphrases.

Reasoning about effort also leads to a phenomenon called *preemption* (Clark & Clark 1979). If Kate wanted to refer to today, yesterday, and tomorrow, she would use *today, yesterday*, and *tomorrow*. She couldn't use *this day, the day before today*, and *the day after today*, even though they are well formed English constructions. Why not? Because *this day* requires more effort than *today*, so to choose it, Kate would have to mean something more specialized. Since she doesn't, she cannot use it and mean the same thing. An entrenched term, like *today*, preempts a more effortful expression, like *this day*, that would mean the same thing.

Preemption is a central force in the use and interpretation of novel expressions. It has two main consequences—blocking and refinement. In English, we can turn nouns into verbs almost to our heart's content, as we sty pigs, corral horses, barn cows, warehouse goods, and on and on. Yet we cannot hospital patients or prison felons. Why not? Because the two novel, hence effortful, verbs *hospital* and *prison* are preempted by the well entrenched verbs *hospitalize* and *imprison*, which would mean the same thing. Their usage is therefore blocked. We can also hip or shoulder people out of the way, and we can knee, elbow, or toe them. But to palm, foot, or fist people would have to be different from slapping, kicking, or slugging them, since otherwise we would have used *slap, kick*, or *slug*. The novel verb *to palm* gets refined by its contrasts with other words in the same lexical neighborhood.

Novel uses of language are a problem for dictionary theories (Chapters 10, and 11, this volume). A newspaper agent once asked a friend of mine, *Is the delivery boy porching your newspaper now?* using *porch* with a meaning that couldn't be in the mental lexicon. It was a meaning the agent and my friend had to create on the spot. How did they manage this? One thing they considered, clearly, was the possible relations that newspapers could have to porches as brought about by delivery boys, and which of these relations was the most salient in their current common ground. But they also tacitly considered the lexical neighborhood; *to porch* had to contrast in meaning with every other expression in that neighborhood. Dictionary theories take neither of these possibilities into account.

5 Momentary Possibilities

Lexical and conceptual possibilities matter. That we know. But if language use is a collective process, what should matter is not the lexical and conceptual possibilities *in general*, but those that are readily accessible in the participants' common ground at the moment the speaker issues an utterance. Let me call these the *momentary possibilities*. The momentary possibilities change from instant to instant in any discourse—in any conversation, narrative, newsstory—as the participants accumulate common ground. More than that, the participants can engineer these momentary possibilities and then exploit them in designing what they say next. Let us see how.

Many momentary possibilities are determined by the situation currently in the participants' focus of attention. Suppose Kate points at a group of ten men jogging and says, *That man's my neighbor*. Which man should Jess infer that she is referring to? That depends on what is salient among the momentary possibilities afforded by their view. If one of the men is naked, or is wearing a business suit, or is only four feet tall, or is running backwards, or is yelling obscenities, or is the only person Jess doesn't know, he would be seen to be the most salient possibility in their current common ground and, because of that uniqueness, the referent of *that man*. What a speaker is taken to mean is, ultimately, the most salient of the momentary possibilities in the speaker and addressees' current common ground (Chapter 3, this volume).

Word meaning is often determined by such momentary salience. Once, at a supermarket checkout counter, the clerk pointed at some radishes I was buying and asked, *Do you have one or two radishes there?* If I had taken *radish* in the conventional sense of *plant of the genus Raphanus*, I would have answered, *No, about thirty*. But given the momentary possibilities in our current common ground—largely determined by the scene in front of us—I created the novel sense *bunch of plants of the genus Raphanus* and answered *Two*. Sense creation like this is common, and it is especially dependent on the momentary possibilities (Chapter 11, this volume).

The momentary possibilities are often engineered by the participants themselves. Take Kate's use of *red*. She may be selecting it from the first six color terms ⟨black, white, red, yellow, green, blue⟩, or from these plus ⟨orange, brown, pink, grey, purple⟩, or from these plus the exotic color terms. Let us call these Set A, Set B, and Set C. She can specify the set she is entertaining at the moment by her choice of contrast. If she says, *Julia just bought a pink dress, and Margaret a red one*, Jess will assume Set B and infer that Margaret's dress is not pink or orange but closer to blood red. For *Julia just bought a maroon dress, and Margaret a red one*, he will assume Set C and infer a color even closer to blood red. But for *Margaret's the woman over there in the red dress*, Jess may assume Set A and infer that Margaret is the woman in the orange dress because the other woman is in black. So whether *red* is taken narrowly as *blood red as opposed to maroon* or less narrowly as *red as opposed to orange or pink* or more broadly as *red as opposed to green, blue, etc.* depends on the momentary lexical possibilities Kate has engineered.

The momentary possibilities can also be determined by the partner. Recall that *some* belongs to two contrast sets: ⟨none, some⟩ and ⟨some, all⟩. To choose *some* from the first set is to reject *none*, but to chose it from the second is to reject *all*. Which set is in focus at the moment can be set up by a question. If Jess asks *Did some of the students leave?* and Kate answers *Yes, in fact, all of them did*, then *some* is taken to mean *some and possibly all*. But if Jess asks *Did all of the students leave?* and Kate answers *No, but some of them did*, then *some* is taken to mean *some but not all*. Or take *two* in Kate's utterance *I have two dollars*. If Jess has just asked *How much money do you have in your hand?* then her *two* means *exactly two*. But if he has just said *I need two more dollars to buy these tickets*, now her *two* means *at least two*.

The momentary lexical possibilities can also be determined by precedent. Suppose Jess and Kate are in front of a video terminal screen full of squares with passageways between them arranged in rows and columns. They are talking about these objects as part of a computer game. This was a set up investigated by Garrod and Anderson (1987). Now the two of them could use the terms *rows, lines,* or *columns* for either the horizontal or vertical paths. So when Jess calls a vertical path *the fifth row*, he sets a temporary precedent. Rows are now vertical. By the choice principle, if Kate wants to refer to a vertical path, she has to use *row* too, and not *line* or *column*. If she wants to refer to a horizontal path, she has to use a term other than *row*, say *line* or *column*. If she were to use *row* unmodified, Jess would be justified in thinking she meant *vertical path*. This type of phenomenon Garrod and Anderson called *entrainment*, and it was pervasive in the talk of their players. It has also been observed in other types of conversation (Chapters 9, and 4, this volume; Isaacs & Clark 1987; Jefferson 1982).

The choice principle, in short, works ultimately from the possibilities in joint focus of attention at each moment in a conversation. These may arise from Jess and Kate's general knowledge of the language and of the objects being talked about. They can also arise from the lexical and conceptual possibilities that become salient to Jess and Kate only for the moment.

6 Conclusion

Words and the world, I have argued, have the meaning they do in part because of the possibilities we see them as being drawn from. This is the principle of possibilities: We understand what a thing is in part by reference to what we infer it could have been. Garner applied his version of the principle mainly to perception. When it is applied to language use, it takes on a special character. In perception, the possibilities Jess infers for a stimulus are determined largely by the *physical* constraints on the situation as Jess perceives them. In language use, the possibilities Jess infers about what Kate means are determined ultimately by *social* constraints. These constraints arise from Jess and Kate trying to coordinate on some mutually accepted purpose. But how?

When Kate and Jess talk to each other, I have argued, they are engaged in a collective activity. To succeed in any collective activity, they have to coordinate on what they are doing, and to coordinate successfully, they have to work on the basis of their common ground at that precise moment. It is ultimately this momentary common ground that determines the possibilities against which they try to interpret both words and the world.

Throughout I have argued against the traditional view of word meanings as fixed entries in a mental lexicon. I have suggested instead that word meanings are the result of a process. This process assesses the lexical and conceptual possibilities readily accessible in common ground at the moment and selects the most salient one. The challenge is to discover how this process works.

Bibliography

Åquist, L. 1972. *Performatives and verifiability by the use of language.* Upsala: Filsofiska Foereningen och Filosofiska Institutionen vid Uppsala Universitet.

Akmajian, A. 1973. The role of focus in the interpretation of anaphoric expressions. In S. R. Anderson and P. Kiparsky (Eds.), *A festshrift for Morris Halle.* New York: Holt, Rinehart, and Winston.

Anderson, J. R. 1985. *Cognitive psychology and its implications* (2nd ed.). New York: W. H. Freeman.

Anderson, J. R. 1976. *Language, memory, and thought.* Hillsdale, NJ: Erlbaum.

Anderson, J. R. 1977. Memory for information about individuals. *Memory and Cognition,* **5**, 430–442.

Anderson, J. R. 1978. The processing of referring expressions within a semantic network. In D. L. Waltz (Ed.), *Theoretical issues in natural language processing-2.* New York: Association for Computing Machinery; 51–56.

Anderson, J. R., and Bower, G. H. 1974. Interference in memory for multiple contexts. *Memory and Cognition,* **2**, 509–514.

Anderson, R. C., Pichert, J. W., Goetz, E. T., Schallert, D. L., Stevens, K. V., and Trollip, S. R. 1976. Instantiation of general terms. *Journal of Verbal Learning and Verbal Behavior,* **15**, 667–679.

Asher, S. R. 1979. Referential communication. In G. J. Whitehurst and B. J. Zimmerman (Eds.), *The functions of language and cognition,* New York: Academic Press; 175–197.

Austin, J. L. 1962. *How to do things with words.* Oxford: Oxford University Press.

Bach, K. 1975. Performatives are statements, too. *Philosophical Studies,* **18**, 229–236.

381

Bach, K., and Harnish, R. M. 1979. *Linguistic communication and speech acts*. Cambridge: MIT Press.

Barenboim, C. 1978. Development of recursive and nonrecursive thinking about persons. *Developmental Psychology*, **14**, 419–420.

Bauer, L. 1979. On the need for pragmatics in the study of nominal compounding. *Journal of Pragmatics*, **3**, 45–50.

Bell, A. 1984. Language style as audience design. *Language in Society*, **13**, 145–204.

Bennett, J. 1973. The meaning-nominalist strategy. *Foundations of Language*, **10**, 141–168.

Bennett, M. 1978. Demonstratives and indexicals in Montague grammar. *Synthese*, **39**, 1–80.

Bever, T. G. 1970. The cognitive basis for linguistic structures. In J. R. Hayes (Ed.), *Cognition and the development of language*. New York: Wiley.

Biederman, I. 1972. Perceiving real world scenes. *Science*, **177**, 77–80.

Bird, G. H. 1975. Confusing the audience. *Analysis*, **35**, 135–139.

Blank, M. A., and Foss, D. J. 1978. Semantic facilitation and lexical access during sentence processing. *Memory and Cognition*, **6**, 644–652.

Boer, S. E., and Lycan, W. G. 1975. Knowing who. *Philosophical Studies*, **28**, 299–344.

Borkin, A. 1970. Coreference and beheaded NPs. *Papers in Linguistics*, **5**, 28–45.

Bower, G. H. 1972. Stimulus-sampling theory of encoding variability. In A. W. Melton and E. Martin (Eds.), *Coding processes in human memory*. Washington, DC: V. H. Winston.

Bower, G. H., Monteiro, K. P., and Gilligan, S. G. 1978. Emotional mood as a context for learning and recall. *Journal of Verbal Learning and Verbal Behavior*, **17**, 573–585.

Bransford, J. D. 1979. *Human cognition: Learning, understanding, and remembering*. Belmont, California: Wadsworth.

Bransford, J. D. 1972. Contextual prerequisites for understanding: Some investigations of comprehension and recall. *Journal of Verbal Learning and Verbal Behavior*, II, 717–726.

Bransford, J. D., and Johnson, M. K. 1973. Considerations of some problems of comprehension. In W. G. Chase (Ed.), *Visual information processing*, New York: Academic Press.

Bransford, J. D., and McCarrell, N. S. 1974. A sketch of a cognitive approach to comprehension: Some thoughts about what it means to comprehend.

In W. B. Weimer and D. S. Palermo (Eds.), *Cognition and the symbolic processes*. Hillsdale, NJ: Lawrence Erlbaum Associates.

Brewer, W. F., and Harris, R. J. 1974. Memory for deictic elements in sentences. *Journal of Verbal Learning and Verbal Behavior*, **13**, 321–327.

Brigell, M., Uhlarik, J., and Goldhorn, P. 1977. Contextual influences on judgements of linear extent. *Journal of Experimental Psychology: Human Perception and Performance*, **3**, 105–118.

Brown, R. 1958. How shall a thing be called? *Psychological Review*, **65**, 14–21.

Brown, R., and Lenneberg, E. H. 1954. A study in language and cognition. *Journal of Abnormal and Social Psychology*, **49**, 454–462.

Bruce, B., and Newman, D. 1978. Interacting plans. *Cognitive Science*, **2**, 195–234.

Burge, T. 1973. Reference and proper names. *Journal of Philosophy*, **70**, 425–439.

Cairns, H. S., and Kamerman, J. 1975. Lexical information processing during sentence comprehension. *Journal of Verbal Learning and Verbal Behavior*, **14**, 170–179.

Carpenter, P. A., and Just, M. A. 1977. Integrative processes in comprehension. In D. LaBerge and S. J. Samuels (Eds.), *Basic processes in reading: Perception and comprehension*. Hillsdale, NJ: Erlbaum.

Carroll, J. M. 1980. Naming and describing in social communication. *Language and Speech*, **23**, 309–322.

Carroll, J. M. 1985. *What's in a name? An essay in the psychology of reference*. New York: Freeman.

Carroll, J. M., and Tanenhaus, M. K. 1975. Prolegomena to a functional theory of word information. In R. E. Grossman, L. J. San, and T. M. Vance (Eds.), *Papers from the parasession on functionalism*. Chicago: Chicago Linguistics Society.

Carroll, J. M., Tanenhaus, M. K., and Bever, T. G. 1978. The perception of relations: The interaction of structural, functional, and contextual factors in the segmention of sentences. In W. J. M. Levelt and G. B. Flores d'Arcais (Eds.), *Studies in the perception of language*. New York: Wiley.

Chafe, W. L. 1970. *Meaning and the structure of language*. Chicago: University of Chicago Press.

Chafe, W. L. 1972. Discourse structure and human knowledge. In J. B. Carroll and R. O. Freedle (Eds.), *Language comprehension and the acquisition of knowledge*. Washington DC: Winston.

Chafe, W. L. 1974. Language and consciousness. *Language*, **50**, 111–133.

Charniak, E. 1972. Towards a model of children's story comprehension. *MIT Artficial Intelligence Laboratory TR-266*.

Chomsky, N. 1965. *Aspects of the theory of syntax*. Cambridge, Mass.: MIT Press.

Chomsky, N. 1971. Deep structure, surface structure, and semantic interpretation. In L. A. Jakobovits and D. D. Steinberg (Eds.), *Semantics: An interdisciplinary reader in philosophy, psychology, linguistics, and anthropology*. Cambridge: Cambridge University Press.

Chomsky, N. 1975. *Reflections on language*. New York: Pantheon.

Christopherson, P. 1939. *The articles: A study of their theory and use in English*. Copenhagen: Munksgaard.

Clark, E. V. 1971. On the acquisition of the meaning of "before" and "after." *Journal of Verbal Learning and Verbal Behavior*, 10, 266–275.

Clark, E. V. 1973. What's in a Word? On the child's acquisition of semantics in his first language. In T. E. Moore (Ed.), *Cognitive development and the acquisition of language*. New York: Academic Press; 65–110.

Clark, E. V. 1978. From gesture to word: on the natural history of deixis in language acquisition. In J. S. Bruner and A. Garton (Eds.), *Human growth and development: Wolfson College lectures 1976*. Oxford: Oxford University Press; 85–120.

Clark E. V. 1983. Meanings and concepts. In J. H. Flavell and E. M. Markman (Eds.), *Handbook of child psychology, vol. 3: Cognitive development*, New York: John Wiley and Sons; 787–840.

Clark E. V. 1987. The principle of contrast: A constraint on language acquisition. In B. MacWhinney (Ed.), *Mechanisms of language acquisition*, Hillsdale, NJ: Erlbaum; 1–33.

Clark, E. V., and Andersen, E. S. 1979. Spontaneous repairs: Awareness in the process of acquiring language. Paper presented at the biennial meeting of the Society for Research in Child Development, San Francisco. March.

Clark, E. V., and Clark, H. H. 1979. When nouns surface as verbs. *Language*, 55, 767–811.

Clark, E. V., and Sengul, C. J. 1978. Strategies in the acquisition of deixis. *Journal of Child Language*, 5, 457–475.

Clark, H. H. 1973. The language-as-fixed-effect fallacy: A critique of language statistics in psychological research. *Journal of Verbal Learning and Verbal Behavior*, 12, 335–359.

Clark, H. H. 1978. Inferring what is meant. In W. J. M. Levelt and G. B. Flores d'Arcais (Eds.), *Studies in the perception of language*. London: Wiley.

Clark, H. H. 1979. Responding to indirect speech acts. *Cognitive Psychology*, **11**, 430–477.

Clark, H. H. 1983b. Language use and language users. In G. Lindzey and E. Aronson (Eds.), *Handbook of social psychology*. Reading, Mass.: Addison-Wesley (Third edition).

Clark, H. H. 1987. Four dimensions of language use. In M. B. Papi and J. Verschueren (Eds.), *The pragmatic perspective*, Amsterdam: John Benjamins; 9–25.

Clark, H. H., and Carlson, T. B. 1982. Speech acts and hearer's beliefs. In N. V. Smith (Ed.), *Mutual knowledge*. London: Academic Press.

Clark, H. H., and Clark, E. V. 1968. Semantic distinctions and memory for complex sentences. *Quarterly Journal of Experimental Psychology*, **20**, 129–138.

Clark, H. H., and Clark, E. V. 1977. *Psychology and language: An introduction to psycholinguistics*. New York: Harcourt Brace Jovanovich.

Clark, H. H., and Haviland, S. E. 1974. Psychological processes as linguistic explanation. In D. Cohen (Ed.), *Explaining linguistic phenomena*. Washington: Hemisphere Publication Corporation.

Clark, H. H., and Haviland, S. E. 1977. Comprehension and the given-new contract. In R. Freedle (Ed.), *Discourse production and comprehension*. Norwood, NJ: Ablex.

Clark, H. H., and Lucy, P. 1975. Understanding what is meant from what is said: A study in conversationally conveyed requests. *Journal of Verbal Learning and Verbal Behavior*, **14**, 56–72.

Clark, H. H., and Marshall, C. R. 1978. Reference diaries. In D. L. Waltz (Ed.), *Theoretical issues in natural language processing-2*. New York: Association for Computing Machinery; 57–63.

Clark, H. H., and Murphy, G. L. 1983. Audience design in meaning and reference. In J. F. LeNy and W. Kintsch (Eds.), *Language and comprehension*, Amsterdam: North-Holland Publishing Company.

Clark, H. H., and Schaefer, E. F. 1987. Collaborating on contributions to conversation. *Language and Cognitive Processes*, **2**, 1–23.

Clark, H. H., and Schunk, D. H. 1980. Polite responses to polite requests. *Cognition*, **8**, 111–143.

Clark, H. H., and Sengul, C. J. 1979. In search of referents for nouns and pronouns. *Memory and Cognition*, **7**, 35–41.

Cohen, P. R. 1978. *On knowing what to say: Planning speech acts*. Unpublished doctoral dissertation, University of Toronto, Toronto.

Cohen, P. R. 1984. The pragmatics of referring, and the modality of communication. *Computational Linguistics*, **10**, 97–146.

Cohen, P. R., and Levesque, H. J. 1990. Rational interaction as the basis for communication. In P. R. Cohen, J. Morgan, and M. E. Pollack (Eds.), *Intentions in communication*. Cambridge: MIT Press.

Cohen, P. R., and Perrault, C. R. 1979. Elements of a plan-based theory of speech acts. *Cognitive Science*, **3**, 197–212.

Comrie, B. 1976. Linguistic politeness axes: Speaker-addressee, speaker-referent, speaker-bystander. *Pragmatics Microfiche* 1:7.

Davison, A. 1975. Indirect speech acts and what to do with them. In P. Cole and J. L. Morgan (Eds.), *Syntax and semantics, vol. 3: Speech acts*. New York: Academic Press; 143–185.

Dixon, R. M. W. 1972. *The Dyirbal language of North Queensland*. Cambridge University Press.

Doll, T. J., and Lapinski, R. H. 1974. Context effects in speeded comprehension and recall of sentences. *Bulletin of the Psychonomic Society*, **3**, 342–344.

Donnellan, K. 1966. Reference and definite description. *Philosophical Review*, **75**, 281–304.

Donnellan, K. 1968. Putting Humpty Dumpty back together again. *Philosophical Review*, **77**, 203–215.

Donnellan, K. S. 1970. Proper names and identifying descriptions. *Synthese*, **21**, 335–358.

Donnellan, K. S. 1978. Speaker reference, descriptions and anaphora. In P. Cole (Ed.), *Syntax and semantics, vol. 9: Pragmatics*, New York: Academic Press; 47–68.

Dooling, D. J. 1972. Some context effects in the speeded comprehension of sentences. *Journal of Experimental Psychology*, **93**, 56–62.

Dorman, M. F. 1974. Discrimination of intensity differences on formant transitions in and out of syllable context. *Perception and Psychophysics*, **16**, 84–86.

Downing, P. A. 1977. On the creation and use of English compound nouns. *Language*, **53**, 810–842.

DuBois, J. W. 1975. Syntax in mid-sentence. In *Berkeley studies in syntax and semantics*, vol. 1. Berkeley, Calif.: Institute of Human Learning and Department of Linguistics, University of California; III-1–III-25.

Duncan, S. D. 1973. Toward a grammar for dyadic conversation. *Semiotica*, **9**, 29–47.

Eich, J. E. 1980. The cue-dependent nature of state-dependent retrieval. *Memory and Cognition*, **8**, 157–163.

Elffers, J. 1976. *Tangram. The ancient Chinese shapes game*. New York: McGraw-Hill.

Espy, W. R. 1978. *Oh thou improper, thou uncommon noun: A bobtailed, generally chronological listing of proper names that have become improper and uncommonly common, together with a smattering of proper names commonly used ..., and certain other diversions.* New York: C. N. Potter.

Ervin-Tripp, S. M. 1976. Is Sybil there? The structure of some American English directives. *Language in Society,* **5,** 25–66.

Evans, G. 1973. The causal theory of names. *Aristotelian Society Supplementary Volume* **47,** 187–208.

Fillmore, C. J. 1972. Subjects, speakers, and roles. In D. Davidson, and G. Harman (Eds.), *Semantics of natural language,* Dordrecht: Reidel; 1–24.

Fillmore, C. J. 1982. Towards a descriptive framework for spatial deixis. In R. J. Jarvella and W. Klein (Eds.), *Speech, place, and action.* New York: Wiley.

Flavell, J. H., Botkin, P. T., Fry, C. L., Wright, J. W., and Jarvis, P. E. 1968. *The development of role taking and communication skills in children.* New York: Wiley.

Fodor, J. A. 1983. *Modulariy of mind.* Cambridge: MIT Press.

Fodor, J. A., Bever, T. G., and Garrett, M. F. 1974. *The psychology of language: An introduction to psycholinguistics and generative grammar.* New York: McGraw-Hill.

Fodor, J. A., and Garrett, M. F. 1966. Some reflections on competence and performance. In J. Lyons and R. J. Wales (Eds.), *Psycholinguistics papers.* Edinburgh: Edinburgh University Press.

Forster, K. 1976. Accessing the mental lexicon. In R. J. Wales and E. C. T. Walker (Eds.), *New approaches to language mechanisms.* Amsterdam: North-Holland.

Foss, D. J., and Hakes, D. T. 1978. *Psycholinguistics: An introduction to the psychology of language.* Englewood Cliffs, NJ: Prentice-Hall.

Foss, D. J., and Jenkins, C. M. 1973. Some effects of context on the comprehension of ambiguous sentences. *Journal of Verbal Learning and Verbal Behavior,* **12,** 577–589.

Fraser, B. 1975. Hedged performatives. In P. Cole and J. L. Morgan (Eds.), *Syntax and semantics, vol. 3: Speech acts.* New York: Academic Press; 187–210.

Frazier, L., and Fodor, J. D. 1978. The sausage machine: A new two-stage parsing model. *Cognition,* **6,** 291–325.

Garfinkel, H. 1967. *Studies in ethnomethodology.* Englewood Cliffs, NJ: Prentice-Hall.

Garner, R. 1975. Meaning. In P. Cole and J. L. Morgan (Eds.), *Syntax and semantics, vol. 3: Speech acts*. New York: Academic Press; 305–361.

Garner, W. R. 1962. *Uncertainty and structure as psychological concepts*. New York: Wiley.

Garrett, M. F. 1978. Word and sentence perception. In R. Held, H. W. Liebowitz, and H. L. Teuber (Eds.), *Handbook of sensory physiology, vol. 8: Perception*. Berlin: Springer-Verlag.

Garrod, S., and Anderson, A. 1987. Saying what you mean in dialogue: A study in conceptual and semantic co-ordination. *Cognition*, **27**, 181–218.

Gazdar, G. 1979. *Pragmatics: Implicature, presupposition, and logical form*. New York: Academic Press.

Gibbs, R. 1979. Contextual effects in understanding indirect requests. *Discourse Processes*, **2**, 1–10.

Gibbs, R. W., Jr. 1981. Your wish is my command: Convention and context in interpreting indirect requests. *Journal of Verbal Learning and Verbal Behavior*, **20**, 431–444.

Giles, H., Mulac, A., Bradac, J. J., and Johnson, P. 1987. Speech accommodation theory: The first decade and beyond. In M. L. McLaughlin (Ed.), *Communication Yearbook 10*, Beverly Hills: Sage; 13–48.

Gleitman, L. R., and Gleitman H. 1970. *Phrase and paraphrase: Some innovative uses of language*. New York: Norton.

Glucksberg, S., Krauss, R. M., and Higgins, E. T. 1975. The development of referential communication skills. In F. E. Horowitz (Ed.), *Review of child development research, vol. 4*, Chicago: University of Chicago Press; 305–345.

Goffman, E. 1963. *Behavior in public places: Notes on the social organization of gatherings*. New York: Free Press of Glencoe.

Goffman, E. 1971. *Relations in public: Microstudies of the public order*. New York: Basic Books.

Goffman, E. 1976. Replies and responses. *Language in Society*, **5**, 257–313.

Goffman, E. 1978. Response cries. *Language*, **54**, 787–815.

Goffman, E. 1979. Footing. *Semiotica*, **25**, 1–29.

Goffman, E. 1981. *Forms of talk*. Philadelphia: University of Pennsylvania Press.

Goldberg, J. 1975. A system for the transfer of instructions in natural settings, *Semiotica*, **14**, 269–296.

Goldman, A. I. 1970. *A theory of human action*. Englewood Cliffs, NJ: Prentice-Hall.

Goodwin, C. 1981. *Conversational organization: Interaction between speakers and hearers*. New York: Academic.

Goodwin, C. 1986. Between and within: Alternative and sequential treatments of continuers and assessments. *Human Studies*, **9**, 205–217.

Gordon, D., and Lakoff, G. 1971. Conversational postulates. *Papers from the Chicago Linguistic Society*, **7**, 257–313.

Green, G. M. 1974. *Semantics and syntactic regularity*. Bloomington: Indiana University Press.

Green, G. M. 1975. How to get people to do things with words: The whimperative question. In P. Cole and J. L. Morgan (Eds.), *Syntax and semantics, vol. 3: Speech acts*. New York: Academic Press; 107–141.

Greenburg, D. 1964. *How to be a Jewish mother: A very lovely training manual*. Los Angeles: Price/Stern/Sloan.

Grice, H. P. 1957. Meaning. *Philosophical Review*, **66**, 377–388.

Grice, H. P. 1968. Utterer's meaning, sentence-meaning, and word-meaning. *Foundations of Language*, **4**, 225–242.

Grice, H. P. 1969. Utterer's meaning and intentions. *Philosophical Review*, **78**, 147–177.

Grice, H. P. 1975. Logic and conversation. In P. Cole and J. L. Morgan (Eds.), *Syntax and semantics, vol. 3: Speech acts*. New York: Academic Press; 225–242.

Grice, H. P. 1978. Some further notes on logic and conversation. In P. Cole (Ed.), *Syntax and semantics, vol. 9: Pragmatics*. New York: Academic Press; 113–128.

Grosz, B. J., and Sidner, C. L. 1986. Attention, intentions, and the structure of discourse. *Computational Linguistics*, **12**, 175–204.

Grosz, B. J., and Sidner, C. L. 1989. Plans for discourse. In P. R. Cohen, J. Morgan, and M. E. Pollack (Eds.), *Intentions in communication*. Cambridge: MIT Press.

Halliday, M. A. K. 1967. Notes on transitivity and theme in English: II. *Journal of Linguistics*, **3**, 199–244.

Halliday, M. A. K. 1970. Language structure and language function. In J. Lyons (Ed.), *New horizons in linguistics*. Baltimore: Penguin.

Harder, P. 1978. Language in action: Some arguments against the concept 'illocutionary'. In Gregersen, K et al. (Eds.), *Papers from the 4th Scandinavian Conference on Linguistics*, Odense: University Press; 193–197.

Harder, P., and Kock, C. 1976. *The theory of presuppostion failure*. Copenhagen: Akademisk Forlag.

Harman, G. 1977. Review of *Linguistic Behavior* by Jonathan Bennett. *Language*, **53**, 417–424.

Haviland, S. E., and Clark H. H. 1974. What's new? Acquiring new information as a process in comprehension. *Journal of Verbal Learning and Verbal Behavior*, **13**, 512–521.

Hawkins, J. A. 1978. *Definiteness and indefiniteness: A study in reference and grammaticality prediction*. London: Croom Helm.

Heal, J. 1974. Explicit performative utterances and statements. *Philosophical Quarterly*, **24**, 106–121.

Heim, I. 1983. File change semantics and the familiarity theory of definiteness. In R. Bauerle, C. Schwarze, and A. von Stechow (Eds.), *Meaning, use and interpretation of language*, Berlin: W. de Gruyter; 294–338.

Hörmann, H. 1983. *Was tun die Worter miteinander im Satz? oder Wieviele sind einige, mehrere und ein paar?* Göttingen: Verlag für Psychologie, Dr. C. J. Hogrefe.

Huttenlocher, J., and Wiener, S. L. 1971. Comprehension of instructions in varying contexts. *Cognitive Psychology*, **2**, 369–385.

Isaacs, E. A., and Clark, H. H. 1987. References in conversations between experts and novices. *Journal of Experimental Psychology: General*, **116**, 26–37.

Jackendoff, R. S. 1972. *Semantic interpretation in generative grammar*. Cambridge: MIT Press.

Jefferson, G. 1972. Side sequences. In D. Sudnow (Ed.), *Studies in social interaction*. New York: Free Press; 294–338.

Jefferson, G. 1973. A case of precision timing in ordinary conversation: Overlapped tag-positioned address terms in closing sequences. *Semiotica*, **9**, 47–96.

Jefferson, G. 1982. On exposed and embedded correction in conversation. *Studium Linguistik*, **14**, 58–68.

Jenkins, J. J. 1974. Remember that old theory of memory? Well, forget it! *American Psychologist*, **29**, 785–795.

Jespersen, O. 1949. *A modern English grammar on historical principles, vol. 7*. Copenhagen: Munksgaard.

Johnson-Laird, P. N. 1983. *Mental models: Towards a cognitive science of language, inference, and consciousness*. Cambridge: Harvard University Press.

Jone, Rev. H. 1959. *Moral theology* (tr. Urban Adelman). Westminster, MD: Newman Press.

Kahn, D. 1967. *The codebreakers: The story of secret writing*. New York: Macmillan.

Kamp, J. A. W. 1981. A theory of truth and semantic representation. In J. Groenendijk, T. Janssen, and M. Stockhof (Eds.), *Formal methods in the study of language, Part 1*, Amsterdam: Mathematical Centre Tracts; 177–321.

Kaplan, R. 1972. Augmented transition networks as psychological models of sentence comprehension. *Artificial Intelligence*, **3**, 77–100.

Kaplan, R. 1973(a). A general syntactic processor. In R. Rustin (Ed.), *Natural language processing*. Englewood Cliffs, NJ: Prentice-Hall.

Kaplan, R. 1973(b). A multi-processing approach to natural language. In *Proceedings of the first national computer conference*. Montvale, NJ: AFIPS Press.

Kaplan, R. 1975. *Transient processing load in sentence comprehension*. Unpublished doctoral dissertation. Harvard University.

Kaplan, R., and Bresnan, J. W. 1982. Lexical-functional grammar: A formal system for grammatical representation. In J. W. Bresnan (Ed.), *The mental representation of grammatical relations*. Cambridge, Mass.: M.I.T. Press.

Karttunen, L. 1977. Presupposition and lingusitic context. In A. Rogers, B. Wall, and J. P. Murphy (Eds.), *Proceedings of the Texas conference on performatives, presuppositions, and implicatures*. Arlington, Va.: Center for Applied Linguistics; 149–160.

Karttunen, L., and Peters, S. 1975. *Conventional implicature of Montague grammar*. Berkeley Linguistic Society, **1**, 266–278.

Katz, J. J. 1964. Semi-sentences. In J. A. Fodor and J. J. Katz (Eds.), *The structure of language: Readings in the philosophy of language*. Englewood Cliffs, NJ: Prentice-Hall.

Katz, J. J. 1972. *Semantic theory*. New York: Harper and Row.

Katz, J. J. 1977. *Propositional structure and illocutionary force*. New York: Crowell.

Kay, P., and Zimmer, K. 1976. *On the semantics of compounds and genitives in English*. Paper presented at the Sixth Annual Meeting of the California Linguistics Association, San Diego, California, May.

Keenan, J. M., MacWhinney, B., and Mayhew, D. 1977. Pragmatics in memory: A study of natural conversation. *Journal of Verbal Learning and Verbal Behavior*, **16**, 549–560.

Kempson, R. 1975. *Presupposition and the delimitation of semantics*. Cambridge: University Press.

Kempson, R. 1977. *Semantic theory*. Cambridge: University Press.

Kimball, J. 1973. Seven principles of surface structure parsing in natural language. *Cognition*, **2**, 15–47.

Kimball, J. 1975. Predictive analysis and over-the-top parsing. In J. Kimball (Ed.), *Syntax and semantics, vol. 4*. New York: Academic Press.

Kintsch, W. 1974. *The representation of meaning in memory.* Hillsdale, NJ: Erlbaum.

Kintsch, W., and van Dijk, T. A. 1978. Toward a model of text comprehension and production. *Psychological Review,* **85**, 363–394.

Krauss, R. M., and Glucksberg, S. 1969. The development of communication: Competence as a function of age. *Child Development,* **40**, 255–256.

Krauss, R. M., and Glucksberg, S. 1977. Social and nonsocial speech. *Scientific American,* **236**, 100–105.

Krauss, R. M., and Weinheimer, S. 1964. Changes in reference phrases as a function of frequency of usage in social interaction: A preliminary study. *Psychonomic Science,* **1**, 113–114.

Krauss, R. M., and Weinheimer, S. 1966. Concurrent feedback, confirmation, and the encoding of referents in verbal communication. *Journal of Personality and Social Psychology,* **4**, 343–346.

Krauss, R. M., and Weinheimer, S. 1967. Effect of referent similarity and communication mode on verbal encoding. *Journal of Verbal Learning and Verbal Behavior,* **6**, 359–363.

Kraut, R. E., Lewis, S. H., and Swezey, L. W. 1982. Listener responsiveness and the coordination of conversation. *Journal of Personality and Social Psychology,* **43(4)**, 718–731.

Kripke, S. 1972. Naming and necessity. In D. Davidson and G. Harman (Eds.), *Semantics of natural languages.* Dordrecht: Reidel; 253–355.

Kripke, S. 1977. Speaker's reference and semantic reference. In P. A. French, T. E. Uehling, Jr., and H. K. Wettstein (Eds.), *Contemporary perspectives in the philosophy of language.* Minneapolis: University of Minnesota Press; 627.

Kuno, S. 1972. Funcional sentence perspective: A case study from Japanese and English. *Linguistic Inquiry,* **3**, 269–320.

Kuno, S. 1975. Three perspectives in the functional approach to syntax. In R. E. Grossman, L. J. San, and T. J. Vance (Eds.), *Papers from the parasession on functionalism.* Chicago: Chicago Linguistic Society.

Lakoff, G. 1971. The role of deduction in grammar. In C. J. Fillmore and D. T. Langendoen (Eds.), *Studies in linguistic semantics.* New York: Holt, Rinehart, and Winston.

Lakoff, G. 1975. Pragmatics in natural logic. In Keenan, E. L. (Ed.), *Formal semantics of natural language,* Cambridge: University Press; 253–286.

Lakoff, R. T. 1972. Language in context. *Language.* **48**, 907–927.

Lakoff, R. 1974. Remarks on *this* and *that. Papers from the Chicago Linguistic Society,* **10**, 345–356.

Lasnik, H. 1976. Remarks on coreference. *Linguistic Analysis.* **2**, 1–22.

Laver, J. D. M. 1973. The detection and correction of slips of the tongue. In V. A. Fromkin (Ed.), *Speech errors as linguistic evidence*, The Hague: Mouton; 132–143.

Lees, R. B. 1960. The grammar of English nominalizations. *International Journal of American Linguistics*, **26**, Publication 12.

Lehrer, A. 1969. Semantic cuisine. *Journal of Linguistics*, **5**, 39–55.

Lerner, G. H. 1987. *Collaborative turn sequences: Sentence construction and social action*. Unpublished Ph.D. dissertation, University of California, Irvine, CA.

Lesgold, A. M., Roth, S. F., and Curtis, M. E. 1979. Foregrounding effects in discourse comprehension. *Journal of Verbal Learning and Verbal Behavior*, **18**, 291–308.

Levelt, W. J. M. 1983. Monitoring and self-repair in speech. *Cognition*, **14**, 41–104.

Levi, J. N. 1978. *The syntax and semantics of complex nominals*. New York: Academic Press.

Levinson, S. C. 1979. Pragmatics and social deixis: Reclaiming the notion of conventional implicature. *Berkeley Linguistic Society*, **5**, 206–223.

Lewis, D. K. 1969. *Convention: A philosophical study*. Cambridge: Harvard University Press.

Lewis, D. K. 1970. General semantics. *Synthese*, **22**, 18–67.

Lewis, D. K. 1979. Scorekeeping in a language game. *Journal of Philsophical Logic*, **8**, 339–359.

Li, C. N. 1971. *Semantics and the structure of compounds in Chinese*. Unpublished doctoral dissertation. University of California, Berkeley.

Liberman, A. M., Cooper, F. S., Shankweiler, D. P., and Studdert-Kennedy, M. 1967. Perception of the speech code. *Psychological Review*, **74**, 431–461.

Litman, D. J., and Allen, J. F. 1987. A plan recognition model for subdialogues in conversation. *Cognitive Science*, **11**, 163–200.

Lockman, A., and Klappholz, A. D. 1980. Toward a procedural model of contextual reference resolution. *Discourse Processes*, **3**, 25–71.

Lyons, J. 1975. Deixis as the source of reference. In E. L. Keenen (Ed.), *Formal semantics of natural language*. Cambridge: Cambridge Univ. Press.

Lyons, J. 1977. *Semantics, vols. 1 and 2*. London: Cambridge Univ. Press.

McCawley, J. D. 1978. Conversational implicature and the lexicon. In P. Cole (Ed.), *Syntax and semantics, vol. 9: Pragmatics*. New York: Academic Press; 245–259.

394 / ARENAS OF LANGUAGE USE

McCawley, J. D. 1979. Presupposition and discourse structure. In C. K. Oh (Ed.), *Syntax and semantics, vol. 13: Presupposition*. New York: Academic Press.

McCawley, J. M. 1971. Prelexical syntax. In R. J. O'Brien (Ed.), *Linguistic developments of the sixties–Viewpoints for the seventies. Monograph Series on Languages and Linguistics.* Georgetown University, **24**, 19–33.

McGregor, G. 1986. Listening outside the participation framework. In G. McGregor and R. S. White (Eds.), *The art of listening*, London: Croom Helm; 55–72.

MacKay, D. G. 1970. Mental diplopia: Towards a model of speech perception. In G. B. Flores d'Arcais and W. J. M. Levelt (Eds.), *Advances in Psycholinguistics*. Amsterdam: North-Holland.

Maclaran, R. 1980. On two asymmetrical uses of the demonstrative determiners in English. *Linguistics*, **18**, 803–820.

Maclay, H., and Osgood, C. E. 1959. Hesitation phenomena in spontaneous English speech. *Word*, **75**, 19–44.

Mandler, J. M., and Johnson, N. S. 1977. Remembrance of things parsed: Story structure and recall. *Cognitive Psychology*, **9**, 111–151.

Maratsos, M. P. 1976. *The use of definite and indefinite reference in young children: An experimental study of semantic acquisition*. Cambridge: Cambridge University Press.

Marslen-Wilson, W. D., and Tyler, L. K. 1980. The temporal structure of spoken language understanding. *Cognition*, **8**, 1–71.

Marlsen-Wilson, W. D., and Welsh, A. 1978. Processing interactions and lexical access during word recognition in continuous speech. *Cognitive Psychology*, **10**, 29–63.

McGeoch, J. A. 1939. Learning. In E. G. Boring, H. S. Langfeld, and H. P. Weld (Eds.), *Introduction to psychology*, New York: Wiley.

Merritt, M. W. 1976. On questions following questions (in service encounters). *Language in Society*, **5**, 315–357.

Meyer, D. E., Schvaneveldt, R. W., and Ruddy, M. G. 1975. Loci of contextual effects on visual word-recognition. In P. Rabbitt and S. Dornic (Eds.), *Attention and performance, vol. 5*. New York: Academic Press.

Millar, M., and Brown, K. 1979. Tag questions in Edinburgh speech. *Linguistische Berichte*, **60**, 24–45.

Miller, G. A. 1951. *Language and communication*. New York: McGraw-Hill.

Miller, G. A., Heise, G., and Lichten, W. 1951. The intelligibility of speech as a function of the context of the test materials. *Journal of Experimental Psychology*, **4**, 329–335.

Miller, G. A. 1978. Semantic relations among words. In M. Halle, J. Bresnan, and G. A. Miller (Eds.), *Linguistic theory and psychological reality*. Cambridge: MIT Press.

Miller, G. A., and Chomsky, N. 1963. Finitary models of language users. In R. D. Luce, R. R. Bush, and E. Galanter (Eds.), *Handbook of mathematical psychology, vol. 1*. New York: Wiley.

Miller, P. H., Kessel, F. S., and Flavell, J. H. 1970. Thinking about people thinking about people thinking about...: A study of social-cognitive development. *Child Development*, 41, 613–623.

Minsky, M. 1975. A framework for representing knowledge. In P. Winston (Ed.), *The psychology of computer vision*. New York: McGraw-Hill, pp. 211–277.

Moravcsik, E. A. 1969. Determination. *Working Papers in Language Universals*. Stanford, Calif.: Stanford University, 1, 64–98.

Morgan, J. L. 1977. Conversational postulates revisited. *Language*, 53, 277–284.

Morgan, J. L. 1978. Two types of convention in indirect speech acts. In Cole, P. (Ed.), *Syntax and semantics, vol. 9: Pragmatics*. New York: Academic Press; 261–280.

Morrow, D. G., and Clark, H. H. 1988. Interpreting words in spatial descriptions. *Language and Cognitive Processes*, 3, 275–291.

Morton, J. 1964. The effects of context on the visual duration threshold for words. *British Journal of Psychology*, 55, 165–180.

Morton, J. 1969. The interaction of information in word recognition. *Psychological Review*, 76, 165–178.

Morton, J. 1970. A functional model for memory. In D. A. Norman (Ed.), *Models of human memory*. New York: Academic Press.

Munro, A. 1977. *Speech act understanding in context*. Unpublished doctoral dissertation. University of California at San Diego.

Nunberg, G. D. 1977. *The pragmatics of reference*. Unpublished doctoral dissertation, City University of New York.

Nunberg, G. 1978. Slang, usage conditions, and l'abitraire‾ du signe. In D. Farkas, W. M. Jacobsen, and K. W. Todrys (Eds.), *Papers from the parasession on the lexicon*. Chicago: Chicago Linguistic Society; 301–311.

Nunberg, G. 1979. The non-uniqueness of semantic solutions: Polysemy. *Linguistics and Philosophy*, 3, 143–184.

Olson, D. R. 1970. Language and thought: Aspects of cognitive theory of semantics. *Psychological Review*, 77, 257–273.

Oreström, B. 1983. *Turn-taking in English conversation*. Lund, Sweden: Gleerup.

Ortony, A., and Anderson, R. C. 1977. Definite descriptions and semantic memory. *Cognitive Science*, 1, 74–83.

Palmer, S. E. 1975. The effects of contextual scenes on the identification of objects. *Memory and Cognition*, 3, 519–526.

Pechmann, T., and Deutsch, W. 1982. The development of verbal and non-verbal devices for reference. *Journal of Experimental Child Psychology*, 34, 330–341.

Perrault, C. R., and Cohen, P. R. 1981. It's for your own good: A note on inaccurate reference. In A. Joshi, B. Webber, and I. A. Sag (Eds.), *Elements of discourse understanding*, 217–230. Cambridge: Cambridge University Press.

Polanyi, L., and Scha, R. 1985. A discourse model for natural language. In L. Polanyi (Ed.), *The structure of discourse*. Norwood, NJ: Ablex.

Prince, E. F. 1978. On the function of existential presupposition in discourse. In *Papers from the Chicago Linguistics Society*, 14, 362–376.

Prince, E. F. 1981. Toward a taxonomy of given-new information. In P. Cole (Ed.), *Radical pragmatics*. New York: Academic Press.

Psathas, G. (Ed.) 1979. *Everyday language: Studies in ethnomethodology*. New York: Wiley.

Ragan, S. L. 1983. Alignment and conversational coherence. In R. T. Craig and K. Tracy (Eds.), *Conversational coherence: Form, structure, and strategy*. Beverly Hills: Sage Publications; 157–171.

Randolph, V. 1928. Verbal modesty in the Ozarks. *Dialect Notes*, 6, 57–64.

Reichman, R. 1978. Conversational coherency. *Cognitive Science*, 2, 283–327.

Reiff, R. R., and Scheerer, M. 1959. *Memory and hypnotic age regression*. New York: International Universities Press.

Rescher, N. 1966. *The logic of commands*. London: Routledge and Kegan Paul.

Ross, J. R. 1970. On declarative sentences. In R. A. Jacobs and P. S. Rosenbaum (Eds.), *Readings in English transformational grammar*. Waltham: Ginn; 222–272.

Rubenstein, H., and Pollack, I. 1963. Word predictability and intelligibility. *Journal of Verbal Learning and Verbal Behavior*, 2, 147–158.

Rubin, A. 1978. A framework for comparing language experiences. In D. Waltz (Ed.), *TINLAP-2: Theoretical issues in natural language processing-2*. New York: Association for Computing Machinery; 133–140.

Rumelhart, D. E., and Ortony, A. 1977. The representation of knowledge in memory. In R. C. Anderson, R. J. Spiro, and W. E. Montague (Eds.),

Schooling and the acquisition of knowledge. Hillsdale, N.J.: Lawerence Erlbaum Associates.

Rumelhart, D. E., Lindsay, P. H., and Norman, D. A. 1972. A process model for long-term memory. In E. Tulving and W. Donaldson (Eds.), *Organization of Memory.* New York: Academic Press; 197–246.

Russell, B. 1905. On denoting. *Mind,* **14,** 479–493.

Sacks, H., and Schegloff, E. 1979. Two preferences in the organization of reference to persons in conversation and their interaction. In G. Psathas (Ed.), *Everyday language: Studies in ethnomethodology.* New York: Irvington; 15–21.

Sacks, H., Schegloff, E. A., and Jefferson, G. A. 1974. A simplest systematics for the organization of turn-taking in conversation. *Language,* **50,** 696–735.

Sadock, J. M. 1974. *Toward a linguistic theory of speech acts.* New York: Academic Press.

Schank, R. C., and Abelson, R. P. 1977. *Scripts, plans, goals, and understanding: An inquiry into human knowledge.* Hillsdale, N.J.: Lawerence Erlbaum Associates.

Schegloff, E. A. 1968. Sequencing in conversational openings. *American Anthropologist,* **70,** 1075–1095.

Schegloff, E. A. 1972. Notes on a conversational practice: Formulating place. In D. Sudnow (Ed.), *Studies in social interaction.* New York: Free Press.

Schegloff, E. A. 1982. Discourse as an interactional achievement: Some uses of 'uh huh' and other things that come between sentences. In D. Tannen (Ed.), *Analyzing discourse: Text and talk. 32nd Georgetown University Roundtable on Languages and Linguistics 1981.* Washington, DC: Georgetown University Press; 71–93.

Schegloff, E. A. 1984. On some gestures' relation to talk. In J. M. Atkinson, and J. Heritage (Eds.), *Structures of social action: Studies in conversation analysis.* Cambridge: Cambridge University Press.

Schegloff, E. A., Jefferson, G., and Sacks, H. 1977. The preference for self-correction in the organization of repair in conversation. *Language,* **53,** 361–382.

Schegloff, E. A., and Sacks, H. 1973. Opening up closings. *Semiotica,* **8,** 289–327.

Schelling, T. C. 1960. *The strategy of conflict.* Cambridge, Mass.: Harvard University Press.

Schiffer, S. 1972. *Meaning.* Oxford: Clarendon Press.

Schuberth, R. E., and Eimas, P. D. 1977. Effects of context on the classification of words and nonwords. *Journal of Experimental Psychology: Human Perception and Performance,* **3,** 27–36.

398 / Arenas of Language Use

Schweller, K. G. 1978. *The role of expectation in the comprehension and recall of direct and indirect requests.* Unpublished doctoral dissertation. University of Illinois, Champaign-Urbana.

Searle, J. 1958. Proper names. *Mind*, **67**, 166–173.

Searle, J. 1965. What is a speech act? In M. Black (Ed.) *Philosophy in America.* London: Allen and Unwin; 221–239.

Searle, J. R. 1969. *Speech acts.* Cambridge: Cambridge University Press.

Searle, J. R. 1975. Indirect speech acts. In P. Cole, and J. L. Morgan (Eds.), *Syntax and semantics, vol. 3: Speech acts.* New York: Academic Press; 59–82.

Searle, J. R. 1989. Collective intentions and actions. In P. R. Cohen, J. Morgan, and M. E. Pollack (Eds.), *Intentions in communication.* Cambridge: MIT Press.

Seidenberg, M. S., Tanenhaus, M. K., Leiman, J. M., and Bienkowski, M. 1982. Automatic access of the meanings of ambiguous words in context: Some limitations of knowledge-based processing. *Cognitive Psychology*, **14**, 489–537.

Simpson, G. B. 1981. Meaning, dominance and semantic context in the processing of lexical ambiguity. *Journal of Verbal Learning and Verbal Behavior*, **20**, 120–136.

Smith, S. M., Glenberg, A., and Bjork, R. A. 1978. Environmental context and human memory. *Memory and Congition*, **6**, 342–353.

Smith, K. H., and McMahon, L. E. 1970. Understanding order information in sentences: Some recent work at Bell Laboratories. In G. Flores d'Arcais and W. J. M. Levelt (Ed.), *Advances in psycholinguistics.* Amsterdam: North Holland.

Sperber, D., and Wilson, D. 1986. *Relevance.* Oxford: Basil Blackwell.

Stalnaker, R. C. Pragmatic presuppositions. In A. Rogers, B. Wall, and J. P. Murphy (Eds.), *Proceedings of the Texas Conference on Performatives, Presuppositions, and Implicatures.* Arlington, VA: Center for Applied Lingusitics; 135–48.

Stalnaker, R. C. 1978. Assertion. In P. Cole (Ed.), *Syntax and semantics, vol. 9: Pragmatics.* New York: Academic; 315–332.

Stenström, A. B. 1984. *Questions and responses in English conversation.* Lund, Sweden: Gleerup.

Sternberg, S. 1966. High-speed scanning in human memory. *Science*, **153**, 652–654.

Strawson, P. F. 1950. On referring. *Mind*, **59**, 320–344.

Strawson, P. F. 1964. Intention and convention in speech acts. *Philosophical Review*, **73**, 439–460.

Strawson, P. F. 1965. *Individuals*. London: Methuen.

Strawson, P. F. 1974. *Subject and predicate in logic and grammar*. London: Methuen.

Street, R. L., Jr., and Giles, H. 1982. Speech accommodation theory: A social cognitive approach to language and speech behavior. In M. E. Roloff and C. R. Berger (Eds.), *Social cognition and communication* Beverly Hills: Sage Publications; 193–226.

Sudnow, D. N. (Ed.) 1972. *Studies in social interaction*. New York: Free Press.

Sully, J. 1896. *Studies of childhood*. New York: Appleton.

Svartvik, J., and Quirk, R. 1980. *A corpus of English conversation*. Lund, Sweden: Gleerup.

Swinney, D. A. 1979. Lexical access during sentence comprehension: (Re)consideration of context effects. *Journal of Verbal Learning and Verbal Behavior*, **18**, 645–659.

Swinney, D. A., and Hakes, D. T. 1976. Effects of prior context upon lexical access during sentence comprehension. *Journal of Verbal Learning and Verbal Behavior*, **15**, 681–689.

Tanenhaus, M. K., Carroll, J. M., and Bever, T. G. 1976. Sentence-picture verification models as theories of sentence comprehension: A critique of Carpenter and Just. *Psychological Review*, **83**, 310–317.

Tanenhaus, M. K., Leiman, J. M., and Seidenberg, M. S. 1979. Evidence for multiple stages in the processing of ambiguous words in syntactic contexts. *Journal of Verbal Learning and Verbal Behavior*, **18**, 427–440.

Thakerar, J. N., Giles, H., and Cheshire, J. 1982. Psychological and linguistic parameters of speech accommodation theory. In C. Fraser and K. R. Scheerer (Eds.), *Advances in the social psychology of language*. New York: Cambridge University Press.

Thavenius, C. 1983. *Referential pronouns in English conversation*. Lund, Sweden: Gleerup.

Thomson, D. F. 1935. The joking relation and organized obscenity on North Queensland. *American Anthropologist*, **37**, 460–490.

Thorne, J. P. 1972. On the notion "definite". *Foundations of Language*, **8**, 562–568.

Thorne, J. P. 1978. Notes on "notes on 'on the notion "definite." '" *Foundations of Language*, **11**, 111–114.

Townsend, J. T. 1972. Some results concerning the identifiability of parallel and serial processes. *British Journal of Mathematical and Statistical Psychology*, **25**, 168–169.

Tulving, E., and Gold, C. 1963. Stimulus information and contextual information as determinants of tachistoscopic recognition of words. *Journal of Experimental Psychology*, **66**, 319–327.

Tulving, E., and Thomson, D. M. 1973. Encoding specificity and retrieval processes in episodic memory. *Psychological Review*, **80**, 352–373.

Tversky, A. 1977. Features of similarity. *Psychological Review*, **84**, 327–352.

van Dijk, T. A., and Kintsch, W. 1983. *Strategies of discourse comprehension*. New York: Academic.

Verschueren, J. 1978. Reflections on presuppostion failure: A contribution to an integrated theory of pragmatics. *Journal of Pragmatics*, **2**, 107–151.

Wanner, E., and Maratsos, M. 1978. An ATN approach to comprehension. In M. Halle, J. Bresnan, and G. A. Miller (Eds.), *Linguistic theory and psychological reality*. Cambridge: MIT Press.

Warden, D. A. 1976. The influence of context on children's use of identifying expressions and references. *British Journal of Psychology*, **67**, 101–112.

Warnock, G. J. 1973. *Some types of performative utterances. Essays on J. L. Austin*, ed. Sir Isaiah Berlin et al., Oxford: University Press; 69–89.

Warren, R. M., and Obusek, C. J. 1971. Speech perception and phonemic restorations. *Perception and Psychophysics*, **9**, 345–349.

Wason, P. C. 1965. The context of plausible denial. *Journal of Verbal Learning and Verbal Behavior*, **4**, 7–11.

Wiggins, D. 1971. On word-sense, sentence-sense, and difference of word-sense: Towards a philosophical theory of dictionaries. In Steinberg, D., and Jakobovits, L. (Eds.), *Semantics*. Cambridge: University Press; 14–34.

Wilkes-Gibbs, D. 1986. *Collaborative processes of language use in conversation*. Unpublished doctoral dissertation. Stanford University, CA.

Winograd, T. 1972. *Understanding natural language*. New York: Academic Press.

Woods, W. A. 1970. Transition network grammars for natural language analysis. *Communications of the A.C.M.*, **13**, 591–606.

Woods, W. A. 1973. An experimental parsing system for transition network grammars. In R. Rustin (Ed.), *Natural language processing*. Englewood Cliffs, NJ: Prentice-Hall.

Yngve, V. H. 1970. On getting a word in edgewise. In *Papers from the Chicago Linguistic Society*, **6**, 567–578.

Ziff, P. 1964. On understanding 'understanding utterances'. In J. A. Fodor and J. J. Katz (Eds.), *The structure of language: Readings in the philosophy of language*. Englewood Cliffs, NJ: Prentice-Hall.

Zimmer, K. E. 1971. Some general observations about nominal compounds. *Working papers on language universals*, Stanford University, **5**, C1–C21.

Zimmer, K. E. 1972. Appropriateness conditions for nominal compounds. *Working papers on language universals*, Stanford University, **8**, 3–20.

Zipf, G. K. 1935. *The psychobiology of language*. New York: Houghton-Mifflin.

Name Index

Subject Index

407

Library of Congress Cataloging-in-Publication Data

Clark, Herbert H.
  Arenas of language use / Herbert H. Clark.
    p. cm.
  Includes bibliographical references and indexes.
  ISBN 0-226-10781-7 (cloth); 0-226-10782-5 (paper)
  1. Conversation. 2. Oral communication. 3. Psycholinguistics.
  4. Pragmatics. I. Title.
  P95.45.C59 1992
  302.3′46–dc20   92–38874
                                                                              CIP

♾ This book is printed on acid-free paper

We gratefully acknowledge permission to publish the following chapters:

Chapter 1: Clark, H.H., & Marshall, C.R. (1981). Definite reference and mutual knowledge. In A.K. Joshi, B. Webber, & I. Sag (Eds.), Linguistics structure and discourse setting (pp. 10-63). Cambridge: Cambridge University Press.

Chapter 2: Clark, H.H., & Carlson, T.B. (1981). Context for comprehension. In J. Long & A. Baddeley (Eds.), Attention and performance IX (pp. 313-330). Hillsdale, NJ: Lawrence Erlbaum Associates.

Chapter 3: Clark, H.H., Schreuder, R., & Buttrick, S. (1983). Common ground and the understanding of demonstrative reference. Journal of Verbal Learning and Verbal Behavior, 22, 245-258.

Chapter 4: Clark, H.H., & Wilkes-Gibbs, D. (1986). Referring as a collaborative process. Cognition, 22, 1-39.

Chapter 5: Clark, H.H., & Schaefer, E.F. (1989). Contributing to discourse. Cognitive Science, 13, 259-294.

Chapter 6: Schober, M. F., & Clark, H.H. (1989). Understanding by addressees and overhearers. Cognitive Psychology, 21, 211-232.

Chapter 7: Clark, H.H., & Carlson, T.B. (1982). Hearers and speech acts. Language, 58, 332-373.

Chapter 9: Clark, H.H., & Schaefer, E.F. (1987). Concealing one's meaning from overhearers. Journal of Memory and Language, 26, 209-225.

Chapter 10: Clark, H. H. (1983). Making sense of nonce sense. In G. B. Flores d'Arcais & R. J. Jarvella (Eds.), The process of language understanding (pp. 297-331). London: Wiley.

Chapter 11: Clark, H.H., & Gerrig, R.J. (1983). Understanding old words with new meanings. Journal of Verbal Learning and Verbal Behavior, 22, 591-608.

Chapter 12 Clark, H.H. (1991) Words, the world, and their possibilities. In G. Lockhead & J. Pomerantz (Eds.) The perception of structure. Washington, DC: APA.

Detail on front cover of the paperback edition of this book is from "The Luncheon of the Boating Party," 1881, by Pierre Auguste Renoir, courtesy of The Phillips Collection, Washington, D.C.

Oil on canvas
51 x 68 (129.5 x 172.7)
Signed and dated
Acquired 1923